No. 952
$12.95

# Microprocessor Programming for Computer Hobbyists

By Neill Graham

FIRST EDITION

FIRST PRINTING—AUGUST 1977
SECOND PRINTING—DECEMBER 1978

Copyright © 1977 by TAB BOOKS

Printed int he United States of America

Reproduction or publication of the content in any manner, without express permission of the publisher, is prohibited. No liability is assumed with respect to the use of the information herein.

---

**Library of Congress Cataloging in Publication Data**

Graham, Neill, 1941-
    Microprocessor programming for computer hobbyists.
    Bibliography: p.
    Includes index.
    1. Microprocessors—Programming. I. Title.
QA76.6.G69    001.6′42    77-22868
ISBN 0-8306-7952-9
ISBN 0-8306-6952-3 pbk.

---

Cover photo courtesy of Radio Electronics Magazine.

# Preface

This book is for the computer hobbyist interested in intermediate and advanced techniques of programming and data structuring. It was written to take up where the computer manufacturers' instruction manuals and the introductory programming language texts leave off.

The book is divided into six parts:

*Part 1. Number Systems.* A computer programmer has to be familiar with three number systems besides the decimal system we all learn as school children. These are the binary, octal, and hexadecimal systems. After reviewing the basics of these systems, Chapter 1 proceeds to more advanced topics such as the representation of signed and floating point numbers.

A computer programmer also occasionally has to convert from one number system to another. A computer can be programmed to do these conversions, but often neither the computer nor the program is handy when needed. Paper and pencil methods are laborious. The conversion tables found in programming manuals usually do not extend to large enough numbers, nor do they provide for floating point numbers. Chapter 2 describes a method of base conversion adapted to the now commonplace pocket calculator. The method does apply to large numbers and does apply to floating point numbers.

*Part 2. A High-Level Language for Machine-Level Programming.* Most computer hobbyists program at the machine level. That is, they work with the bits, bytes, and words built into the computer, rather than with the more advanced data structures found in high level languages. It might seem, then, that the programs in a book aimed at computer hobbyists should be written in assembly language, which, next to machine code, is the most machine oriented of computer languages.

Unfortunately different microprocessors have different assembly languages. If the reader is using a different microprocessor than the author used, then he will have to translate each program into the assembly language for his machine.

Nor is this just a matter of substituting one set of mnemonics for another. An assembly language program achieves its characteristic efficiency by using special tricks based on the hardware features of a particular machine. The translator has first to decipher the purpose of each trick, and then think up a new set of tricks that will have the same effect on his own machine.

Furthermore, assembly language has no provisions for displaying advanced program and data structures. Such structures may be used, of course, but their use is not obvious from the assembly code. These, too, the translator has to dig painfully out of the original program.

In short, it is easier to translate *downward*, from a high level language to an assembly language, then it is to translate *crosswise*, from one assembly language to another.

Therefore, the programs in this book are all written in a high level language. The language chosen is an extension of PL/M, the PL/I-like language developed for the Intel 8080 microprocessor. The major additions to PL/M were the addition of new data and control structures, to make the language more expressive. Where possible, the new structures were borrowed from PL/I. Several minor changes were made to eliminate confusing notations and, in one case, (signed comparisons) to provide for hardware feature found on some computers, but not on the 8080.

Part 2 also contains a chapter on program design, with suggestions on how to best use the features of the language in creating your own programs.

*Part 3. Arithmetic.* Most microprocessors provide only addition and subtraction for 8-bit bytes and (sometimes!) 16-bit words. Addition and subtraction of large numbers, multiplication and division of *any* numbers, and floating point arithmetic, must all be programmed by the user. Chapter 7 and 8 cover the needed techniques.

Also included are chapters on numeric input and output routines, and on the arithmetic based "linear congruential" method of generating random numbers. The latter will be of particular interest to computer games fans.

*Part 4. Data Structures.* Data inside a computer often represents objects in the real world, or perhaps in our imagination. The more sophisticated the data structures we use, the more complex and interesting the objects we can represent. Part 4 covers the most widely used data structures, and some of the algorithms by which they are manipulated.

*Part 5. Searching.* Computers spend far more time than most people realize in searching through tables, as well as through more complicated data structures such as chains and trees. The techniques for searching are at least as important as those for doing arithmetic. Part 5 covers techniques for searching data structures ranging from simple lists to the inverted files and multilists used in advanced information retrieval systems.

Chapter 22 introduces another kind of searching, the kind used in artificial intelligence work to search for the best solution to a problem among a number of possible ones. Here we focus on the problem of a game playing computer (such as a chess playing machine) searching for the best next move.

*Part 6. Sorting.* Sorting is an aid to searching. We store items in a particular order to make it easier to find them later.

There are two kinds of sorting: internal sorting, for data stored in the computer's main memory; and external sorting, for data on auxiliary storage devices such as tape or disk. Chapter 23 focuses on three internal sorting routines that will meet almost all the needs of the computer hobbyist. Chapter 24 takes up external sorting techniques. The discussion is general rather than specific so that the reader may adapt the techniques to whatever auxiliary storage devices are present in his system.

Neill Graham

# Contents

## Part I  Number Systems — 13

### 1 The Binary and Related Systems — 13
Integers—Binary Arithmetic—Signed Numbers—Ranges—Fractions—Floating Point Numbers.

### 2 Base Conversion with a Pocket Calculator — 28
Basic Techniques—Conversion to Decimal—Conversion From Decimal—Computing Large Powers—Scaling and Logarithms—Rounding.

## Part II  A High Level for Machine Level Programs — 41

### 3 Data Definition — 41
Primitive Data Types—Constants—Names, Addresses, and Values—Structures—Arrays—Pointers—Macros—Initialization.

### 4 Data Manipulation — 59
The Assignment Operator—The Arithmetic Operations—The Logical Operations—The Rotate and Shift Operations—The Relational Operations—Expressions.

### 5 Control Structures — 73
Sequencing—Selection—Evaluating Conditions—Repetition—Procedures.

### 6 Program Design — 96
Comments—A Case Study.

## Part III Arithmetic — 108

### 7 Multiple Precision Arithmetic — 108
Addition—Subtraction—Incrementation and Negation—Shifting—Integer Multiplication—Integer Divide—Multiplication and Division of Binary Fractions.

## 8 Floating Point Arithmetic — 124
Floating Point Representations—The Load and Store Routines—The Arithmetic Routines.

## 9 Numeric Input and Output — 141
Integer Input—Integer Output—Floating Point Input—Floating Point Output.

## 10 Pseudo-Random Numbers — 158
The Linear Congruential Generator—Choosing A and C—How to Get Random Numbers With Different Ranges—Improving Random Number Generators.

# Part IV Data Structures — 166

## 11 Structures and Arrays — 166
Structures—Linear Arrays—Multidimensional Arrays.

## 12 Stacks, Queues and Deques — 184
Stacks—Circular Arrays—Queues—Deques.

## 13 Strings — 201
Descriptors—Declarations—String Input and Output—Operations on Strings—Garbage Collection.

## 14 Chains — 220
Plexes—Chains and Rings—Insertion and Deletion.

## 15 Trees — 238
Definitions—Linear Representations of Trees—Bit Tables—Plex Representations—Recursive Definition of Trees—Recursive Programming.

## 16 Graphs — 258
Definitions—Representations of Graphs—Lists.

# Part V Searching — 273

## 17 Searching Lists — 273
Entities, Attributes, Values, and Relations—Sequential Search: Linear Arrays—Sequential Search: Chains—Block Search—Binary Search.

## 18 Hashing — 285
Hashing—Hashing Functions—Collision Handling.

## 19 Searching Binary Trees — 299
Definitions—Searching—Insertion—Deletion—Sequential Traversal—Performance.

## 20 Indexes — 311
Arguments—Functions—Sequential and Nonsequential Files—Maintenance of Indexed Sequential Files—Multilevel Indexes.

## 21 Secondary and Multiple Key Retrieval — 324
Inverted Files—Chained Files—Multidimensional Binary Trees.

## 22 Searching Game Trees — 338
Termination Criteria—Static Evaluation—The Minimax Method.

# Part VI Sorting — 346

## 23 Internal Sorting — 346
Definitions—Sorting Lists of Two or Three Records—The Bubble Sort—The Shell Sort—Quicksort.

## 24 External Sorting — 361
Merging—Runs—Sorting by Merging—Balanced Merging—The Polyphase Sort—Generating the Initial Runs—A Priority Queue.

## Index — 379

# Part I
# Number Systems

## Chapter 1
## The Binary and Related Systems

Computer programmers use four number systems: binary or base-2, octal or base-8, decimal or base-10, and hexadecimal or base-16. The binary system is the one required by most computer hardware, and the decimal system is the one we all learned in school and use in everyday life. Octal and hexadecimal are closely related to binary. But octal requires only a third as many digits as binary to represent a given number, and hexadecimal only a fourth as many, so that these systems are better suited for use by human beings.

### INTEGERS

We start out by seeing how integers, or whole numbers, are represented and manipulated in each system. We will then find it easy to extend our results to fractions and floating point numbers.

*Digits.* The digits are the symbols each system uses to represent numbers. The number of digits used equals the *base* or *radix* of the system. Thus the binary system uses 2 digits, octal uses 8, decimal uses 10, and hexadecimal uses 16. The digits each system uses are:

| | |
|---|---|
| Binary | 0, 1 |
| Octal | 0, 1, 2, 3, 4, 5, 6, 7 |
| Decimal | 0, 1, 2, 3, 4, 5, 6, 7, 8, 9 |
| Hexadecimal | 0, 1, 2, 3, 4, 5, 6, 7, 8, 9, A, B, C, D, E, F |

Newcomers to the hexadecimal system find it strange to see letters of the alphabet used as digits. But the technique has a long history: Both the Greeks and the Romans used the letters of their alphabets to represent numbers.

*Basic Designation.* The digits 100 could be a binary number with value 4, an octal number with value 64, a decimal number with value 100, or a hexadecimal number with value 256. Mathematicians write the base as a subscript for systems other than decimal. They would write:

$$100_2 = 4 \qquad\qquad 100 = 100 \text{ (Of course!)}$$
$$100_8 = 64 \qquad\qquad 100_{16} = 256$$

Since most computer input and output devices cannot handle subscripts, programmers need another method for base designation. In this book we will follow the system used in PL/M: we designate binary by B, octal by O or Q, decimal by D, and hexadecimal by H. Thus we could write

$$100B = 4 \qquad\qquad 100D = 100$$
$$100Q = 64 \qquad\qquad 100H = 256$$

The D for decimal may be omitted, and usually is. The letter Q is preferred to O for octal, since "oh" and "zero" are easily confused. In a program, a hexadecimal number must start with one of the digits 0-9, since otherwise the computer would confuse it with a name. Thus CFH would be written 0CFH. The leading zero does not affect the value of the number: CFH = 0CFH.

*Powers of the Base.* As we remember from school, the digits of a decimal number, read from right to left, represent "units," "tens," "hundreds," "thousands," and so on. If we replace the words by the corresponding numbers, we get the series: 1, 10, 100, 1000, .... These numbers are called the *powers of ten*. Each is equal to 1 multiplied by a certain number of tens. Thus 1 equals 1 multiplied by 0 tens, or $10^0$; 10 equals 1 multiplied by 1 ten or $10^1$; 100 equals 1 multiplied by 2 tens or $10^2$; 1000 equals 1 multiplied by 3 tens or $10^3$; and so on. Once we get beyond $10^1$, we can forget about the 1, and just say that $10^2$ is 2 tens multiplied together, $10^3$ is 3 tens multiplied together, and so on.

This method of writing numbers is called *exponential notation*. The raised number—3 in $10^3$—is the *exponent*.

Exponential notation is convenient since it allows us to express our results in the same form in different systems. For instance, the series corresponding to $10^0$, $10^1$, $10^2$, $10^3$, ...would be $2^0$, $2^1$, $2^2$, $2^3$, ...for the binary system, $8^0$, $8^1$, $8^2$, $8^3$, ...for octal, and $16^0$, $16^1$, $16^2$, $16^3$, ...for hexadecimal. In each case the number is to be multiplied by itself the number of times indicated by the exponent: $8^3 = 8*8*8* = 512$.

(In this book I will follow the programming languages by using an asterisk, "*", to indicate multiplication.)

*The Place Value System.* Each of the four number systems uses a *positional notation* or *place value system*. This means that we find the value of a number by mulitplying each digit by a *weight*, and adding up the products. The weight a particular digit is multiplied by depends on its position in the number.

To arrive at a general rule for which weight should multiply which digit, let us set up a scheme for numbering the digit positions in the representation of a number. We will number the positions from right to left, starting with 0 for the rightmost digit. The following examples illustrate the scheme:

Binary System: 10010101B
1 0 0 1 0 1 0 1     Digits
7 6 5 4 3 2 1 0     Position Numbers

Octal System: 1537Q
1 5 3 7     Digits
3 2 1 0     Position Numbers

Decimal System: 9745
9 7 4 5     Digits
3 2 1 0     Position Numbers

Hexadecimal System: 3CH
3 C     Digits
1 0     Position Numbers

We can now state the rule for finding the value of a number in any system. Let B stand for the base of the number system (2, 8, 10, or 16), and P for the position number of a particular digit (0, 1, 2, 3,...). The rule is:

*To evaluate a base-B number, multiply each digit by $B^P$, where P is the position number of the digit, and add up the resulting products.*

The following examples illustrate the application of this rule in each number system. The weights—$2^4$, $8^3$, etc.—were all worked out by doing the appropriate multiplications on a calculator. In the next chapter we shall see how to do these calculations without having to explicitly work out the values of the weights.

Binary System: 11011011B
$$\begin{aligned}11011011B &= 1*2^7 + 1*2^6 + 0*2^5 + 1*2^4 \\ &\quad + 1*2^3 + 0*2^2 + 1*2^1 + 1*2^0 \\ &= 1*128 + 1*64 + 0*32 + 1*16 + 1*8 + 0*4 \\ &\quad + 1*2 + 1*1 \\ &= 128 + 64 + 16 + 8 + 2 + 1 \\ &= 219\end{aligned}$$

Octal System: 3641100Q
$$\begin{aligned}3641100Q &= 3*8^6 + 6*8^5 + 4*8^4 + 1*8^3 + 1*8^2 + 0*8^1 + 0*8^0 \\ &= 3*262144 + 6*32768 + 4*4096 + 1*512 + 1*64 \\ &\quad + 0*8 + 0*1 \\ &= 786432 + 196608 + 16384 + 512 + 64 \\ &= 1000000\end{aligned}$$

For the decimal system the answer is, of course, obvious, but the way it is arrived at will help illustrate how the technique works in less familiar systems:

Decimal System: 9754
$$\begin{aligned}9754 &= 9*10^3 + 7*10^2 + 5*10^1 + 4*10^0 \\ &= 9*1000 + 7*100 + 5*10 + 4*1 \\ &= 9000 + 700 + 50 + 4 \\ &= 9754\end{aligned}$$

In doing the arithmetic for the hexadecimal system, we must replace the digits A, B, C, D, E, and F by their decimal equivalents 10, 11, 12, 13, 14, and 15. These equivalences should be memorized.

Hexadecimal System: F4240H
$$\begin{aligned}F4240H &= 15*16^4 + 4*16^3 + 2*16^2 + 4*16^1 + 0*16^0 \\ &= 15*65536 + 4*4096 + 2*256 + 4*16 + 0*1 \\ &= 983040 + 16384 + 512 + 64 \\ &= 1000000\end{aligned}$$

*Correspondence between Binary, Octal, and Hexadecimal.* Since 8 equals $2^3$, it follows that one octal digit corresponds to exactly three binary digits (or bits); and since 16 equals $2^4$, one hexadecimal digit corresponds to four bits. These correspondences are illustrated in Fig. 1-1 and Fig. 1-2. To

| THREE-BIT GROUP | OCTAL DIGIT |
|---|---|
| 000 | 0 |
| 001 | 1 |
| 010 | 2 |
| 011 | 3 |
| 100 | 4 |
| 101 | 5 |
| 110 | 6 |
| 111 | 7 |

Fig. 1-1. Correspondence between three-bit groups and octal digits.

convert a binary number to octal, then, we divide it up into groups of three bits (supplying 0s on the left, if necessary, to make the groups come out even), and replacing each three-bit group by the corresponding octal digit:

$$111101000010010000000B = 011, 110, 100, 001, 001, 000, 000B$$
$$= 3641100Q$$
$$= 1111, 0100, 0010, 0100, 0000B$$
$$= F4240H$$

Obviously, the process can also be carried out in reverse, replacing each octal digit with the corresponding three-bit group, or each hexadecimal digit with the corresponding

| FOUR-BIT GROUP | HEXADECIMAL DIGIT | DECIMAL VALUE |
|---|---|---|
| 0000 | 0 | 0 |
| 0001 | 1 | 1 |
| 0010 | 2 | 2 |
| 0011 | 3 | 3 |
| 0100 | 4 | 4 |
| 0101 | 5 | 5 |
| 0110 | 6 | 6 |
| 0111 | 7 | 7 |
| 1000 | 8 | 8 |
| 1001 | 9 | 9 |
| 1010 | A | 10 |
| 1011 | B | 11 |
| 1100 | C | 12 |
| 1101 | D | 13 |
| 1110 | E | 14 |
| 1111 | F | 15 |

Fig. 1-2. Correspondence between four-bit groups and hexadecimal digits. The decimal value of each hexadecimal digit is also given.

four-bit group. Any leading 0s in the resulting binary number are discarded:

$$3641100Q = 011, 110, 100, 001, 001, 000, 000B$$
$$= 11110100001001000000B$$
$$F4240H = 1111,0100,0010,0100,0000B$$
$$= 11110100001001000000B$$

With practice you will find you can perform these conversions without effort. You will read 101 as 5, or 1010 as A, as readily as if the digit itself has been written.

On most computers bits are grouped in *cells* or *words*. If the number of bits in a cell is divisible by 3, then octal notation is appropriate for indicating the contents of the cell. If the number of bits is divisible by 4, then hexadecimal notation is indicated. Occasionally some other consideration enters. The 8080 microprocessor, for instance, uses cells containing 8 and 16 bits, and hence hexadecimal would seem to be indicated. But it turns out that the 8080 instruction codes are easier to decipher if written in octal, so many 8080 users prefer octal.

## BINARY ARITHMETIC

In discussing arithmetic operations we will find it convenient to work with a fixed number of bits, as does the computer. We will therefore assume that our operands and results are all *8-bit bytes*. The byte will be the basic data type for the programming language developed in Part 2 of the book.

*Addition.* The rules for binary addition are as follows:

$0 + 0 = 0$      $1 + 0 = 1$
$0 + 1 = 1$      $1 + 1 = 10$ (0 with 1 to carry)

Consider the addition of the two 8-bit numbers 10010111B and 01011101B. We arrange our work as in ordinary arithmetic:

```
   10010111
 + 01011101
   ────────
   11110100
```

The reader unfamiliar with binary addition is advised to work through the example using the above rules.

Now suppose we add 10110001B and 11001010B. We have:

```
   10110001
 + 11001010
   ────────
  101111011
```

Now the answer has 9 bits, because of the carry out of the leftmost position. However we have assumed memory cells that hold only 8 bits. What happens to the extra bit?

Most computers provide a *carry bit* for just this purpose. After an addition, the carry bit will be 1 if a carry out of the leftmost position occurred, and 0 otherwise. We could write the above examples as follows, to indicate the value of the carry bit in each case:

$$\begin{array}{r} 10010111 \\ +\ 01011101 \\ \hline 11110100 \end{array}$$

(carry = 0)

and

$$\begin{array}{r} 10110001 \\ +\ 11001010 \\ \hline 01111011 \end{array}$$

(carry = 1)

*Subtraction.* The rules for binary subtraction are:

$0 - 0 = 0$  
$0 - 1 = 1$ and borrow 1  
$1 - 0 = 1$  
$1 - 1 = 0$

During subtraction the carry bit serves as a "borrow bit" by indicating whether or not a borrow was needed to do the subtraction in the leftmost position. On some machines the carry bit will be 0 if there was no borrow, and 1 if there was. On other machines the indication is reversed: 1 indicates no borrow and 0 the opposite.

Now consider two examples:

$$\begin{array}{r} 10010100 \\ -\ 01110111 \\ \hline 00011101 \end{array}$$

(borrow = 0)

and

$$\begin{array}{r} 10011101 \\ -\ 11001010 \\ \hline 11010011 \end{array}$$

(borrow = 1)

If we are dealing with unsigned numbers, then borrow = 1 is an error condition, indicating that we attempted to subtract a larger number from a smaller one.

*Multiplication.* The rules are:

$0 * 0 = 0$       $1 * 0 = 0$
$0 * 1 = 0$       $1 * 1 = 1$

In carrying out a binary multiplication with paper and pencil, we can arrange our work in the usual way (for clarity I have written some lines of all 0s that would not usually be written out in paper and pencil multiplication):

```
        11011010
       *10111001
        11011010
        00000000
        00000000
        11011010
        11011010
        11011010
        00000000
        11011010
 1001110110001010
```

Notice that multiplying two 8-bit numbers gives a 16-bit product. In general, the number of bits in the product is the sum of the number bits in the two operands. Thus multiplying an 8-bit number by a 16-bit number would give a 24-bit product. And multiplying two 16-bit numbers yields a 32-bit product.

Thus when we multiply the contents of two memory cells, we must assume we have a cell large enough to hold the complete product, or else that the numbers being multiplied are small enough that all the excess bits on the left will be zeros.

*Division.* Division is carried out using the rules for multiplication and subtraction, again very much as in ordinary arithmetic. As an example we divide 11010100B by 00010111B:

```
              1001
      10111)11010100
            10111
            000111
             00000
             001110
              00000
              011100
               10111
               00101
```

Thus the quotient is 00001001B and the remainder is 00000101B. As in the multiplication example, I have for clarity written down some rows of zeros that are not usually written down. We will study these examples in more detail in Chapter 7, when we undertake to write software multiplication and division routines.

## SIGNED NUMBERS

There are three methods used to represent signed numbers in binary notation: the sign-magnitude representation, the twos-complement representation, and the ones-complement representation.

*Sign-Magnitude Representation.* The sign-magnitude representation is closest to everyday usage. The leftmost bit in a cell represents the sign—0 for + and 1 for −. The remaining bits represent the magnitude. Thus we would represent +1000000B as 01000000 and −1000000B as 11000000.

*Twos Complement Representation.* Let us define a negative number in the obvious way, as the result of subtracting the corresponding positive number from zero. That is,

$$-X = 0 - X$$

where the subtraction is done using binary arithmetic and the borrow into the leftmost position is ignored.

With this definition,

$-00000000B = 00000000B - 00000000B = 00000000B$
$-00000001B = 00000000B - 00000001B = 11111111B$
$-00000010B = 00000000B - 00000010B = 11111110B$
$-00000011B = 00000000B - 00000011B = 11111101B$

and so on.

When we subtract a number other than 0 from 0, the subtraction in the leftmost position borrows a 1 from a nonexistent position to the left of it. We are in fact subtracting from 100000000B or $2^8$. Thus we can write

$$-X = 2^8 - X$$

or, more generally, for N-bit numbers,

$$-X = 2^N - X$$

This will work for $X = 0$, too, provided only the bits in positions 0 through $N - 1$ are retained in the result, and the bit in position N is ignored.

The negative of a number computed in this way is called its *twos complement*, since we form it by subtracting the given number from a power of *two*.

Fig. 1-3 shows a twos complement representation. For simplicity we use three-bit numbers in the example, so that there will only be eight possible bit patterns, and we can discuss them all individually.

The three-bit groups whose leftmost bits are 0 represent positive numbers:

> 000 represents 0
> 001 represents 1
> 010 represents 2
> 011 represents 3

The three-bit groups whose leftmost bits are 1 represent negative numbers:

> 100 represents $-4$
> 101 represents $-3$
> 110 represents $-2$
> 111 represents $-1$

Thus the leftmost bit serves as a sign bit, just as it did in the sign-magnitude representation. If the leftmost bit is 0, the number is positive; if it is 1, the number is negative.

With one exception, the representative of each negative number is the twos complement of the representative of the

| BIT PATTERN | NUMBER REPRESENTED |
|---|---|
| 000 | 0 |
| 001 | 1 |
| 010 | 2 |
| 011 | 3 |
| 100 | -4 |
| 101 | -3 |
| 110 | -2 |
| 111 | -1 |

| NEGATION |
|---|
| -000B = 000B − 000B = 000B |
| -001B = 000B − 001B = 111B ⟶ -111B = 000B − 111B = 001B |
| -010B = 000B − 010B = 110B ⟶ -110B = 000B − 110B = 010B |
| -011B = 000B − 011B = 101B ⟶ -101B = 000B − 101B = 011B |
| -100B = 000B − 100B = 100B (?) |

Fig. 1-3. A twos complement representation using 3-bit numbers.

corresponding positive number, and vice versa. (Zero is its own twos complement as it should be: $-0 = 0$.) The exception is 100, the representative of $-4$, which is its own twos complement! (See the bottom line of Fig. 1-3.) Because of this anomalous behavior, this smallest negative number is sometimes omitted from a twos complement representation, and its occurrence regarded as an error.

We add and subtract in the twos complement representation by adding and subtracting the representatives as if they were unsigned binary numbers, and ignoring any carry or borrow:

$\quad$ 010B + 101B = 111B $\qquad\qquad$ $2 + (-3) = -1$
$\quad$ 111B + 011B = 010B (carry ignored) $\qquad$ $(-1) + 3 = 2$
$\quad$ 110B − 001B = 101B $\qquad\qquad$ $(-2) - 1 = -3$
$\quad$ 010B − 011B = 111B (borrow ignored) $\qquad$ $2 - 3 = -1$

This is the most useful property of the twos complement representation: The computer may use exactly the same addition and subtraction hardware for twos complement numbers as it does for unsigned binary numbers.

One problem can occur. Consider the following additions:

$\quad$ 010B + 011B = 101B $\qquad\qquad$ $2 + 3 = -3$ (?)
$\quad$ 110B + 101B = 011B (carry ignored) $\quad$ $(-2) + (-3) = 3$ (?)

In each case the correct answer was outside the range $-4$ through 3 that can be represented in a 3-bit twos complement system, and so an incorrect answer having the wrong sign was obtained. This is known as *twos complement overflow*. The carry bit cannot be used to detect twos complement overflow. In the examples in the last paragraph we saw perfectly legitimate additions and subtractions which produced carries and borrows. Instead, a separate overflow bit, which is set to 1 when a twos complement overflow occurs and to 0 otherwise, is required. Without this bit twos complement overflow can be hard to detect; an overflow bit is a good feature to look for when buying a computer!

We can regard the strange behavior of 100B as an example of twos complement overflow. The bit pattern 100 represents $-4$, the negative of which is 4. But 4 is one more than the largest positive number, 3, which we can represent. We have

$\qquad$ 011B + 001B = 100B $\qquad\qquad$ $3 + 1 = -4$ (?)

A similar twos complement system can be set up using any number of bits. We are interested in the cases of 8 and 16 bits. With 8 bits we can represent numbers from −128 through 127. With 16 bits the range is −32768 through 32767. In each case the smallest negative number (−128, −32768) is its own twos complement. Or put another way, if we attempt to negate the smallest negative number, a twos complement overflow will occur.

*Ones Complement Representation.* The ones complement of a number is obtained by subtracting it from (for an 8-bit number) 11111111B instead of 0. The result is the same as the *logical complement*, which results from replacing 0s by 1s and 1s by 0s throughout the number. When ones complement numbers are added, an "end around" carry must be used: Any carry out of the leftmost position is added to the rightmost position of the result. Ones complement representations are not nearly as popular as the other two already discussed, so we will not go into the details of them here.

## RANGES

We may ask: What range of numbers can we represent using a given number of digits in a certain number system?

For the answer we turn to the decimal system. With three digits, for instance, we can represent numbers in the range 0 through 999. Now $999 = 1000 - 1 = 10^3 - 1$. In this range are 1000 or $10^3$ numbers.

A few more examples convince us the rule is general: Using N digits in base B, we can represent $B^N$ numbers ranging from 0 through $B^N - 1$. Thus with 8 bits our range is 0 through $2^8 - 1$ or 0 through 255. With 16 bits the range is 0 through $2^{16} - 1$ or 0 through 65535.

For twos complement numbers, the $2^N$ bit patterns are divided evenly between positive and negative numbers. Thus we have $2^{N-1}$ positive numbers and $2^{N-1}$ negative numbers. The positive numbers run from 0 through $2^{N-1} - 1$. The negative numbers run from −1 through $-2^{N-1}$. The desired range is thus $-2^{N-1}$ through $2^{N-1} - 1$. For 8 and 16 bits the ranges are $-2^7$ through $2^7 - 1$ and $-2^{15}$ through $2^{15} - 1$, or as has already been mentioned, −128 through 127 and −32768 through 32767.

## FRACTIONS

So far we have confined ourselves to integers. We can readily extend our work to numbers having both integer and fractional parts by extending our correspondence between powers of the base and position values.

*Negative Powers.* A negative power is defined as 1 divided by the corresponding positive power. Thus $10^{-1} = 1/10 = .1$, $10^{-2} = 1/100 = .01$, $10^{-3} = 1/1000 = .001$, and so on. Or, for powers of 2, $2^{-1} = 1/2 = .5$, $2^{-2} = 1/4 = .25$, $2^{-3} = 1/8 = .125$, and so on.

*The Extended Place Value System.* Consider the decimal number 25.456. The "." is usually refered to as the "decimal point;" it separates the integer and fractional parts of the number. We will use the more general term "radix point" which applies equally well to all number systems. There is no need for terms like "binary point," "octal point," and "hexadecimal point," since the function of the radix point is independent of any particular number system.

Now let us extend our method of numbering positions as follows. The digit just to the left of the radix point is in position 0. From that position we number to the left with the positive integers 1, 2, 3, . . . , and to the right with the negative integers $-1, -2, -3, \ldots$. Thus for 25.456 the numbering would be:

```
2 5.  4  5  6              Digits
1 0  -1 -2 -3        Position Numbers
```

With this extended method of position numbering, our rule for finding the value of a base-B number still holds: Multiply each digit by $B^N$ where B is the base and N is the position number of the digit, and add up the products.

We first see that for a decimal number this rule gives the expected result:

$$25.456 = 2*10^1 + 5*10^0 + 4*10^{-1} + 5*10^{-2} + 6*10^{-3}$$
$$= 20 + 5 + .4 + .05 + .006$$
$$= 25.456 \text{ (as expected)}$$

The following examples illustrate the rule in other systems:

Binary System: 11001.10011B

$$11001.10011B = 1*2^4 + 1*2^3 + 0*2^2 + 0*2^1 + 1*2^0$$
$$+ 1*2^{-1} + 0*2^{-2} + 0*2^{-3} + 1*2^{-4} + 1*2^{-5}$$
$$= 16 + 8 + 1 + .5 + .0625 + .03125$$
$$= 25.59375$$

Octal System: 31.46Q
$$31.46Q = 3*8^1 + 1*8^0 + 4*8^{-1} + 6*8^{-2}$$
$$= 3*8 + 1*1 + 4*.125 + 6*015625$$
$$= 24 + 1 + .5 + .09375$$
$$= 25.59375$$

Hexadecimal System: 19.98H
$$19.98H = 1*16^1 + 9*16^0 + 9*16^{-1} + 8*16^{-2}$$
$$= 1*16 + 9*1 + 9*.0625 + 8*.00390625$$
$$= 25.59375$$

We may as before convert between binary and octal or binary and hexadecimal by dividing the binary number into groups of 3 or 4 bits. Only two additional points need be noted: 1) The radix point must always fall between such groups, never inside one. 2) When necessary, the integer part of a binary number may be extended on the *left* with extra 0s, and the fractional part may be extended on the *right* in the same way. Using 11001.10011B as an example, we have:

$$011,001.100,110B = 31.46Q$$
$$0001,1001.1001,1000B = 19.98H$$

The arithmetical operations may be extended to numbers with fractional parts exactly as in ordinary arithmetic. The twos complement system for representing signed numbers is also easily extended. We will delve into these matters further in the chapter on floating point arithmetic.

## FLOATING POINT NUMBERS

Numbers in which the radix point may be in any position are termed *floating point* numbers. Such numbers frequently contain many zeros whose only purpose is to show the position of the radix point. Two examples from elementary physics are

602300000000000000000000.

and

0.0000000000000000000000000000000000663

For numbers such as these we are better off using *scientific notation* or *exponential format*:

$$6.023 \times 10^{23}$$
$$6.63 \times 10^{-34}$$

(We use the "times sign," which is traditional, in place of the "*" to denote multiplication.)

Multiplying a decimal number by 10 shifts the radix point one place to the right. So $6.023 \times 10^{23}$ instructs us to take 6.023 and move the radix point 23 places to the right, filling in zeros once we get beyond the 3. In the same way, dividing by 10 shifts the radix point one place to the left. So $6.63 \times 10^{-34}$ instructs us to start with 6.63 and shift the radix point 34 places to the left, filling in zeros once we get beyond the 6.

The number which is multiplied by the power of 10—6.023 in $6.023 \times 10^{23}$—is called the *mantissa*. (This is not the same as the mantissa used in logarithms.) The power to which 10 is raised—the 23—is called the *exponent*.

Binary, octal, and hexadecimal numbers may also be written in scientific notation, except that the 10 is replaced by 2, 8, or 16. Here are some examples:

$$1.0110101B \times 2^5 = 101101.01B$$
$$1.101B \times 2^{-3} = .001101B$$
$$2.73Q \times 8^9 = 2730000000Q$$
$$5.3Q \times 8^{-1} = .53Q$$
$$2.A3FH \times 16^3 = 2A3FH$$
$$4.AEH \times 16^{-4} = .0004AEH$$

Notice that in each example the exponent is in decimal notation. This is usually convenient when the number is to be used by a person, since the person must shift the radix point the required number of places. Should the number be stored inside a computer, then both mantissa and exponent would be in binary notation.

# Chapter 2

# Base Conversion with a Pocket Calculator

Programmers often need to convert from binary, octal, or hexadecimal to decimal, and vice versa. It is easy, of course, to program a computer to do these conversions, but one often needs to do them when no computer is handy. Programming manuals sometimes contain tables for base conversion. These tables are often clumsy to use, especially for large numbers, and like the computer they are seldom at hand when needed.

In this chapter we will examine conversion techniques that require only an inexpensive pocket calculator. The techniques are general, and will work for floating point numbers as well as integers. The calculator should feature floating point arithmetic, and display as many digits as possible. (The examples were worked using a 10-digit calculator.) The logarithm function—either natural or common—is helpful but not essential.

**BASIC TECHNIQUES**

We face two problems: 1) Given the digits of the representation of a number to some base, compute the decimal value of the number. (This was done in the last chapter, but the techniques used for illustrative purposes there are not the most efficient ones.) 2) Given the decimal value of a number, compute the digits of its representation to some base. In this section we shall look at the basic techniques for doing these conversions, and illustrate them with the trivial "decimal to decimal" conversion.

*Digits to Decimal Value.* Suppose we have the digits of the representation of an integer to a given base. We can compute the decimal value of the integer as follows:

1) Clear the calculator display.
2) Working from left to right through the digits of the number to be converted, repeat the following for each digit:
   - 2.1) Multiply the number displayed on the calculator by the base of the number being converted.
   - 2.2) Add the decimal value of the current digit to the number displayed on the calculator.
3) The number displayed on the calculator is the decimal value of the number to be converted.

Let us illustrate this algorithm by converting the digits 9, 7, 3, and 2 to the decimal number 9732:

| Operation | Number Displayed on Calculator |
|---|---|
| Clear Display | 0 |
| *Multiply by 10 | 0 |
| Add 9 | 9 |
| Multiply by 10 | 90 |
| Add 7 | 97 |
| Multiply by 10 | 970 |
| Add 3 | 973 |
| Multiply by 10 | 9730 |
| Add 2 | 9732 |

The step marked by a "*" may be omitted; however, it is often most convenient to treat each digit in exactly the same way, even at the expense of an occasional unnecessary operation.

*Decimal Value to Digits.* We assume the number to be converted has the form of the mantissa of a number in scientific notation. More precisely, the number M must satisfy

$$1 \le M < B$$

where B is the base of the number system being converted to. The technique is as follows:

1) Enter the decimal value to be converted into the calculator.

2) We obtain the digits of the converted number in left to right order by repeating the following for each digit:
   - 2.1) The integer part of the number displayed is the decimal value of the current digit. Write down that digit.
   - 2.2) Subtract the integer part of the number displayed, leaving the fractional part.
   - 2.3) Multiply the number displayed by the base of the system being converted to.

We illustrate by converting the number 9.732 to its digits in the decimal system: 9, 7, 3, and 2.

| Operation | Number Displayed | Digit |
|---|---|---|
| Enter 9.732 | 9.732 | |
| Record Digit | | 9 |
| Subtract 9 | .732 | |
| Multiply by 10 | 7.32 | |
| Record Digit | | 7 |
| Subtract 7 | .32 | |
| Multiply by 10 | 3.2 | |
| Record Digit | | 3 |
| Subtract 3 | .2 | |
| Multiply by 10 | 2 | |
| Record Digit | | 2 |
| Subtract 2 | 0 | |

For obvious reasons, this technique is often called "digit stripping".

When actually converting to binary, octal, or hexadecimal, the display will rarely go to zero. Therefore, we simply compute the number of digits needed, and then stop. With a 10-digit calculator, we can obtain a maximum of 33 binary digits, 11 octal digits, and 8 hexadecimal digits. Any digits computed beyond these will be "garbage" resulting from round-off errors.

**CONVERSION TO DECIMAL**

The algorithm just given for converting to decimal works for integers only. We now wish to extend it to any floating point number. We assume that the number to be converted has been written in scientific notation:

1) Move the radix point to the right until the mantissa is an integer. Decrease the exponent by 1 for each shift.

2) Convert the mantissa—which is now an integer—using the algorithm given in the last section.

3) For small exponents: If the exponent is positive, multiply the converted mantissa by the base a number of times equal to the exponent. If the exponent is negative, divide by the base a number of times equal to the magnitude of the exponent. For large exponents, see the section on computing large powers for methods which are easier to use and give better accuracy.

Figure 2-1 summarizes the complete conversion algorithm. Figures 2-2, 2-3, and 2-4 show worked out examples of binary to decimal, octal to decimal, and hexadecimal to decimal conversion.

## CONVERSION FROM DECIMAL

The decimal number to be converted must be scaled until it is greater than or equal to 1 but less than the base of the system we are converting to. The scaling can be done by repeated multiplication or division by the base in question. If many multiplications or divisions are called for, see the section on computing large powers for methods that will be simpler to apply and give greater accuracy.

The algorithm for converting from decimal to base-B is:

1) Enter the number to be converted into the calculator.
2) Set the exponent of the converted number to 0. While the number displayed is less than 1 or greater than or equal to B, repeat the following:

---

1) Move the radix point to the right until the mantissa is an integer. Decrease the exponent by 1 for each shift.
2) Convert the mantissa to decimal as follows:
  2.1) Clear the calculator display.
  2.2) Working from right to left through the digits of the mantissa, repeat the following for each digit:
    2.2.1) Multiply the number displayed on the calculator by B.
    2.2.2) Add the decimal value of the current digit to the number displayed
3) Multiply the number displayed by $B^E$ where E is the exponent at the end of step 1. For small positive E, multiply by B, E times. For small negative E, divide by B, $-E$ times. For large E, if E is positive compute $B^E$ as described in the section COMPUTING LARGE POWERS and multiply the number displayed by it. If E is negative, compute $B^{-E}$ in the same way and divide by it.

Fig. 2-1. Algorithm for converting a floating point number from base B to decimal.

Convert $1.1101B \times 2^2$ to decimal.
1) Write the number to be converted in the form
$$11101B \times 2^{-2}$$
2) Convert the mantissa to decimal:

| OPERATION | NUMBER DISPLAYED |
|---|---|
| Clear display | 0 |
| Multiply by 2 | 0 |
| Add 1 | 1 |
| Multiply by 2 | 2 |
| Add 1 | 3 |
| Multiply by 2 | 6 |
| Add 1 | 7 |
| Multiply by 2 | 14 |
| Add 0 | 14 |
| Multiply by 2 | 28 |
| Add 1 | 29 |

3) Since $-2$ is the exponent at the end of step 1, divide the number displayed by 2, twice.

| OPERATION | NUMBER DISPLAYED |
|---|---|
|  | 29 |
| Divide by 2 | 14.5 |
| Divide by 2 | 7.25 |

Thus $1.1101B \times 2^2 = 7.25$.

Fig. 2-2. Worked-out example of binary to decimal conversion.

---

  2.1) If the number displayed is less than 1, multiply by B and decrease the exponent by 1.
  2.2) If the number displayed is greater than or equal to B, divide by B and increase the exponent by 1.
 3) The number displayed may now be converted using the digit stripping technique previously given. The result is the mantissa of the converted number. The radix point goes after the leftmost digit, the first one calculated.
 4) Using the exponent and mantissa obtained, write the converted number in scientific notation.

Figure 2-5 gives the complete conversion algorithm. Figures 2-6, 2-7, and 2-8 show worked out examples of decimal to binary, decimal to octal, and decimal to hexadecimal conversion.

## COMPUTING LARGE POWERS

Both of the conversion algorithms call for multiplication or division by some power of 2, 8, or 16. When the exponent is

Convert $4.56Q \times 8^4$ to decimal.
1) Write the number to be converted in the form:
$$456Q \times 8^2$$
2) Convert the mantissa to decimal:

| OPERATION | NUMBER DISPLAYED |
|---|---|
| Clear Display | 0 |
| Multiply by 8 | 0 |
| Add 4 | 4 |
| Multiply by 8 | 32 |
| Add 5 | 37 |
| Multiply by 8 | 296 |
| Add 6 | 302 |

3) Since 2 is the exponent at the end of step 1, multiply the number displayed by 8, twice.

| OPERATION | NUMBER DISPLAYED |
|---|---|
|  | 302 |
| Multiply by 8 | 2416 |
| Multiply by 8 | 19328 |

Thus $4.56Q \times 8^4 = 19328 = 1.9328 \times 10^4$

Fig. 2-3. Worked-out example of octal to decimal conversion.

---

small we may simply multiply or divide by the base the required number of times. But faced with powers like $2^{100}$, $8^{55}$, or $16^{75}$, it is worth devoting some time to determining how to compute them quickly and accurately.

---

Convert $6.CFDH \cdot 16^2$ to decimal.
1) Write the number to be converted in the form:
$$6CFDH \times 16^{-1}$$
2) Convert the mantissa to decimal:

| OPERATION | NUMBER DISPLAYED |
|---|---|
| Clear Display | 0 |
| Multiply by 16 | 0 |
| Add 6 | 6 |
| Multiply by 16 | 96 |
| Add 12 | 108 |
| Multiply by 16 | 1728 |
| Add 15 | 1743 |
| Multiply by 16 | 27888 |
| Add 13 | 27901 |

3) Since $-1$ is the exponent at the end of step 1, divide the number displayed by 16, once.

| OPERATION | NUMBER DISPLAYED |
|---|---|
|  | 27901 |
| Divide by 16 | 1743.8125 |

Thus $6.CFDH \times 16^2 = 1743.8125 = 1.7438125 \times 10^3$

Fig. 2-4. Worked-out example of hexadecimal to decimal conversion.

1) Enter the number to be converted into the calculator.
2) Set the exponent of the converted number to 0. While the number displayed is less than 1 or greater than or equal to B, repeat the following:
  2.1) If the number displayed is less than 1, multiply by B and decrease the exponent by 1.
  2.2) If the number displayed is greater than or equal to B, divide by B and increase the exponent by 1.
3) Compute the mantissa digits of the converted number in left to right order by repeating the following for each digit:
  3.1) The integer part of the number displayed is the decimal value of the current digit. Write down that digit.
  3.2) Subtract the integer part from the number displayed, leaving the fractional part.
  3.3) Multiply by B
4) Write the result in the form
$$(\text{mantissa}) \times B^{(\text{exponent})}$$
where the mantissa was computed in step 3 and the exponent in step 2. The radix point is in the usual position: immediately to the right of the first mantissa digit computed.

Fig. 2-5. Algorithm for converting a decimal floating point number to base B.

Our strategy will be to do as many multiplications as possible using the largest power of the base that can be represented accurately inside the calculator. For a 10 digit

Convert 6.5 to binary.
1) Enter 6.5 into the calculator.
2) Divide the number displayed by 2 until it becomes less than 2. Initialize the exponent to 0 and increase it by 1 for each division.

| OPERATION | NUMBER DISPLAYED | EXPONENT |
|---|---|---|
|  | 6.5 | 0 |
| Divide by 2 | 3.25 | 1 |
| Divide by 2 | 1.625 | 2 |

3) Compute the mantissa digits.

| OPERATION | NUMBER DISPLAYED | DIGIT |
|---|---|---|
|  | 1.625 |  |
| Record digit |  | 1 |
| Subtract 1 | .625 |  |
| Multiply by 2 | 1.25 |  |
| Record Digit |  | 1 |
| Subtract 1 | .25 |  |
| Multiply by 2 | .5 |  |
| Record Digit |  | 0 |
| Subtract 0 | .5 |  |
| Multiply by 2 | 1 |  |
| Record digit |  | 1 |
| Subtract 1 | 0 |  |

4) Combine mantissa computed in step 3 with exponent computed in step 4 to give final answer:
$$6.5 = 1.101B \times 2^2$$

Fig. 2-6. Worked-out example of decimal to binary conversion.

Convert $3.5 \times 10^3$ to octal.
1) Enter $3.5 \times 10^3$ into the calculator.
2) Divide the number displayed by 8 until it becomes less than 8. Initialize the exponent to 0 and increase it by 1 for each division.

| OPERATION | NUMBER DISPLAYED | EXPONENT |
|---|---|---|
|  | 3500 | 0 |
| Divide by 8 | 437.5 | 1 |
| Divide by 8 | 54.6875 | 2 |
| Divide by 8 | 6.8359375 | 3 |

3) Compute the mantissa digits.

| OPERATION | NUMBER DISPLAYED | DIGIT |
|---|---|---|
|  | 6.8359375 |  |
| Record digit |  | 6 |
| Subtract 6 | .8359375 |  |
| Multiply by 8 | 6.6875 |  |
| Record digit |  | 6 |
| Subtract 6 | .6875 |  |
| Multiply by 8 | 5.5 |  |
| Record digit |  | 5 |
| Subtract 5 | .5 |  |
| Multiply by 8 | 4 |  |
| Record digit |  | 4 |
| Subtract 4 | 0 |  |

4) Combine the mantissa computed in step 3 with the exponent computed in step 2 to give the final answer:

$$3.5 \times 10^3 = 6.6540 \times 8^3$$

Fig. 2-7. Worked-out example of decimal to octal conversion.

---

Convert $10^{-1}$ to hexadecimal.
1) Enter $10^{-1}$ into the calculator.
2) Multiply the number displayed by 16 until it is greater than or equal to 1. Initialize the exponent to 0 and decrease it by 1 for each multiplication.

| OPERATION | NUMBER DISPLAYED | EXPONENT |
|---|---|---|
|  | .1 | 0 |
| Multiply by 16 | 1.6 | $-1$ |

3) Compute the mantissa digits.

| OPERATION | NUMBER DISPLAYED | DIGIT |
|---|---|---|
|  | 1.6 |  |
| Record digit |  | 1 |
| Subtract 1 | .6 |  |
| Multiply by 16 | 9.6 |  |
| Record digit |  | 9 |
| Subtract 9 | .6 |  |

Since the display is again .6, the next digit will be 9, and so on indefinitely. Thus the mantissa is 1.9999...H.

4) Combine the mantissa computed in step 3 with the exponent computed in step 2 to give the final answer:

$$10^{-1} = 1.999...H \times 16^{-1}$$

The answer could be rounded off to 8 digits to give

$$1.999999AH \times 16^{-1}$$

Fig. 2-8. Worked-out example of decimal to hexadecimal conversion.

calculator this number is, for each base:

$$2^{33} = 8.589934592 \times 10^9$$
$$8^{11} = 8.589934592 \times 10^9$$
$$16^8 = 4.294967296 \times 10^9$$

These numbers can be calculated when needed by repeated multiplication. But if extensive conversion work is anticipated, they might be memorized or noted in a convenient place. Fortunately, only two numbers are necessary since $2^{33} = 8^{11}$.

Now suppose we wish to compute $2^{100}$. Since $100 = 1 + 33 + 33 + 33$, and since multiplying exponentials adds their exponents, we have:

$$2^{100} = 2 * 2^{33} * 2^{33} * 2^{33} = 1.267650600 \times 10^{30}$$

correct to 10 decimal places. In the same way we can compute $8^{55}$ and $16^{75}$:

$$8^{55} = 8^{11} * 8^{11} * 8^{11} * 8^{11} * 8^{11} = 4.676805240 \times 10^{49}$$

and
$$16^{75} = 16 * 16 * 16 * 16^8 * 16^8 * 16^8 * 16^8 * 16^8$$
$$* 16^8 * 16^8 * 16^8 * 16^8$$
$$= 2.037035977 \times 10^{90}$$

When a negative power is needed, compute the corresponding positive power and divide by it instead of multiplying by it.

Figure 2-9 illustrates the use of the preceding method in an octal to decimal conversion.

## SCALING AND LOGARITHMS

When converting from decimal to another base, we have a problem in using the method just given for computing large powers: We do not know the required exponent in advance. Fortunately there is a technique using logarighms by which this exponent can be computed.

The logarithms we need are not the familiar natural and common logarithms, but logarithms to bases 2, 8, and 16. These are easily computed on a calculator that features *any* logarithm, regardless of the base. We have:

$$\log_2 N = \log N / \log 2$$
$$\log_8 N = \log N / \log 8$$
$$\log_{16} N = \log N / \log 16$$

Convert $3.5Q \times 8^{24}$ to decimal.
1) Write the number to be converted in the form
$$35Q \times 8^{23}$$
2) Convert the mantissa to decimal:

| OPERATION | NUMBER DISPLAYED |
|---|---|
| Clear display | 0 |
| Multiply by 8 | 0 |
| Add 3 | 3 |
| Multiply by 8 | 24 |
| Add 5 | 29 |

3) Compute $8^{23}$ as $8 \cdot 8^{11} \cdot 8^{11}$, and multiply this by the mantissa to obtain the final result.

| OPERATION | NUMBER DISPLAYED |
|---|---|
| Enter 8 | 8 |
| Multiply by $8^{11}$ | $6.871947674 \times 10^{10}$ |
| Multiply by $8^{11}$ | $5.902958104 \times 10^{20}$ |
| Multiply by 29 | $1.711857850 \times 10^{22}$ |

Thus $3.5Q \times 8^{24} = 1.711857850 \times 10^{22}$

Fig. 2-9. Example of an octal to decimal conversion using the method given in the text for computing large powers.

---

where the unadorned "log" may be to any base, and is the *log* function available on your calculator. If more than one log function is available, either may be used. The *log* function may be labeled *ln*.

We need one other function, and this is the INT function familiar to users of BASIC. INT (X) is defined as the largest integer which does not exceed X. More specifically:

1) If X is an integer, then INT (X) = X. Examples: INT (5) = 5; INT ( −3) − 3.
2) If X is not an integer and is positive, INT (X) is the integer part of X. Examples: INT (3.14) = 3; INT (2.718) = 2.
3) If X is not an integer and is negative, then INT (X) is the integer part of X minus 1. Examples: INT (−3.14) = −4; INT (−2.718 = −3.

Now let X be any positive number. Suppose we convert X to base B and write the result in scientific notation. The exponent of the result will be:

$$\text{INT}(\log_B X)$$

That is, to find the exponent, we take the logarithm of X to base B and then apply the INT function to the result.

1) Compute the exponent, E, of the converted number using
$$E = INT(\log_B x)$$
where x is the decimal number to be converted. See the section SCALING AND LOGARITHMS in the text for the details of this calculation.
2) If E is positive compute $B^E$ and divide it into the number to be converted. If E is negative, compute $B^{-E}$ and multiply it by the number to be converted. Use the techniques of the section COMPUTING LARGE POWERS to compute $B^E$ or $B^{-E}$. Leave the result of the multiplication or division displayed on the calculator.
3) Compute the mantissa digits as in step 3 of Fig. 2-5.
4) Write the result in the form
$$(mantissa) \times B^E$$
where the radix point in the mantissa is immediately to the right of the leftmost digit.

Fig. 2-10. Algorithm for converting from decimal to base B modified to use the logarithmic method of computing the exponent.

---

Example: $X = 10^{-20}$ and $B = 8$
$\log_8 (10^{-20}) = \log (10^{-20})/\log 8 = -46.05/2.08 = -22.14$
$INT(-22.14) = -23$
Thus $10^{-20}$ in octal will have the form:

$$(octal\ mantissa) \times 8^{-23}$$

Example: $X = 1.5 \times 10^{35}$ and $B = 16$
$\log_{16} (1.5 \times 10^{35}) = \log (1.5 \times 10^{35})/\log 16$
$= 81.00/2.77 = 29.24$
$INT(29.24) = 29$
Thus $1.5 \times 10^{35}$ in hexadecimal will have the form:
$$(hexadecimal\ mantissa) \times 16^{29}$$

Figure 2-10 shows the algorithm for converting from decimal to some other base modified to use the logarithmic method of computing the exponent. Figure 2-11 shows a worked-out example using that method.

## ROUNDING

In decimal, the rule for rounding is: add 1 to the rightmost digit to be retained if the next digit to the right is 5 or greater. Thus, rounding to two decimal places, 9.453 rounds to 9.45 and 9.457 rounds to 9.46. The corresponding rules for binary, octal, and hexadecimal are:

*Binary.* Add 1 to the rightmost digit to be retained if the next digit to the right is 1.

*Octal.* Add 1 to the rightmost digit to be retained if the next digit to the right is 4 or greater.

Convert $10^{30}$ to octal.
1) $\log_8(10^{30}) = \log(10^{30})/\log 8 = 69.08/2.08 = 33.21$
   $E = \text{INT}(33.21) = 33$
2) Compute $8^{33} = 8^{11} \cdot 8^{11} \cdot 8^{11} = 6.338253001 \times 10^{29}$
   Divide $10^{30}$ by $6.338253001 \times 10^{29}$ to get $1.577721810$
3) Compute the mantissa digits:

| OPERATION | NUMBER DISPLAYED | DIGIT |
|---|---|---|
|  | 1.577721810 |  |
| Record digit |  | 1 |
| Subtract 1 | .577721810 |  |
| Multiply by 8 | 4.621774480 |  |
| Record digit |  | 4 |
| Subtract 4 | .621774480 |  |
| Multiply by 8 | 4.974195840 |  |
| Record digit |  | 4 |
| Subtract 4 | .974195840 |  |
| Multiply by 8 | 7.793566720 |  |
| Record digit |  | 7 |
| Subtract 7 | .793566720 |  |
| Multiply by 8 | 6.348533760 |  |
| Record digit |  | 6 |
| Subtract 6 | .348533760 |  |
| Multiply by 8 | 2.788270080 |  |
| Record digit |  | 2 |
| Subtract 2 | .788270080 |  |
| Multiply by 8 | 6.306160640 |  |
| Record digit |  | 6 |
| Subtract 6 | .306160640 |  |
| Multiply by 8 | 2.449285120 |  |
| Record digit |  | 2 |
| Subtract 2 | .449285120 |  |
| Multiply by 8 | 3.594280960 |  |
| Record digit |  | 3 |
| Subtract 3 | .594280960 |  |
| Multiply by 8 | 4.754247680 |  |
| Record digit |  | 4 |
| Subtract 4 | .754247680 |  |
| Multiply by 8 | 6.033981440 |  |
| Record digit |  | 6 |

Since at most 11 accurate octal digits can be obtained from a 10-digit decimal number, we terminate the calculation of mantissa digits at this point

4) Write out the result:
$$10^{30} = 1.4476262346Q \times 8^{33}$$

Fig. 2-11. A decimal to octal conversion using the logarithmic method of computing the exponent.

---

*Hexadecimal.* Add 1 to the rightmost digit to be retained if the next digit to the right is 8 or greater.

Rounding to two places in the fraction, we find that

$\quad\quad\quad\quad$ 10.100B rounds to 10.10B
$\quad\quad\quad\quad$ 10.101B rounds to 10.11B

$$\begin{aligned}
6.433\text{Q} &\text{ rounds to } 6.43\text{Q} \\
6.434\text{Q} &\text{ rounds to } 6.44\text{Q} \\
9.\text{FC7H} &\text{ rounds to } 9.\text{FCH} \\
9.\text{FC8H} &\text{ rounds to } 9.\text{FDH}
\end{aligned}$$

Note that the 1 added to the rightmost digit to be retained may cause a carry, which may propagate a number of places to the left. Thus 1.111B rounds to 10.00B, 5.774Q rounds to 6.00Q, and 5.FF8H rounds to 6.00H.

# Part II
# A High Level
# for Machine Level Programs

# Chapter 3
# Data Definition

In this chapter we embark on the construction of a high level, PL/I-like, language to serve as a substitute for machine code and assembly language in describing machine level programs.

### PRIMITIVE DATA TYPES

We classify the data items a program can manipulate into different *types*. Integers, real numbers, complex numbers, and character strings are examples of data types.

The *primitive data types* of a programming language are those which are assumed to be already defined, and which the programmer is not required to define in terms of simpler data types. The primitive data types of most versions of BASIC, for instance, are real numbers (floating point numbers) and character strings.

Since we are building a machine level language, the primitive data types of the language should be the same as those offered by the computer itself. Luckily (for standardization is not the computer industry's forte) most hobbyist computers feature the same data types: 8-bit bytes and 16-bit words. These, then, will be the primitive data types of our programming language.

Figure 3-1 illustrates an 8-bit byte and a 16-bit word. Following the conventions of Chapter 1, the bits of a byte or word are numbered from right to left, beginning with 0. For a

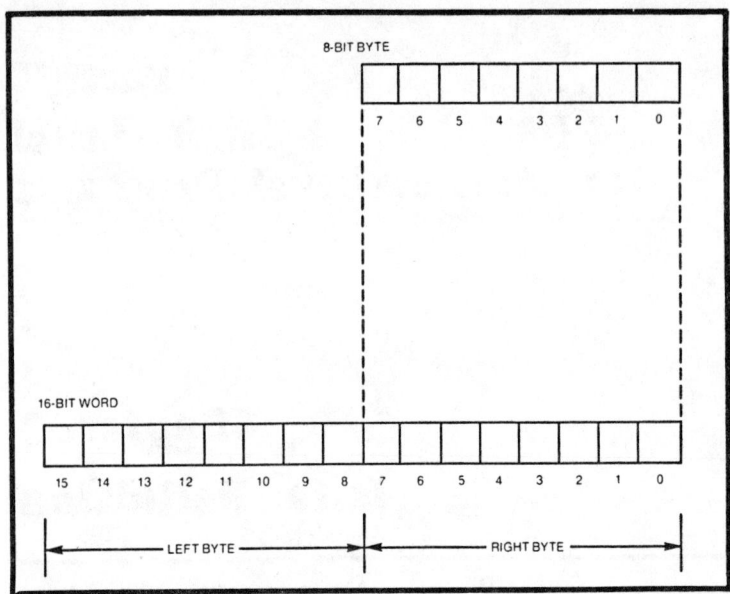

Fig. 3-1. Our primitive data types: The 8-bit byte and the 16-bit word. Note the numbering of the bits.

byte, the rightmost bit is bit 0; the leftmost bit is bit 7. For a word, the rightmost bit is still bit 0, but the leftmost bit is bit 15, Also, a word is made up of two bytes. The right byte is bits 0-7; the left byte is bits 8-15.

The rightmost bit of a byte or word is sometimes called the *least significant bit* and the leftmost bit, the *most significant bit*. The rightmost *byte* is sometimes called the *least significant byte* and the leftmost byte, the *most significant byte*. Still another name for the rightmost byte is the *low order byte*; the leftmost byte is then the *high order byte*.

**CONSTANTS**

Constants denote bit patterns which are to be placed in bytes or words. We shall use five kinds of constants: binary, octal, decimal, hexadecimal, and character. As a rule, we use a decimal constant when we wish to denote a numerical value; a binary, octal, or hexadecimal constant to denote a bit pattern; and a character constant to denote the code for a character.

The notation for binary, octal, decimal, and hexadecimal constants is the same used in Chapter 1. The specified bit pattern is always *right justified* in the byte or word—that is, moved as far to the right as possible. Thus 101B denotes the pattern 00000101 for a byte and 0000000000000101 for a word.

Two hexadecimal digits denote the contents of one byte, and four hexadecimal digits denote the contents of one word. This makes hexadecimal particularly useful for denoting bit patterns, and we shall generally use hexadecimal rather than binary or octal for this purpose. Remember that in programs, a hexadecimal constant must start with one of the digits 0-9. Thus in a program FCH would be written 0FCH; in either case it would denote the bit pattern 11111100.

A character constant consists of a character enclosed in single quote marks, and denotes the bit pattern that corresponds to the character in question in whatever character code is being used. Thus if we are using ASCII, then 'A' = 41H, 'B' = 42H, '.' = 2EH, '+' = 2BH, and so on. Note that ' ' is the code for a *blank space*; in ASCII it would equal 20H.

We may enclose more than one character between the quote marks. The code for the characters enclosed are stored in adjacent bytes. Thus 'ABCDE' denotes a block of 5 bytes; the first byte contains the code 'A', the second 'B', the third 'C', the fourth 'D', and the fifth 'E'.

## NAMES, ADDRESSES, AND VALUES

We may visualize a computer memory as a long list of bytes. The bytes are numbered, starting with 0. The number of a byte is called its *address*. Figure 3-2 illustrates this memory layout.

A *word* consists of two adjacent bytes. The address of the word is the address of its first byte, that is, the byte having the smallest address. Some computers, such as the PDP-11, require that the first byte of a word have an even address, and the second an odd address. Thus the addresses of all words are even numbers. Most hobbyist computers, however, do not impose this restriction, and allow words to start on either even or odd addresses.

Another variation: on some computers the first byte of a word is the low order byte, and the second is the high order byte. On others, the reverse is true. Therefore we will avoid programs which depend on the order in which the bytes of a word are stored, since such programs would not work correctly on computers that use a different order.

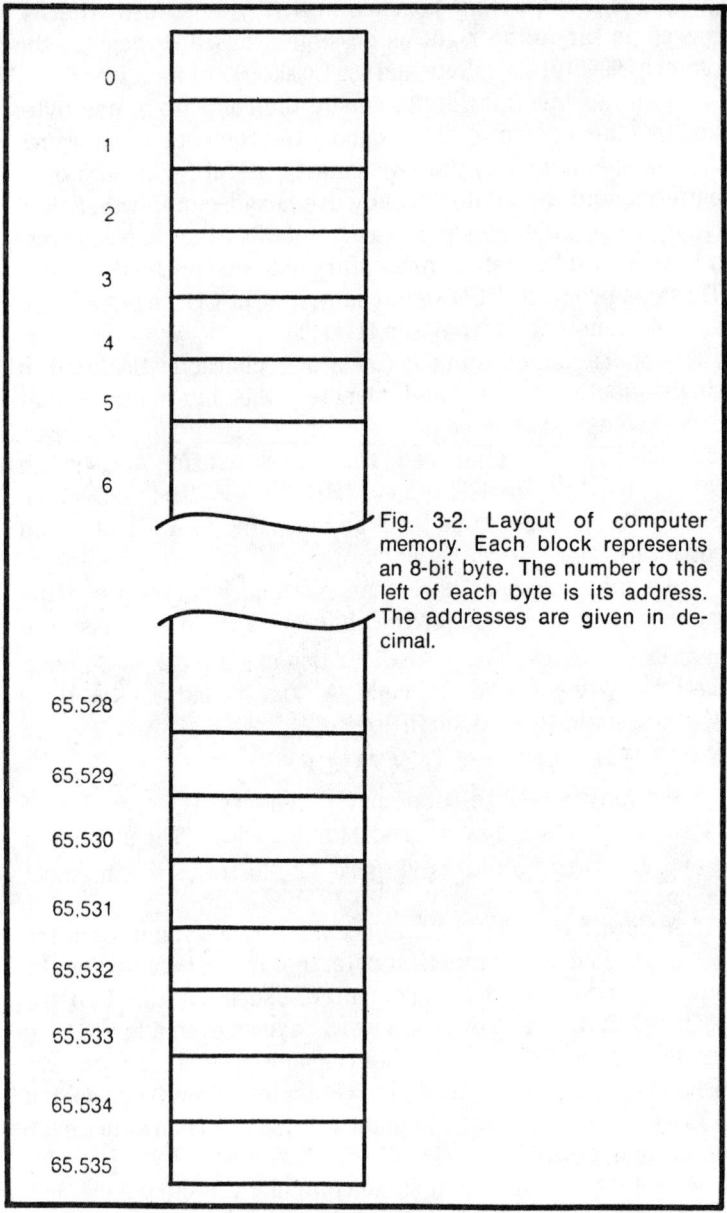

Fig. 3-2. Layout of computer memory. Each block represents an 8-bit byte. The number to the left of each byte is its address. The addresses are given in decimal.

Figure 3-3 illustrates the various conventions for building words from bytes.

*Declarations.* It is inconvenient to refer to memory locations by their numerical addresses. Instead, we refer to them by name. We make up the names in such a way as to suggest the nature of the contents of a location, or the use to which it will be put in the program.

The correspondence between names and memory locations is established using the DECLARE statement. Thus

DECLARE COUNTER BYTE;

will establish COUNTER as the name of a byte. In the same way

DECLARE POINTER WORD;

would establish POINTER as the name of a word.

The words BYTE and WORD are *attributes*. Thus COUNTER has the BYTE attribute and POINTER has the WORD attribute.

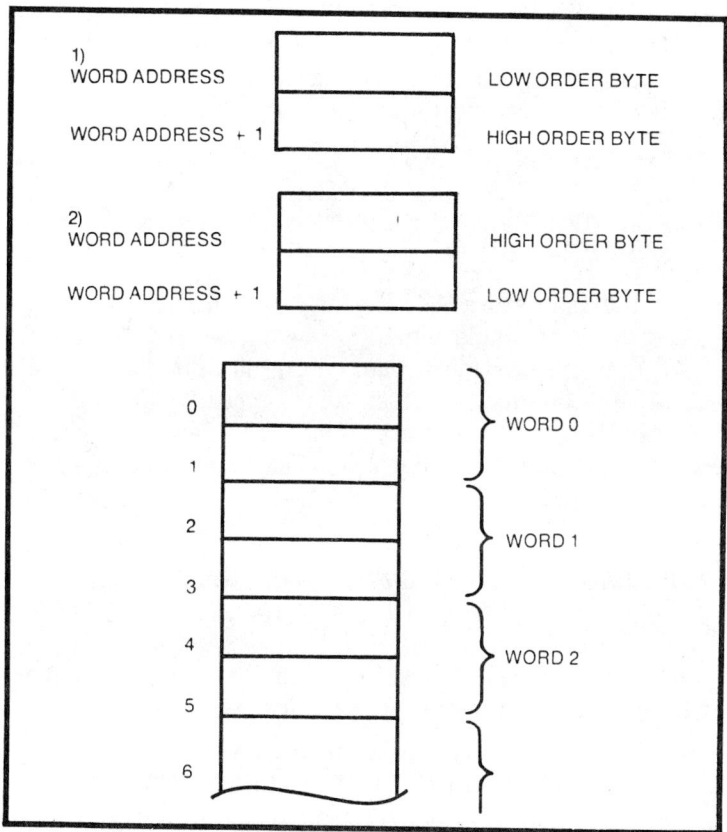

Fig. 3-3. Conventions for building words from bytes: 1) Low order byte stored first. 2) High order byte stored first. 3) Words begin only on even addresses.

The data currently stored in the named location is the current *value* of the name. Thus if the byte named counter currently contains (the bit pattern representing) 25, then we would say that the value of COUNTER is 25. If the word denoted by POINTER currently holds 3F2CH, then 3F2CH is the current value of POINTER.

A name is also often called a *variable*, since its value can *vary* during program execution.

When a name appears in a mathematical expression, such as POINTER + 1, it stands for its value, that is, the data stored at the named location. If we wish to refer to the address of the location, rather than its contents, we prefix the name with an "@" sign. Thus @ POINTER stands for the address of the byte POINTER while POINTER stands for its value.

Usually we will need to name more than one memory location in a program. We can use a separate DECLARE statement for each name:

DECLARE COUNTER BYTE;
DECLARE TEMPORARY BYTE;
DECLARE LOW_VALUE BYTE;
DECLARE HIGH_VALUE BYTE;

(We use the underscore character "_" to join separate words together to form a single name.)

We may include more than one declaration in a single DECLARE statement, rather than repeating the word DECLARE as in the above example. The declarations are separated by commas; a single semicolon appears at the end of the entire DECLARE statement:

DECLARE COUNTER BYTE, TEMPORARY BYTE,
    LOW_VALUE BYTE, HIGH_VALUE BYTE;

If all the names of a set have the same attribute, the attribute may be "factored out" like this:

DECLARE (COUNTER, TEMPORARY,
    LOW_VALUE, HIGH_VALUE) BYTE;

The attribute BYTE applies to each of the names inside the parentheses—that is, each one names a one byte location.

Figure 3-4 illustrates the correspondence between names, addresses, values, and memory locations.

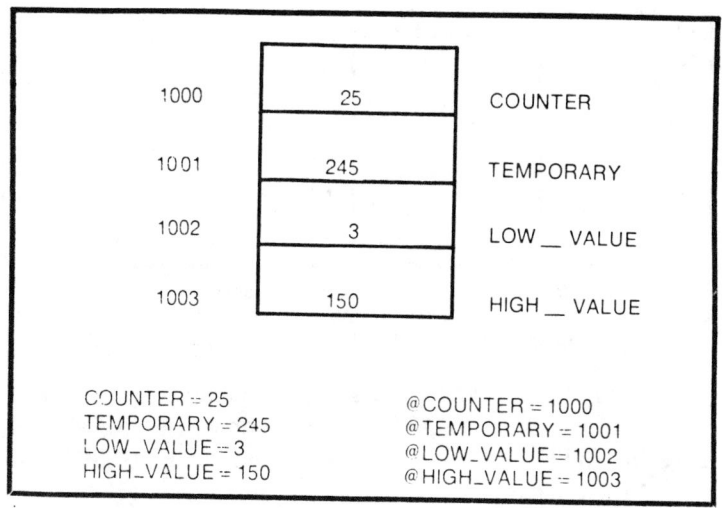

Fig. 3-4. Correspondence between names, addresses, values, and memory locations.

## STRUCTURES

We have assumed that the computer hardware provides only two kinds of memory location—the byte and the word. Nevertheless, it is often convenient to take a group of bytes or words and treat them as a single memory location. Or, looking at the matter another way, we would like to define more complex data types in terms of the primitive ones built into the language.

For instance, suppose the data we are working with consists of dates. Each date is written in the usual month/day/year form: 6/18/76, for instance. Such a date could be stored in three bytes: the first byte would hold the month, the second byte the day, and the third byte the year. What we need is a memory location consisting of three bytes. The location should be *structured*, that is, it should be made up of three parts or *components*: month, day, and year.

We declare such a structured location, or *structure*, as follows:

DECLARE 1 DATE,
        2 MONTH BYTE,
        2 DAY BYTE,
        2 YEAR BYTE;

DATE is the name of a three-byte memory location, as shown in Fig. 3-5. It is subdivided into three components: MONTH,

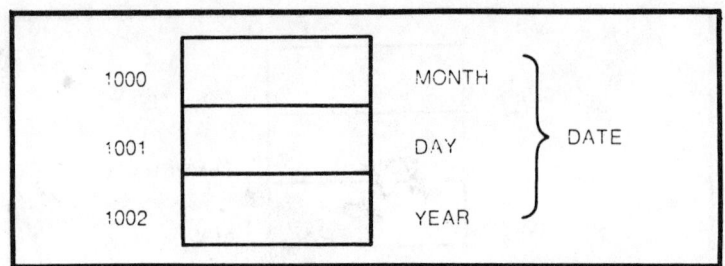

Fig. 3-5. The structured location DATE is represented by three adjacent bytes in memory. The first byte is the MONTH compnoent; the second, the DAY component; and the third, the YEAR component.

DAY, and YEAR. We refer to the components by *qualifying* the structure name: DATE.MONTH names the first byte of DATE, DATE.DAY names the second, and DATE.YEAR names the third.

The numbers 1 and 2 are *level numbers*. Level 1 is the level of the entire structure; Level 2 is the first level of subdivision; we could use additional levels so that the components themselves would be structures, which could be further subdivided still. Consider the following:

```
DECLARE 1 DATE_AND_TIME,
         2 DATE,
           3 MONTH BYTE,
           3 DAY BYTE,
           3 YEAR BYTE,
         2 TIME,
           3 HOUR BYTE,
           3 MINUTE BYTE,
           3 SECOND BYTE;
```

DATE_AND_TIME means a six-byte location. DATE_AND_TIME.DATE and DATE_AND_TIME.TIME each names a three-byte location. And each of the following names a one-byte location:

DATE_AND_TIME.DATE.MONTH<br>
DATE_AND_TIME.DATE.DAY<br>
DATE_AND_TIME.DATE.YEAR<br>
DATE_AND_TIME.TIME.HOUR<br>
DATE_AND_TIME.TIME.MINUTE<br>
DATE_AND_TIME.TIME.SECOND

Figure 3-6 shows the layout of the location DATE_AND_TIME.

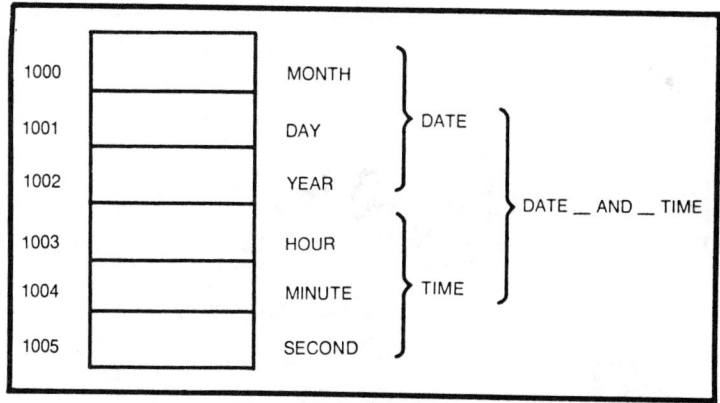

Fig. 3-6. Memory layout for the structure DATE __ AND __ TIME.

A structure may incorporate both bytes and words as components. Thus if we wished to store the complete year—1976 as opposed to 76—we could declare DATE as follows:

    DECLARE 1 DATE,
            2 MONTH BYTE,
            2 DAY BYTE,
            2 YEAR WORD;

Figure 3-7 shows the layout of the revised structure DATE.

Often we would like to declare several memory locations as having the same structure. We do not wish to have to recopy all the subdivisions in each declaration. Instead, we may use a declaration with the following form:

    DECLARE 1 INSTANT LIKE DATE_AND_TIME;

INSTANT is given the same subdivisions as

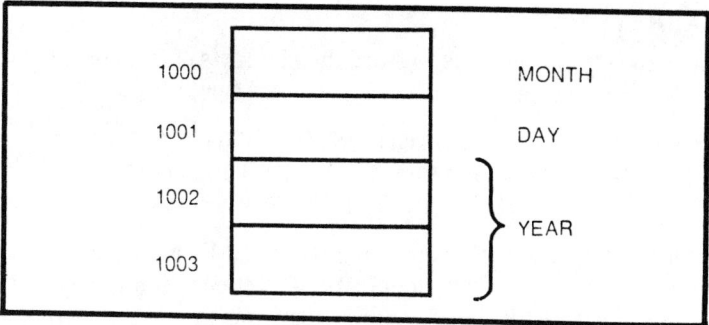

Fig. 3-7. A structure containing both byte and word components.

49

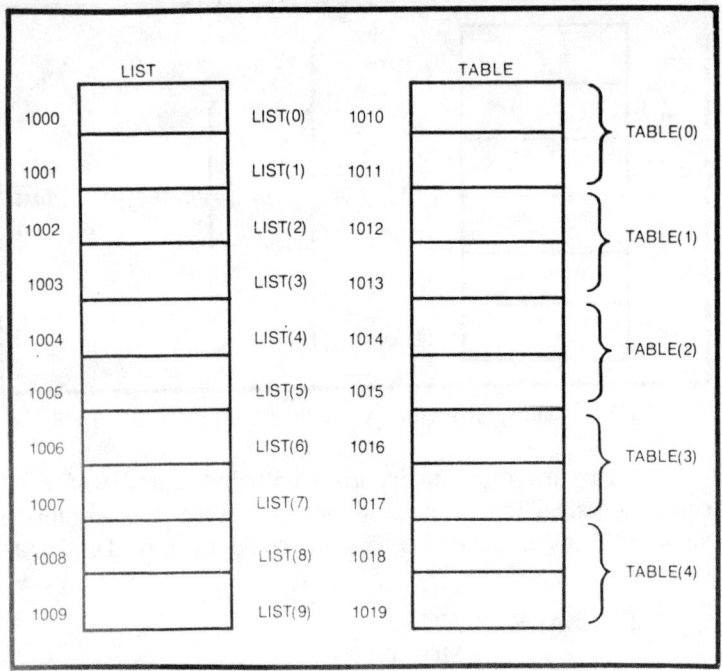

Fig. 3-8. Memory layouts for the 10-byte array, LIST and the 5-word array, TABLE.

DATE_AND_TIME. Thus it is a six-byte location, and we can refer to INSTANT.DATE, INSTANT.DATE.MONTH, and so on. The attribute LIKE TIME_AND_DATE functions much like BYTE or WORD in describing the kind of memory location that INSTANT refers to. It allows us—in a somewhat roundabout way—to add a new data type to the language. With the aid of LIKE, every structure defines a new data type.

## ARRAYS

An array allows us to store the elements of a list or table in adjacent memory locations. The declaration

DECLARE LIST(10) BYTE;

defines an array of 10 bytes named LIST. In the same way

DECLARE TABLE (5) WORD;

defines an array of 5 words named TABLE. Figure 3-8 shows the effects of these two declarations. Notice that although both LIST and TABLE each occupies the same amount of memory, in one case this memory is divided up into 10 bytes; and in the other, into 5 words. The elements of an array are numbered 0-9, and the 5 elements of table are numbered 0-4. We name a particular array element by putting its number in parentheses after the name of the array. The names of the elements of LIST are

LIST(0)   LIST(5)

LIST(1)   LIST(6)

LIST(2)   LIST(7)

LIST(3)   LIST(8)

LIST(4)   LIST(9)

and the names of the elements of TABLE are:

TABLE(0)
TABLE(1)
TABLE(2)
TABLE(3)
TABLE(4)

The number in parentheses is called the *subscript* or *index*. We would read LIST(5) as "LIST subscripted by 5" or, for short, "LIST sub 5".

A subscript is not always a number. More commonly, in fact, it is the name of a byte or word. The value of the name—the contents of the named location—determines which array element will be referenced.

Suppose, for instance, that ENTRY names a byte. Consider the name of an element of LIST, LIST(ENTRY). If the value of ENTRY is 0, then LIST(ENTRY) will be the name of element 0 of LIST; if the value of ENTRY is 1, then LIST(ENTRY) will be the name of element 1 of LIST; and so on.

When we use a name such as COUNTER or TEMPORARY or LIST(1), we choose which location will be referred to when the program is written. But when we use a name like LIST(ENTRY), the value of ENTRY will be computed as the program runs on the computer, and only at "run time" will it be determined what location LIST(ENTRY) refers to. Thus we defer until run time the choice of which location we wish to refer to, rather than having to make that choice when we write the program.

The subscript may also be an algebraic expression. The value of the expression determines which array element will be referenced.

We may declare arrays of structured locations as well as arrays of bytes or words. Consider the following:

  DECLARE 1 DATE(5),
     2 MONTH BYTE,
     2 DAY BYTE,
     2 YEAR BYTE;

This declares an array of 5 elements, each element of which is a 3-byte structured location. DATE(0), DATE(1), and so on each names such a 3-byte location. DATE(0).MONTH refers to a 1-byte location, the MONTH component of DATE(0). In the same way DATE(1).YEAR refers to the YEAR component of DATE(1), DATE(4).DAY refers to the DAY component of DATE(4), and so on.

If we define BIRTH_DATE by
  DECLARE 1 BIRTH_DATE LIKE DATE;
then BIRTH_DATE would have the same components as the elements of DATE, but would not itself be an array. If we wish BIRTH_DATE to refer to an array, we would write:
  DECLARE 1 BIRTH_DATE(10) LIKE DATE;
Now BIRTH_DATE refers to a 10-element array each element of which has the same components as each element of DATE.

The components of a structure may themselves be arrays. Thus

  DECLARE 1 PERSON,
     2 NAME (40) BYTE,
     2 ADDRESS(60) BYTE;

declares a 100-byte structure PERSON. Forty bytes are used for NAME and 60 for ADDRESS. (Presumably the name and address are stored one character per byte.) PERSON.NAME refers to a 40-byte array. PERSON.NAME(0) is the first byte in that array, PERSON.NAME(1) is the second byte, and so on.

Finally, we can have an array of structures each of which contains arrays as components. Consider the following:

```
DECLARE 1 PERSONS(100),
          2 NAME(40) BYTE,
          2 ADDRESS(60) BYTE;
```

PERSONS is an array of 100 elements, each element of which is a 100-byte structure. (So the array PERSONS occupies 10,000 bytes.) PERSONS(5) refers to element 5 of PERSONS and is a 100-byte structure. PERSONS(5).NAME is the NAME component of PERSONS, and is a 40-byte array. PERSONS(5).NAME(3) refers to element 3 in the array PERSONS(5).NAME, and is a byte.

We may also declare *multidimensional arrays* in which more than one subscript is needed to specify an element. For instance, we may think of

```
DECLARE TABLE (3, 5) BYTE;
```

as declaring a table of 3 rows (numbered 0-2) and 5 columns (numbered 0-4). TABLE(1, 3) refers to the byte at the intersection of row 1 and column 3.

In the same way, we may think of

```
DECLARE BOOK (10, 3, 5) BYTE;
```

as declaring a book of tables having 10 pages (numbered 0-9), with each page containing a table of 3 rows and 5 columns. BOOK(3, 0, 2) refers to the byte at the intersection of row 0 and column 2 in the table on page 3.

For one-dimensional arrays, it is convenient to have a notation for 1) the number of elements in the array, and 2) the subscript of the last element.

We adopt the following notation, where LIST is the name of a one-dimensional array:

LENGTH (LIST) = number of elements in LIST
LAST (LIST) = subscript of last element of LIST

If LIST was declared by

```
DECLARE LIST(100) WORD;
```

then:

LENGTH (LIST) = 100
LAST (LIST) = 99

In general:

LAST (LIST) = LENGTH (LIST) − 1

**POINTERS**

A pointer is a word that contains the address of another location. We say that the pointer "designates" or "points to"

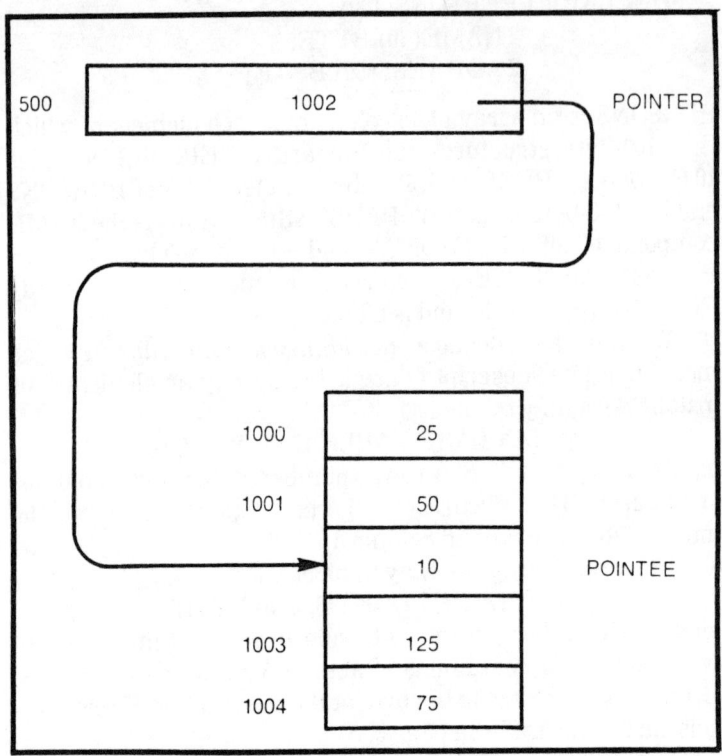

Fig. 3-9. The relation between a pointer and the byte that it points to. In illustrations, an arrow is always used to indicate that one memory location points to another.

the location whose address it contains. Since the value of the pointer is set and changed as the program runs, pointers offer another way of deferring until run time the choice of the memory location referred to in a particular step of a program.

We need some way of designating the memory location pointed to by a particular pointer. Our language offers two methods of doing this.

*The BASED attribute.* Consider the following declaration:

DECLARE POINTER WORD,
        POINTEE BASED POINTER BYTE;

POINTEE is declared to be a byte. Which byte? The byte whose address is contained in POINTER. If the contents of POINTER changes, then the byte named by POINTEE also changes. Figure 3-9 illustrates the relation between POINTER

54

and POINTEE. The use of an arrow to show that one location points to another is customary.

Pointers may also point to structures and arrays. Thus

```
DECLARE 1 TIME BASED POINTER
          2 HOUR BYTE,
          2 MINUTE BYTE,
          2 SECOND BYTE;
```

declares TIME to be the 3-byte structure whose address is contained in POINTER. (The address of a structure or array is the address of its first byte.) Thus TIME.MINUTE refers to the second byte of the 3-byte structure the address of the first byte of which is contained in POINTER.

Arrays may be designated by pointers also:
```
DECLARE TABLE(5) BASED POINTER BYTE;
```
Now TABLE(3) refers to element 3 of the 5-byte array the address of whose first byte is in POINTER.

Figure 3-10 illustrates structures and arrays designated by pointers.

*Qualified Names.* A name may be "qualified" by the name of a pointer. The qualified name then refers to the location designated by the pointer.

Consider the declaration:

```
DECLARE P WORD,
        COUNT BYTE,
        VALUE WORD;
```

Then

$$P - > COUNT$$

names the *byte* pointed to by P, since COUNT was declared as a byte. In the same way,

$$P - > VALUE$$

names the *word* pointed to by P, since VALUE is declared to be a word.

(The sign $- >$ is made up of a minus sign followed by a greater than sign.)

Qualified names are most useful when the name being qualified is that of a structure. Suppose we define CHESS_PIECE by:

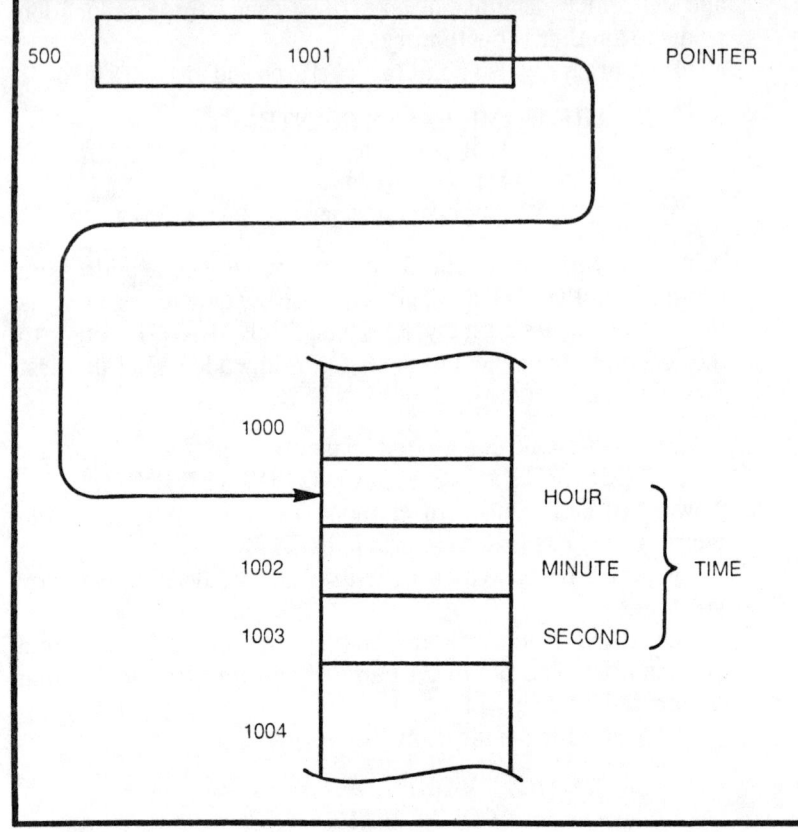

Fig. 3-10. Structure and array designated by pointers. In each case we may think of the structure or array definition as an "overlay," which is superimposed on the block of memory whose address is the value of the pointer.

```
DECLARE 1 CHESS_PIECE,
          2 KIND BYTE,
          2 COLOR BYTE,
          2 POSITION,
            3 ROW BYTE,
            3 COLUMN BYTE;
```

Now suppose that P, Q, and R are pointers, all pointing to locations having the same structure as CHESS_PIECE. Then

P – > CHESS_PIECE is the location like CHESS_PIECE pointed to by P;

Q – > CHESS_PIECE is the location like CHESS_PIECE pointed to by Q;

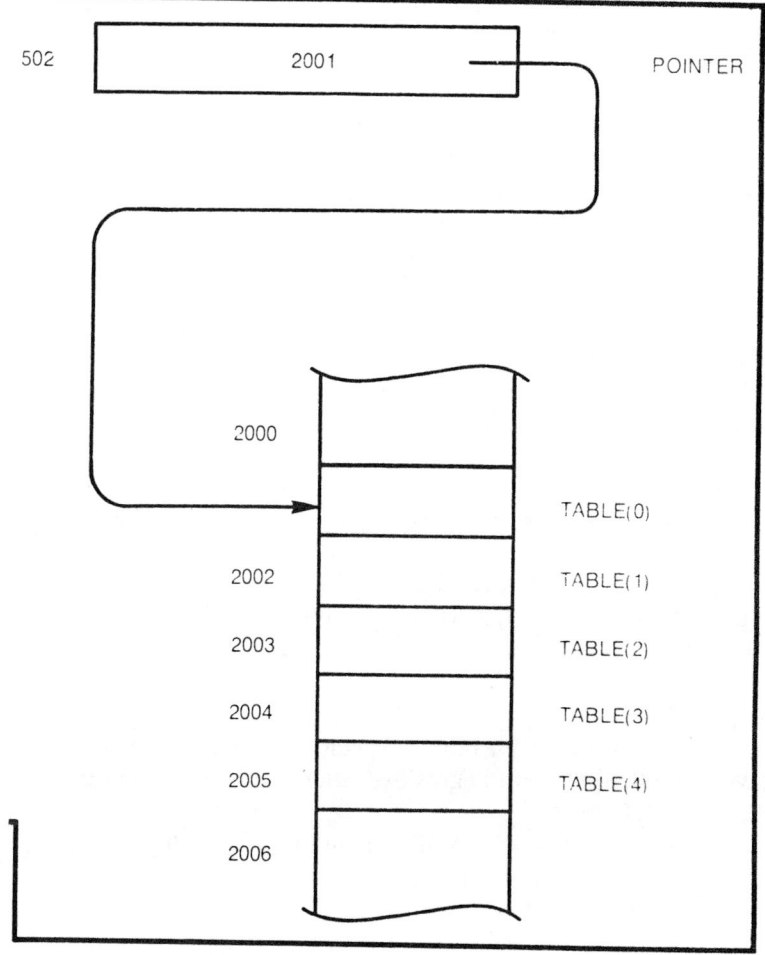

R −> CHESS_PIECE is the location like CHESS_PIECE pointed to by R; and so on.

Thus the structure CHESS_PIECE serves as a "prototype" of all the locations with the same structure that might be pointed to by P, Q, or R.

Since P −> CHESS_PIECE names a location with the same structure as CHESS_PIECE, we can refer to its components:

> P −> CHESS_PIECE.KIND
> P −> CHESS_PIECE.COLOR
> P −> CHESS_PIECE.POSITION.ROW
> P −> CHESS_PIECE.POSITION.COLUMN

Each of the above refers to one of the bytes in the 4-byte structured location pointed to by P.

## MACROS

A *macro* is a word that stands for a piece of program text. Wherever the word appears in the program, the text it stands for is substituted. Macros are declared using the LITERALLY attribute:

DECLARE COUNT_UP LITTERALLY
'COUNT = COUNT + 1' ;

Wherever COUNT_UP appears thereafter, COUNT = COUNT + 1 will be substituted. Thus the statement

COUNT_UP;

would have the same effect as:

COUNT = COUNT + 1;

Macros are particularly useful in assigning meaningful names to numerical constants, as in:

DECLARE CARRIAGE_RETURN LITERALLY 'ODH';

Wherever the word CARRIAGE_RETURN subsequently appears in the program, it will be replaced by ODH, the ASCII code for a carriage return.

## INITIALIZATION

We can initialize variables—specify the values they will have when the program begins execution—using the INITIAL attribute, as follows:

DECLARE LIST (5) WORD INITIAL (25, 5, 0, OFCH, 1110B); When the program begins to execute, the elements of LIST will have the following values:

| Name | Value |
| --- | --- |
| LIST(0) | 25 |
| LIST(1) | 5 |
| LIST(2) | 0 |
| LIST(3) | OFCH |
| LIST(4) | 1110B |

These are, of course, initial values only; the program can change them as it executes.

# Chapter 4
# Data Manipulation

In the last chapter we saw how to define memory locations and assign names to them. Now we turn to the manipulation of the data stored in those locations. Just as in the last chapter we built our data structures from bytes and words, the basic memory locations available on small computers, so in this chapter we focus our attention on the basic *operations* a small computer can carry out.

## THE ASSIGNMENT OPERATOR

*Data Movement.* The assignment operator moves data into a storage location. In the PL/I family of languages the assignment operator is represented by an equal sign.

LET SOURCE and DESTINATION be defined as bytes:

DECLARE (SOURCE, DESTINATION) BTYE;

Then the statement

DESTINATION = SOURCE;

causes the bit pattern in SOURCE to be copied into DESTINATION. The contents of SOURCE are not changed. The old contents of DESTINATION are lost, having been replaced by the contents of SOURCE. Fig. 4-1 illustrates the assignment operation.

More generally, every assignment statement has the form:

$$location = value;$$

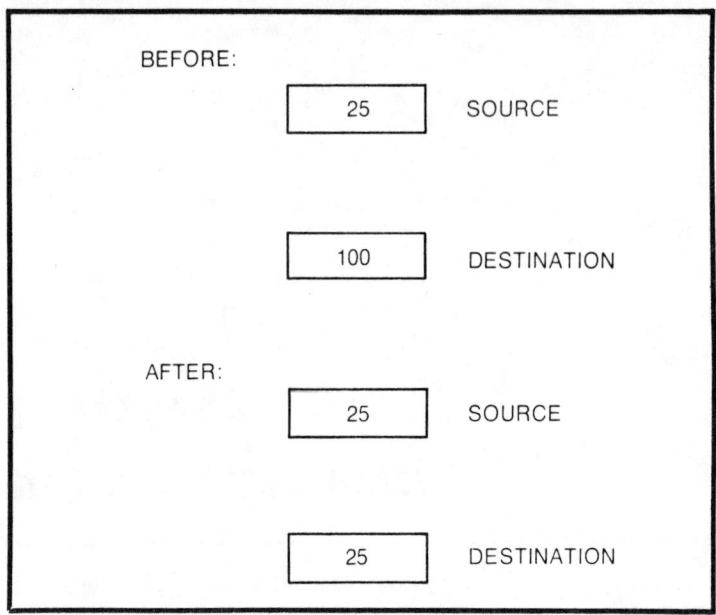

Fig. 4-1. Assignment.

The part of the assignment statement to the left of the equal sign specifies a location into which data is to be stored. This might be a simple name (DESTINATION), a subscripted name (LIST(ENTRY)) or a qualified name (DATE.MONTH), but it will always specify the location where data is to be stored.

The right side of the assignment statement specifies the *value* to be stored in the location named on the left. When a *name* appears on the right side of an assignment statement, it always stands for its value, that is, the bit pattern stored in the named location.

*Other ways of Specifying Values.* The value on the right of an assignment statement may be specified by a constant. The statement

DESTINATION = 25;

causes (the bit pattern whose value in binary notation is) 25 to be stored in the location named DESTINATION.

The value may also be specified by an expression. Consider:

DESTINATION = A + B − C;

Since the names A, B, and C are on the right side of the equal sign, they all stand for the contents of the named locations. Thus the value of A is added to the value of B, the value of C is subtracted from the sum, and the difference is stored in DESTINATION. We will examine expressions further after having defined all the operators that may appear in them.

When a name is prefixed by the @ sign, it stands for the *address* rather than the *contents* of the named location. The statement

$$\text{POINTER} = @\text{SOURCE};$$

causes the address of SOURCE to be stored in the word POINTER.

*Type Conversion.* If the value specified on the right of an assignment statement is a byte, and the location named on the left is a word, then the byte is extended on the left with 8 zeros so as to fill out the word. On the other hand, if the value is a word, and the location it is to be stored in is a byte, then bits 0-7 (the right byte) of the word are stored in the named location, and bits 8-15 (the left byte) are *lost*.

*Other Uses of the Equal Sign.* Unfortunately, the equal sign has many uses in mathematics and programming other than specifying assignments. It may be used to make a statement ($2 + 2 = 4$), ask a question (Does $2 + 2 = 4$?), or set a problem (Find the $x$ such that $x + 2 = 4$). We must take care not to confuse these other uses of the equal sign with its use as the assignment operator.

*Multiple Assignment.* We may assign the same value to more than one location in a single assignment statement. The statement

$$A, B, C, D, E = 25;$$

stores 25 in locations A, B, C, D, and E. It is equivalent to the 5 statements:

$$A = 25;$$
$$B = 25;$$
$$C = 25;$$
$$D = 25;$$
$$E = 25;$$

## THE ARITHMETIC OPERATIONS

Binary arithmetic has already been taken up in Chapter 1. We need only concern ourselves, therefore, with how the arithmetical operations are expressed in our language.

*Addition and Subtraction.* We indicate addition and subtraction with the usual + and − signs:

$$\text{RESULT} = \text{DATA\_1} + \text{DATA\_2};$$
$$\text{RESULT} = \text{DATA\_1} - \text{DATA\_2};$$

If DATA_1 and DATA_ 2 are both bytes, then an 8-bit addition or subtraction will be done, and the result will be a byte. If both are words, a 16-bit addition will be done, and the result will be a word. If one is a byte and the other a word, then the byte is extended with zeros on the left to form a word, a 16-bit addition is done, and the result is a word.

The bit patterns involved may represent either unsigned binary numbers, or signed numbers in the twos complement representation. The addition and subtraction operations are the same in each case; the computer does not have to "know" which interpretation the user intends.

*CARRY and OVERFLOW.* We assume that the computer has carry and overflow bits. After an addition, the carry bit will be 0 if no carry occurred out of the leftmost position, and 1 if a carry did occur. After a subtraction the carry bit will be 0 if the subtraction in the leftmost position did not necessitate a borrow, and 1 if it did. After either an addition or subtraction, the overflow bit will be 0 if a twos complement overflow did not occur, and 1 if it did.

CARRY and OVERFLOW are the names of *bytes*, not *bits*, whose values depend on the settings of the corresponding bits. If the carry or overflow bit is 0, then the value of CARRY or OVERFLOW will be 00000000B. If the carry or overflow bit is 1, then CARRY or OVERFLOW will be 11111111B.

It is convenient to think of 00000000B and 11111111B as representing the logical values FALSE and TRUE. We shall assume that every program includes the declaration:

    DECLARE TRUE LITERALLY '11111111B',
        FALSE LITERALLY '00000000B';

We can thus say that CARRY or OVERFLOW will have the value TRUE if the corresponding bit is set to 1, and the value FALSE otherwise.

*PLUS and MINUS.* The PLUS and MINUS operators are equivalent to the "add with carry" and "subtract with borrow" instructions found on many computers. The PLUS operator causes its operands to be added, and then the carry bit to be added to the rightmost position of the result. The

MINUS operator causes its operands to be subtracted, and then the carry bit to be subtracted from the rightmost position of the result. In Chapter 7 we will see how PLUS and MINUS can be used to implement *multiple precision* arithmetic—arithmetic on numbers more than one or two bytes long.

*Negation.* We assume that signed numbers are represented using the twos complement system. We negate a number by subtracting it from 0, and ignoring the borrow. Thus $-X$ is defined to be equal to $0 - X$. If X is a byte, the subtraction will be done using 8-bit arithmetic; otherwise, 16-bit arithmetic will be used.

*Multiplication and Division.* The multiplication and division operators are:

|        |                |
|--------|----------------|
| *      | multiplication |
| /      | division       |
| MOD    | remainder      |

MOD is the only one of these which might be unfamiliar; X MOD Y is the *remainder* obtained when X is divided by Y.

All three operations share the following two properties:

1) The operands are assumed to represent *unsigned* numbers. Unlike addition and subtraction, the multiplication and division operations will not yield the correct results when applied to signed numbers in the twos complement representation. (Since signed and unsigned multiplication and division are not equivalent, we had to choose one for our operators to carry out. For machine level programming, the unsigned operations are the most useful.)

2) The result of a multiplication or division operation is always a word, regardless of the types of the operands. If a multiplication yields a result longer than 16 bits, the rightmost 16 bits are retained and the rest discarded. The operations / and MOD are undefined if the second operand has the value 0.

## THE LOGICAL OPERATIONS

The logical operations are defined in terms of the English logical connectives "and", "or", and "not". They may be used to implement these connectives in a program. But they may also be used as general bit manipulating operators in applications that have nothing to do with logic.

The logical operations are all "bitwise" operations. That is, bit 0 of the result will depend only on bit 0 of each of the two operands; bit 1 of the result will depend only on bit 1 of the operands, and so on. The bits in a given position in the operands influence only that position in the result.

*AND.* The AND operation is defined by the following rules:

$$0 \text{ AND } 0 = 0 \qquad 1 \text{ AND } 0 = 0$$
$$0 \text{ AND } 1 = 0 \qquad 1 \text{ AND } 1 = 1$$

The result bit is 1 if and only if the first operand *and* the second operand bits are 1, hence the name of the operation.

For operands of more than one bit, we apply the above rules to each position:

$$\begin{array}{r} 10101110 \\ \text{AND } \underline{10011011} \\ 10001010 \end{array}$$

Let us focus our attention on one of the operands in this example, say the second one. Wherever a 0 occurs in the second operand, the result bit in that position is also 0. But wherever a 1 occurs in the second operand, the result bit is the same as the bit in that position in the first operand.

This means we can set selected bits in a byte or word to 0, and leave the others unchanged, by ANDing with another byte or word, called a *mask*. Wherever a 0 appears in the mask, a 0 will appear in the result. But wherever a 1 appears in the mask, the corresponding bit in the other byte or word will appear unchanged in the result.

*OR.* The rules for OR are:

$$0 \text{ OR } 0 = 0 \qquad 1 \text{ OR } 0 = 1$$
$$0 \text{ OR } 1 = 1 \qquad 1 \text{ OR } 1 = 1$$

The result bit is 1 if and only if the first *or* the second operand bit is 1. Also, the result bit is 1 when both operand bits are 1. This case distinguishes the present "inclusive or" from the "exclusive or" which will be taken up next.

The following example shows two bytes ORed together:

$$\begin{array}{r} 10011010 \\ \text{OR } \underline{10100110} \\ 10111110 \end{array}$$

Just as AND could be used to set selected bits in a byte or word to 0, OR can be used to set selected bits to 1. Again let us focus our attention on the second operand. Wherever a 1 appears in the second operand a 1 appears in the result. But wherever a 0 bit appears, the first operand bit is reproduced unchanged.

*XOR (Exclusive Or)*. The rules for XOR are:

$$0 \text{ XOR } 0 = 0 \qquad 1 \text{ XOR } 0 = 1$$
$$0 \text{ XOR } 1 = 1 \qquad 1 \text{ XOR } 1 = 0$$

The OR and XOR operations differ only in the case where both operands are 1. For OR the result is 1 in that case, and for XOR it is 0.

The following illustrates the XOR of two bytes:

```
     00001111
XOR  00110011
     --------
     00111100
```

We can use XOR to *logically complement* selected bits, that is, to replace 1s by 0s and 0s by 1s. As before, focus attention on the second operand in the example. Wherever a 0 occurs, then the result bit is the same as the first operand bit. But wherever a 1 occurs, the result bit is the logical complement of the corresponding bit in the first operand.

*NOT*. The rules for NOT are:

$$\text{NOT } 0 = 1 \qquad \text{NOT } 1 = 0$$

NOT takes one operand, and logically complements each bit in that operand:

$$\text{NOT } 10110010 = 01001101$$

An entire byte or word can be complemented using either the XOR or the NOT operator. The following two statements have the same effect:

```
RESULT =   NOT DATA;
RESULT =   DATA XOR 11111111B
```

## THE ROTATE AND SHIFT OPERATIONS

The rotate and shift operations shift the bit pattern in a byte or word a certain number of places to the left or right. This results in bits being shifted out of one end of the byte or

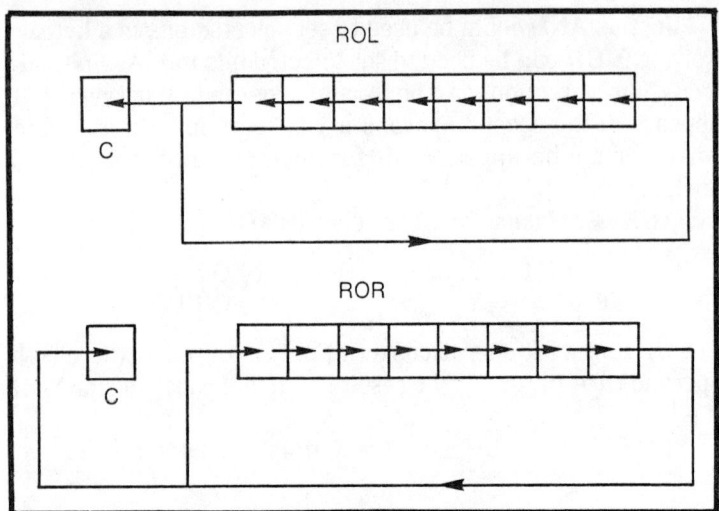

Fig. 4-2. **Rotate left** and **rotate right**. The arrows indicate the movement of the bits. The box marked **C** is the carry bit.

word and other bits being shifted in at the other end. It is with respect to the shifted-in bits that the various rotate and shift operations differ.

For all rotate and shift operations, the carry bit is set to the last bit rotated or shifted out of the byte or word. If that bit was 0 then CARRY will have the value FALSE when the operation is completed. Otherwise it will have the value TRUE.

For a rotate, bits shifted out of one end of the word are shifted into the other. Thus the bits circulate around the byte or word, and none are lost. We have two rotate operations:

        ROL    rotate left

        ROR   rotate right

Figure 4-2 illustrates ROL and ROR both diagrammatically and by example.

The shift operations are similar to the rotates, but differ as to the source of the bits shifted in. We have three cases:

1) *Zeros are shifted in.* This gives us the two operations:

        SHL    shift left

        SHR   shift right

Figure 4-3 illustrates these operations.

2) *The carry bit is shifted in.* The operations are:

SCL    shift left with carry

SCR    shift right with carry

These operations are illustrated in Fig. 4-4. Notice that, since the bit shifted out of the byte or word is shifted into the carry bit, and the carry bit is always shifted into the byte or word, the effect is of a rotate in which the carry bit is included. "Shift with carry" could also be called "rotate through carry", and often is.

3) *The sign bit (leftmost bit) is shifted in (right shift only)*. The operation is:

ASR  arithmetic right shift

Figure 4-5 illustrates ASR. An arithmetic right shift shifts a twos complement signed number to the right, while preserving its sign.

*Functional Notation.* A rotate or shift operation requires two operands: the byte or word to be rotated or shifted, and the number of places through which to rotate or shift. The operation yields a single result: the rotated or shifted byte or word. (There is also a *side effect*, the setting of the carry bit, but that does not concern us at the moment.)

We could use *operator notation* for rotates and shifts, as we have for the arithmetical and logical operations. If that

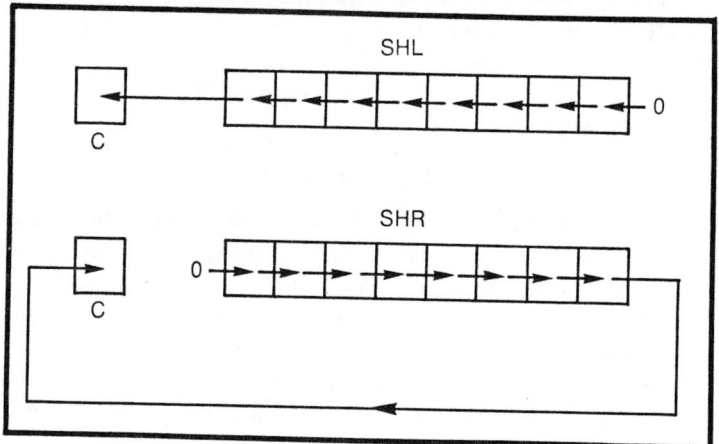

Fig. 4-3. **Shift left** and **shift right**.

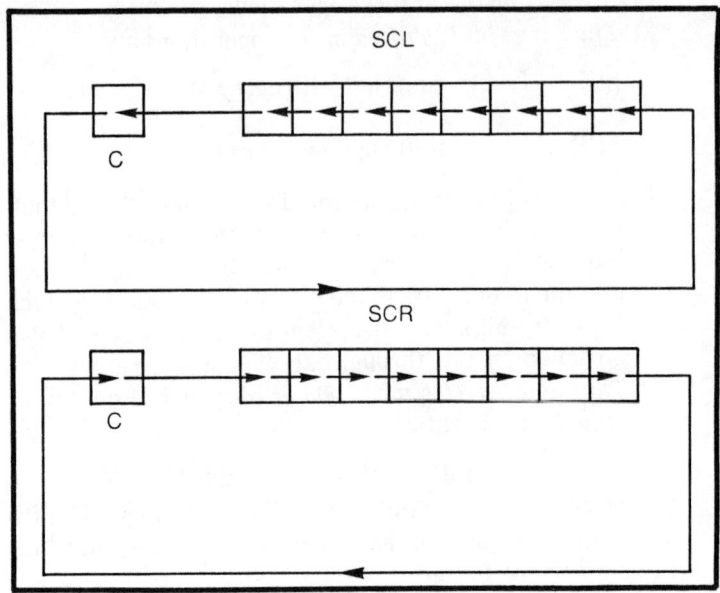

Fig. 4-4. **Shift left with carry** and **shift right with carry**.

were done we would write, for instance,

$$RESULT = DATA\ SHL\ 3;$$

to assign to RESULT the result of shifting the contents of DATA 3 places to the left.

In fact, however, we will follow XPL and PL/M and use *functional notation* for the rotate and shift operations. The operands follow the operator (now called a function), enclosed in parentheses and separated by a comma. Thus the example just given would become:

$$RESULT = SHL\ (DATA, 3);$$

The entire expression SHL (DATA, 3) stands for the result obtained by carrying out the shift. Thus SHR (11011001B, 3) stands for 00011011B and ROL (11011001B, 4) stands for 10011101B. The constants, names, or expressions inside the parentheses are called the *arguments* of the function.

The first argument of a rotate or shift function—the data to be rotated or shifted—may be either a byte or a word. The result will be a byte or word accordingly. The second argument—the one that specifies the number of places to be shifted or rotated through—must always be a byte. It is treated as an unsigned integer.

## THE RELATIONAL OPERATIONS

A relational operator tests its operands to determine if a particular relation holds. If the relation holds, then the result of the operation is 11111111B or TRUE. Otherwise, the result is 00000000B or FALSE. (Remember, we assume that TRUE and FALSE are declared LITERALLY as 11111111B and 00000000B.)

The "less than" and "greater than" relations differ depending on whether we consider the bit patterns being compared to represent signed or unsigned numbers. Consider the bit patterns 01111111 and 10000001. If these represent *unsigned numbers*, then 01111111B = 127, 10000001B = 129, and 01111111 is less than 10000001. On the other hand, in the twos complement representation, 01111111 still represents 127, but 10000001 represents −127, and hence 10000001 is less than 01111111.

*Unsigned Relationals.* The relational operators for unsigned numbers are:

|     |                                          |
| --- | ---------------------------------------- |
| =   | equal to                                 |
| >   | greater than                             |
| <   | less than                                |
| > = | greater than or equal to (not less than) |
| < = | less than or equal to (not greater than) |
| < > | not equal to                             |

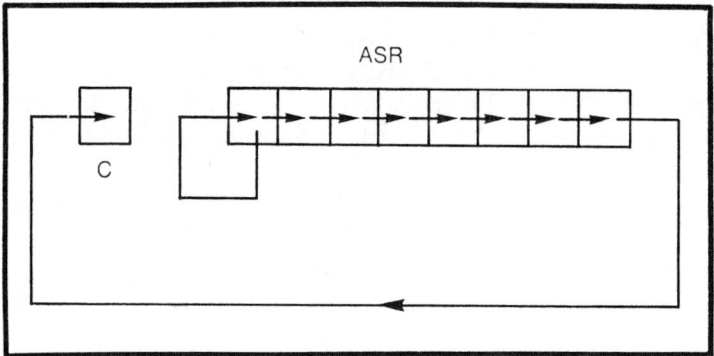

Fig. 4-5. Arithmetic right shift.

The following are some relational expressions and their values:

| Relational Expression | Value |
|---|---|
| 25 = 30 | FALSE |
| 50 > 40 | TRUE |
| 35 < 35 | FALSE |
| 80 > = 70 | TRUE |
| 35 < = 35 | TRUE |
| 23 < > 24 | TRUE |

Relational operators, like all the others we have discussed, can occur in the right hand sides of assignment statements. For instance,

RESULT = DATA_1 > DATA_2;

will cause TRUE to be stored in RESULT if the value of DATA_1 is greater than the value of DATA_2; otherwise, FALSE will be stored in RESULT.

We must take care not to confuse the assignment operator with the relational operator "equals." for instance, the following could cause confusion:

RESULT = DATA_1 = DATA_2;

The leftmost equal sign is the assignment operator. Any equal signs to the right of that are TRUE to be assigned to RESULT if DATA_1 and DATA_2 have the same value, and FALSE otherwise.

Enclosing the relational expression in parentheses improves clarity, since the assignment operator can never occur inside parentheses:

RESULT = (DATA_1 = DATA_2);

*Signed Relationals.* The relational operators = and < > apply equally well to signed and unsigned numbers. For the rest, we need a different set of operators for signed and unsigned numbers:

|  | Unsigned | Signed |
|---|---|---|
| greater than | > | GT |
| less than | < | LT |
| greater than or equal to | > = | GE |
| less than or equal to | < = | LE |

The signed relational operators behave just like the unsigned ones, except they assume the bit patterns they operate on represent signed numbers in the twos complement representation. Thus the value of

$$-1>$$

is TRUE, since
$-1 = 00000000B - 00000001B = 11111111B = 255$. On the other hand, the value of

$$-1 \, GT \, 1$$

is FALSE, since GT treats its operands as signed numbers.

## EXPRESSIONS

An expression directs the computer to calculate a value. The value of the expression is the result of the calculation. Thus $2 + 3$ is an expression which directs the computer to add two numbers. The value of the expression is 5, the result of the addition.

So far we have dealt with expressions that each contained only a single operator: DATA_1 + DATA_2, DATA_1 AND DATA_2, DATA_1 < DATA_2, and so on. But it is often convenient to specify more than one operation in the same expression, as in:

$$DATA\_1 + DATA\_2 * DATA\_3$$

The question now is which of the operations, + or *, should be done first? The result will certainly be different depending on our choice. Consider the expression $3 + 4 * 5$. If we do the addition first, we get $7 * 5 = 35$. But if we do the multiplication first, we get $3 + 20 = 23$.

To resolve such questions we assign a *priority* to each operator. In evaluating an expression, the highest priority operators are applied first, then those with the next lowest priority, and so on. Operators with the same priority are applied in left to right order as they occur in the expression.

The priorities we shall use are:

```
highest priority   * / MOD
       │           + -  PLUS MINUS
       │           = > < >= <= <> GT LT GE LE
       │           NOT
       ▼           AND
lowest priority    OR XOR
```

Operators on the same line have the same priority.

71

The priorities of the arithmetic operations are the usual ones: multiplications and divisions are done before additions and subtractions. (So 3 + 4 * 5 would equal 23, not 35.) MOD has the same priority as multiplication and division, while PLUS and MINUS, being variations on + and −, share with them the same priority.

The relational operators have a lower priority than the arithmetic operators. Therefore, in an expression like

$$X - Y > A + B$$

the arithmetic operations on each side of the relational operator will be carried out first. Then, the results of the two operators have still lower priorities, so that in expressions like

$$X > Y \text{ AND } A <= B$$

the relational expressions will be evaluated first, and the results of those combined by the logical operator. In such expressions the logical operators behave much like the corresponding English words. For instance, the expression

$$A < B + 5 \text{ AND } X = Y \text{ AND } U >= V$$

will have the value true if and only if the English sentence "A is less than B + 5 and X equals Y and U is greater than or equal to V" is also true. One must be careful, however, not to forget the distinction between OR and XOR, a distinction not made in English.

We may change the order of evaluation of operators by using parentheses: operators inside a set of parentheses are always applied before any operators outside that set of parentheses. Thus (3 + 4) * 5 = 35; the parentheses cause the + to be applied before the *, contrary to the normal priorities of + and *.

Parentheses often lend clarity even when their use is not strictly required. This is particularly true in connection with the logical and relational operations, whose priorities are not well known and may vary from one language to another. The expression

$$(A < B + 5) \text{ AND } (X = Y) \text{ AND } (U >= V)$$

seems clearer than the unparenthesized version, even though the two have precisely the same meaning.

# Chapter 5
# Control Structures

In a program it is insufficient to merely state what actions the computer is to carry out. We must specify the *order* in which those actions will be executed. We must say which actions are to be carried out only *under certain conditions*, and which are to be executed *repeatedly*. We may wish to *invoke* a complex sequence of actions with a single command. Providing for these possibilities in a programming language is the function of control structures.

## SEQUENCING

*Sequencing* refers to the actions of a program being carried out in a certain order, or sequence. This order is the same as the order in which the program statements appear in the program text, unless some other order is specifically called for by control statements.

Thus if a part of a program had the form

>   *statement-1;*
>   *statement-2;*
>   .
>   .
>   .
>   *statement-n;*

then the computer would execute all these statements in top to bottom order, *provided* none was a control statement which explicitly changed the order of execution.

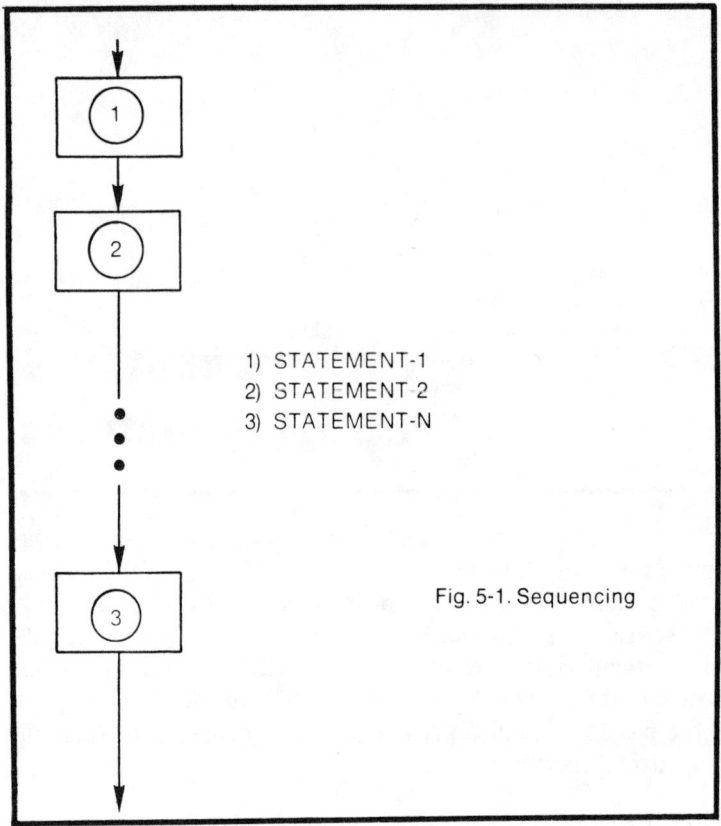

Fig. 5-1. Sequencing

1) STATEMENT-1
2) STATEMENT-2
3) STATEMENT-N

If the statements were written on a single line

*statement-1; statement-2; ... statement-n;*

then they would be excuted in left-to-right order.

Each of the control structures in this chapter will be illustrated by a flowchart. Fig. 5-1 illustrates sequencing.

## SELECTION

*Selection* statements allow the computer to select some program statements for execution, and reject others, depending on the "conditions that prevail" when the program is executed.

*If...Then....* The simplest selection statement has the form:

IF *condition* THEN *statement;*

*Condition* can be a relational expression such as

$$X > Y$$

or a group of relational expressions joined by logical operators:

$$(X > Y) \text{ OR } ((Y > Z) \text{ AND } (X > Z))$$

Variables whose values are TRUE or FALSE may also be included. After the assignment

$$C = (Y > Z);$$

the above condition could be written:

$$(X > Y) \text{ OR } (C \text{ AND } (X > Z))$$

Note that CARRY and OVERFLOW are names which always have TRUE or FALSE values.

When the computer encounters an IF statement, it first evaluates *condition*. (The details of evaluating conditions are taken up in the next section of this chapter.) If the value of the condition is TRUE, then *statement* is executed. Otherwise, the computer passes on to the next statement in the program. This is illustrated by a flowchart in Fig. 5-2.

In the following example

```
IF POINTER < UPPER_LIMIT THEN
    POINTER = POINTER + 1;
```

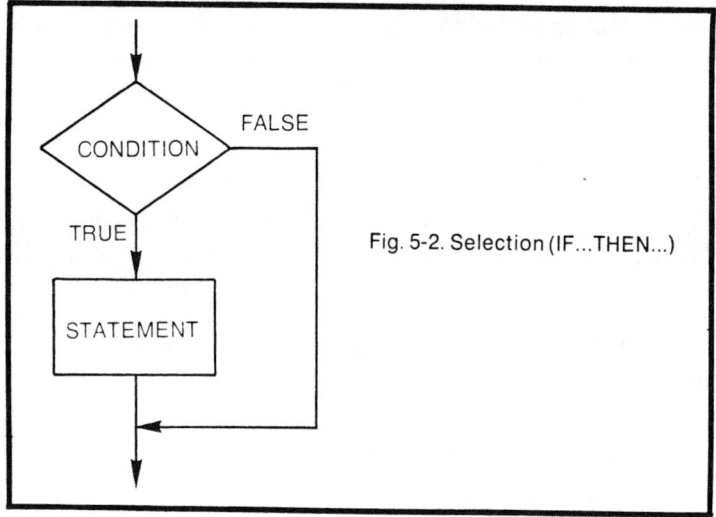

Fig. 5-2. Selection (IF...THEN...)

the assignment POINTER = POINTER + 1 will be executed if and only if the value of POINTER is less than the value of UPPER_LIMIT.

*Do...END.* The definition of the IF statement provides for only a single statement following the THEN. This is no limitation, however, since we can make any number of statements behave as a single statement by enclosing them between the statements DO and END. Thus in

```
IF POINTER < UPPER_LIMIT THEN
    DO;
        POINTER = POINTER + 1;
        NOT_EMPTY_FLAG = TRUE;
        COUNT = COUNT - 1;
    END;
```

all three assignment statements will be executed if the value of POINTER is less than the value of UPPER_LIMIT. Otherwise, none of them will be executed, and control will be passed to the statement following the END statement.

Notice the use of indentation to show when one statement or group of statements is part of another. The entire DO-END group is part of the IF statement, and so is indented with respect to IF. The three assignment statements are part of the DO-END group, and so are indented with respect to DO and END. We shall use indentation extensively to display which statements are part of, or subordinate to, other statements.

*If...THEN...ELSE....* Instead of specifying that a certain statement will or will not be executed, we can provide two alternatives one of which will always be executed. For this purpose we use the "ELSE form" of the IF statement:

> IF *condition* THEN *statement-1*;
> ELSE *statement-2*;

Fig. 5-3 illustrates this form of the IF statement. If *condition* is TRUE, *statement-1* is executed and *statement-2* is not. If *condition* is FALSE, *statement-2* is executed and *statement-1* is not.

As before, *statement-1* and *statement-2* can be single statements, as in

```
IF POINTER < UPPER_LIMIT THEN
    POINTER = POINTER + 1;
ELSE ERROR_FLAG = TRUE;
```

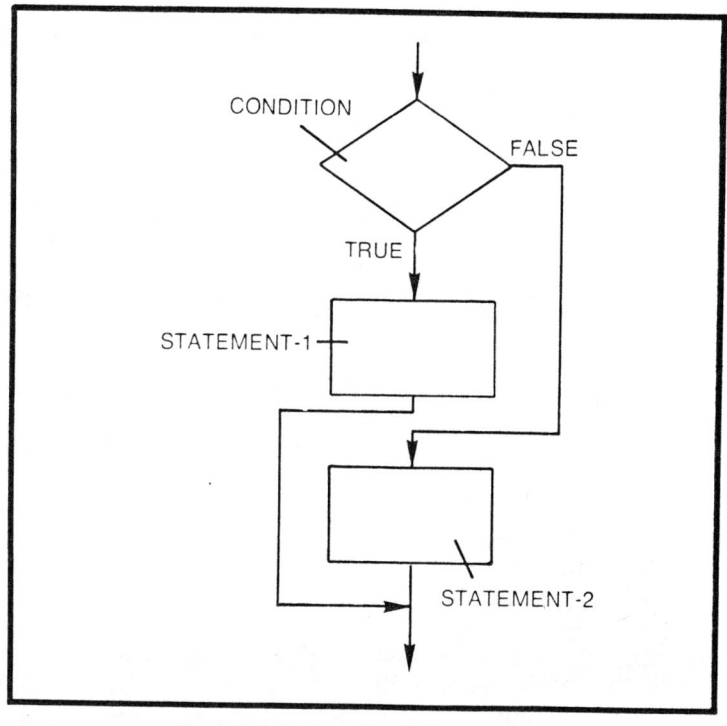

Fig. 5-3. Selection (IF...THEN...ELSE...)

or DO-END groups, as in:

```
IF POINTER < UPPER_LIMIT THEN
   DO;
      POINTER = POINTER + 1;
      COUNT = COUNT - 1;
   END;
ELSE
   DO;
      ERROR_FLAG = TRUE;
      NOT_EMPTY_FLAG = FALSE;
   END;
```

If the value of POINTER is less than the value of UPPER_LIMIT, then the statements in the DO-END group following THEN will be executed. Otherwise, those in the DO-END group following ELSE will be executed.

The statements following THEN and ELSE in an IF statement may themselves be IF statements. When THEN is followed by another IF statement, a problem arises. Consider the following, written without indentation:

    IF *condition-1* THEN IF *condition-2* THEN *statement-1*;
    ELSE *statement-2*;

The problem: Which IF does the ELSE go with? We must have a "disambiguating rule" to decide the issue. We will adopt the rule used in PL/I and XPL: *An ELSE statement is paired with the nearest preceding IF statement that does not already have an ELSE part.*

Thus in the above example, the ELSE should be paired with the second, not the first, IF. We can make this obvious by writing the statement in indented form:

IF *condition-1* THEN
    IF *condition-2* THEN
        *statement-1*;
    ELSE
        *statement-2*;

No problem occurs when an IF statement is used in the ELSE part of another IF statement.

*Multiway Selection.* At some point in a program we may wish the computer to select one action out of many possible ones. We may formulate such multiway selections in two ways: using IF statements and using a special DO CASE statement.

The scheme for making a multiway selection with IF statements is as follows:

        IF *condition-1* THEN statement-1;
        ELSE IF *condition-2* THEN statement-2;
        ELSE IF *condition-3* THEN statement-3;

            .
            .
            .

        ELSE *statement-n*;

The statement corresponding to the first condition that is true will be executed. If none of the conditions are true, then the last statement—the one following the final ELSE—is executed. Once one statement has been executed, all the remaining ones are skipped over. Fig. 5-4 shows a flowchart of this multiway selection.

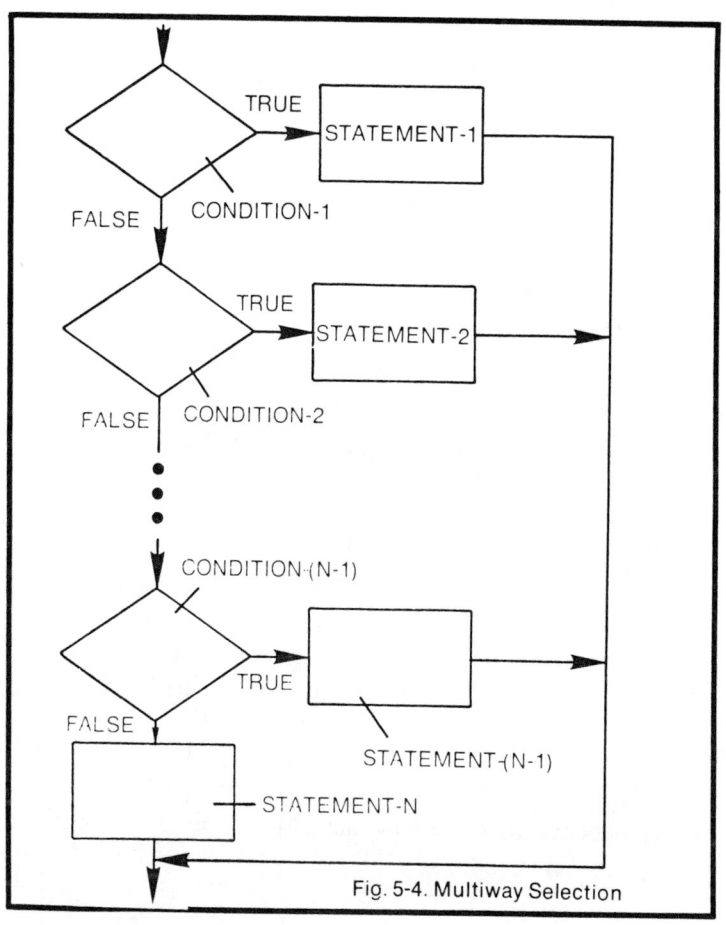

Fig. 5-4. Multiway Selection

Suppose, for instance, we wished to execute different statements under different conditions as follows:

| Condition | Statement |
|---|---|
| X > Y | A = TRUE; |
| U = V | B = FALSE; |
| Y < U | C = TRUE; |
| none of the above | D = FALSE; |

We could write:

IF X > Y THEN A = TRUE;
ELSE IF U = V THEN B = FALSE;
ELSE IF Y < U THEN C = TRUE;
ELSE D = FALSE;

The DO CASE statement allows the value of an expression to determine which of several statements is executed. It has the form:

DO CASE *expression*;
    *statement-0*;
    *statement-1*;
    .
    .
    .
    *statement-n*;
END;

First *expression* is evaluated. If its value is 0 then *statement-0* is executed; if its value is 1 then *statement-1* is executed, and so on. If the value of *expression* is greater than *n*, then the behavior of the DO CASE statement is unpredictable.

Fig. 5-5 illustrates the DO CASE statement.

Suppose we wished to execute one out of four statements depending on the value of Z:

| Condition | Statement |
|---|---|
| $Z = 0$ | $A = TRUE$; |
| $Z = 1$ | $B = FALSE$; |
| $Z = 2$ | $C = TRUE$; |
| $Z = 3$ | $D = FALSE$; |

We could accomplish this selection with:

DO CASE Z;
    $A = TRUE$;
    $B = FALSE$;
    $C = TRUE$;
    $D = FALSE$;
END;

## EVALUATING CONDITIONS

The selection statements just studied, and the repetition statement to be taken up next, base their actions on the values of conditions such as:

$$(X > Y) \text{ AND } (Z = 5)$$

Theoretically, the relational expressions would first be evaluated, obtaining a TRUE or FALSE value for each. These TRUE and FALSE values would be combined by the logical

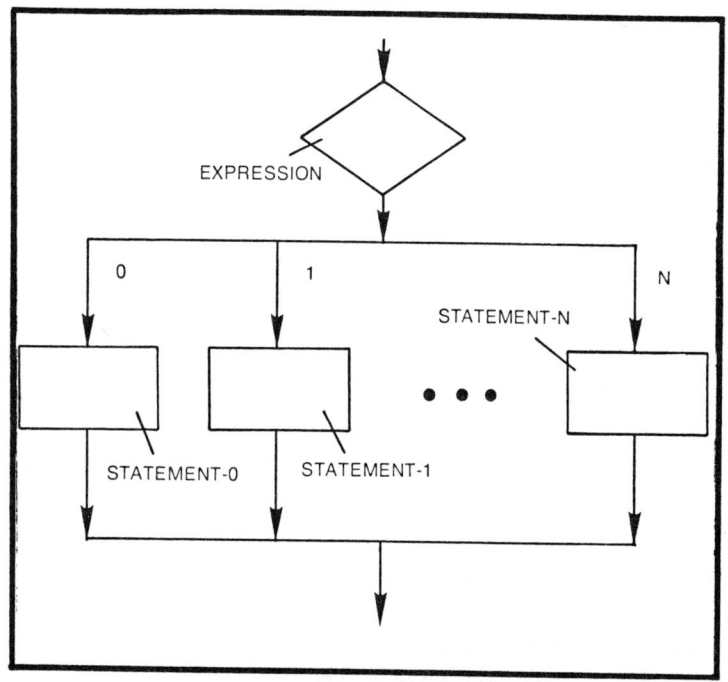

Fig. 5-5. Selection (DO CASE)

operators to obtain a single TRUE or FALSE value for the entire expression.

In practice, conditions are usually handled in a quite different way.

Let us first consider the relational expressions such as X < Y and X > = Y. We start by comparing the contents of X and Y using a *compare* instruction:

CMP X,Y

The computer will subtract Y from X, and set the hardware *carry, overflow, sign,* and *zero* bits according to the result of the subtraction.

The computer's instruction set features a group of branch (sometimes called jump) instructions. Each tests the hardware *carry, overflow, sign,* and *zero* bits for a certain condition; if the condition holds, the computer branches to a designated location.

Figure 5-6 shows the branch instructions for the PDP-11/LSI-11. The M6800 features an equivalent set. Notice

| CONDITION | BRANCH IF TRUE | BRANCH IF FALSE |
|---|---|---|
| X = Y    | BEQ  | BNE  |
| X > Y    | BHI  | BLOS |
| X < Y    | BLO  | BHIS |
| X >= Y   | BHIS | BLO  |
| X <= Y   | BLOS | BHI  |
| X <> Y   | BNE  | BEQ  |
| X GT Y   | BGT  | BLE  |
| X LT Y   | BLT  | BGE  |
| X GE Y   | BGE  | BLT  |
| X LE Y   | BLE  | BGT  |

Fig. 5-6. Branch instructions for the PDP-11/LSI-11. It is assumed that a CMP X, Y (Compare X with Y) instruction has been executed before the branch instruction.

that for each condition there is an instruction that will branch if the condition is true, and one that will branch if it is false. If you examine the flowcharts in this chapter, you will find that in almost every case we wish to "detour around" a statement when a condition is false. We can do this using the branch instruction in the *Branch If False* column.

Let us consider an example. The statement

$$IF\ X > Y\ THEN\ A = A + 1;$$

would be translated into assembly language as

```
        CMP X,Y
        BLOS LABEL
        (Assembly code for A = A + 1)
LABEL:  (Assembly code for following statement)
```

Thus if X is *not* greater than Y, if it is "LOw or Same", then we branch around the code for A = A + 1.

Now consider the statement:

IF X LE Y THEN A = A + 1;
ELSE B = B + 1;

The assembly code would be:

```
         CMP X,Y
         BGT LABEL1
         (Assembly code for A = A + 1)
         BR LABEL2
LABEL 1: (Assembly code for B = B + 1)
LABEL 2: (Assembly code for following statement)
```

BR is an unconditional branch which branches around the code for the ELSE part after the code for the THEN part has been executed.

Tests of CARRY and OVERFLOW can be handled with the BCC (Branch if Carry Clear) and BVC (Branch if oVerflow Clear) instructions. (Here "clear" means "is zero".) Thus

> IF CARRY THEN A = A + 1;

would be implemented by:

> BCC LABEL
> (Assembly code for A = A + 1)
> LABEL: (Assembly code for following statement)

Different conventions exist for testing a byte expected to have a TRUE or FALSE value. We will follow the convention of PL/M: Test the right most bit of the byte. If the rightmost bit is 0, take the value of the byte to be FALSE. If the rightmost bit is 1, take the value to be TRUE.

One way to test the rightmost bit would be to rotate it into *carry* with a RORB instruction. With this method

> IF X THEN A = A + 1;

would be implemented as

> RORB X
> BCC LABEL
> (Assembly code for A = A + 1)
> LABEL: (Assembly code for following statement)

When several conditions are ANDed together, we branch if *any* of them is FALSE. Thus

IF (X > Y) AND (U > V) AND (W > Z) THEN A = A + 1;

would be implemented by:

> CMP X, Y
> BLOS LABEL
> CMP U, V
> BLOS LABEL
> CMP W, Z
> BLOS LABEL
> (Assembly code for A = A + 1)
> LABEL: (Assembly code for following statement)

When the conditions are ORed together, we branch to the THEN part if any of the conditions is TRUE. Thus

IF (X > Y) OR (U > V) OR (W > Z) THEN A = A + 1;

becomes

```
            CMP X, Y
            BGT LABEL1
            CMP U,V
            BGT LABEL1
            CMP W,Z
            BLOS LABEL2
LABEL1: (Assembly code for A = A + 1)
LABEL2: (Assembly code for following
        statement)
```

All the branch instructions except the last are taken from the *Branch If True* column of Fig. 5-6, and branch *to* (not around) the code for the THEN part of the IF statement. The final branch instruction, as before, comes from the *Branch If False* column and branches *around* the THEN part.

For an IF-THEN-ELSE statement we implement ORed conditions like ANDed ones but with two changes:

1) The branch instructions are taken from the *Branch If True* column of Fig. 5-6.
2) The code segments for the THEN part and the ELSE part are interchanged.

Thus

IF (X > Y) OR (U > V) OR (W > Z) THEN A = A + 1;
ELSE B = B + 1;

becomes

```
            CMP X,Y
            BGT LABEL1
            CMP U,V
            BGT LABEL1
            CMP W,Z
            BGT LABEL1
            (Assembly code for B = B + 1)
            BR LABEL2
LABEL1: (Assembly code for A = A + 1)
LABEL2: (Assembly code for following
        statement)
```

Note the interchange of the THEN and ELSE parts.

The same techniques can be used to handle complicated expressions involving OR, AND, and NOT. But such expressions are perhaps unwise; they are difficult to understand in expression form and even more difficult to translate.

When a logical expression occurs in an assignment statement, we can implement the assignment using an IF statement. Thus

$$X = (Y < Z) \text{ AND } (A > = B);$$

would be implemented as if it had been written:

X = FALSE;
IF (X < Z) AND (A > = B) THEN X = TRUE;

The IF statement is implemented as just described.

A word on the DO CASE statement: It is implemented using table lookup. The value of *expression* is used as a subscript to select an address from a table of addresses. The address selected is the address of the code to be executed for the case corresponding to the value of *expression*.

## REPETITION

Frequently a program statement must be executed repeatedly in order to have the desired effect. Not only must the programmer specify that a repetition is to take place, he must specify most carefully the condition for the repetition to terminate, since the repetition which fails to terminate is one of the most common of programming errors. Our language provides three repetition statements, and hence three ways to specify the all important termination condition.

*DO WHILE.* The form of the DO WHILE statement is as follows:

DO WHILE *condition;*
   *statement-1;*
   *statement-2;*
     .
     .
     .
   *statement-n;*
END;

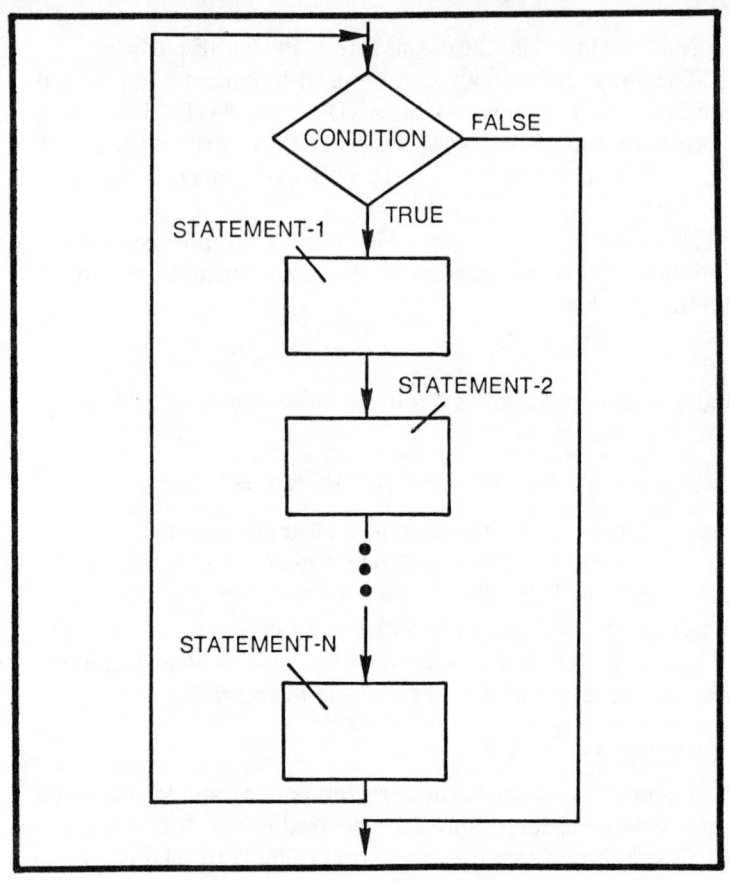

Fig. 5-7. Repetition (DO WHILE)

*Statement-1* through *statement-n* are executed repeatedly. Before each repetition, *condition* is checked. If it is TRUE, the repetition takes place. If it is FALSE, then control passes to the statement following the END statement. Note that *condition* is checked before the first repetition. If it is FALSE then, the statements will not be executed at all.

Fig. 5-7 shows a flowchart of the DO WHILE statement. Notice that we have a branch when the condition is FALSE, just as in the IF statement, and so the implementation techniques of the last section may be applied here without change.

As an example, the following statements will form the sum of the integers from 1 through 99:

```
SUM = 0;
N = 1;
DO WHILE N < > 100;
    SUM = SUM + N;
    N = N + 1;
END;
```

Note that 100 is *not* included in the sum. The condition N < > 100 is checked before each repetition. When it is FALSE, that is, when N = 100, then the repetitions are terminated. Thus the 100th repetition never takes place.

*DO UNTIL.* Sometimes it is better to check for termination *after* each repetition rather than before. The DO UNTIL statement accomplishes this. It has the form:

```
DO UNTIL condition;
    statement-1;
    statement-2;
        .
        .
        .
    statement-n;
END;
```

*Statement-1* through *statement-n* are executed repeatedly. After each repetition, *condition* is checked. If it is TRUE, the repetition terminates; control is transferred to the statement following the END statement. Otherwise, another repetition is initiated. Note that the statements will always be executed at least once, since the terminating condition is not checked until after they have been executed once.

Fig. 5-8 is a flowchart of the DO UNTIL statement. Note that it, too, involves a branch when the condition is FALSE, and hence can be implemented using the techniques of the last section.

The following code also forms the sum of the integers from 1 through 99:

```
SUM = 0;
N = 1;
DO UNTIL N = 100;
    SUM = SUM + N;
    N = N + 1;
END;
```

After the 99th repetition, N will have been incremented by 1 to equal 100, and so the N = 100 will be TRUE and the repetition will terminate.

*The Iterative DO Statement.* The iterative DO statement is best illustrated by example. The statements:

DO I = 0 TO 99;
    LIST(I) = 0;
END;

will set LIST(0) through LIST(99) to 0, since the statement LIST(I) = 0 will be executed for I = 0, I = 1, and so on through I = 99.

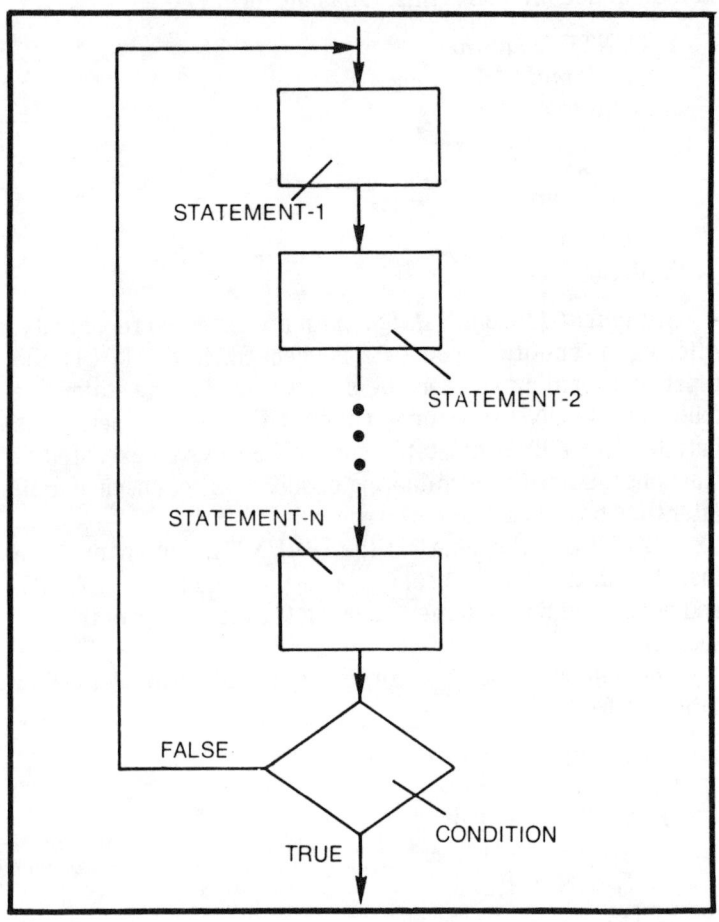

Fig. 5-8. Repetition (DO UNTIL)

We could set only the odd numbered entries to 0:

```
DO I = 1 TO 99 BY 2;
    LIST(I) = 0;
END;
```

Now LIST(I) = 0 will be executed for I = 1, 3, 5, ..., 99. We could process these elements in reverse order if we wished:

```
DO I = 99 DOWNTO 1 BY 2;
    LIST(I) = 0;
END;
```

LIST(I) = 0 will now be executed for I = 99, 97, 95, ..., 1.

The statements

```
DO I = L TO M BY N;
    .
    .
    .
END;
```

are equivalent to

```
I = L;
DO WHILE I <= M;
    .
    .
    .
    I = I + N;
END;
```

and the statements
```
DO I = L DOWNTO M BY N;
    .
    .
    .
END;
```

are equivalent to

```
I = L;
DO WHILE I >= M;
    .
    .
    .
    I = I - N;
END;
```

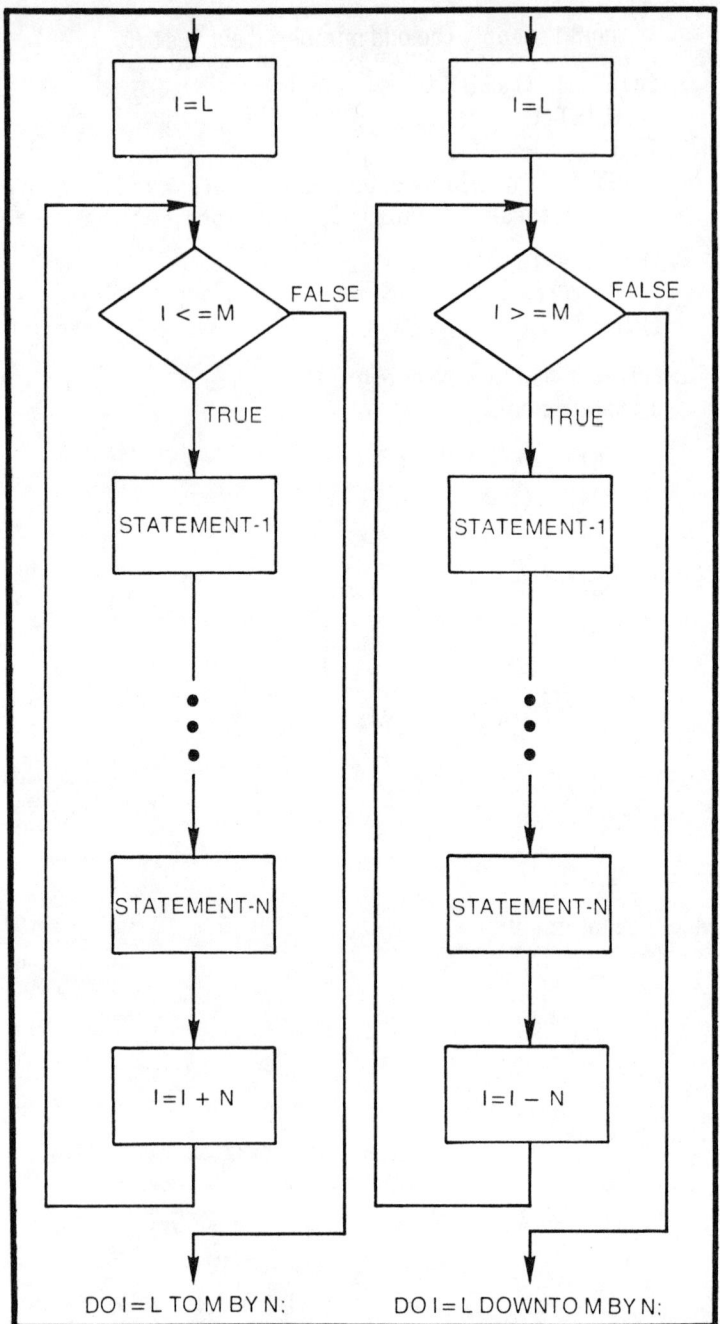

Fig. 5-9. Repetition (Iterative DO)

The names L, M, and N may be replaced by expressions. If "BY N" is omitted, N is assumed to be 1.

Fig. 5-9 shows flowcharts for both the TO and DOWNTO forms of the iterative DO statement.

Since the iterative DO statement is defined in terms of DO WHILE, it is possible that *no* executions of the repeated statements will take place. Consider the following:

DO I = 5 TO P;
   LIST(I) = 0;
END;

If, when the computer reaches the DO statement, P is less than 5, then LIST(I) = 0 will not be executed, but control will pass immediately to the statement following the END statement.

## PROCEDURES

A procedure can be:

1) A *main program*, whose execution is initiated either by the computer's operating system or directly by the computer operator.
2) A *subroutine*, which is a program that is called by another program to do a particular job, and which returns control to the calling program when it is finished.
3) A *function*, which is similar to a subroutine, except that it returns a value, which is used in evaluating an expression.

A main program may be conveniently considered to be a subroutine which is called by the computer's operating system, rather than by another user written program. Thus we need only consider cases 2 and 3.

*Subroutines*. A subroutine has the following form:

*label*: PROCEDURE (*arg-1, arg-2, ..., arg-n*);
          .
          .
          .
END *label*;

*Label* is the name of the subroutine. This is the name by which the subroutine is referred to when it is called from elsewhere in the program.

The *arguments—arg-1* through *arg-n*—are names of locations declared inside the subroutine. When the subroutine is called, these locations are assigned values provided by the calling program.

Consider the subroutine SQUARE defined as follows:

SQUARE: PROCEDURE (X, P);
    DECLARE X BYTE, P WORD, Y BASED P BYTE;
    Y = X * X;
END SQUARE;

SQUARE has two arguments, X and P. X contains the value to be squared. P contains the address of the location in which the square of X is to be stored.

A procedure is invoked by means of a CALL statement. The subroutine call

CALL SQUARE (5, 1000);

requests SQUARE to square 5, store the result in location 1000, and then return to the calling program. After the SQUARE has returned, location 1000 will contain 25, and execution of the calling program will continue with the statement following the CALL statement.

The effect of the CALL statement is precisely the same as if the following had been executed:

X = 5;
P = 1000;
Y = X * X;

Since Y is declared to be the byte pointed to by P, 25 will be stored in location 1000.

Normally we would refer to the location in which the result is to be stored by name, rather than by address. The same holds true for the location containing the data. Thus we would have

CALL SQUARE (DATA, @RESULT);

which has the same effect as the statements

X = DATA;
P = @RESULT;
Y = X * X;

The contents of X—which is the same as the contents of DATA because of X = DATA—is squared. The result is stored in the location pointed to by P—which is RESULT, because of P = @RESULT.

The values of the subroutines arguments can be given by expressions, as well as constants and names; the statement

    CALL SQUARE (DATA_1 – DATA_2,
      @TABLE + OFFSET);

would cause:

    X = DATA_1 – DATA_2;
    P = @TABLE + OFFSET;
    Y = X * X;

The difference between the contents of DATA_1 and DATA_2 would be squared. The result would be stored at the address obtained by adding the contents of OFFSET to the address of TABLE.

*Global and Local Names.* Arguments may be used to supply a subroutine with data and with the addresses at which to store its results. Another method of passing data to and from a subroutine by using *global names* (or *global variables*) will now be explained.

Procedure declarations may appear inside other procedure declarations. Consider the following situation:

    OUTER: PROCEDURE;
      DECLARE (A, B, C) BYTE;
        .
        .
        .
      INNER: PROCEDURE;
        DECLARE (X, Y, Z) BYTE;
          .
          .
          .
        END INNER;
        .
        .
        .
      END OUTER;

Names declared inside a procedure, but not inside another procedure contained in it, are said to be *local* to that procedure. Thus A, B, and C are local to OUTER; X, Y, and Z are local to INNER. Names declared in a procedure containing a given procedure are *global* to the *contained* procedure. Thus A, B, and C are global to INNER.

A procedure has access to all the names that are either local or global to it. Thus INNER may use the names A, B, C, X, Y, and Z in any manner consistent with the language. OUTER, on the other hand, only has access to A, B, and C. Since X, Y, and Z are local to INNER they are inaccessible to OUTER.

If a local name is the same as a global one, the local declaration takes precedence, and the name refers to the location declared in the current procedure. The procedure forfeits the right to refer to the global location, since the name of the global location has been taken over by the local location.

A subroutine can obtain data from the calling procedure, and return data to it, simply by using global names. In particular, if a global name appears on the right side of an assignment statement, its value will be fetched. If the global name appears on the left side, it will be assigned a new value. Since the global names are accessible to the calling procedure as well as the subroutine, data can be passed between the two in this way.

*Functions.* Consider the following version of SQUARE:

```
SQUARE: PROCEDURE (X) BYTE;
    DECLARE X BYTE;
    RETURN X * X;
END SQUARE;
```

These statements define a *function*. The word BYTE following PROCEDURE (X) indicates that the function returns a BYTE value.

The value a function returns occurs in a RETURN statement, which terminates the function and returns as a value the value of the expression following the word RETURN. Every function must contain at least one RETURN statement.

A function may contain more than one RETURN statement. Because of selection statements, different parts of the function procedure may be executed under different conditions, and hence the return may have to be made from different points. An example is the function ABS which returns the magnitude of a twos complement number:

```
ABS: PROCEDURE (X) BYTE;
    DECLARE X BYTE;
    IF X GE 0  THEN RETURN X;
    ELSE RETURN - X;
END ABS;
```

A subroutine may also contain RETURN statements, therefore allowing returns from different parts of the subroutine. The RETURN statement for a subroutine is just

RETURN;

and includes no expression.

A function is called by using it in an expression. In evaluating the expression the function call is replaced by the value the function returned. Thus

$$A = SQUARE (5);$$

will cause 25 to be assigned to A. In

$$A = 3 + 5 * SQUARE (3);$$

SQUARE (3) is replaced by the value returned—which is 3 * 3 or 9:

$$A = 3 + 5 * 9;$$

On completion of the evaluation, A is assigned the value 48.

Of course, the arguments of a function may be expressions as well as names or constants:

$$A = X + Y * SQUARE (U + V);$$

The sum of the values of U and V is first computed. This value is passed to SQUARE. The value that SQUARE returns is multiplied by the value of Y, and the product is added to the value of X. The sum is stored in location A.

Some additional features of procedures (subroutines and functions) are taken up in other chapters, where their applications can be better illustrated. These include *interrupt procedures* whose calls are forced by external devices demanding attention (Chapter 12) and *recursive procedures* which are defined in terms of themselves (Chapter 15).

# Chapter 6
# Program Design

Throughout most of the short history of programming, programs have been created in a haphazard and undisciplined manner. This has had two consequences.

First, it has been difficult to teach people how to program. It was easy enough to teach them the instruction set of a computer or the statements of a high level language. But either they learned from reading other people's programs or from experimenting with the computer how to create their own programs, or they did not learn how to do this at all.

Second, programs created haphazardly tend to be error prone. This is true even for programs written by skilled professional programmers working for reputable computer manufacturers. It has been estimated, for instance, that the operating system for the IBM 360 contains about 1000 bugs (errors), and that this number remains about the same from one release of the system to another.

In recent years two powerful techniques of program design have been developed. These are *structured programming* and *top-down design*. They aid the beginner in learning how to program, and the experienced programmer in writing error free programs.

*Structured programming* means conceiving every program in terms of four control structures: *sequencing, selection, repetition*, and *subroutine (or function) invocation*. To be avoided are maze-like flowcharts and the equally maze-like programs that result from the unrestricted use of the GO TO statement found in most languages. Structured programming requires a programming language in which the needed control structures can be conveniently expressed. The language used in this book meets that requirement.

In *top-down design* we think of a program as a collection of hierarchically related *modules*. A module is often a procedure, but need not be. Any collection of statements that performs a definite function may be a module.

The modules are related as shown in Fig. 6-1. The top level module is the program itself. The lowest level ones do not call on any other modules, but are expressed directly in the statements of the programming language. All other modules call on lower level modules.

We start out by expressing the program in terms of modules on the next lowest level. Even if the program is to be a complex one, this first step may be very simple, because we can assume that the modules on the next level themselves perform complicated functions. This is like starting out the design of a car by deciding that it will have an engine, an electrical system, a transmission, and so on; and deciding on the specifications of each system and how the various systems will be connected together; but postponing for the moment any consideration of the detailed operation of any one system.

The process continues by realizing the second level modules in terms of the third level ones. At each stage, we express a module in terms of those on the next lowest level. As we go to lower and lower levels the functions of the modules get simpler and simpler, until eventually the lowest level modules may be easily expressed directly in terms of the programming language.

## COMMENTS

*Documentation.* Every program worth writing must be documented. That is, it should contain, or be accompanied by, an explanation of what each part of the program does. Most programming languages provide a means of including *comments* in the program itself, so that program and documentation may be intermixed.

In the PL/I family of languages, comments are enclosed between the symbols /* and */:

/* THIS IS AN EXAMPLE OF A COMMENT */

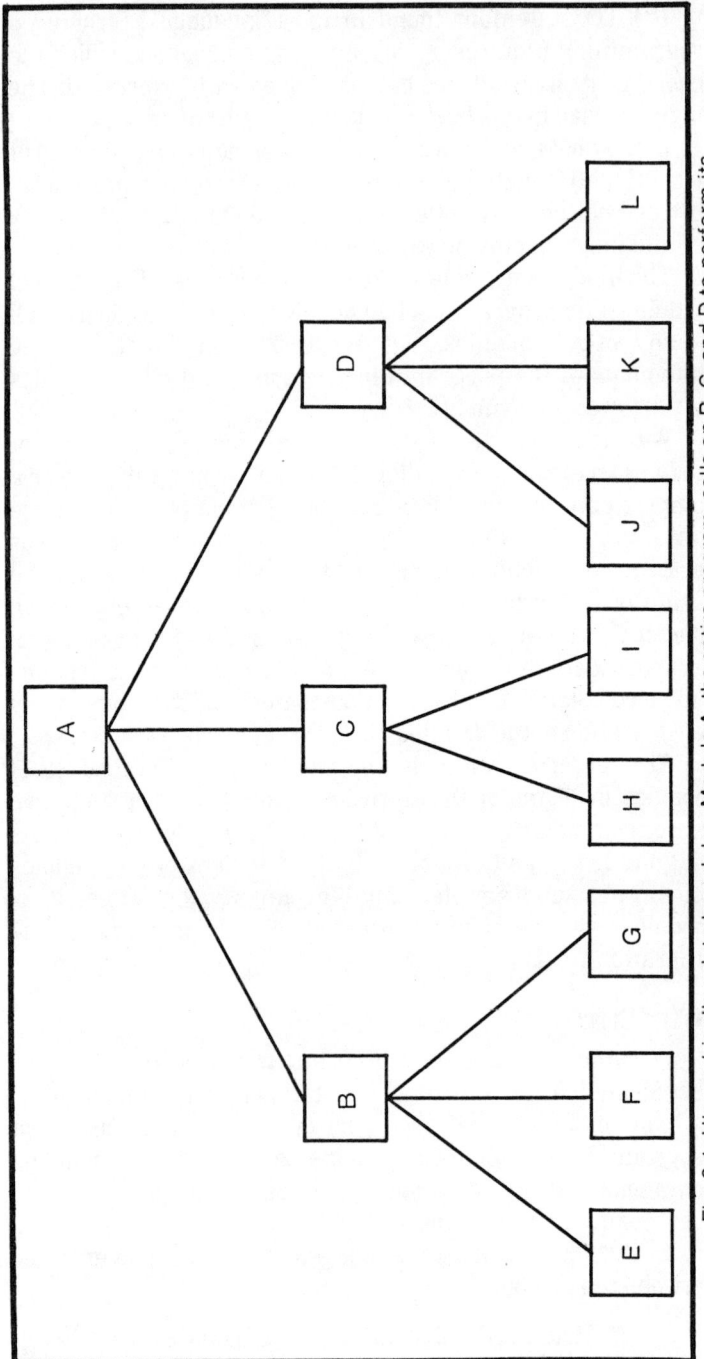

Fig. 6-1. Hierarchically related modules. Module A, the entire program, calls on B, C, and D to perform its function. B in turn calls on E, F, and G; C calls on H and I; and so on. Modules E through L do not call on any other modules, but are implemented entirely with operations available in the programming language being used.

A comment may be inserted anywhere in a program as long as it does not break up a name or a constant. Thus things such as

X = /* THE TABLE ENTRY JUST FOUND */ A(I);

are permissible. The above would have the same effect as

X = A(I);

since the comment would be ignored when translating the program into machine code. But one can doubt whether such intermixing of comments and parts of a statement really improves clarity. With rare exceptions, the comments in the programs in this book are written on separate lines from the program statements.

*Comments and Top-Down Design.* One way of going about top-down design is to *program with comments*. That is, when we are writing a program, and discover that a complicated job must be done at a certain point, we describe that job in a comment and go on. For instance, if at a certain point we had to find the smallest element in a list, we might write something like

/* FIND SMALLEST ENTRY IN LIST_A */

and go on. Each such comment would describe a lower level module.

After the first draft of the program is complete, we go back and place beneath each "unresolved" comment the program statements necessary to do the job described. (The comment should be left in place for documentation.) These statements might contain additional comments, which would be resolved in a third draft, and so on.

*Procedure Names as Comments.* Another technique would be to write a descriptive procedure call, such as

CALL FIND_SMALLEST_ENTRY_IN_LIST_A;

in the first (and possibly final) draft of the program. Then, instead of revising the program to include program statements which implement the comments, we would simply write the called-for procedures. In the case above we would write a procedure FIND_SMALLEST_ENTRY_IN_LIST_A to carry out the operation described in its name.

## A CASE STUDY

The techniques of program design are often easier to illustrate than to describe. The rest of this chapter, therefore is devoted to applying the techniques just discussed to a practical (and typical) programming problem.

*The Problem.* The problem is to print decimal numbers in a appropriate format. We wish to print the numbers in the ordinary, or nonexponetial, format if this is possible using at most 7 digits including any leading or trailing zeros. If this is not possible for some number, then it will be printed in exponential format (scientific notation).

Thus $3.51 \times 10^3$ and $2.6 \times 10^{-4}$ can both be printed in nonexponential format:

$$3.51 \times 10^3 = 3510$$
$$2.6 \times 10^{-4} = .00026$$

On the other hand, neither $6.54 \times 10^7$ nor $3.71 \times 10^{-6}$ can be written in nonexponential format without using more than 7 digits (8 would be required in each case). These would be printed in the computer printout version of exponential format:

$6.54 \times 10^7$ would be printed as $6.54E+7$
$3.71 \times 10^{-6}$ would be printed as $3.71E-6$

The number to be printed is stored inside the computer in exponential format in three named locations:

SIGN:            A byte whose value is TRUE if the number is negative and FALSE if it is positive.

DIGITS:           A 7-byte array which holds the character codes for the digits of the mantissa.

DECIMAL_EXPONENT:    A byte containing the exponent as a twos-complement binary number.

The decimal point is assumed to be between the first and second mantissa digits—between DIGITS (0) and DIGITS (1). Thus $3.51 \times 10^3$ would be represented as

SIGN = FALSE
DIGITS = '3510000'
DECIMAL_EXPONENT = 3

and $-2.6 \times 10^{-4}$ would be represented as

SIGN = TRUE
DIGITS = '2600000'
DECIMAL_EXPONENT = -6

We wish to write a procedure which will print out a number represented in this way in the appropriate format as described above. The procedure, PRINT_NUMBER, is similar to, but slightly more flexible than, the output routines of BASIC interpreters. In Chapter 9 we will use PRINT_NUMBER as part of a floating point output routine.

*The Top Level.* PRINT_NUMBER, the procedure we wish to write, will occupy the top level of a hierarchy of modules. We begin by expressing PRINT_NUMBER in terms of lower level modules.

Some thought about the problem leads us to the following: We can start by printing the sign, a trivial operation. Before we can decide whether to use exponential or nonexponetial format, the number of significant digits—the number of digits other than trailing zeros—in the number to be printed must be known. Finally, we should print in nonexponential format if possible; otherwise, we will print in exponential format.

These considerations lead to the following first draft of our program:

```
PRINT_NUMBER: PROCEDURE;
   DECLARE SIGNIFICANT_DIGITS BYTE;
   /* PRINT SIGN */
   /* COMPUTE SIGNIFICANT_DIGITS */
   IF /* NONEXPONENTIAL FORMAT POSSIBLE */
   THEN
       CALL PRINT_NONEXPONENTIAL;
   ELSE
       CALL PRINT_EXPONENTIAL;
END PRINT_NUMBER;
```

Three second-level modules have been represented by comments: /* PRINT SIGN */, /* COMPUTE SIGNIFICANT_DIGITS */, and /* NONEXPONENTIAL FORMAT POSSIBLE */ (a condition!). Two others are represented by procedures: PRINT_NONEXPONENTIAL and PRINT_EXPONENTIAL. The choice was made on the belief that the first three would be straightforward, hardly justifying separate procedures. The latter two promise to be more complex and thus, for clarity, had best be taken up separately rather than as part of another procedure. Obviously, this is a subjective judgement, and someone else might well make different choices.

*On the Second Level.* Now we start to work on the second level modules. Printing the sign is trivial: if the sign is negative a minus sign is printed. Nothing is printed if the sign is positive. We have:

```
/* PRINT SIGN */
    IF SIGN THEN CALL PRINT_CHAR ( ' − ' );
```

We assume that the procedure PRINT_CHAR, which prints the character whose code is supplied as an argument, is already available, say as part of the computer's operating system.

The number of significant digits is the number of digits (7) minus the number of trailing zeros. We start by setting SIGNIFICANT_DIGITS to 7 and then work backwards through the array DIGITS, decreasing SIGNIFICANT_DIGITS by 1 for every trailing zero found. However, if all the digits are zero, then we want to consider at most 6 of them "insignificant." We will always print one digit even if it is zero. We use the auxiliary variable I to make sure that SIGNIFICANT_DIGITS is not decremented more than 6 times:

```
/* COMPUTE SIGNIFICANT_DIGITS */
    SIGNIFICANT_DIGITS = 7;
    I = 6;
    DO WHILE DIGITS(I) = '0' AND I > 0;
        SIGNIFICANT_DIGITS =
            SIGNIFICANT_DIGITS − 1;
        I = I − 1;
    END;
```

Now we have to check whether the number can be printed in nonexponential format, or whether exponential printing will be necessary.

The decimal point is assumed to be following the first digit of the mantissa. If we are to stay within our 7 digit limit, we certainly cannot move the decimal point more than 6 places to the right. Thus one requirement for nonexponential format is that

$$\text{DECIMAL\_EXPONENT LE 6}$$

What if DECIMAL_EXPONENT is negative? Then we must shift the decimal point DECIMAL_EXPONENT (using its absolute value) places to the left. The first shift will take it past the leftmost digit. Each remaining shift will require that a leading zero be supplied. The number of leading zeros needed is $-\text{DIGITS} - 1$. (For instance, $3.5 \times 10^{-3} = .0035$. The number of leading zeros needed is $-(-3) - 1 = 3 - 1 = 2$.)

Now the number of leading zeros plus the number of significant digits cannot exceed 7 if we are to print in nonexponential format. Therefore we must have:

$$-\text{DECIMAL\_EXPONENT} - 1 + \text{SIGNIFICANT\_DIGITS}$$
$$\text{LE 7}$$

We may manipulate this algebraically into a more convenient form, moving DECIMAL_EXPONENT to the right of LE and 7 to the left:

$$\text{SIGNIFICANT\_DIGITS} - 8 \text{ LE DECIMAL\_EXPONENT}$$

If we are to print in nonexponential format, then, DECIMAL_EXPONENT must lie in the range SIGNIFICANT_DIGITS − 8 through 6 (notice that SIGNIFICANT_DIGITS − 8 is always a negative number). Thus the condition for nonexponential printing is:

(SIGNIFICANT_DIGITS − 8 LE
 DECIMAL_EXPONENT)
AND (DECIMAL_EXPONENT LE 6)

We have now provided program statements to go with each of the comments in our first draft. With the understanding that the procedures PRINT_NONEXPONENTIAL and PRINT_EXPONENTIAL are still to be provided, we can write a final draft of PRINT_NUMBER. This draft is shown in Program 6-1.

*PRINT_NONEXPONENTIAL.* The procedure PRINT_NONEXPONENTIAL must clearly do three things:

1) Print decimal point and leading zeros if any when the exponent is negative.

```
PRINT_NUMBER: PROCEDURE;
    DECLARE (SIGNIFICANT_DIGITS, I) BYTE;
    /* PRINT SIGN */
        IF SIGN THEN CALL PRINT_CHAR('-');
    /* COMPUTE SIGNIFICANT DIGITS */
        SIGNIFICANT_DIGITS=7;
        I=6;
        DO WHILE DIGITS(I) = '0' AND I > 0;
            SIGNIFICANT_DIGITS = SIGNIFICANT_DIGITS - 1;
            I = I - 1;
        END;
    /* PRINT IN EXPONENTIAL OR NONEXPONENTIAL FORMAT */
        IF (SIGNIFICANT_DIGITS - 8 LE DECIMAL_EXPONENT)
            AND (DECIMAL_EXPONENT LE 6) THEN
            CALL PRINT_NONEXPONENTIAL;
        ELSE
            CALL PRINT_EXPONENTIAL;
END PRINT_NUMBER;
```

Program 6-1. PRINT_NUMBER formats and prints a decimal number.

2) Print the significant digits, putting the decimal point in the proper position if it occurs among the significant digits.
3) If the exponent was greater than the number of significant digits minus 1, the print trailing zeros.

These considerations lead to our first draft for PRINT_NONEXPONENTIAL:

```
PRINT_NONEXPONENTIAL: PROCEDURE;
    /* PRINT DECIMAL POINT AND LEADING ZEROS
        FOR NUMBERS WITH NEGATIVE EXPONENTS */
    /* PRINT SIGNIFICANT DIGITS */
    /* PRINT TRAILING ZEROS */
END PRINT_NONEXPONENTIAL;
```

Printing the decimal point and leading zeros is straightforward if we remember that, when DECIMAL_EXPONENT is negative, the number of leading zeros is $-$DECIMAL_EXPONENT $- 1$:

```
/* PRINT DECIMAL POINT AND LEADING ZEROS
   FOR NUMBERS WITH NEGATIVE EXPONENTS */
IF DECIMAL_EXPONENT LT 0 THEN
    DO;
        CALL PRINT_CHAR ('.');
        DO J = 1 TO -DECIMAL_EXPONENT - 1;
            CALL PRINT_CHAR ('0');
        END;
    END;
```

Note that if DECIMAL_EXPONENT = −1, then −DECIMAL_EXPONENT − 1 will be 0, and *no* leading zeros will be printed.

Printing the significant digits causes no trouble, but we must be sure to insert the decimal point in the correct position should it fall among the significant digits. We can handle that by counting down DECIMAL_EXPONENT as we print significant digits. When DECIMAL_EXPONENT goes to zero, then that is where the decimal point should go:

```
/* PRINT SIGNIFICANT DIGITS */
CALL PRINT_CHAR (DIGITS(0));
DO J = 1 TO SIGNIFICANT_DIGITS - 1;
    IF DECIMAL_EXPONENT = 0 THEN
        CALL PRINT_CHAR ('.');
    CALL PRINT_CHAR (DIGITS(J));
    DECIMAL_EXPONENT =
        DECIMAL_EXPONENT - 1;
END;
```

The leftmost digit—DIGITS(0)—is treated as a special case since any decimal point in front of it has already been printed.

If DECIMAL_EXPONENT has not gone to zero or become negative, then we must continue counting it down and printing trailing zeros:

```
/* PRINT TRAILING ZEROS */
DO WHILE DECIMAL_EXPONENT GT 0;
    CALL PRINT_CHAR ('0');
    DECIMAL_EXPONENT =
        DECIMAL_EXPONENT - 1;
END;
```

Putting these refinements into our first draft of PRINT_NONEXPONENTIAL gives us Program 6-2, the final draft of PRINT_NONEXPONENTIAL.

```
PRINT__NONEXPONENTIAL: PROCEDURE;
   DECLARE J BYTE;
   /* PRINT DECIMAL POINT AND LEADING ZEROS FOR NUMBERS
      WITH NEGATIVE EXPONENTS */
      IF DECIMAL__EXPONENT LT 0 THEN
         DO;
            CALL PRINT__CHAR('.');
            DO J=1 TO -DECIMAL__EXPONENT-1;
               CALL PRINT__CHAR('0');
            END;
         END;
   /* PRINT SIGNIFICANT DIGITS */
      CALL PRINT__CHAR(DIGITS(0));
      DO J=1 TO SIGNIFICANT__DIGITS-1;
         IF DECIMAL__EXPONENT=0 THEN
            CALL PRINT__CHAR('.');
         CALL PRINT__CHAR(DIGITS(J));
         DECIMAL__EXPONENT=DECIMAL__EXPONENT-1;
      END;
   /* PRINT TRAILING ZEROS */
      DO WHILE DECIMAL__EXPONENT GT 0;
         CALL PRINT__CHAR('0');
         DECIMAL__EXPONENT=DECIMAL__EXPONENT-1;
      END;
END PRINT__NONEXPONENTIAL;
```

Program 6-2. PRINT__NONEXPONENTIAL prints a decimal number in everyday (nonexponential) format.

PRINT_EXPONENTIAL is extremely straightforward, partly because the exponential format is much more rigid than the nonexponential one. Thinking about the parts of the exponential format gives us this first draft for PRINT_EXPONENTIAL:

```
PRINT_EXPONENTIAL: PROCEDURE;
   /* PRINT FIRST DIGIT */
   /* PRINT DECIMAL POINT */
   /* PRINT REMAINING SIGNIFICANT DIGITS */
   /* PRINT 'E' */
   /* PRINT EXPONENT */
END PRINT_EXPONENTIAL;
```

```
PRINT _ EXPONENTIAL: PROCEDURE;
   DECLARE J BYTE;
   /* PRINT FIRST DIGIT */
      CALL PRINT _ CHAR(DIGITS(0));
   /* PRINT DECIMAL POINT */
      IF SIGNIFICANT _ DIGITS > 1 THEN CALL PRINT _ CHAR('.');
   /* PRINT REMAINING SIGNIFICANT DIGITS */
      DO J = 1 TO SIGNIFICANT _ DIGITS - 1;
         CALL PRINT _ CHAR(DIGITS(J));
      END;
   /* PRINT 'E' */
      CALL PRINT _ CHAR('E');
   /*PRINT EXPONENT */
      IF DECIMAL _ EXPONENT GE 0 THEN
         CALL PRINT _ CHAR(' + ');
      ELSE
         DO;
            CALL PRINT _ CHAR(' - ');
            DECIMAL _ EXPONENT = - DECIMAL _ EXPONENT;
         END;
      CALL PRINT _ UNSIGNED _ INTEGER(DECIMAL _ EXPONENT);
END PRINT _ EXPONENTIAL;
```

Program 6-3. PRINT _ EXPONENTIAL prints a decimal number in exponential format.

---

Adding the necessary statements to implement these comments gives us Program 6-3, the final draft of PRINT_EXPONENTIAL. The necessary statements are sufficiently obvious so that only two further explanations are necessary:

We make the printing of the decimal point conditional upon there being more than one significant digit. Thus $1 \times 10^9$ will print as 1E+9 instead of 1.E+9, as it would if the decimal point were always printed.

The procedure PRINT_UNSIGNED_INTEGER will be written in Chapter 9. For the moment we assume that it is available as it indeed is on many systems.

# Part III
# Arithmetic

# Chapter 7
# Multiple Precision Arithmetic

A typical hobby computer is equipped to carry out arithmetical, logical, shifting, and relational operations on bytes. Some of these operations—but usually not all—may also be available for words. The only arithmetical operations provided are addition and subtraction; multiplication and division are rarely included.

In practice we must often work with larger numbers than can be stored in a byte or word. Often 3, 4, or more bytes are needed. We need to extend the arithmetical, logical, and shifting operations available for bytes and words to these multi-byte values. Also we need to implement multiplication and division for bytes and words as well as multi-byte values.

We will refer to numbers that require more than one byte of storage as *multiple precision numbers*. (Whether words are treated as multiple precision numbers will depend on the computer, and on what word operations are implemented in the hardware.) Arithmetic on multiple precision numbers is called *multiple precision arithmetic*, and that (together with a few other multiple precision operations) is the subject of this chapter.

We will concentrate on 4-byte numbers, although the techniques developed may easily be extended to numbers having less or more bytes—even single byte numbers in the case of multiplication and division.

We define three 4-byte registers which will be treated as global variables by all the procedures in this chapter:

DECLARE (AC0, AC1, AC2, AC3) BYTE,
/* ACCUMULATOR */
(OP0, OP1, OP2, OP3) BYTE,
/* OPERAND */
(MQ0, MQ1, MQ2, MQ3) BYTE;
/* MULTIPLIER-QUOTIENT */

These registers are illustrated in Fig. 7-1. Note that the bytes of each register are numbered, from right to left, 0-3. Thus AC0 is the rightmost byte of the accumulator, and AC3 is the leftmost byte.

It would have been more elegant to define structures AC, OP, and MQ; and to let AC0, AC1, and so on be components of these structures. But structures offer no technical advantages for fixed locations—as opposed to array elements and locations designated by pointers—and their use would have made our names clumsier: AC.AC0 instead of just AC0, for instance. Nevertheless, we shall often informally use AC to refer to the entire accumulator, OP to refer to the entire operand, and MQ to refer to the entire MQ.

Whenever an arithmetic procedure is called, the first operand will be in AC and the second (if any) will be in OP. The

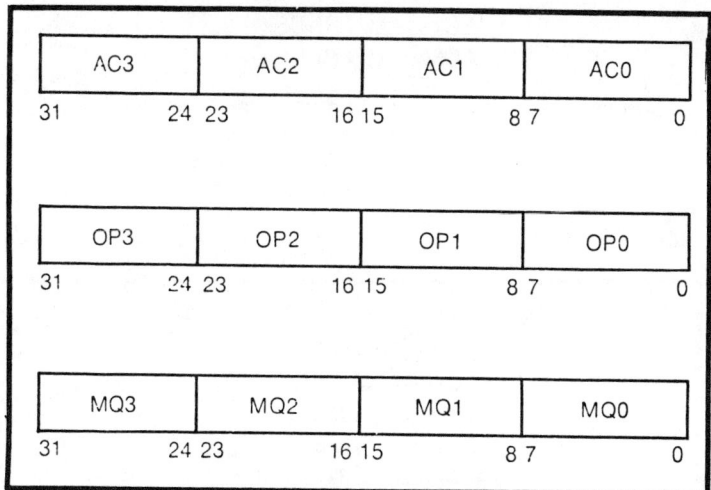

Fig. 7-1. The 4-byte registers AC, OP and MQ. The bits of each register are numbered 0-31 as shown.

109

procedure will leave the result in AC. As its name implies, MQ is used to temporarily store multipliers and quotients.

## ADDITION

Multiple precision addition is accomplished using the + operation, which corresponds to the "add" instruction on computers, and with the PLUS operation, which corresponds to "add with carry."

The statement

$$AC0 = AC0 + OP0;$$

adds the rightmost bytes of AC and OP, and stores the result in the rightmost byte of AC. In addition, the carry bit is set to 1 if there was a carry out of the leftmost position of the addition, and to 0 otherwise.

Now

$$AC1 = AC1 \text{ PLUS } OP1;$$

adds the contents of AC1, the contents of AC2, and the carry bit, and stores the result in AC1. The carry bit is added in the rightmost position—that is, if the carry bit is 1 then 00000001 is added to the sum of AC1 and OP1.

We complete the 4-byte addition using the PLUS operator:

$$AC2 = AC2 \text{ PLUS } OP2;$$
$$AC3 = AC3 \text{ PLUS } OP3;$$

Incorporating these four statements into a procedure gives Program 7-1, ADD _ OP _ TO _ AC. When this procedure returns, CARRY will be TRUE or FALSE depending on whether there was a carry out of the leftmost position of the entire 4-byte addition.

```
ADD _ OP _ TO _ AC: PROCEDURE:
    AC0 = AC0 + OP0;
    AC1 = AC1 PLUS OP1:
    AC2 = AC2 PLUS OP2:
    AC3 = AC3 PLUS OP3:
END ADD _ OP _ TO _ AC;
```

Program 7-1. ADD _ OP _ TO _ AC adds the contents of OP to the contents of AC and leaves the result in AC.

```
SUBTRACT _ OP _ FROM _ AC: PROCEDURE:
   AC0 = AC0 - OP0;
   AC1 = AC1 MINUS OP1;
   AC2 = AC2 MINUS OP2;
   AC3 = AC3 MINUS OP3;
END SUBTRACT _ OP _ FROM _ AC;
```

Program 7-2. SUBTRACT _ OP _ FROM _ AC subtracts the contents of OP from the contents of AC and leaves the result in AC.

## SUBTRACTION

Multiple precision subtraction is very similar to multiple precision addition. The statement

$$AC0 = AC0 - OP0;$$

subtracts OP0 from AC0 and sets the carry bit to 1 or 0 depending on whether or not the subtraction in the leftmost position generated a borrow.

We continue the subtraction to the left using MINUS, which subtracts both the carry bit and the second operand from the first operand. (MINUS is equivalent to the "subtract with borrow" instruction on many computers);

$$AC1 = AC1 \text{ MINUS } OP1;$$
$$AC2 = AC2 \text{ MINUS } OP2;$$
$$AC3 = AC3 \text{ MINUS } OP3;$$

Program 7-2 shows the procedure SUBTRACT_OP_FROM_AC incorporating the above statements. When the procedure returns, CARRY will be TRUE or FALSE depending on whether or not the subtraction in the leftmost position of the entire 4-byte number generated a borrow.

## INCREMENTATION AND NEGATION

Incrementation adds 1 to the contents of a register. Negation subtracts the contents of a register from zero, thus replacing the contents of the register by its twos complement.

Incrementation is a special case of addition; negation is a special case of subtraction. Therefore Program 7-3, INCREMENT_AC, and Program 7-4, NEGATE_AC, are special cases of programs already covered, and require no further discussion.

```
INCREMENT_AC: PROCEDURE;
   AC0 = AC0 + 1;
   AC1 = AC1 PLUS 0;
   AC2 = AC2 PLUS 0;
   AC3 = AC3 PLUS 0;
END INCREMENT_AC;
```

Program 7-3. INCREMENT_AC adds 1 to the contents of AC.

We could write similar procedures INCREMENT_OP and NEGATE_OP for OP. We shall not bother to actually write these out.

**SHIFTING**

Multiple precision shifting is needed to implement multiplication and division, and occasionally for other purposes. The procedures in this section will be written for AC. But in later work we will also assume equivalent procedures to exist for OP and MQ.

The idea of multiple precision shifting may be illustrated with the SHL or "shift left" operation. The statement

$$AC0 = SHL\,(AC0, 1);$$

shifts AC0 one place to the left. A 0 is shifted into bit 0 of AC1, and the bit which formerly occupied position 7 has been shifted into the carry bit.

Moving on to AC1, we now use SCL instead of SHL, so that the bit that was shifted out of the left end of AC0 and into the carry bit will be shifted into the right end of AC1:

$$AC1 = SCL\,(AC1, 1);$$

AC2 and AC3 are handled in the same way:

$$AC2 = SCL\,(AC2, 1);$$
$$AC3 = SCL\,(AC3, 1);$$

```
NEGATE_AC: PROCEDURE;
   AC0 = 0 - AC0;
   AC1 = 0 MINUS AC1;
   AC2 = 0 MINUS AC2;
   AC3 = 0 MINUS AC3;
END NEGATE_AC;
```

Program 7-4. NEGATE_AC replaces the contents of AC by its twos complement.

```
SHL_AC: PROCEDURE:
    AC0 = SHL (AC0, 1):
    AC1 = SCL (AC1, 1):
    AC2 = SCL (AC2, 1):
    AC3 = SCL (AC3, 1):
END SHL_AC:
```

Program 7-5. SHL_AC shifts the contents of AC one place to the left.

A right shift works the same way except that we must start with AC3 and work to the right:

$$AC3 = SHR\ (AC3, 1);$$
$$AC2 = SCR\ (AC2, 1);$$
$$AC1 = SCR\ (AC1, 1);$$
$$AC0 = SCR\ (AC0, 1);$$

Program 7-5, SHL_AC, and Program 7-6, SHR_AC, implement the left and right shift. When either of these procedures returns, CARRY will be TRUE or FALSE depending on whether the bit shifted out of AC was 1 or 0.

The arithmetical right shift, ASR, which preserves the value of the sign bit, is easy to implement if the computer itself features the ASR operation:

$$AC3 = ASR\ (AC3, 1);$$
$$AC2 = SCR\ (AC2, 1);$$
$$AC1 = SCR\ (AC1, 1);$$
$$AC0 = SCR\ (AC0, 1);$$

Program 7-7 uses this code to implement the procedure ASR_AC.

If the computer does not feature the ASR operation, then the sign bit before shifting must be saved and reinserted in the sign position after the shift. The exact method of best doing

Program 7-6. SHR_AC shifts the contents of AC one place to the right.

```
SHR_AC: PROCEDURE:
    AC3 = SHR (AC3, 1):
    AC2 = SCR (AC2, 1):
    AC1 = SCR (AC1, 1):
    AC0 = SCR (AC0, 1):
END SHR_AC:
```

```
ASR __ AC: PROCEDURE:
   AC3 = ASR(AC3, 1);
   AC2 = SCR(AC2, 1);
   AC1 = SCR(AC1, 1);
   AC0 = SCR(AC0, 1);
END ASR __ AC;
```

Program 7-7. ASR __ AC shifts the contents of AC one place to the right **arithmetically**, that is, preserving the value of bit 31, the sign bit.

this will vary from one computer to another; the following is one way:

$$\text{TEMP} = \text{AC3 AND 80H};$$
$$\text{CALL SHR\_AC};$$
$$\text{AC3} = \text{AC3 OR TEMP};$$

## INTEGER MULTIPLICATION

A worked-out binary multiplication is shown in Chapter 1. Examining it, we notice the following:

1) The product is the sum of a series of *partial products*—the numbers between the horizontal lines.
2) There is one partial product for each digit of the multiplier. If a multiplier digit is 1, the corresponding partial product is equal to the multiplicand. If the multiplier digit is 0 the corresponding partial product is 0.
3) Reading from bottom to top, the significant digits of each partial product are shifted one place to the right with respect to those of the partial product just below it.

In computer multiplication, it is more convenient to add up the partial products as they are formed, rather than adding them all up at once as in the paper and pencil method. We will use AC to hold the sum of all the partial products formed so far.

For integer multiplication, at least, it turns out to be most convenient to form the partial products from bottom to top, which is equivalent to processing multiplier digits from left to right (as opposed to right to left in the paper and pencil method). Before adding a partial product to AC, we shift AC one place to the *left*. This gives the same effect as if each partial product had been shifted one place to the *right* with respect to the one just below it.

These considerations lead to the following first draft for our multiplication algorithm:

```
INTEGER_MULTIPLY: PROCEDURE;
   DECLARE I BYTE;
   /* MOVE AC TO MQ. CLEAR AC TO HOLD SUM
      OF PARTIAL PRODUCTS */
   DO I = 1 TO 32;
      /* SHIFT AC AND MQ EACH ONE PLACE TO
         THE LEFT. IF BIT SHIFTED OUT OF MQ IS
         1, ADD OP TO AC */
   END;
END INTEGER_MULTIPLY;
```

The comments are easily implemented, as shown in Program 7-8. We note that after CALL SHL_MQ, the carry bit holds the current multiplier digit. We can test this by testing CARRY. Thus

IF CARRY THEN CALL ADD_OP_TO_AC;

adds the multiplicand to the sum of the partial products if and only if the multiplier digit is 1.

```
INTEGER_MULTIPLY: PROCEDURE:
   DECLARE I BYTE:
   /* MOVE AC TO MQ. CLEAR AC TO HOLD SUM OF
      PARTIAL PRODUCTS */
      MQ0 = AC0; MQ1 = AC1; MQ2 = AC2; MQ3 = AC3;
      AC0 = 0; AC1 = 0; AC2 = 0; AC3 = 0;
   DO I = 1 TO 32;
      /* SHIFT AC AND MQ EACH ONE PLACE TO THE LEFT.
         IF THE BIT SHIFTED OUT OF MQ IS 1, ADD OP
         TO AC */
      CALL SHL_AC;
      CALL SHL_MQ;
      IF CARRY THEN CALL ADD_OP_TO_AC;
   END;
END INTEGER_MULTIPLY;
```

Program 7-8. INTEGER_MULTIPLY multiplies the contents of OP by the contents of AC, and leaves the result in AC. The operands are treated as integers.

**INTEGER DIVIDE**

As before, we start by examining the worked-out division in Chapter 1 and making observations as follows:

1) Only the significant bits of the divisor are used; leading zeros are eliminated. Thus, in effect, the divisor is shifted to the left until all leading zeros have been shifted out, and the leftmost significant bit is in the leftmost position.
2) The number of quotient digits is one more than the number of leading zeros that were shifted out of the divisor.
3) The numbers just below the horizontal lines are *partial remainders*. The first partial remainder is the dividend. The last one is the remainder of the entire division (that is, the result of the MOD operation).
4) At each step of the division process, the divisor is compared with the current partial remainder. If the divisor is less than or equal to the partial remainder, it is subtracted from the partial remainder, and a 1 is placed in the quotient. Otherwise a 0 goes in the quotient and the partial remainder remains unchanged.

After each step the divisor is shifted one place to the right.

The division procedure may be asked to divide by zero, an illegal operation. In that case it should display an error message and return with divisor and dividend unchanged.

Computer division is similar to the paper and pencil method. We keep the partial remainders in AC, the divisor in OP, and form the quotient in MQ. Here is the outline of the division procedure:

```
INTEGER_DIVIDE: PROCEDURE;
    DECLARE (I, COUNT) BYTE;
    /* IF DIVISION BY ZERO IS BEING ATTEMPTED,
       PRINT ERROR MESSAGE AND RETURN */

    /* SHIFT OP LEFT UNTIL LEFTMOST
       SIGNIFICANT BIT IS IN LEFTMOST POSITION.
       SET COUNT TO NUMBER OF ZEROS SHIFTED
       OUT */

    /* INCREMENT COUNT TO GIVE NUMBER OF
```

DIGITS IN QUOTENT. CLEAR MQ TO HOLD
QUOTIENT */

DO I = 1 TO COUNT;
    /* SHIFT MQ LEFT. IF OP IS LESS THAN OR EQUAL TO AC, SUBTRACT OP FROM AC AND INSERT 1 (THE QUOTIENT DIGIT) INTO LOW ORDER BIT OF MQ. SHIFT OP RIGHT */
END;
/* MOVE MQ TO AC (OMIT IF REMAINDER DESIRED INSTEAD OF QUOTIENT) */
END INTEGER_DIVIDE;

Program 7-9 shows the complete INTEGER_DIVIDE procedure. The implementation of the comments in the outline are largely straightforward. But the following points are worth noting:

We must test whether the divisor is zero to determine whether or not the procedure is being requested to perform an illegal operation. A simple way to test a multi-byte number for being zero is to OR together all its bytes, that is, to form:

OP0 OR OP1 OR OP2 OR OP3

If there is a 1 in a given position in any of the bytes then a 1 will appear in that position in the result. Thus if the result is zero then all the bits in all the bytes must be zeros, and so OP must be zero.

Errors are reported by calling a subroutine ERROR which takes two arguments: The first argument is the number of characters in the error message and the second argument is the address of the first byte of the error message. Thus

CALL ERROR (26, @ 'DIVISION BY ZERO ATTEMPTED');

will print the error message that appears between the quote marks.

We have to shift OP left until its leftmost significant bit is in the leftmost position. Also we must keep count of the

```
INTEGER __ DIVIDE: PROCEDURE;
    DECLARE (I, COUNT) BYTE;
    /* IF DIVISION BY ZERO IS BEING ATTEMPTED, PRINT
        ERROR MESSAGE AND RETURN */
        IF (OP0 OR OP1 OR OP2 OR OP3) = 0 THEN
            DO;
                CALL ERROR (26, @ 'DIVISION BY ZERO ATTEMPTED');
                RETURN;
            END;
    /*SHIFT OP LEFT UNTIL LEFTMOST SIGNIFICANT BIT
        IS IN LEFTMOST POSITION. SET COUNT TO NUMBER OF
        ZEROS SHIFTED OUT */
        COUNT = 0;
        DO WHILE (OP3 AND 80 H) = 0;
            CALL SHL __ OP;
            COUNT = COUNT + 1;
        END;
    /*INCREMENT COUNT TO GIVE NUMBER OF DIGITS IN QUOTIENT.
        CLEAR MQ TO HOLD QUOTIENT */
        COUNT = COUNT + 1;
        MQ0 = 0; MQ1 = 0; MQ2 = 0; MQ3 = 0;
    DO I = 1 TO COUNT;
        /* SHIFT MQ LEFT. IF OP IS LESS THAN OR EQUAL TO
            AC, SUBTRACT OP FROM AC AND INSERT 1 (THE QUOTIENT
            DIGIT) INTO LOW ORDER BIT OF MQ. SHIFT OP RIGHT */
            CALL SHL __ MQ;
            CALL SUBTRACT __ OP __ FROM __ AC;
            IF CARRY THEN CALL ADD __ OP __ TO __ AC;
            ELSE MQ0 = MQ0 OR 1;
            CALL SHR __ OP;
    END;
    /* MOVE MQ TO AC (OMIT IF REMAINDER DESIRED INSTEAD OF
        QUOTIENT) */
        AC0 = MQ0; AC1 = MQ1; AC2 = MQ2; AC3 = MQ3;
END INTEGER __ DIVIDE;
```

Program 7-9. INTEGER __ DIVIDE divides the contents of AC by the contents of OP and leaves the result in AC. The operands are treated as integers. The procedure is easily modified to return the remainder, or both quotient and remainder.

---

number of leading zeros shifted out in COUNT. The following repetition accomplishes these things:

```
COUNT = 0;
DO WHILE (OP3 AND 80H) = 0;
    CALL SHL_OP;
    COUNT = COUNT + 1;
END;
```

The expression OP3 AND 80H masks off all but the leftmost bit of OP3. If that bit is 0, then OP3 AND 80H will equal 0; otherwise it will not.

Moving on to the division itself, at each step we shift the quotient (MQ) one place to the left, to make room for a new quotient digit. Then we subtract the divisor (OP) from the partial remainder (AC). If CARRY is TRUE—indicating a borrow occurred—then the divisor was greater than the partial remainder. We restore the partial remainder by adding OP back to AC. If the subtraction did not cause a borrow (CARRY = FALSE) then the difference becomes the new partial remainder, and the current quotient digit—the rightmost bit in MQ—is set to 1. Finally, the divisor is shifted one place to the right. All of this is easier to program than to describe:

```
CALL SHL_MQ;
CALL SUBTRACT_OP_FROM_AC;
IF CARRY THEN CALL ADD_OP_TO_AC;
ELSE MQ0 = MQ0 OR 1;
CALL SHR_OP;
```

When the division is complete, the remainder will be in AC and the quotient in MQ. If the remainder is to be the result—we are programming MOD—or if both quotient and remainder are needed, then nothing further need be done. Otherwise, the contents of MQ are moved to AC.

## MULTIPLICATION AND DIVISION OF BINARY FRACTIONS

Addition and subtraction are independent of the position of the radix point, as long as that position is the same in both operands. Multiplication and division *are* dependent on the position of the radix point: Although the significant digits of a product or quotient will always be the same, the positioning of those digits in the result register will depend on the assumed location of the radix point. Thus if we wish to multiply and divide fractions—as we will in the next chapter—we need separate multiplication and division procedures.

For our work in this chapter, we will assume that the radix point is between bits 30 and 31 of AC and OP. Bit 31 of AC and OP is reserved for use by the procedures and in the result. It must be zero in the operands.

Fraction multiplication is quite similar to integer multiplication, except that we examine the multiplier digits from right to left and shift the sum of the partial products in AC one place right after each step. This assures that excess bits will be lost on the right and not on the left.

Assuming that the multiplier has been moved to MQ, and AC has been cleared, we multiply fractions as follows:

```
DO I = 1 TO 31;
    CALL SHR_MQ;
    IF CARRY THEN CALL ADD_OP_TO_AC;
    CALL SHR_AC;
END;
```

This routine has one disadvantage. It is possible that bit 30, the bit just to the right of the radix point, will be 0 (just as .3* .3 = .09 in decimal). In that case our result contains only 30 significant bits instead of 31.

We can remedy this by generating not the product of the operands but the product times two—the product shifted one place to the left. Then bit 31 will be the leftmost bit of the product. If it happens to be 0, then we still have 31 significant bits remaining—the same number that was in the operands.

To generate the product times two, we merely shift AC right before adding the current partial product, rather than after. This avoids a final shift to the right, which is the same as a division by two. The code is:

```
DO I = 1 TO 31;
    CALL SHR_AC;
    CALL SHR_MQ;
    IF CARRY THEN CALL ADD_OP_TO_AC;
END;
```

Using this we get Program 7-10, FRACTION_MULTIPLY.

Fraction division can be done in the same way as integer division, except that no alignment step is needed. Fractions are already aligned on the left. Also we will shift the partial

```
FRACTION _ MULTIPLY: PROCEDURE;
   DECLARE I BYTE;
   /* MOVE AC TO MQ. CLEAR AC TO HOLD SUM OF PARTIAL
      PRODUCTS */
   MQ0 = AC0; MQ1 = AC1; MQ2 = AC2; MQ3 = AC3;
   AC0 = 0; AC1 = 0; AC2 = 0; AC3 = 0;
   DO I = 1 TO 31;
      /* SHIFT AC AND MQ EACH ONE PLACE TO THE RIGHT
         IF BIT SHIFTED OUT OF MQ IS 1, ADD OP TO AC*/
         CALL SHR _ AC;
         CALL SHR _ MQ;
         IF CARRY THEN CALL ADD _ OP _ TO _ AC;
   END;
END FRACTION _ MULTIPLY
```

Program 7-10. FRACTION _ MULTIPLY multiplies the contents of OP by the contents of AC and leaves the result in AC. The operands are treated as fractions. The result left in AC is two time the true product.

remainder left rather than shifting the divisor right. This will prevent any bits being lost out of the right end of the divisor—a situation that could not occur in the integer division procedure but could occur here.

The following code, like that used for integer division, restores the partial remainder by adding back the divisor if subtracting the divisor caused a borrow. Thus it is known as *restoring division*:

```
DO I = 1 TO 32;
   CALL SHL_MQ;
   CALL SUBTRACT_OP_FROM_AC;
   IF CARRY THEN CALL ADD_OP_TO_AC;
   ELSE MQ0 = MQ0 OR 1;
   CALL SHL_AC;
END;
```

This code generates a 32-bit quotient, so bit 31 may be used as a quotient bit. Thus the dividend must be less than twice the divisor, since the quotient can only be as large as 1.11111...B, which is just less than 2.

The restoring division algorithm is slowed down because sometimes both a subtraction and an addition are done in the same step. We can speed up the procedure by using

```
FRACTION_DIVIDE: PROCEDURE:
    DECLARE I BYTE:
    /* IF DIVISION BY ZERO IS BEING ATTEMPTED, PRINT
        ERROR MESSAGE AND RETURN */
        IF (OP0 OR OP1 OR OP2 OR OP3) = 0 THEN
            DO:
                CALL ERROR (26, @ 'DIVISION BY ZERO ATTEMPTED'):
                RETURN:
            END:
    /* NONRESTORING FRACTION DIVISION */
        CALL SUBTRACT_OP_FROM_AC:
        DO I = 1 TO 32:
            CALL SHL_MQ:
            CALL SHL_AC:
            IF CARRY THEN        /* IF AC WAS NEGATIVE */
                CALL ADD_OP_TO_AC:
            ELSE
                DO:
                    CALL SUBTRACT_OP_FROM_AC:
                    MQ0 = MQ0 OR 1:
                END:
        END:
END FRACTION_DIVIDE:
```

Program 7-11. FRACTION_DIVIDE divides the contents of AC by the contents of OP and leaves the result in AC. The operands are treated as fractions.

---

*nonrestoring division*, which does an addition *or* a subtraction at each step, but never both.

Nonrestoring division uses the difference

partial remainder - divisor

in place of the partial remainder. In each step the sign of this quantity is tested. If the sign is positive, the quantity is shifted one place to the left and the divisor is subtracted; the quotient digit is 1. If the sign is negative, the quantity is shifted one place to the left and the divisor is added; the quotient digit is 0.

The following is the code for nonrestoring division. Note that the call to SHL_AC shifts the sign bit of AC into the carry bit, so CARRY is TRUE if AC was negative and FALSE otherwise:

```
CALL SUBTRACT_OP_FROM_AC;
DO I = 1 TO 32;
   CALL SHL_MQ;
   CALL SHL_AC;
   IF CARRY THEN
      CALL ADD_OP_TO_AC;
   ELSE
      DO;
         CALL SUBTRACT_OP_FROM_AC;
         MQ0 = MQ0 OR 1;
      END;
END;
```

Nonrestoring division is well suited to dividing fractions. Since we are seldom interested in a remainder with fraction division, no extra step is needed at the end to restore the remainder. Also the reserved bit 31 is needed as a sign bit, since AC must hold a signed number in nonrestoring division.

Program 7-11, FRACTION_DIVIDE, uses nonrestoring division.

# Chapter 8
# Floating Point Arithmetic

Floating point numbers are represented inside the computer in a manner similar to scientific notation. Floating point representations offer several advantages:

*Accuracy.* All digit positions are available to store significant digits. No positions are wasted on nonsignificant leading zeros.

*Range.* A typical range for floating point numbers is $10^{-38}$ through $10^{38}$, far larger than would be practical with a fixed point representation.

*Ease of Use.* The computer automatically aligns radix points for addition and subtraction, and locates the radix point after a multiplication or division. Such "scaling" often calls for tedious and complex programming when all values must be represented as fixed point numbers.

On the other hand, the arithmetic routines for floating point arithmetic take up more memory space, and require more time to execute, than do the routines for fixed point arithmetic. Also both a mantissa and an exponent must be stored for a floating point number, so that for the same precision a floating point number will take up more memory space than the corresponding fixed point number.

But when the data to be processed is in floating point form—as in scientific calculations—then the advantages of floating point representations far outweigh their disadvantages.

## FLOATING POINT REPRESENTATIONS

In this chapter we will use two floating point representations: an "internal" representation, which is used by the floating point procedures while they are processing a number; and an "external" representation, which is used to store floating point numbers when they are not being processed.

*The Internal Representation.* For the moment let us—for purposes of illustration—consider floating point numbers whose mantissas consist of a single byte. With such a representation we could write 1010B as

$$0.1010000B \times 2^4$$

and .000101B as

$$0.1010000B \times 2^{-3}$$

As with ordinary scientific notation the exponent (4, −3) indicates the number of positions to the right or left that the radix point must be moved.

The mantissa differs slightly from the one in ordinary scientific notation. In ordinary scientific notation 1010B would be written

$$1.0100000B \times 2^3$$

whereas in internal flaoting point format we write it

$$0.1010000B \times 2^4$$

The mantissa has been shifted one place to the right, and the exponent increased by 1 to compensate.

Specifically, the mantissa is a *fraction* such that the bit immediately following the radix point must be 1. The 0 to the left of the radix point is reserved for internal use by the floating point procedures.

The exponent, like the mantissa, must be represented in binary notation inside the computer. Furthermore, we need to represent both positive and negative exponents.

We could use the twos complement system for this purpose. But often manipulation is simplified if we add to each exponent a positive number—called the *bias*—and use the resulting positive number to represent the exponent.

Suppose, for instance, that our exponents can range from −128 through 127. We choose the *bias* to be 128; we represent each exponent by the *biased* exponent obtained by adding 128 to the true exponent. The biased exponents range from 0 through 255 and may be stored in a single byte.

The following are some examples of biased exponents:

| True Exponent | Biased Exponent | Binary Representation |
|---|---|---|
| −128 | 0 | 00000000B |
| −3 | 125 | 01111101B |
| 0 | 128 | 10000000B |
| 4 | 132 | 10000100B |
| 127 | 255 | 11111111B |

In the internal representation of sign of the number is represented by a single byte which has the value TRUE for negative numbers and FALSE for positive numbers.

Thus we could represent $1010B = 0.1010000B \times 2^4$ as

00000000     (sign)<br>
10000100     (exponent)<br>
01010000     (mantissa)

and $-.000101B = -0.1010000B \times 2^{-3}$ as

11111111     (sign)<br>
01111101     (exponent)<br>
01010000     (mantissa)

The representation we shall actually use is the same as the one just illustrated, except that we will use 4 bytes for the mantissa rather than just 1. Thus the mantissa is a 4-byte fraction with the radix point between bits 31 and 32. This is precisely the fraction format we considered in the last chapter, and we can call upon the arithmetic routines developed there when writing our floating point procedures.

As an example of the 4-byte mantissa, consider the representation of .1, whose binary representation is the repeating fraction .000110011001100...B where the digits 1100 repeat indefinitely. We have

00000000     (sign)<br>
01111101     (exponent)<br>
01100110 01100110 01100110 01100110     (mantissa)

The repeating binary representation has been truncated to 31 bits.

We will define several floating point registers to hold numbers in internal representation. AC_SIGN, AC_EXP, and AC0 through AC3 hold one complete floating point number, as do OP_SIGN, OP_EXP, and OP0 through OP3. MQ0 through MQ3 hold the mantissa only of a multiplier or quotient:

| | |
|---|---|
| DECLARE AC_SIGN BYTE, | /* ACCUMULATOR SIGN */ |
| AC_EXP WORD, | /* ACCUMULATOR EXPONENT */ |
| (AC0, AC1, AC2, AC3) BYTE, | /* ACCUMULATOR MANTISSA */ |
| OP_SIGN BYTE, | /* OPERAND SIGN */ |
| OP_EXP BYTE, | /* OPERAND EXPONENT */ |
| (OP0, OP1, OP2, OP3) BYTE, | /* OPERAND MANTISSA */ |
| (MQ0 MQ1, MQ2, MQ3) BYTE; | /* MULTIPLIER-QUOTIENT */ |

Note that AC_EXP is declared as a word rather than a byte. The reason is that the biased exponent may occasionally go out of the range 0-255 during an arithmetic routine, but be brought back into the legal range before the routine terminates. By reserving a word for AC_EXP, we prevent the routine from having to announce an error prematurely.

Figure 8-1 illustrates the floating point registers. These registers are global to all the floating point procedures. We will use the word AC to refer to the entire accumulator: AC_SIGN, AC_EXP, and AC0-AC3. "AC mantissa" will refer to AC0-AC3. Similar terminology holds for OP.

Each arithmetic routine assumes that its operands are in AC and OP, and leaves its result in AC.

*The External Representation.* In our external representation the mantissa will consist of 24 significant bits. The exponent will consist of 1 byte.

(The additional 7 bits of the internal representation serve as *guard bits*, to prevent errors due to the limited size of the floating point registers from working their way into the 24 bits

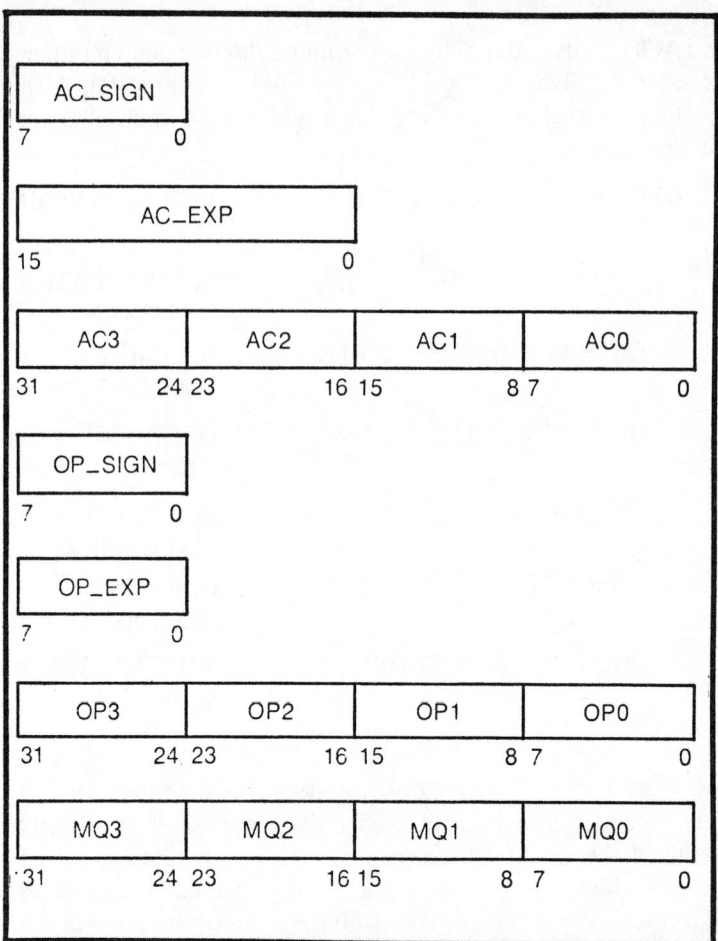

Fig. 8-1. The floating point registers.

we are going to keep. For the purposes of this chapter a single guard bit would be sufficient. But in the next chapter we will see how additional guard bits defend against loss of accuracy during binary-decimal conversion. They can serve the same purpose during the evaluation of scientific functions, such as SIN, EXP, and LOG.)

We can thus use four bytes to store a number in external representation. The first of these we use for the exponent; the remaining three for the mantissa. The mantissa in internal representation is rounded off to 24 bits and shifted one place to the left, so that the 24 bits will fit into three bytes. (That is, the "reserved bit" on the left is eliminated.) Bits 0-23 in the external representation mantissa correspond to bits 7-30 in the internal representation mantissa.

We have still not said how the sign bit is stored in external representation. The leftmost bit of the mantissa is always 1, unless the entire mantissa is 0, a situation we will ignore for the moment. Therefore the leftmost bit of the mantissa need not actually be stored, since we already know what it must be. We can replace it with the sign bit, which is 0 for positive numbers and 1 for negative numbers.

We of course need to be able to recover the leftmost mantissa bit—the one the sign bit replaced—when we convert from external to internal representation. The bit in question will be 1 *unless the entire mantissa is 0*. What we need, then, is some way of indicating a 0 mantissa.

We can do this by limiting slightly the range of the exponent. Instead of allowing it to range from −128 through 127 (biased exponent 0-255) we restrict it to the range −127 through 127 (biased exponent 1-255). We then use a biased

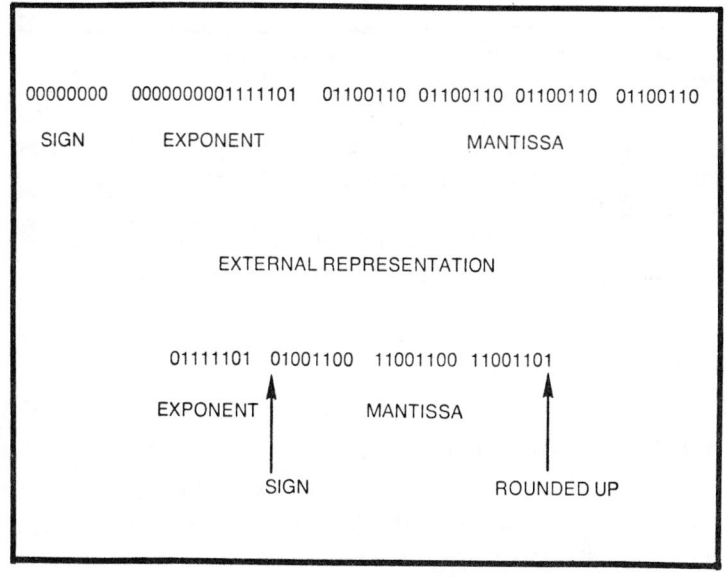

Fig. 8-2. Comparison of the internal and external representations of the floating point number 0.1. In the external representation notice that 1) the mantissa bits have been shifted one place to the left; 2) the mantissa has been rounded off to 23 bits; and 3) the leftmost bit of the mantissa has been replaced by the sign bit.

```
LOAD__AC: PROCEDURE (POINTER);
   DECLARE POINTER WORD,
           MEMORY__BYTE BASED POINTER BYTE;
   /* LOAD THE BYTES */
      AC__EXP = MEMORY__BYTE; POINTER = POINTER + 1;
      AC0 = 0;
      AC1 = MEMORY__BYTE; POINTER = POINTER + 1;
      AC2 = MEMORY__BYTE; POINTER = POINTER + 1;
      AC3 = MEMORY__BYTE;
   /*GET SIGN */
      IF (AC3 AND 80H) = 0 THEN AC__SIGN = FALSE;
      ELSE AC__SIGN = TRUE;
   /* IF EXPONENT IS NOT ZERO, SET ``HIDDEN'' LEFTMOST
      BIT TO 1*/
      IF AC__EXP < > 0 THEN AC3 = AC3 OR 80H;
   /* SHIFT ONE PLACE TO THE RIGHT */
      CALL SHR__AC;
END LOAD__AC;
```

Program 8-1. LOAD__AC converts to internal format the number pointed to by the argument, and stores it in AC.

exponent of 0 to indicate that the mantissa is 0. The floating point number 0, then, is represented by four bytes all 32 bits of which are 0.

When converting from external to internal representation, then, the leftmost bit will be set to 0 if the biased exponent is 0, and to 1 if it is not.

Figure 8-2 contrasts the external and internal representations using the number .1 as an example.

## THE LOAD AND STORE ROUTINES

Two procedures, LOAD__AC and STORE__AC, convert between the internal and external representations. The argument of LOAD__AC is the address of a number in the external representation; LOAD__AC converts this to the internal representation and places it in AC. The argument of STORE__AC is the address of a 4-byte location. STORE__AC converts the number in AC to the external representation, and stores it in the location addressed.

Programs 8-1 and 8-2 show the procedures LOAD_AC and STORE_AC. These procedures assume that the exponent byte is stored first, followed by the rightmost mantissa byte, the middle mantissa byte, and finally the leftmost mantissa byte. Only slight modifications are required if it is desired to store the bytes in some other order.

STORE_AC must round off the contents of AC to 24 bits before converting to external form.

A decimal number may be rounded off by adding 5 to the leftmost position to be dropped, and then truncating the result

```
STORE _ AC: PROCEDURE (POINTER):
   DECLARE POINTER WORD.
         MEMORY _ BYTE BASED POINTER BYTE:
   "ROUND _ AC TO 24 BITS "'
      AC0 = AC0 + 40H:
      AC1 = AC1 PLUS 0:
      AC2 = AC2 PLUS 0:
      AC3 = AC3 PLUS 0:
   " CHECK FOR ROUNDING OVERFLOW "'
      IF (AC3 AND 80H) < > 0 THEN
         DO:
            CALL SHR _ AC:
            AC _ EXP = AC _ EXP + 1:
            IF AC _ EXP GT 255 THEN
               CALL ERROR (17. @ 'EXPONENT OVERFLOW'):
         END:
   "SHIFT ONE PLACE LEFT "'
      CALL SHL _ AC:
   " INSERT SIGN "'
      AC3 = (AC3 AND 7FH) OR (AC _ SIGN AND 80H):
   " STORE BYTES "'
      MEMORY _ BYTE = AC _ EXP: POINTER = POINTER + 1:
      MEMORY _ BYTE = AC1: POINTER = POINTER + 1:
      MEMORY _ BYTE = AC2: POINTER = POINTER + 1:
      MEMORY _ BYTE = AC3:
END STORE _ AC:
```

Program 8-2. STORE_AC converts to external format the number in AC, and stores it at the location pointed to by the argument.

to the desired number of places. Thus to round off 5.674 to one decimal place, we add .05 getting 5.724, and truncate the result to one decimal place getting 5.7. If the number had been 8.637, then adding .05 would have given 8.687, which would become 8.6 after truncation.

In binary, .5 is .1B, so we add a 1 instead of a 5. Thus we round the AC mantissa to 24 bits by adding a 1 to bit 6, and then discardng bits 0-6. Rounding may cause an overflow (via carries) into bit 31; when it does, we shift the mantissa one place to the right and compensate by adding 1 to the exponent.

A routine LOAD_OP, similar to LOAD_AC, could be written for OP. There is normally no reason to *store* OP, since the result of an operation always appears in AC.

**THE ARITHMETIC ROUTINES**

*Addition.* In principle floating point addition is simple: we first align the binary points of the operand mantissas by shifting the mantissa of the operand with the smallest exponent to the right. We then add the mantissas if the operands had the same sign and subtract them otherwise. Finally we must *normalize* the result—shift it to the right or left until the leftmost significant bit is in position 31, immediately to the right of the radix point.

In practice a few technicalities complicate matters somewhat.

We begin by outlining the floating point addition routine using comments:

```
FLOATING_ADD: PROCEDURE;
    /* EXCHANGE OP AND AC, IF NECESSARY, SO
       THAT THE OPERAND WITH THE LARGEST
       EXPONENT WILL BE IN AC */
    /* DETERMINE HOW MANY PLACES THE OP
       MANTISSA MUST BE SHIFTED TO THE
       RIGHT TO ALIGN RADIX POINTS. IF THIS
       NUMBER IS GREATER THAN 30, AC
       ALREADY CONTAINS THE RESULT,
       SO RETURN √/
    /* IF THE SIGNS OF THE TWO OPERANDS
       DIFFER, NEGATE THE OP MANTISSA */
    /* SHIFT THE OP MANTISSA RIGHT
       ARITHMETICALLY TO ALIGN RADIX POINTS */
```

```
      /* ADD THE MANTISSAS */
      /* IF THE SIGNS OF THE TWO PERANDS DIFFER,
         CHECK TO SEE IF THE RESULT OF
         THE ADDITION WAS NEGATIVE. IF
         IT WAS, NEGATE THE AC MANTISSA,
         AND STORE OP_SIGN IN AC_SIGN */
      /* NORMALIZE THE RESULT */
      END FLOATING_ADD;
```

Program 8-3 shows the complete FLOATING_ADD procedure.

The routine begins by putting the operand with the largest exponent in AC. This assures that we can always align radix points by shifting the OP mantissa to the right. And if we find that the required shift is so large that no significant bits would be left in the OP mantissa—we would be adding zero to AC—then AC will contain the result and we can simply return.

The number of bits by which the OP mantissa must be shifted to the right to align radix points is simply AC_EXP − OP_EXP. (The biases cancel out in the subtraction.) If the difference exceeds 30, then all the significant bits will be shifted out of the OP mantissa, and the result will equal the other operand, the one now in AC. Hence in that case the routine can simply return.

If the signs of the operands differ, we negate (in twos complement fashion) the OP mantissa, so that a subtraction rather than an addition will take place. We do not at the moment worry about whether it is OP (rather than AC) which is negative.

The operations of negation and shifting to align the radix point are not interchangeable, as the following example illustrates:

0.1000001

| *Negate* | *Shift 3 Places Right* |
|---|---|
| 1.0111111 | 0.0001000 |
| *Shift 3 Places Right* | *Negate* |
| 1.1110111 | 1.11110000 |

(Note that the right shifts are arithmetical: bits equal to the leftmost bit—which now functions as a sign bit—are shifted in on the left.)

```
FLOATING __ ADD: PROCEDURE:
   DECLARE (I, SHIFT __ COUNT) BYTE:
   /* EXCHANGE OP AND AC, IF NECESSARY, SO THAT THE
       OPERAND WITH THE LARGEST EXPONENT WILL BE IN AC */
       IF OP __ EXP > AC __ EXP THEN
          DO:
             I = AC __ SIGN: AC __ SIGN = OP __ SIGN: OP __ SIGN = I:
             I = AC __ EXP: AC __ EXP = OP __ EXP: OP __ EXP = I:
             I = AC0: AC0 = OP0: OP0 = I:
             I = AC1: AC1 = OP1: OP1 = I:
             I = AC2: AC2 = OP2: OP2 = I:
             I = AC3: AC3 = OP3: OP3 = I:
          END:
   /* DETERMINE HOW MANY PLACES THE OP MANTISSA MUST BE
      SHIFTED TO THE RIGHT TO ALIGN THE RADIX POINTS. IF
      THIS NUMBER IS GREATER THAN 30, AC ALREADY CONTAINS
      THE RESULT, SO RETURN */
      SHIFT __ COUNT = AC __ EXP - OP __ EXP:
      IF SHIFT __ COUNT > 30 THEN RETURN:
   /* IF THE SIGNS OF THE TWO OPERANDS DIFFER, NEGATE
      THE OP MANTISSA */
      IF AC __ SIGN <> OP __ SIGN THEN CALL NEGATE __ OP:
   /* SHIFT THE OP MANTISSA RIGHT ARITHMETICALLY TO
      ALIGN RADIX POINTS */
      DO I = 1 TO SHIFT __ COUNT:
          CALL ASR __ OP:
      END:
   /* ADD THEN MANTISSAS */
      CALL ADD __ OP __ TO __ AC:
   /* IF THE SIGNS OF THE TWO OPERANDS DIFFER,
      CHECK TO SEE IF THE RESULT OF THE ADDITION
      WAS NEGATIVE. IF IT WAS, NEGATE THE AC MANTISSA,
      AND STORE OP __ SIGN IN AC __ SIGN */
      IF (AC __ SIGN <> OP __ SIGN) AND (AC3 LE 0) THEN
          DO:
              CALL NEGATE __ AC:
              AC __ SIGN = OP __ SIGN:
          END:
   /* NORMALIZE RESULT */
      CALL NORMALIZE __ AC:
END FLOATING __ ADD:
```

Program 8-3. FLOATING __ ADD adds OP to AC and leaves the result in AC.

It is negating first and then shifting which gives the desired answer, since the negation can be influenced by bits—the rightmost 1 in the example—which are lost during shifting. This observation leads us to two rules:

1) When the operand signs differ, the register to be shifted—in this case OP—must be negated.
2) The negation must be done before the shifting.

If OP has been shifted far enough to the right to cause any bits to be lost—the only case that can cause trouble—then the magnitude of OP is less than that of AC, so the result of the signed addition will be positive, and will not have to be negated again. Only one negation will take place, and Rule 2 assures that it will take place before and not after shifting.

Thus, having negated the OP mantissa if necessary, we shift the OP mantissa right to align the radix points.

And now, *finally*, we get around to doing the addition. We call the multiple precision addition routine written in the last chapter, ADD_OP_TO_AC, to add the OP mantissa to the AC mantissa and place the result in the AC mantissa.

If the result is a negative twos complement number, the AC mantissa must be negated and AC_SIGN set appropriately. Just to keep things from being too simple, an overflow may have taken place into bit 31, the twos complement sign bit.

We reason as follows:

The only case in which an overflow could have occurred would be if both operands had the same sign. But in that case, the sign of the result will be the same as the sign of the operands, so AC_SIGN already has the correct value. Also the result cannot be a negative twos complement number, since the OP mantissa is not negated when the two signs are the same.

If the operands had opposite signs then a subtraction rather than an addition took place. There can be no overflow from the subtraction, but the results might be negative number in twos complement form. We check the sign of the AC mantissa by checking bit 31, the leftmost bit in AC3.

If the AC mantissa is positive, then the magnitude of AC was greater than that of OP, so the sign of the result will be the sign of AC. Hence AC_SIGN need not be changed.

If the AC mantissa is negative, then the magnitude of OP was greater than that of AC, and so the sign of the result will be the sign of OP. Hence we move OP_SIGN to AC_SIGN and negate the AC mantissa, making it positive again.

These actions will be taken provided that the operand signs differ *and* the AC mantissa is negative:

(AC_SIGN < > OP_SIGN) AND (AC3 LE 0)

On a computer that does not permit signed comparisions, AC3 LE 0 may be replaced by (AC3 AND 80H) < > 0.

Finally, we must place the result in normal form, with its most significant bit in position 31. Since this job must be done after every arithmetic operation, we write a subroutine for it and invoke the subroutine with:

CALL NORMALIZE_AC;

Normalization completes the addition routine.

*Subtraction.* With addition in hand, subtractionbecomes easy. We merely change the sign of OP and call FLOATING_ADD. Program 8-4 shows FLOATING_SUBTRACT.

*Normalization.* At the end of an arithmetic routine AC may not be in normal form: the leftmost significant bit may not be in position 30. An overflow into bit 31 may have occurred. Significant digits may have cancelled out, leaving unwanted leading zeros. We may have a zero mantissa without the mandatory zero exponent. The exponent may be outside the required range of 1-255.

The normalization routine handles all these matters. We outline it as follows:

NORMALIZE_AC: PROCEDURE;
   /* IF THE AC MANTISSA IS ZERO, SET AC_SIGN TO FALSE, AC_EXP TO ZERO, AND RETURN */
   /* IF BIT 31 OF THE AC MANTISSA IS NOT 0, THEN SHIFT THE AC MANTISSA ONE PLACE TO THE RIGHT, AND ADD 1 TO AC_EXP */
   /* SHIFT AC MANTISSA LEFT UNTIL WE GET A 1 IN BIT 30. SUBTRACT 1 FROM AC_EXP FOR EACH LEFT SHIFT */
   /* IF AC_EXP IS GREATER THAN 255 ANNOUNCE EXPONENT OVERFLOW */
   /* IF AC_EXP IS LESS THAN 1 THEN ANNOUNCE EXPONENT UNDERFLOW */
END NORMALIZE_AC;

```
FLOATING_SUBTRACT: PROCEDURE:
  /* CHANGE SIGN OF OP AND ADD */
  OP_SIGN = NOT OP_SIGN;
    CALL FLOATING_ADD:
  END FLOATING_SUBTRACT;
```

Program 8-4. FLOATING_SUBTRACT subtracts OP from AC and leaves the result in AC.

Program 8-5 shows the complete NORMALIZE_AC routine. The implementation of the comments is straightforward and should require no further comment.

*Multplication.* Floating point multiplication and division are much simpler than addition. The routines FRACTION_MULTIPLY, FRACTION_DIVIDE, (from the last chapter) and NORMALIZE_AC do all the work. All we have to worry about at this point is calculating the sign and exponent of the result.

The sign of a product will be plus if the two operands have the same sign, and minus otherwise. Thus

$$AC\_SIGN = ACIGN \times OR\, OP\_SIGN;$$

The true exponent of a product is the sum of the true exponents of the operands. When we add biased exponents, however, the result will be doubly biased—it will have a bias of 256 instead of 128, since *each* of the two operand exponents had a bias of 128, and both biases appear in the sum. We must subtract 128 from the sum to restore the correct bias.

Furthermore, we recall that FRACTION_MULTIPLY was written to generate twice the product rather than the product itself, to make sure that we have at least 31 significant bits. We must compensate for this by subtracting 1 from the exponent of the result. The exponent calculation thus becomes

$$AC\_EXP = AC\_EXP + OP\_EXP - 128 - 1;$$

Or, combining the last two terms:

$$AC\_EXP = AC\_EP + OP\_EXP - 129;$$

```
NORMALIZE__AC: PROCEDURE:
    /* IF AC MANTISSA IS ZERO, SET AC__SIGN TO FALSE,
        AC__EXP TO ZERO, AND RETURN */
        IF (AC0 OR AC1 OR AC2 OR AC3) = 0 THEN
            DO:
                AC__SIGN = FALSE:
                AC__EXP = 0:
                RETURN:
            END:
    /* IF BIT 31 OF THE AC MANTISSA IS NOT 0, THEN
        SHIFT THE AC MANTISSA ONE PLACE TO THE RIGHT,
        AND ADD 1 TO AC__EXP */
        IF (AC3 AND 80H) <> 0 THEN
            DO:
                CALL SHR__AC:
                AC__EXP = AC__EXP + 1:
            END:
    /* SHIFT AC MANTISSA LEFT UNTIL WE GET A 1 IN
        BIT 30. SUBTRACT 1 FROM AC__EXP FOR EACH LEFT
        SHIFT */
        DO WHILE (AC3 AND 40H) = 0:
            CALL SHL__AC:
            AC__EXP = AC__EXP - 1:
        END:
    /* IF AC__EXP IS GREATER THAN 255 ANNOUNCE EXPONENT
        OVERFLOW */
        IF AC__EXP GT 255 THEN
            CALL ERROR (17, @'EXPONENT OVERFLOW'):
    /* IF AC__EXP IS LESS THAN 1 THEN ANNOUNCE EXPONENT
        UNDERFLOW */
        IF AC__EXP LT 1 THEN
            CALL ERROR (18, @'EXPONENT UNDERFLOW'):
END NORMALIZE__AC;
```

Program 8-5. NORMALIZE__AC puts the number in AC into normal form.

Since AC__EXP is a word, there is no danger of intermediate results in this calculation causing overflow.

With sign and exponent calculated, we need only to call FRACTION__MULTIPLY and NORMALIZE__AC. Program

```
FLOATING_MULTIPLY:   PROCEDURE:
   /* COMPUTE SIGN AND EXPONENT OF RESULT. MULTIPLY THE
      FRACTIONS. AND NORMALIZE THE PRODUCT */
      AC_SIGN = AC_SIGN XOR OP_SIGN:
      AC_EXP = AC_EXP + OP_EXP - 129:
      CALL FRACTION_MULTIPLY:
      CALL NORMALIZE_AC:
END FLOATING_MULTIPLY:
```

Program 8-6. FLOATING_MULTIPLY multiplies AC by OP and leaves the result in AC.

8-6 shows the complete multiply routine, FLOATING_MULTIPLY.

*Division.* In our floating point representation we have a simple way to detect if the divisor is zero: OP will be zero if and only if OP_EXP is 0. We may use this to check for division by zero, and the more cumbersome test in FRACTION_DIVIDE may be removed.

Signs are handled in division the same as in multiplication:

   AC_SIGN = AC_SIGN × OR OP_SIGN;

The exponent of a quotient is the difference between the exonent of the dividend and the exponent of the divisor.

```
FLOATING_DIVIDE: PROCEDURE:
   /* CHECK FOR DIVISION BY ZERO */
      IF OP_EXP = 0 THEN
         DO:
            CALL ERROR(26. @'DIVISION BY ZERO ATTEMPTED'):
            RETURN:
         END:
   /* COMPUTE SIGN AND EXPONENT OF RESULT. DIVIDE THE
      FRACTIONS. AND NORMALIZE THE QUOTIENT */
      AC_SIGN = AC_SIGN XOR OP_SIGN:
      AC_EXP = AC_EXP - OP_EXP + 128:
      CALL FRACTION_DIVIDE:
      CALL NORMALIZE_AC:
END FRACTION_DIVIDE:
```

Program 8-7. FLOATING_DIVIDE divides AC by OP and leaves the result in AC.

Subtracting biased exponents causes the biases to cancel; we must add 128 to the difference to obtain a biased result:

AC_EXP = AC_EXP − OP_EXP + 128;

Since the operands are normalized, we know that the dividend mantissa is less thn 1 and the divisor mantissa is greater than or equal to .5. Thus the quotient mantissa is less than $1/.5 = 2$. This can be accommodated provided we allow overflow into bit 31 of the AC mantissa.

We complete the division routine with calls to FRACTION_DIVIDE and NORMALIZE_AC. Program 8-7 shows the result.

# Chapter 9
# Numeric Input and Output

Binary numbers are convenient for computers but not for people. *We* prefer decimal, octal, or hexadecimal. We need, then, routines that will read a number in decimal, octal, or hexadecimal, and convert it to binary; as well as those which do the reverse, and print a binary number in a human oriented number system.

## ASSUMPTIONS

We shall assume two routines to already exist: READ_CHAR, which reads the next character from the input device and stores it in location CHAR; and PRINT_CHAR, which takes a character code as its argument and prints the corresponding character on the output device.

We shall also make some assumptions about the character code being used. We assume that the codes for adjacent digits are adjacent binary numbers. Thus:

$$'1' = '0' + 1$$
$$'2' = '0' + 2$$
$$\vdots$$
$$'9' = '0' + 9$$

141

We make the same assumption for the letters A through F:

$$'B' = 'A' + 1$$
$$'C' = 'A' + 2$$
$$'D' = 'A' + 3$$
$$'E' = 'A' + 4$$
$$'F' = 'A' + 5$$

These assumptions hold for the ASCII and EBCDIC codes, but *not* for the Baudot code.

Because of these assumptions, if the value of I is an octal or decimal digit, or a hexadecimal digit not greater than 9, then the corresponding character code is:

$$'0' + I$$

If the value of I is greater than 9 the code for the corresponding hexadecimal digit is:

$$'A' + (I - 10)$$

Conversely, if the character code lies in the range '0' through '9' the corresponding value is

$$CHAR - '0'$$

whereas if the code lies in the range 'A' through 'F' the corresponding value is:

$$CHAR - 'A' + 10$$

## INTEGER INPUT

For integer input we use the same algorithm that, in Chapter 2, was used to convert integers from binary, octal, or hexadecimal to decimal.

Suppose the word VALUE is to hold the number read in. We have:

1) Clear VALUE:

$$VALUE = 0;$$

2) For each digit in the number being read, multiply VALUE by the base, B, of the number system and add the value of the digit read:

$$VALUE = B*VALUE + DIGIT\_VALUE;$$

We will assume that when a conversion routine is called, CHAR already contains the code for the first digit of the number to be read in. (The main program must often examine this first digit to determine that a number follows, and so the numeric input routine is to be called.)

With this assumption we can read in a decimal number as follows:

```
VALUE = 0;
DO WHILE ('0' < = CHAR) AND (CHAR < = '9');
    VALUE = 10*VALUE;
    VALUE = VALUE + (CHAR - '0');
    CALL READ_CHAR;
END;
```

If a general purpose multiplication routine is not available, we can multiply by 10 by multiplying by 2 and by 8, and adding the two products. Since 2 and 8 are powers of 2, multiplication by these numbers may be implemented by left shifts (of 1 and 3 places, respectively). This gives:

```
VALUE = 0;
DO WHILE ('0' < = CHAR) AND (CHAR < = '9');
    VALUE = SHL(VALUE, 1) + SHL(VALUE, 3);
    VALUE = VALUE + (CHAR - '0');
    CALL READ_CHAR;
END;
```

This code is the basis for Program 9-1, READ_UNSIGNED_DECIMAL_INTEGER.

---

```
READ_UNSIGNED_DECIMAL_INTEGER: PROCEDURE (POINTER);
    DECLARE POINTER WORD,
            VALUE BASED POINTER WORD;
    VALUE = 0;
    DO WHILE ('0' < = CHAR) AND (CHAR < = '9');
        VALUE = SHL (VALUE, 1) + SHL (VALUE, 3);
        VALUE = VALUE + (CHAR - '0');
        CALL READ_CHAR;
    END;
END READ_UNSIGNED_DECIMAL_INTEGER;
```

Program 9-1. READ_UNSIGNED_DECIMAL_INTEGER.

```
READ_UNSIGNED_OCTAL_INTEGER: PROCEDURE (POINTER);
   DECLARE POINTER WORD,
           VALUE WORD;
   VALUE = 0;
   DO WHILE ('0' <= CHAR) AND (CHAR <= '7');
      VALUE = SHL (VALUE, 3);
      VALUE = VALUE + (CHAR - '0');
      CALL READ_CHAR;
   END;
END READ_UNSIGNED_OCTAL_INTEGER;
```

Program 9-2. READ_UNSIGNED_OCTAL_INTEGER.

---

For octal, we must multiply VALUE by 8 before adding the value of the next digit. The multiplication by 8 is implemented with a single left shift:

$$\text{VALUE} = \text{SHL (VALUE, 3)};$$

Program 9-2 shows the complete octal input routine.

For hexadecimal input, we must multiply by 16, which we can accomplish with a 4-place left shift:

$$\text{VALUE} = \text{SHL (VALUE, 4)};$$

The hexadecimal input routine is made more complicated by the fact that the digits lie in two nonadjacent ranges. Thus the test in the DO WHILE, which tells us whether there is another digit to be read, has the following form:

$$(('0' <= \text{CHAR}) \text{ AND } (\text{CHAR} <= '9'))$$
$$\text{OR } (('A' <= \text{CHAR}) \text{ AND } (\text{CHAR} <= 'F'))$$

When we add the numerical value of the character to VALUE, we must know whether the character is in the range '0' through '9' or 'A' through 'F'. We can determine this with a single test provided we know which range comes first, whether $'9' < 'A'$ or $'F' < '0'$.

Unfortunately this is a point on which ASCII and EBCDIC disagree. In ASCII the numbers come before the letters; in EBCDIC, the letters come first. For ASCII we can use

```
IF CHAR <= '9' THEN
   VALUE = VALUE + (CHAR - '0');   ELSE
   VALUE = VALUE + (CHAR - 'A' + 10);
```

while for EBCDIC we use

```
IF CHAR > = '0' THEN
   VALUE = VALUE + (CHAR - '0');
ELSE
   VALUE = VALUE + (CHAR - 'A' + 10);
```

Program 9-3 shows the complete hexadecimal input routine.

The preceding programs read unsigned integers. But numbers preceded by signs are just as easily hndled:

```
SIGN = FALSE;
IF CHAR = ' + ' THEN CALL READ_CHAR;
IF CHAR = '-' THEN
   DO;
      CALL READ_CHAR;
      SIGN = TRUE;
   END;
CALL   READ_UNSIGNED_DECIMAL_INTEGER
   (+VALUE);
IF SIGN THEN VALUE = -VALUE;
```

## INTEGER OUTPUT

We can obtain the digits of a number in a particular number system by repeatedly dividing by the base of the

```
READ_UNSIGNED_HEXADECIMAL_INTEGER: PROCEDURE (POINTER);
   DECLARE POINTER WORD,
         VALUE BASED POINTER WORD;
   VALUE = 0;
   DO WHILE (('0' < = CHAR) AND (CHAR < = '9'))
         OR (('A' < = CHAR) AND (CHAR < = 'F'));
      VALUE = SHL (VALUE, 4);
      IF CHAR < = '9' THEN
         VALUE = VALUE + (CHAR - '0');
      ELSE
         VALUE = VALUE + (CHAR - 'A' + 10);
      CALL READ_CHAR;
   END;
END READ_UNSIGNED_HEXADECIMAL_INTEGER;
```

Program 9-3. READ_UNSIGNED_HEXADECIMAL_INTEGER.

```
PRINT_UNSIGNED_DECIMAL_INTEGER: PROCEDURE (VALUE);
   DECLARE VALUE WORD,
           DIGITS(5) BYTE;
   COUNT = 0;
   DO UNTIL VALUE = 0;
      DIGITS (COUNT) = (VALUE MOD 10) + '0';
      VALUE = VALUE / 10;
      COUNT = COUNT + 1;
   END;
   DO UNTIL COUNT = 0;
      COUNT = COUNT - 1;
      CALL PRINT_CHAR (DIGITS (COUNT));
   END;
END PRINT_UNSIGNED_DECIMAL_INTEGER;
```

Program 9-4. PRINT_UNSIGNED_DECIMAL_INTEGER.

---

number system. The successive remainders are the desired digits. The digits are generated in right to left order, a minor inconvenience.

We illustrate using the decimal system and 9315:

|  | Quotient | Remainder |
|---|---|---|
| Start with 9315 | 9315 | |
| Divide by 10 | 931 | 5 |
| Divide by 10 | 93 | 1 |
| Divide by 10 | 9 | 3 |
| Divide by 10 | 0 | 9 |

Since the digits are generated in right-to-left order, we must store them as they are generated, and then afterwards print them out in normal left-to-right order. We use a 5-byte array, DIGITS, to store the digits as they are generated.

The following code will print out in decimal the unsigned number stored in VALUE:

```
COUNT = 0;
DO UNTIL VALUE = 0;
    DIGITS(COUNT) = (VALUE MOD 10) + '0';
    VALUE = VALUE / 10;
    COUNT = COUNT + 1;
END;
DO UNTIL COUNT = 0;
    COUNT = COUNT - 1;
    CALL PRINT_CHAR (DIGITS(COUNT));
END;
```

There is no simple technique for dividing by 10; the general purpose integer division routine discussed in Chapter 7 should be used. This routine yields both the quotient and the remainder.

The above code gives us Program 9-4, PRINT_UNSIGNED_DECIMAL_INTEGER.

With octal and hexadecimal there *are* simpler ways to do the division.

For octal a division by 8 is simply a 3-place shift to the right. And the remainder is simply the 3 rightmost bits before the shift. Thus we have:

DIGITS(COUNT) = (VALUE AND 7Q) + '0';
VALUE = SHR (VALUE, 3);

Program 9-5 shows the complete octal output routine.

For hexadecimal we shift 4 places to the right to divide by 16. And the remainder is the rightmost 4 bits before the shift. As before, the fact that we have a discontinuous range of digits causes a slight increase in complexity:

TEMP = VALUE AND OFH
  IF TEMP < = 9 THEN
    DIGITS(COUNT) = TEMP + '0';
  ELSE
    DIGITS(COUNT) = TEMP − 10 + 'A';

Program 9-6 shows the complete hexadecimal output routine.

```
PRINT _ UNSIGNED _ OCTAL _ INTEGER: PROCEDURE (VALUE);
  DECLARE VALUE WORD,
          DIGITS (6) BYTE;
  COUNT = 0;
  DO UNTIL VALUE = 0;
      DIGITS (COUNT = (VALUE AND 7Q) + '0';
      VALUE = SHR (VALUE, 3);
      COUNT = COUNT + 1;
  END;
  DO UNTIL COUNT = 0;
      COUNT = COUNT − 1;
      CALL PRINT _ CHAR (DIGITS(COUNT));
  END;
END PRINT _ UNSIGNED _ OCTAL _ INTEGER ;
```
    Program 9-5. PRINT_UNSIGNED_OCTAL_INTEGER.

```
PRINT__UNSIGNED__HEXADECIMAL__INTEGER : PROCEDURE (VALUE);
   DECLARE VALUE WORD,
           DIGITS(4) BYTE;
           TEMP BYTE;
   COUNT = 0;
   DO UNTIL VALUE = 0;
      TEMP = VALUE AND 0FH;
      IF TEMP <= 9 THEN
         DIGITS(COUNT) = TEMP + '0';
      ELSE
         DIGITS(COUNT) = TEMP - 10 + 'A';
      VALUE = SHR(VALUE, 4);
      COUNT = COUNT + 1;
   END;
   DO UNTIL COUNT = 0;
      COUNT = COUNT - 1;
      CALL PRINT__CHAR (DIGITS(COUNT));
   END;
END PRINT__UNSIGNED__HEXADECIMAL__INTEGER;
```

Program 9-6. PRINT__UNSIGNED__HEXADECIMAL__INTEGER.

---

If we wish to output signed values we may use:

```
IF VALUE LT 0 THEN
   DO;
      VALUE = -VALUE;
      CALL PRINT__CHAR ('-');
   END;
CALL PRINT__UNSIGNED__DECIMAL__INTEGER;
```

If your computer does not have provisions for signed comparisons, the test VALUE LT 0 may be replaced by (VALUE AND 8000H) <> 0. Only the leftmost byte of VALUE need be included in the test.

## FLOATING POINT INPUT

For floating point input we shall use the same technique that was used in Chapter 2 to convert binary, octal, and hexadecimal floating point numbers to decimal.

We begin by reading in the sign:

```
AC_SIGN = FALSE;
IF CHAR = '+' THEN CALL READ_CHAR;
IF CHAR = '−' THEN
    DO;
        CALL READ_CHAR;
        AC_SIGN = TRUE;
    END;
```

Next we read in the digits preceding the decimal point (if any) and use them to form an integer in AC0-AC3. We use a routine INSERT_RIGHTMOST_DIGIT which multiplies AC by 10 and adds the value of the digit whose character code is in CHAR.

We limit the number of digits in the input to 9, the maximum number that can be stored in AC without overflow. For digits in excess of 9, we add 1 to the decimal exponent if the digit is to the left of the decimal point, and ignore the digit if it is to the right. In either case the excess digits count as zeros:

```
AC0, AC1, AC2, AC3 = 0;
DECIMAL_EXPONENT = 0;
COUNT = 9;
DO WHILE ('0' <= CHAR) AND (CHAR <= '9');
    IF COUNT > 0 THEN
        DO;
            CALL INSERT_RIGHTMOST_DIGIT;
            COUNT = COUNT − 1;
        END;
    ELSE
        DECIMAL_EXPONENT =
            DECIMAL_EXPONENT + 1;
    CALL READ_CHAR;
END;
```

Next we read in the digits following the decimal point, if any. These are still read in as digits in an integer, but the decimal exponent is decreased for 1 for each digit. For instance, 12.345 would be read as $12345 \times 10^{-3}$.

```
IF CHAR = '.' THEN
   DO;
      CALL READ_CHAR;
      DO WHILE ('0' < = CHAR) AND (CHAR < =
        '9');
         IF COUNT > 0 THEN
         DO;
            CALL INSERT_RIGHTMOST_DIGIT;
            DECIMAL_EXPONENT =
              DECIMAL_EXPONENT - 1;
            COUNT = COUNT - 1;
         END;
         CALL READ_CHAR;
      END;
   END;
```

We now read in the exponent part, if any.

```
IF CHAR = 'E' THEN
   DO;
      CALL READ_CHAR;
      EXP_SIGN = FALSE;
      IF CHAR = ' + ' THEN CALL READ_CHAR;
      IF CHAR = ' - ' THEN
         DO;
            CALL READ_CHAR;
            EXP_SIGN = TRUE;
         END;

      CALL READ_UNSIGNED_DE-
        CIMAL_INTEGER (@EXP_VALUE);
      IF EXP_SIGN THEN
         DECIMAL_EXPONENT =
           DECIMAL_EXPONENT - EXP_VALUE;
      ELSE
         DECIMAL_EXPONENT =
         DECIMAL_EXPONENT + EXP_VALUE;
   END;
```

If the exponent part had a negative sign, it was subtracted from the current value of DECIMAL_EXPONENT. Otherwise, it was added.

AC0-AC3 now contains an integer. The radix point is to the right of bit 0. If we set AC_EXP to $31 + 128 = 159$, then we have a floating point number in AC, although it is not necessarily in normal form. But that deficiency can be remedied with a call to NORMALIZE_AC:

AC_EXP = 159;
CALL NORMALIZE_AC;

Finally, DECIMAL_EXPONENT specifies a positive or negative power of 10 by which AC must be multiplied. That is, we must multiply AC by:

$$_{10}\text{DECIMAL\_EXPONENT}$$

We can do this by successive multiplicaions by 10 if DECIMAL_EXPONENT is positive, or successive divisions by 10 if DECIMAL_EXPONENT is negative.

These sucessive multiplications or divisions will introduce error, since the intermediate results cannot be accurately represented using only 31 bits. Here is where our 7 guard digits come in. Some of these—typically 4 or 5—will be in error, but the errors should not work their way to the left far enough to contaminate the 24 bits we are goint to store. *The technique of successive multiplication or division by 10 is not recommended unless 6 or 7 guard bits are available.*

We start by loading a floating point 10—$0.101B \times 2^4$—into OP:

OP_SIGN = FALSE;
OP_EXP = 32; /*4 + 128*/
OP0, OP1, OP2 = 0;
OP3 = 50H;

If the decimal exponent is positive, multiply by 10 repeatedly:

DO WHILE DECIMAL_EXPONENT GT 0;
  CALL FLOATING_MULTIPLY;
  DECIMAL_EXPONENT =
    DECIMAL_EXPONENT − 1;
END;

If the decimal exponent is negative, divide by 10 repeatedly:

DO WHILE DECIMAL_EXPONENT LT 0;
  CALL FLOATING_DIVIDE;
  DECIMAL_EXPONENT =
    DECIMAL_EXPONENT + 1;
END;

```
FLOATING_POINT_INPUT: PROCEDURE;
    DECLARE (COUNT, DECIMAL_EXPONENT, EXP_SIGN) BYTE,
            EXP_VALUE WORD;
    /* THE FOLLOWING PROCEDURE MULTIPLIES AC0-AC3 BY 10
        AND ADDS TO THE RESULT THE DIGIT WHOSE CHARACTER
        CODE IS IN CHAR */


    INSERT_RIGHTMOST_DIGIT: PROCEDURE;
        /* MULTIPLY AC0-AC3 BY 10 */
            CALL SHL_AC;
            OP0 = AC0; OP1 = AC1; OP2 = AC2; OP3 = AC3;
            CALL SHL_AC;
            CALL SHL_AC;
            CALL ADD_OP_TO_AC;
        /* ADD DIGIT WHOSE CHARACTER CODE IS IN CHAR */
            AC0 = AC0 + (CHAR AND 0FH);
            AC1 = AC1 PLUS 0;
            AC2 = AC2 PLUS 0;
            AC3 = AC3 PLUS 0;
    END INSERT_RIGHTMOST_DIGIT;


    /* EXECUTION OF FLOATING_POINT_INPUT BEGINS HERE */
    /* READ IN SIGN */
        AC_SIGN = FALSE;
        IF CHAR = '+' THEN CALL READ_CHAR;
        IF CHAR = '-' THEN
            DO;
                CALL READ_CHAR;
                AC_SIGN = TRUE;
            END;


    /* READ IN DIGITS TO LEFT OF DECIMAL POINT */
        AC0, AC1, AC2, AC3 = 0;
        DECIMAL_EXPONENT = 0;
        COUNT = 9;
        DO WHILE ('0' <= CHAR) AND (CHAR <= '9');
            IF COUNT > 0 THEN
                DO;
                    CALL INSERT_RIGHTMOST_DIGIT;
                    COUNT = COUNT - 1;
                END;
            ELSE
                DECIMAL_EXPONENT = DECIMAL_EXPONENT + 1;
            CALL READ_CHAR;
        END;
```

Program 9-7. FLOATING_POINT_INPUT reads in a floating point number in either expoential or nonexponential format.

```
/* READ IN DIGITS TO THE RIGHT OF DECIMAL POINT */
   IF CHAR = '.' THEN
      DO;
         CALL READ_CHAR;
         DO WHILE ('0' <= CHAR) AND (CHAR <= '9');
            IF COUNT > 0 THEN
               DO;
                  CALL INSERT_RIGHTMOST_DIGIT;
                  DECIMAL_EXPONENT = DECIMAL_EXPONENT - 1;
                  COUNT = COUNT - 1;
               END;

            CALL READ_CHAR;
         END;
      END;
/* READ IN EXPONENT PART */
   IF CHAR = 'E' THEN
      DO;
         CALL READ_CHAR;
         EXP_SIGN = FALSE;
         IF CHAR = '+' THEN CALL READ_CHAR;
         IF CHAR = '-' THEN
            DO;
               CALL READ_CHAR;
               EXP_SIGN = TRUE;
            END;
         CALL READ_UNSIGNED_DECIMAL_INTEGER(@EXP_VALUE);
         IF EXP_SIGN THEN
            DECIMAL_EXPONENT = DECIMAL_EXPONENT - EXP_VALUE;
         ELSE
            DECIMAL_EXPONENT = DECIMAL_EXPONENT + EXP_VALUE;
      END;
/* PUT AC IN NORMAL FORM */
   AC_EXP = 159;
   CALL NORMALIZE_AC;

/* MULTIPLY OR DIVIDE AC BY POWER OF 10 SPECIFIED BY
   DECIMAL EXPONENT */
   /* LOAD FLOATING POINT 10 INTO OP */
      OP_SIGN = FALSE;
      OP_EXP = 132; /* 4 + 128 */
      OP0, OP1, OP2 = 0;
      OP3 = 50H;
   /* IF DECIMAL EXPONENT IS POSITIVE, MULTIPLY BY 10 */
      DO WHILE DECIMAL_EXPONENT GT 0;
         CALL FLOATING_MULTIPLY;
         DECIMAL_EXPONENT = DECIMAL_EXPONENT - 1;
      END;
   /* IF DECIMAL EXPONENT IS NEGATIVE, DIVIDE BY 10*/
      DO WHILE DECIMAL_EXPONENT LT 0;
         CALL FLOATING_DIVIDE;
         DECIMAL_EXPONENT = DECIMAL_EXPONENT + 1;
      END;
END FLOATING_POINT_INPUT;
```

Program 9-7. Con'd.

A call to STORE_AC will now round the result to 24 bits and store it—in external form—in the desired location.

Program 9-7 shows the complete FLOATING_POINT_INPUT routine. This includes the procedure INSERT_RIGHTMOST_DIGIT, which multiplies AC0-AC3 by 10 and adds the value of the current digit.

**FLOATING POINT OUTPUT**

Our floating point output routine uses the same technique that was used in Chapter 2 to convert decimal floating point numbers to binary, octal, or hexadecimal.

Our strategy is to multiply or divide AB by 10 until its value is greater than or equal to 1 and less than 10. We can then extract the decimal digits using digit stripping.

DECIMAL_EXPONENT is initialized to 0. It is then increased by 1 for each division by 10 and decreased by 1 for each multiplication by 10.

The digits obtained by digit stripping, together with DECIMAL_EXPONENT, are passed to the routine PRINT_NUMBER which was developed as a case study in program design in Chapter 6. PRINT_NUMBER prints a properly formatted decimal number.

We start by getting AC in the range $1 <= AC < 10$. Since $1 = 0.1B \times 2^1$, and $10 = 0.101B \times 2^4$, we start by bringing our binary exponent into the range 1-4. For the biased exponents the range becomes 129-132.

After initializing DECIMAL_EXPONENT to 0, and loading a floating point 10 into OP, we multiply or divide by 10 to bring the exponent into the desired range:

```
DO WHILE AC_EXP > 132;
   CALL FLOATING_DIVIDE;
   DECIMAL_EXPONENT =
     DECIMAL_EXPONENT + 1;
END;
DO WHLE AC_EXP < 129;
   CALL FLOATING_MULTIPLY;
   DECIMAL_EXPONENT =
     DECIMAL_EXPONENT - 1;
END;
```

If AC_EXP = 132 (true exponent = 4), then the integer part of AC may be as large as 15. If it is 10 or greater, then an additional division by 10 is needed:

```
IF (AC_EXP = 132) AND (AC3 > = 50H) THEN
    DO;
        CALL FLOATING_DIVIDE;
        DECIMAL_EXPONENT =
            DECIMAL_EXPONENT + 1;
    END;
```

To aid in extracting the decimal digits from AC, we wish to convert it to a fixed point format, the radix point lying between bits 27 and 28. The leftmost 4 bits (28-31) will be the integer part, and the remainder (bits 0-27) will be the fraction part. This arrangement is illustrated in Fig. 9-1.

We can obtain the desired format as follows:
```
IF AC_EXP = 132 THEN
    CALL SHL_AC;
ELSE
    DO WHILE AC_EXP < 131;
        CALL SHR_AC;
        AC_EXP = AC_EXP + 1;
    END;
```

We wish to round AC to 7 decimal digits, the maximum number that can be represented accurately using 24 bits. Since, as AC is now formatted, the radix point is to the right of the leftmost decimal digit, we need to round to 6 decimal places. We can do this by adding $.5 \times 10^{-6} = 5 \times 10^{-7} = 0.0000086H$. The rounding is thus done by:

```
AC0 = AC0 + 86H;     AC2 = AC2 PLUS 0;
AC1 = AC1 PLUS 0;    AC3 = AC3 PLUS 0;
```

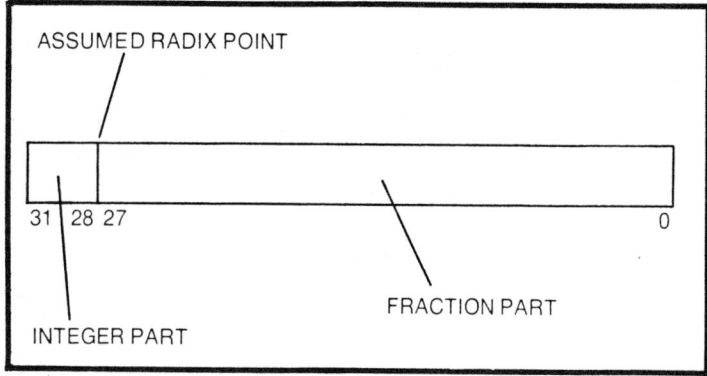

Fig. 9-1. The fixed point format for the AC mantissa used during digit stripping.

```
FLOATING_POINT_OUTPUT: PROCEDURE:
    DECLARE (SIGN, DIGITS(7), I) BYTE:
    /* MULTIPLY OR DIVIDE AC BY 10 TO GET IT IN THE
        RANGE 1 <= AC < 10 */
        /* LOAD FLOATING POINT 10 INTO OP */
            OP_SIGN = FALSE:
            OP_EXP = 132: /* 4 + 128 */
            OP0, OP1, OP2 = 0:
            OP3 = 50H
        /* INITIALIZE DECIMAL_EXPONENT, WHICH WILL BE USED
            TO KEEP TRACK OF THE NUMBER OF MULTIPLICATIONS
            OR DIVISIONS DONE */
            DECIMAL_EXPONENT = 0:

        /* DIVIDE BY 10 */
            DO WHILE AC_EXP > 132:
                CALL FLOATING_DIVIDE:
                DECIMAL_EXPONENT = DECIMAL_EXPONENT + 1:
            END:
        /* MULTIPLY BY 10 */
            DO WHILE AC_EXP < 129:
                CALL FLOATING_MULTIPLY:
                DECIMAL_EXPONENT = DECIMAL_EXPONENT - 1:
            END:

        /* IF AC IS GREATER THAN OR EQUAL TO 10, DIVIDE
            BY 10 AGAIN */
            IF (AC_EXP = 132) AND (AC3 > 50H) THEN
                DO:
                    CALL FLOATING_DIVIDE:
                    DECIMAL_EXPONENT = DECIMAL_EXPONENT + 1:
                END:
        /* POSITION CONTENTS OF AC SO THAT RADIX POINT IS
            BETWEEN BITS 27 AND 28 */
            IF AC_EXP = 132 THEN
                CALL SHL_AC:
            ELSE
                DO WHILE AC_EXP < 131:
                    CALL SHR_AC:
                    AC_EXP = AC_EXP + 1:
                END:
        /* ROUND AC TO 7 DECIMAL DIGITS */
            AC0 = AC0 + 86H:
            AC1 = AC1 PLUS 0:
            AC2 = AC2 PLUS 0:
            AC3 = AC3 PLUS 0:

        /* BEWARE OF ROUNDING OVERFLOW */
            IF AC3 >= 0A0H THEN
                DO:
                    AC0, AC1, AC2 = 0:
                    AC3 = 10H:
                    DECIMAL_EXPONENT = DECIMAL_EXPONENT + 1:
                END:
        /* GET DECIMAL DIGITS BY DIGITS STRIPPING */
            DIGITS(0) = SHR(AC3, 4) + '0':    /* GET LEFTOMOST DIGIT */
            DO I = 1 TO 6:
                AC3 = AC3 AND 0FH:    /* CLEAR BITS 28-31 */
                CALL SHL_AC:          /* MULTIPLY BY 10 */
                OP0 = AC0: OP1 = AC1: OP2 = AC2: OP3 = AC3:
                CALL SHL_AC:
                CALL SHL_AC:
                CALL ADD_OP_TO_AC:
                DIGITS(I) = SHR(AC3, 4) + '0': /* GET NEXT DIGIT */
            END:
        /* FORMAT AND PRINT RESULT */
            SIGN = AC_SIGN:
            CALL PRINT_NUMBER:
END FLOATING_POINT_OUTPUT:
```

Program 9-8. FLOATING_POINT_OUTPUT prints a floating point number in exponential or nonexponential format.

The roundup may cause the contents of AC to become 10 (for instance, 9.9999995 would round to 10.000000). If that occurs we set AC0-AC3 to 1 and add 1 to DECIMAL_EXPONENT:

```
IF AC3 > = 0A0H THEN
   DO;
      AC0, AC1, AC2 = 0;
      AC3 = 10H;
      DECIMAL_EXPONENT =
         DECIMAL_EXPONENT + 1;
   END;
```

We now proceed with the digit stripping, as described in Chapter 2. Each multiplication by 10 shifts the next decimal digit into bits 28-31 of the AC mantissa:

```
DIGITS(0) = SHR              /* GET LEFTMOST
   (AC3, 4) + '0';              DIGIT */
DO I = 1 TO 6;
   AC3 = AC3 AND 0FH;        /* CLEAR BITS 28-31 */
   CALL SHL_AC;              /* MULTIPLY BY 10 */
   OP0 = AC0; OP1 =
      AC1; OP2 = AC2;
      OP3 = AC3;
   CALL SHL_AC;
   CALL SHL_AC;
   CALL ADD_OP_TO_AC;
   DIGITS(I) =               /* GET NEXT DIGIT */
      SHR (AC3, 4) + '0';

END
```

The sign of the converted number is just the sign of AC:

$$SIGN = AC\_SIGN;$$

Our decimal number is now specified by the contents of DIGITS, SIGN, and DECIMAL_EXPONENT. a call to PRINT_NUMBER, the formatting routine developed in Chapter 6, will cause a properly formatted decimal number to be printed.

Program 9-8 shows the complete procedure FLOATING_POINT_OUTPUT.

# Chapter 10
# Pseudo-Random Numbers

A sequence of pseudo-random numbers appears to be the result of some random process such as throwing dice, spinning a roulette wheel, or drawing raffle tickets from a drum. But actually the numbers are not random at all: they are generated by a subroutine inside the computer. They appear to be random only to someone who does not know the technique used to generate them.

We generate a sequence of pseudo-random numbers by applying some arithmetical, logical, or shifting operations to the last member of the sequence, the result of those operations being the next member. Each new member of the sequence is generated from the previous one in the same way. The particular operations used distinguish one pseudo-random number generator from another.

(For convenience we will hereafter drop the "pseudo" and speak of "random numbers" and "random number generators.")

A common fallacy among programmers is that some randomly or haphazardly chosen sequence of operations will yield a good random number generator. The sequences produced by such haphazardly constructed generators often quickly degenerate, the same number or the same short sequence being generated repeatedly. The only safe course is to rely on operations which are known—through mathematical analysis—to yield good random number generators.

One of the simplest, and most thoroughly analyzed, random number generation techniques is the so-called *linear congruential* method. We shall confine our attention to it for the remainder of this chapter.

## THE LINEAR CONGRUENTIAL GENERATOR

We define the linear congruential random number generator as follows: Let X be the previously generated random number. We generate the next number in the sequence, and assign it to X, with the following,

$$X = (A*X + C) \text{ MOD } M;$$

where A, C, and M are *carefully chosen* constants.

In words, we generate a new value of X by taking the old one, multiplying by the value of A, adding the value of C, dividing by the value of M, and taking the remainder from that division as the new value of X. The successive values of X form the random sequence.

As an example, consider the random number generator defined by:

$$X = (5*X + 3) \text{ MOD } 8$$

We may take any number in the range 0-7 as the initial value of X. Choosing 0, we get the sequence:

$$0\ 3\ 2\ 5\ 4\ 7\ 6\ 1$$

This sequence will repeat itself indefinitely.

We see that the numbers 0 through 7 have been rearranged into what, at first glance, seems to be a random sequence. At second glance we notice some obvious patterns, such as pairs of numbers which differ by 3-0-3, 2-5, and 4-7. Also the sequence is very short. Both of these problems, however, can be remedied by choosing a larger number for M, and by choosing A and C appropriately.

When we multiply or add two words, and ignore any bits that are lost out of the left side of the word through carries or shifting, then the result we get is the true result MOD $2^N$, where N is the number of bits in the word. By choosing $M = 2^N$ we do not actually have to carry out the division by M. It is automatically carried out by the computer's multiplication and addition routines. Our random number generator simplifies to:

$$X = A*X + C;$$

By using the multiple precision arithmetic techniques discussed in Chapter 7, we can let N be any multiple of 8: 8, 16, 24, 32, and so on. In general, 8 bits are too few for a random number generator. The sequence generated is too short—only 256 values before repeating—and the numbers are insufficiently random. For many applications 16 bits are adequate. For critical applications, however, 24 or 32 bits would be preferred.

In the rest of this chapter we will consider random number generators built on 16 bit words. These will generate $2^{16} = 65536$ numbers without repeating, those numbers consisting of all the values in the range 0 through $2^{15} - 1 = 65535$, rearranged in a hopefully random appearing sequence.

## CHOOSING A AND C

The following rules can be shown (although not easily!) to yield random number generators with good properties. It is assumed that M is a power of 2:

1) A MOD 8 = 5. That is, A should be chosen so that dividing it by 8 will yield a remainder of 5. This means that in octal, the right most digit of A should be 5, and in hexadecimal it should be 5 or D. In binary the rightmost 3 digits of A should be 101.

2) When A is written in binary notation, the digits should not exhibit any simple pattern. Also, large uninterrupted blocks of zeros or ones should be avoided.

3) C should be an odd number near:

$$M*(1 - 1/\sqrt{3})/2$$

For $M = 2^{16}$ this works out to be 13849. For $M = 2^{32}$ it is 907633385.

Only Rule 2 calls for further comment. The requirement that no simple patterns occur would exclude

$$0101010101010101B$$

which consists of 01 repeated 8 times, and

$$1011101001011101B$$

which is bilaterally symmetrical. The prohibition against large blocks of one or zeros would exclude

$$0000000010110101B$$
$$1111111101110101B$$

as well as $1000000001000101B$

Numbers having only a few ones—as in the last example—are sometimes chosen because multiplication by such a number is easily implemented with a few add and shift operations. But such a choice adversely affects the quality of the resulting random number generator. General purpose multiplication routines are easy enough to write, if none are included in the hardware, firmware, or software of your computer.

Here is an example of a random number generator constructed according to these rules. We choose:

$A = 58653 = 162435Q = 1110010100011101B$
$C = 13849$
$M = 2^{16} = 65536$

Notice that the octal representation of A ends in a 5 or, equivalently, its binary representation ends in 101. The binary representation of A exhibits no simple pattern and no large block of zeros or ones. C is an odd number and equals value recommended for $M = 2^{16}$. The formula for generating the random numbers is:

$$X = (58653*X + 13849) \text{ MOD } 65536$$

As mentioned, the MOD 65536 will take care of itself if the multiplication and addition is done on 16-bit words, with overflow ignored.

If the initial value of X—the so-called "seed"—is taken to be zero, the first 18 numbers produced by the generator are:

| 00000 | 13849 | 46062 | 32271 | 59596 | 04405 |
| 37402 | 01291 | 40792 | 64273 | 56326 | 32967 |
| 53156 | 28589 | 40370 | 19779 | 58800 | 43785 |

## HOW TO GET RANDOM NUMBERS WITH DIFFERENT RANGES

The random numbers produced by the generator just exhibited range from 0 through 65535. For reasons already given, we usually choose $M = 2^N$, and then the random numbers generated will range from 0 through $2^N - 1$.

But what about other ranges we may need? If we are simulating the cast of a die, we would need random number in the range 1-6. Or to simulate a drawing from a box containing 100 raffle tickets, we would have to have random numbers ranging from 1 through 100.

Here is a technique for generating random numbers in the range 0 through K - 1, where K is some constant, given N bit random numbers to start with. By adding a constant we can cause our range to start anywhere we wish. Thus if we wanted our random numbers to range from 1 through K instead of 0 through K - 1, we would add a 1 to each random number.

The idea is to form the integer part of the product

$$K*X/2^N$$

where X is the N-bit random number. Since $X/2^N$ is less than 1, multiplying by K must give a product less than K. Taking the integer part will give an integer in the range 0 through K - 1, since K - 1 is the largest integer less than K.

Dividing by $2^N$ is the same as an N-bit right shift. It is convenient to break this shift down into two parts.

Let n be the number of bits in K when it is expressed in binary notation. Thus if $K = 6 = 110B$, then $n = 3$. If $K = 100 = 1100100B$, then $n = 7$, and so on. We start by shifting X to the right n places.

Next we multiply the shifted value of X by K. Since we are multiplying an n-bit number by an N - n bit number, the result will be an N-bit number.

Finally, shift the product of the multiplication N - n places to the right (or extract the leftmost n bits of the product in some other way). This will be an integer in the desired range, 0 through K - 1.

For example, suppose $K = 100 = 1100100B$, so $n = 7$, and $N = 16$. Then the statements

$$X = SHR\ (X, 7);$$
$$X = 100*X;$$
$$X = SHR\ (X, 9);$$

will convert the 16-bit random number X to an integer in the range 0-99.

Suppose $X = 59596 = 1110100011001100B$. Then SHR (X, 7) = 0000000111010001B = 465. Multiplying by 100 gives

46500 = 1011010110100100B. Finally, shifting 9 places to the right gives 0000000001011010B = 90.

Applying this technique to the numbers yielded by the random number generator constructed in the last section gives:

| 00 | 21 | 70 | 49 | 90 | 06 |
| 57 | 01 | 62 | 98 | 85 | 50 |
| 81 | 43 | 61 | 30 | 89 | 66 |

## IMPROVING RANDOM NUMBER GENERATORS

The linear congruential generators just discussed are sufficient for most purposes. Occasionally greater randomness is desired, often by people who find it hard to believe that so simple an algorithm will really yield random-seeming numbers. Those seeking greater randomness may try the following technique, which combines the outputs of two random number generators to produce a highly random sequence.

The idea is this: We have two random number generators, say, generator #1 and generator #2. The last K numbers produced by generator #1 are stored in a table named TABLE. Generator #2 is used to select a number at random from TABLE. This number is the next random number; it is replaced with the next number produced by generator #1.

Suppose our two random number generators are:

$$X = (A*X + C) \text{ MOD } M$$

and

$$Y = (B*X + D) \text{ MOD } M$$

where $M = 2^{16}$.

We choose TABLE to be 64 words long:

DECLARE TABLE (64) WORD;

We need to convert the 16-bit random number Y into a random subscript from 0–63 for TABLE. For K a power of 2 the technique of the last section reduces to a single shift:

I = SHR (Y, 10);

which sets I the value of I to a random number in the range 0–63.

Suppose X and Y have been given their initial values. We initialize table using generator #1:

```
DO I = 0 TO 63;
    TABLE(I) = X;
    X = A*X + C; /* ASSUME ARITHMETIC MOD M */
END;
```

To generate a random number, Z, we first use generator #2 to select at random an entry in TABLE:

$$I = SHR(Y, 10);$$

The value of the selected entry is the desired random number:

$$Z = TABLE(I);$$

This entry is replaced by the current value of X, the output of generator #1:

$$TABLE(I) = X;$$

Finally, new values are generated for X and Y:

```
X = A*X + C; /* ASSUME MOD M ARITHMETIC */
Y = B*Y + D;
```

This process is repeated every time a new random number, Z, is desired.

Figure 10-1 illustrates this process using $M = 2^4 = 16$ and K (the number of elements in TABLE) = 4. The random number generators are:

$$X = (13*X + 3) \text{ MOD } 16$$
$$Y = (13*X + 1) \text{ MOD } 16$$

(Normally, A and B would *not* be chosen the same. But for $M = 16$, the only possible values for A and B are 5 and 13; choosing both A and B equal to 5 gave better results than choosing one 5 and the other 13.)

The output, Z, goes through the initial sequence

0  4  5  3  14  8  10

and then the following sequence, which repeats itself thereafter:

7  2  12  9  11  6  0  13

15  10  4  1  3  14  8  5

| X | Y | I | TABLE | | | | Z |
|---|---|---|---|---|---|---|---|
| 4 | 0 | 0 | <u>0</u> | 3 | 10 | 5 | 0 |
| 7 | 1 | 0 | <u>4</u> | 3 | 10 | 5 | 4 |
| 14 | 14 | 3 | <u>7</u> | 3 | 10 | <u>5</u> | 5 |
| 9 | 7 | 1 | 7 | <u>3</u> | 10 | 14 | 3 |
| 8 | 12 | 3 | 7 | <u>9</u> | 10 | <u>14</u> | 14 |
| 11 | 13 | 3 | 7 | 9 | 10 | <u>8</u> | 8 |
| 2 | 10 | 2 | 7 | 9 | <u>10</u> | 11 | 10 |
| 13 | 3 | 0 | <u>7</u> | 9 | 2 | 11 | 7 |
| 12 | 8 | 2 | 13 | 9 | <u>2</u> | 11 | 2 |
| 15 | 9 | 2 | 13 | 9 | <u>12</u> | 11 | 12 |
| 6 | 6 | 1 | 13 | <u>9</u> | 15 | 11 | 9 |
| 1 | 15 | 3 | 13 | <u>6</u> | 15 | <u>11</u> | 11 |
| 0 | 4 | 1 | 13 | <u>6</u> | 15 | 1 | 6 |
| 3 | 5 | 1 | 13 | <u>0</u> | 15 | 1 | 0 |
| 10 | 2 | 0 | <u>13</u> | 3 | 15 | 1 | 13 |
| 5 | 11 | 2 | 10 | 3 | <u>15</u> | 1 | 15 |
| 4 | 0 | 0 | <u>10</u> | 3 | 5 | 1 | 10 |
| 7 | 1 | 0 | <u>4</u> | 3 | 5 | 1 | 4 |
| 14 | 14 | 3 | <u>7</u> | 3 | 5 | <u>1</u> | 1 |
| 9 | 7 | 1 | 7 | <u>3</u> | 5 | 14 | 3 |
| 8 | 12 | 3 | 7 | <u>9</u> | 5 | <u>14</u> | 14 |
| 11 | 13 | 3 | 7 | 9 | 5 | <u>8</u> | 8 |
| 2 | 10 | 2 | 7 | 9 | <u>5</u> | 11 | 5 |

Fig. 10-1. Using two random number generators and a table to generate a highly random sequence. In each step an underline indicates the selected table entry.

Note that the *period* of the generator—the length of the repeating sequence—has not been increased. It is the same—16—for the two generators individually as it is for the combined generator. It is the randomness of the numbers in that sequence which is increased.

# Part IV
# Data Structures

## Chapter 11
## Structures and Array

The computers we are interested in offer only two sizes of memory cells: 8-bit bytes and 16-bit words. But frequently the data items we have to store require larger cells, cells having more complex structures, or cells related to one another in specified ways. In this chapter—and the remaining ones in this part of the book we will look at the *data structures* or *information structures* and the relations between them.

In this chapter we focus our attention on *structures* and *arrays*. These were defined in Chapter 3. Now we are ready to look in more detail at how the computer goes about accessing the components of a structure or the elements of an array. The techniques are similar for each, which is why both are taken up in the same chapter.

### STRUCTURES

Let us begin by trying to clear up a troublesome problem of terminology. The terms *data structure* and *structure* are not the same and should not be confused.

*Data structure* is the more general term. It refers to any of the methods of organizing data taken up in this part of the book: Structures, arrays, stacks, queues, deques, strings, plexes, trees, graphs, and so on.

*Structure*, on the other hand, is a PL/I term and refers to block of memory defined by a Pl/I structure declaration. Having taken the structure declaration from PL/I, we (not too willingly) take the name with it.

A structure is also a data structure, but not the other way around.

*An Example.* Consider the following declaration:

    DECLARE 1 PIECE,
          2 TYPE BYTE,
          2 COLOR BYTE,
          2 POSITION,
             3 ROW BYTE,
             3 COLUMN BYTE;

PIECE is the name of a 4-byte block of data. We may think of the block named as a 4-byte memory location, or cell, even if 4-byte locations are not implemented in the computer hardware. This location is divided into three parts which are themselves named locations: TYPE, COLOR, and POSITION. TYPE and COLOR are bytes and hence indivisible. But POSITION is subdivided into two byte-sized locations, ROW and COLUMN. Figure 11-1 shows the layout of PIECE and its subdivisions in memory.

We want to use piece to store a description of a chess piece. We encode information about the piece as follows: For TYPE let 0 indicate a pawn, 1 a knight, 2 a rook, 3 a bishop, 4 a queen, and 5 a king. For COLOR let 0 stand for white and 1 for black. For POSITION, assume that the rows and columns of the chessboard are numbered from 0 through 7, with the square in row 0 and column 0 being in the lower left hand corner, as seen by White.

A *value* of PIECE—a data item that can be stored in the location named PIECE—will be a 4-byte block of data. Using the code just given we can interpret *some* such blocks of data as describing chess pieces.

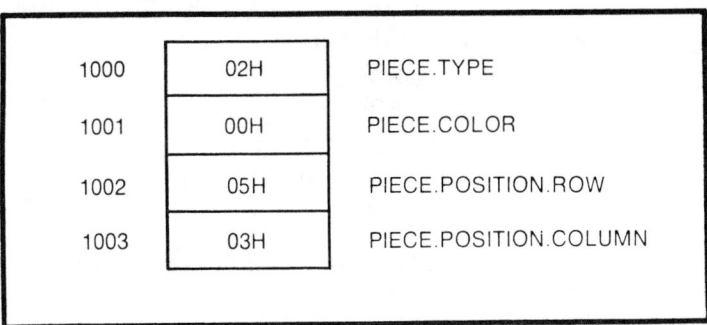

Fig. 11-1. The structure PIECE

We may write the 4-byte values of PIECE as 8-digit hexadecimal numbers, using two hexadecimal digits for each byte. The value 02000503H, for instance, describes a white rook located at the intersection of row 5 and column 3. And 04010206H represents a black queen located at the intersection of row 2 and column 6.

On the other hand, 2C4135CAH does not describe any chess piece, since the values of its parts cannot be interpreted according to the code just given. It is a *possible* value of PIECE, but not a *legal* value.

When we assign a value to a structure, we at the same time assign values to each of its components. Thus if the value of PIECE is 02000503H, the values of its components must be:

>    PIECE.TYPE = 02H
>    PIECE.COLOR = 00H
>    PIECE.POSITION = 0503H
>    PIECE.POSITION.ROW = 05H
>    PIECE.POSITION.COLUMN = 03H

*Address Calculations.* Of course the structured locations we define with structure declarations do not exist as such in computer memory. In memory there are only bytes and words. When we refer to a component of a structure, we are referring to a byte or word, or block of bytes or words, somewhere in memory. Since computers refer to memory locations by *address*, the computer must calculate the address of the location or locations being referred to. This is known as *address calculation*.

Suppose, for instance, that PIECE has been assigned bytes 1000 through 1003, as shown in Fig. 11-1. Then @PIECE, the address of PIECE, is 1000. From Fig. 11-1 we see that the addess of each component is as follows:

>    @PIECE.TYPE = 1000
>    @PIECE.COLOR = 1001
>    @PIECE.POSITION = 1002
>    @PIECE.POSITION.ROW = 1002
>    @PIECE.POSITION.COLUMN = 1003

We can calculate these addresses by assigning to each component an *offset* or *displacement*, which is the number that must be added to the address of the structure to get the address of the component. In PIECE, for instance, the offsets for TYPE, COLOR, and POSITION are 0, 1, and 2. We have:

|  | Structure Address |  | Offset |  |  |
|---|---|---|---|---|---|
| @PIECE.TYPE = | 1000 | + | 0 | = | 1000 |
| @PIECE.COLOR = | 1000 | + | 1 | = | 1001 |
| @PIECE.POSITION = | 1000 | + | 2 | = | 1002 |

The address of the minor structure POSITION is 1002, and its components ROW and COLUMN have offsets 0 and 1 respectively. Thus:

|  | Structure Address |  | Offset |  |  |
|---|---|---|---|---|---|
| @PIECE.POSITION.ROW = | 1002 | + | 0 | = | 1002 |
| @PIECE.POSITION.COLUMN = | 1002 | + | 1 | = | 1003 |

Often it is most useful to consider the offsets of components of minor structures to be with respect to the start of the major structure rather than the minor structure. Then ROW and COLUMN would have offsets of 2 and 3 with respect to the beginning of PIECE, and we would have:

|  | Structure Address |  | Offset |  |  |
|---|---|---|---|---|---|
| @PIECE.POSITION.ROW = | 1000 | + | 2 | = | 1002 |
| @PIECE.POSITION.COLUMN = | 1000 | + | 3 | = | 1003 |

*Translation Time vs Run Time.* An address calculation can be carried out at translation time—when the program is translated into machine code—or at run time—when the translated program is running on the computer.

Doing address calculations at translation time is always to be preferred. Then a calculation need only be done once, when the structure reference is translated. If the address calculation is put off until run time, then it may have to be done many times, since the structure reference may occur inside a loop. Also if the calculation is done at translation time, no instructions for doing it have to be inserted in the translated machine code. Such instructions are always needed for a run-time calculation.

*Structures in Fixed Locations.* If a structure is in a fixed location—that is, it is not an array element or designated by a pointer—then the address calculation can always be done at translation time. Both the address of the structure and the offsets of the components are known at translation time.

Using PIECE as an example, a reference to PIECE.TYPE is a reference ot the byte located at @PIECE + 0; a reference to PIECE.COLOR is a reference to the byte located at @PIECE + 1, and so on.

Now most assemblers allow expression such as @PIECE + 1, @PIECE + 2, and so on, to be used in the address fields of instructions. (In assembly language, the @-sign is omitted, since names in assembly language stand for the addresses, rather than the contents, of the named locations. To keep a consistent notation in this book I will always use the @-sign when referring to addresses, even in an assembly language context.)

Thus when writing an instruction to manipulate PIECE.POSITION.ROW we would simply use @PIECE + 2 in the address field. If PIECE.POSITION.COLUMN was the object of our instruction, then the address field would contain @PIECE + 3.

*Structures Designated by Pointers.* Define POINTER and VALUE by:

DECLARE POINTER WORD,
        1 VALUE BASED POINTER LIKE PIECE;

VALUE names a block of four bytes, structured like PIECE, whose address is the value of POINTER. To access the byte VALUE.POSITION.COLUMN we must add the offset 3 to the contents of POINTER. The offset is known at translation time, but the contents of POINTER is not, so this must be a run time address calculation.

We have:

    @VALUE = POINTER
    @VALUE.TYPE = POINTER + 0
    @VALUE.COLOR = POINTER + 1
    @VALUE.POSITION.ROW = POINTER + 2
    @VALUE.POSITION.COLUMN = POINTER + 3

Some computers feature one or more *index registers*, each of which can hold an address. An instruction that uses an index register contains a *displacement field*. When the instruction is executed, the contents of the displacement field is added to the contents of the index register, the sum being taken as the address of the memory location to be referenced.

On such a computer we can load the value of POINTER into an index register, and then refer to the components of VALUE using instructions whose displacement fields contain the corresponding offsets. To refer to VALUE.POSITION. ROW, for instance, we would use an instruction whose displacement field was 3.

On a computer that does not have index registers, we must use an 'add' instruction to add the offset to the value of POINTER. Sometimes one or more uses of the 'increment' instruction—which adds 1 to the contents of a register—may be the most efficient way to add a small offset to a pointer.

## LINEAR ARRAYS

Arrays are similar to structures in that they allow us to access a particular group of bytes or words inside a block of memory. But whereas with a structure the offset is known at translation time, with an array it must be calculated at run time.

Thus accessing an element of an array is slightly less efficient than accessing a component of a structure. On the other hand, we often need the flexibility of calculating at run time which element we wish to access, instead of being stuck with a choice made when the program was written.

We may think of the elements of a linear array as being laid out along a straight line (hence *linear*). The elements are in sequential order: We have a 0th element, a 1st element, a 2nd element, and so on. The order of elements in a linear array is the same as the order of the locations in computer memory (the entire computer memory is just one large linear array). This makes the address calculation for linear arrays particularly simple.

Consider the linear array LIST defined by:

DECLARE LIST (10) BYTE;

The elements of LIST are numbered 0 through 9, as shown in Fig. 11-2. If @LIST—the address of the first byte of LIST—is 1000, then LIST will occupy bytes 1000-1009.

```
@LIST = 1000

@LIST(0) = 1000                    LIST(0)
@LIST(1) = 1001                    LIST(1)
@LIST(2) = 1002                    LIST(2)
@LIST(3) = 1003                    LIST(3)
@LIST(4) = 1004                    LIST(4)
@LIST(5) = 1005                    LIST(5)
@LIST(6) = 1006                    LIST(6)
@LIST(7) = 1007                    LIST(7)
@LIST(8) = 1008                    LIST(8)
@LIST(9) = 1009                    LIST(9)
```

Fig. 11-2. The array LIST

The subscripted name LIST(I) refers to the element of LIST whose number is stored in location I. The address of that element is:

$$@LIST(I) = @LIST + I$$

If, at a certain instant during the program run, the value of I is 3, then @LIST(I) = 1003 and LIST(I) refers to the value stored at byte 1003. If at another instant the value of I is 5, then @LIST(I) = 1005, and LIST(I) refers to the contents of byte 1005. And so on.

If by some mischance the value of I should be 100, then LIST(I) will refer to location 1100, which is outside the memory area allocated to LIST. Disaster!

The address calculation must be done at run time, since only at run time is the value of I known. If the array is at a fixed location (not designated by a pointer), then @LIST *is* known at translation time. If the computer has an index register, *and* the displacement field of an instruction will hold a 16-bit word, then we can use @LIST in the displacement field of the instruction and load the value of I into the index register. The PDP-11/LSI-11 is one computer that satisfies these conditions; array access is particularly simple on a PDP-11.

If each element in an array is longer than 1 byte, then the subscript must be multiplied by the element size before being added to the array address. Consider the following:

DECLARE WORD_LIST(10) WORD;

If we assume @WORD_LIST = 1000, then WORD_LIST will occupy 20 bytes, 1000-1019, as shown in Fig. 11-3.

Since the size of an element is 2 bytes, increasing I by 1 must increase the element address by 2. Thus the address calculation must be:

@WORD_LIST(I) = @WORD_LIST + 2*I

Thus, since @WORD_LIST = 1000, @WORD_LIST(5) = 1010, @WORD_LIST(7) = 1014, and so on.

In assembly language, the multiplication by 2 can be done either by a left shift or by adding the contents of a register to itself.

*Arrays of Structures.* The elements of arrays may be structures instead of bytes or words, and in that case one encounters element sizes greater than 2. For example:

DECLARE 1 PIECES (5) LIKE PIECE;

PIECES consists of 5 four-byte structures, for a total of 20 bytes. If, as usual, we let @PIECES = 1000, then PIECES will occupy locations 1000-1019. (See Fig. 11-4.)

The address calculation for PIECES is:

@PIECES(I) = PIECES + 4*I

The multiplication by 4 can be implemented by means of a 2 place shift to the left. (When working with arrays of structures, we try, if at all possible, to make the size of the structure a power of 2. Then the multiplication in the address calculation can be implemented with left shifts.)

Now suppose we wish to access:

PIECES(I).POSITION.COLUMN

Since the offset for PIECE.POSITION.COLUMN is 3, we have

@PIECES(I).POSITION.COLUMN = @PIECES(I) + 3
= @PIECES + 4*I + 3

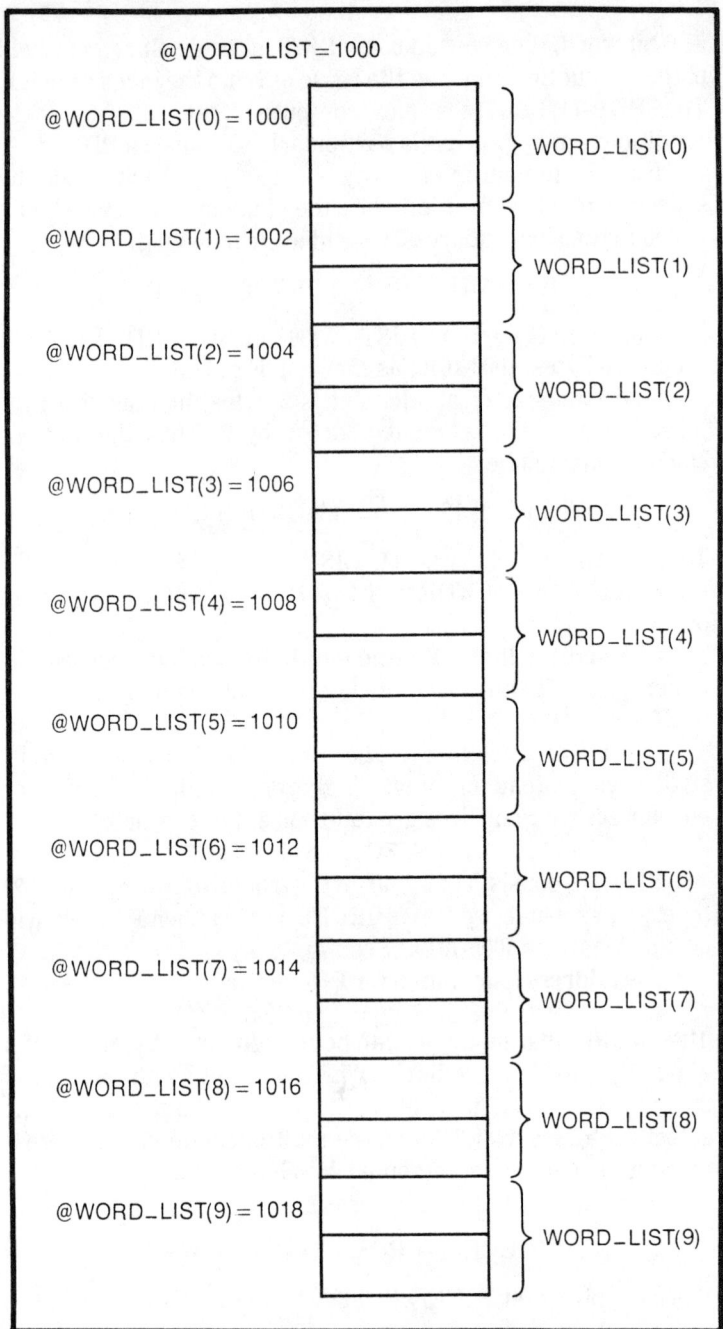

Fig. 11-3. An array of words, WORD_LIST

Thus:

@PIECES(2).POSITION.COLUMN = 1000 + 4*2 + 3 = 1011

For specifying this access in assembly language, it is often advantageous to rearrange the above expression:

@PIECES(I).POSITION.COLUMN = (@PIECES + 3) + 4*I

The address @PIECES + 3 can be computed at translation time, and only 4*I need be computed and added at run time. In particular, we could use an instruction with @PIECES + 3 in

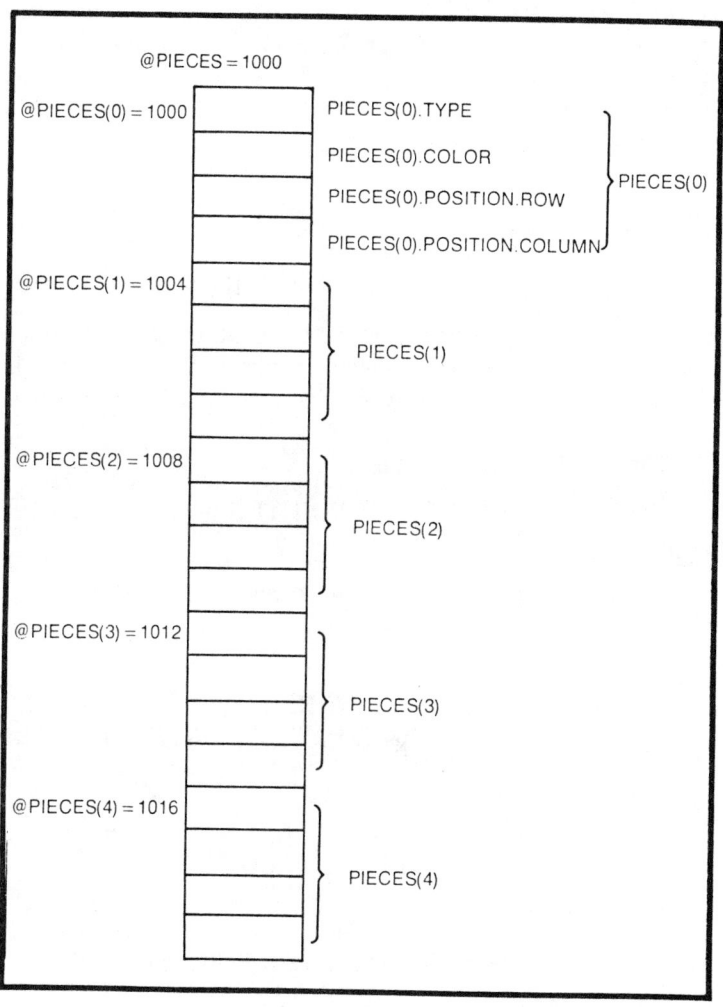

Fig. 11-4. An array of structures, PIECES

the displacement field, and load 4*I into the index register at run time.

On the other hand, this is not always the best strategy. Suppose we were going to access each of the components

@PIECES(I).TYPE
@PIECES(I).COLOR
@PIECES(I).POSITON.ROW
@PIECES(I).POSITION.COLUMN

in turn, all for the same value of I. In that case it would be better to compute @PIECES + 4*I once and for all and put this value in the index register. We could then use instructions with displacements of 0, 1, 2, and 3 to access the various components of PIECES(I).

*Arrays Designated by Pointers.* An array of either bytes, words, or structures can be designated by a pointer. Consider the following:

DECLARE POINTER WORD,
        VALUE BASED POINTER (10) BYTE;

No memory is allocated for VALUE at translation time. Instead, the name VALUE always refers to the 10-byte block the address of whose first byte is the value of POINTER. (See Fig. 11-5.)

The address calculation is

@VALUE(I) = POINTER + I

Neither the value of POINTER nor the value of I is known at translation time, so neither can be put in the displacement field of an instruction.

Suppose we had defined:

DECLARE POINTER WORD,
        1 VALUE BASED POINTER (10)   LIKE
        PIECE.

If we wish to access

VALUE(I).POSITION.COLUMN

the address calculation is:

@VALUE(I).POSITION.COLUMN = POINTER + 4*I + 3

No part of this calculation can be done at translation time, since the values of neither POINTER nor I are known then.

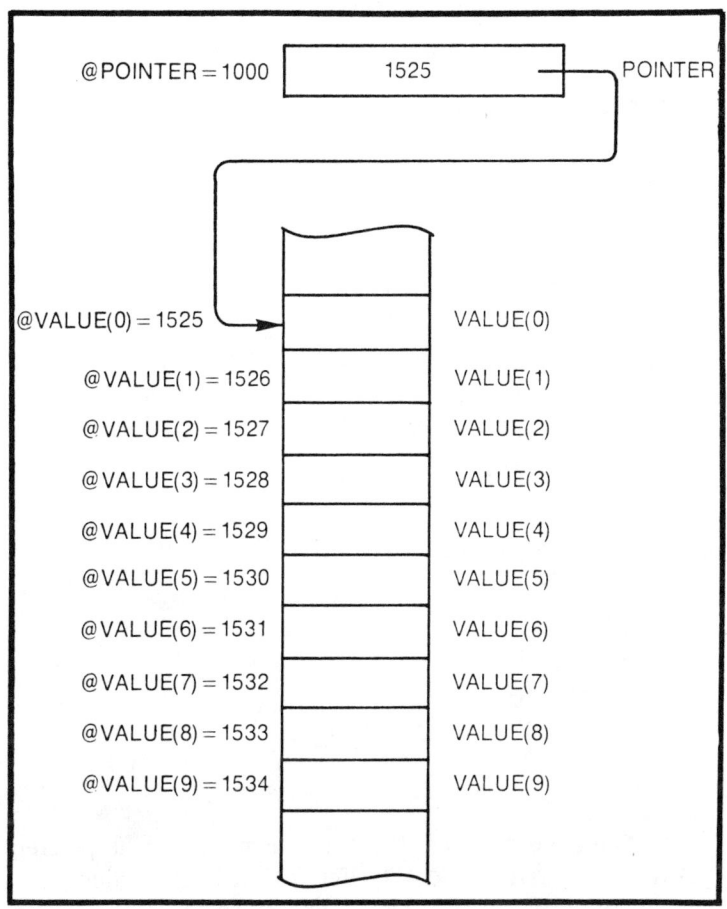

Fig. 11-5. An array designated by a pointer

However, the offset 3 is known, and may be included in the displacement field of an instruction. Then at run time POINTER + 4*I will be calculated and put into the index register.

*Subscripts vs Pointers.* When we wish to access an arbitrary element of a linear array—a so-called "random access"—then the address calculations just discussed are appropriate. But when we wish to access the array sequentially, to process all its elements in order from start to finish (or from finish to start), then it is often more efficient to access the array elements via pointers instead of subscripted names.

Consider the array defined by:

DECLARE TABLE (100) BYTE

and suppose we wish to set every element of TABLE to 0. Using subscripts, we could write:

```
I = 99;
DO UNTIL I = 0;
    VALUE(I) = 0;
    I = I - 1;
END;
```

The address calculation @VALUE(I) = @VALUE + I must be done 100 times.

Now let us add the declaration

DECLARE POINTER WORD,
          POINTEE BASED POINTER BYTE;

and rewrite the above code as follows:

```
POINTER = @VALUE;
I = 99;
DO UNTIL I = 0;
    POINTEE = 0;
    POINTER = POINTER + 1;
    I = I - 1;
END;
```

We have substituted the incrementation of a pointer (POINTER = POINTER + 1) for the address calculation implied by VALUE(I). On most machines the pointer incrementation is at least marginally simpler or faster, and on some (the M6800) it is drastically so. The gap between the two is widened for word arrays or arrays of structures, where the address calculation is correspondingly more complicated.

Most experienced assembly language programmers would probably write code equivalent to our second example, the one using pointers.

*Parallel Linear Arrays.* Here is a way to implement arrays of structures in high level languages such as BASIC, FORTRAN, and PL/M, which allow arrays but do not allow structures.

Recall the 20-byte array, PIECES, which we declared to be structured like PIECE. Instead of the single 20-byte array, we could have used 4 five-byte arrays instead:

```
DECLARE TYPE(5)TYPE,
        COLOR(5)BYTE,
        ROW(5)BYTE,
        COLUMN(5)BYTE;
```

For any I, TYPE(I) would contain the type of the entry whose number is stored in I, COLOR(I) its color, ROW(I) its row number, and COLUMN(I) its column number.

Arrays such as TYPE, COLOR, ROW, and COLUMN are sometimes called *parallel arrays*, since it is convenient to imagine them arranged in parallel columns, as in Fig. 11-6. A horizontal row, which cuts across all four columns, contains the information pertaining to a particular piece.

We may compare accesses to the same information using an array of structures and parallel arrays as follows:

| Array of Structures | Parallel Arrays |
|---|---|
| PIECES(I).TYPE | TYPE(I) |
| PIECES(I).COLOR | COLOR(I) |
| PIECES(I).POSITION.ROW | ROW(I) |
| PIECES(I).POSITION.COLUMN | COLUMN(I) |

As mentioned, parallel arrays are best used in languages that feature linear arrays but not structures. When working in assembly language, there seems to be no reason to favor parallel arrays over an array of structures.

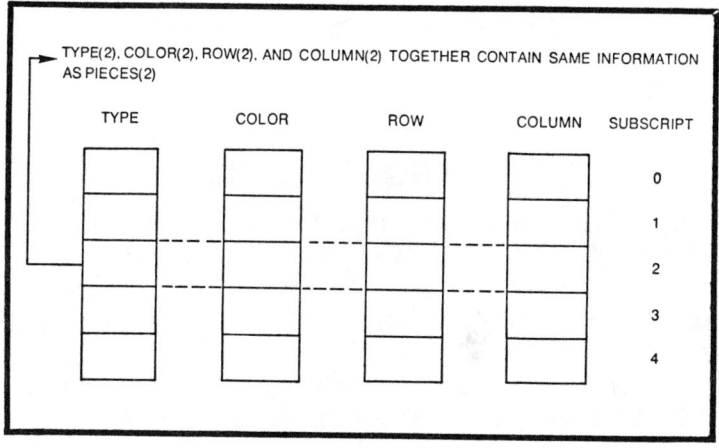

Fig. 11-6. Parallel arrays

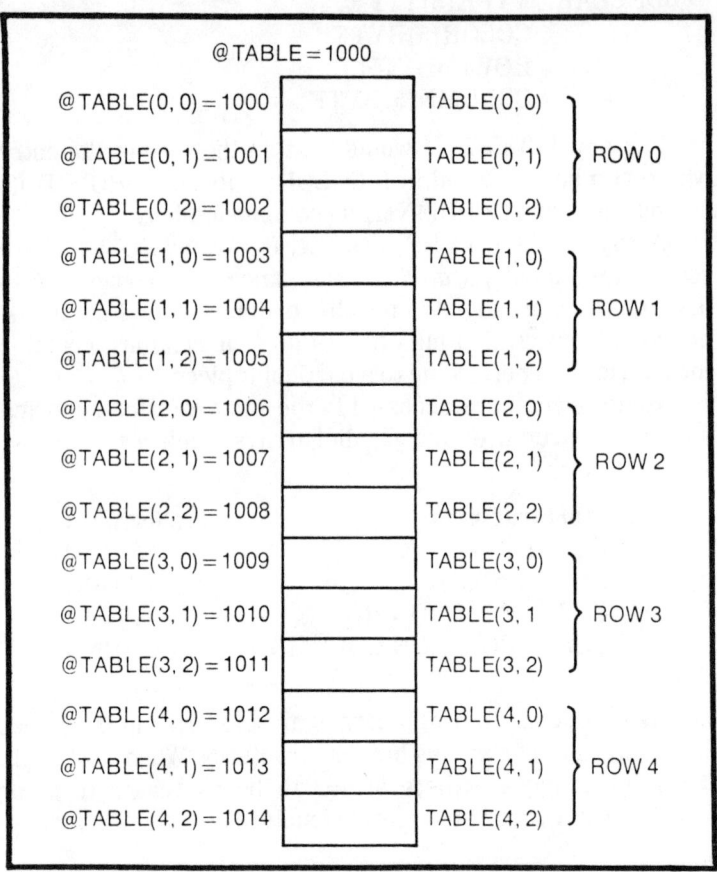

Fig. 11-7. A two-dimensional array stored by rows

## MULTIDIMENSIONAL ARRAYS

The declaration

DECLARE TABLE(5, 3) BYTE;

defines a table having 5 rows and 3 columns. A reference to an element of TABLE needs two subscripts: one to specify the row of the desired element, and one to specify the column. The row subscript can have values in the range 0-4; the column subscript, in the range 0-2.

We can store TABLE in memory either by rows or by columns. If we store by rows, then the first row will be stored first, followed by the second row, and so on. Figure 11-7 illustrates this method of storing a two-dimensional array.

The address calculation is:

$$@TABLE(I, J) = @TABLE + 3*I + J$$

This is reasonable, since when the column subscript J increases by 1, we are moving from one byte to another in the same row, and so the address should increase by 1. But when I increases by 1, we are moving from a certain position in one row to the corresponding position in the next row. Since each row takes up 3 bytes, this move involves jumping 3 bytes. Hence when I increases by 1, @TABLE(I, J) should increase by 3.

On the other hand, we could store TABLE by columns, as shown in Fig. 11-8.

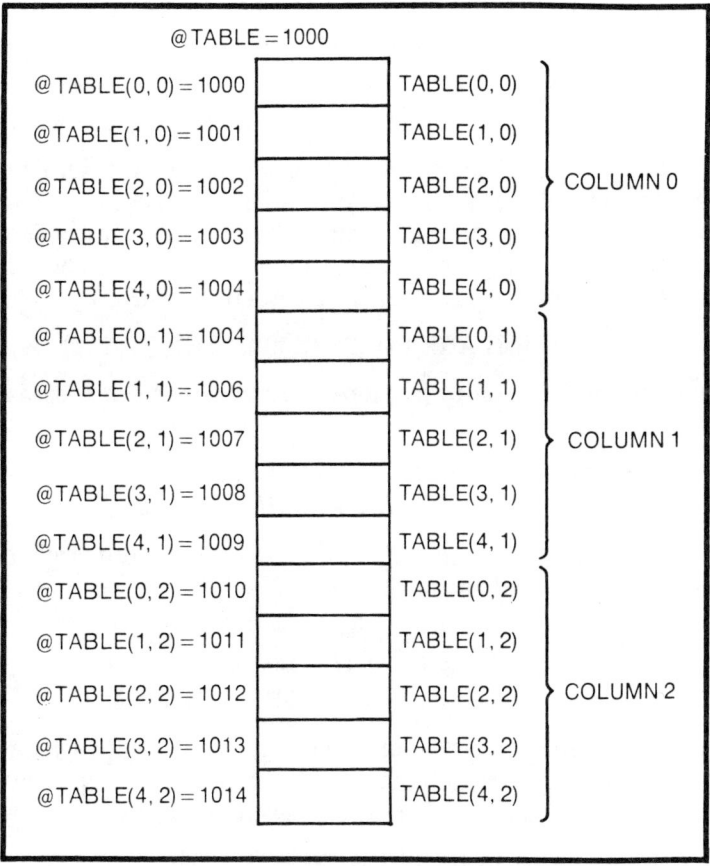

Fig. 11-8. A two-dimensional array stored by columns

Now when I increases by 1 we are moving to the next byte, and so @TABLE(I, J) increases by 1. But when J increases by 1, we are moving from one column to the next, and have to jump forward 5 bytes, since each column is 5 bytes long. These considerations yield the address calculation:

$$@TABLE(I, J) = @TABLE + I + 5*J$$

If the table elements are larger than bytes, then each subscript has to be multiplied by the element size. Suppose the elements are 7-byte structures. Then we would have

@TABLE(I,   J) = @TABLE + 3*7*I + 7*J   (by rows)
@TABLE(I,   J) = @TABLE + 7*I + 5*7*J   (by columns)

The products 3*7 and 5*7 would, of course, be worked out at translation time. The run time calculations would be:

@TABLE(I,J) = @TABLE + 21*I + 7*J   (by rows)
@TABLE(I, J) = @TABLE + 7*I + 35*J   (by columns)

With table dimensions, as with element sizes, it is helpful to use powers of 2, since multiplication by these can be implemented with shifting. Computer chess fans can rejoice that the ancient inventors of their game chose a chess board with $8\ (= 2^3)$ rows and columns. If we define BOARD by:

DECLARE BOARD(8, 8) BYTE;

and assume BOARD to be stored by rows, then the address calculation is:

@BOARD(I, J) = @BOARD + 8*I + J
             = @BOARD + SHL (I, 3) + J

If we wanted the elements of BOARD to be words rather than bytes, we would have:

@BOARD(I, J) = @BOARD + 8*2*I + 2*J
             = @BOARD + 16*I + 2*J
             = @BOARD + SHL (I, 4) + SHL (J, 2)

We can go on to higher dimensions if we wish, although the need to do so does not often arise. The following example will illustrate the technique. Let BOOK be defined by:

DECLARE BOOK(30, 10, 7) BYTE;

We may think of this as defining a *book of tables* having 30 pages, with each page containing a table having 10 rows and 7 columns.

Suppose we store by pages, and on each page store by rows. Each page contains a 10 by 7 table and so contains 10*7 bytes. When the page subscript I increases by 1, we jump from a position on one page to the corresponding position on the next page, and so we must jump 10*7 bytes. Everytime the row subscript J increases by 1, then we jump 7 bytes to get to the corresponding position in the next row. When the column subscript K increases by 1, we simply move to the next byte.

These considerations give us the address calculation

$$@BOOK(I, J, K) = @BOOK + 10*7*I + 7*j + K$$

or, with the constants multiplied out:

$$@BOOK(I, J, K) = @BOOK + 70*I + 7*J + K$$

If the elements of book had been 5-byte structures, instead of single bytes, then we would have

$$@BOOK(I, J, K) = @BOOK + 10*7*5*I + 7*5*J + 5*K$$

or, after multiplying out the constants:

$$@BOOK(I, J, K) = @BOOK + 350*I + 35*J + 5*K$$

If a language does not provide for multidimensional arrays, we can use linear arrays and write out the subscript expressions explicitly. To implement the 5 by 3 table declared at the beginning of this section, for instance, we could use the 15 byte linear array LIST:

$$\text{DECLARE LIST}(15) \text{ BYTE};$$

We could refer to the table element in row I and column J by

$$\text{LIST}(3*I + J)$$

Since

$$@LIST(3*I + J) = @LIST + 3*I + J$$

we have the same address calculation as we did for @TABLE(I, J), when the elements were stored by rows.

As long as the language provides for linear arrays, we can use this technique to implement arrays of any dimension.

# Chapter 12
# Stacks, Queues and Deques

Stacks, queues, and deques are basically linear arrays or linear lists, but with two distinctive features:

1) The size of the list may vary, within limits, as the computation proceeds. New elements may be inserted, and old ones deleted.
2) Insertions and deletions may only be made at the ends of the lists. Further restrictions on insertions and deletions distinguish stacks and queues from deques.

**STACKS**

A stack is a linear list for which insertions and deletions are allowed at only one end. The end at which insertions and deletions may be made is the *top* of the stack. The other end is the *bottom*.

We may visualize a stack as a stack of physical objects, such as books or papers or cards. We can put new objects on top of the stack (insertion) and remove old ones (deletion). But never insert or remove objects from the middle of the stack, or from the bottom.

Another mental image for a stack is the stack of plates in a cafeteria, where a spring loaded device assures that only the top plate is at counter level, and hence accessible. This image yields several metaphors: We sometimes speak of a "push down list" or a "push down stack." We "push" items onto the stack, and "pop" them or "pull" them off.

One feature of this picture is misleading: In a computer implementation of a stack, we *do not* move all the items up or down when an item is pushed on or popped off. Only the top item is affected.

Items are inserted and deleted from a stack according to a Last In First Out, or LIFO, discipline. This means that the last item pushed onto the stack is always the first one removed. Items are popped off of a stack in exactly the reverse of the order in which they were pushed on.

*Stack Implementations.* We implement a stack as a block of memory with a pointer at one end. The pointer designates the current position of the top of the stack:

We define:

```
DECLARE  TOP_POINTER WORD,
         TOP BASED TOP_POINTER BYTE;
```

There are four possible variations on the stack.

The stack may grow either forward or backward in memory. If it grows forward in memory, then top is the end having the largest address, and when new items are pushed on, they are stored at successively higher addresses. If the stack grows backwards in memory, then the top is the end having the *smallest* address, and when new items are pushed on, they are stored at successively lower addresses.

The other source of variation is that TOP—the byte pointed to by TOP_POINTER—can either be the location where the last item to be pushed on *was* stored, or it can be the location where the next item to be pushed on *will be* stored.

The four possible variations of the stack are listed below and illustrated in Fig. 12-1:

1) Stack grows forward in memory. TOP is location of last item pushed on.
2) Stack grows forward in memory. TOP will receive the next item to be pushed on.
3) Stack grows backward in memory. TOP is location of last item pushed on.
4) Stack grows backward in memory. TOP will receive the next item to be pushed on.

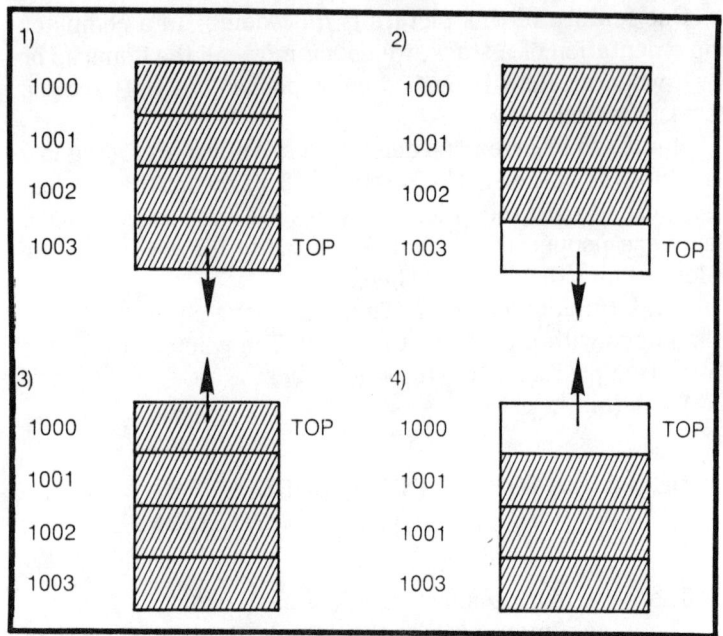

Fig. 12-1. Four variations of stack. Shaded locations are filled. Unshaded ones are empty. Arrows show the direction of growth for each stack.

A stack that grows backward is convenient, since it can share a block of memory with some other table that grows forward.

For example, Fig. 12-2 shows the layout of the user's workspace for a typical BASIC interpreter. The symbol table contains all variables used so far in the program, together with their current values. It grows forward as new variables are defined. The stack is used to evaluate algebraic expressions and process FOR-NEXT and GOSUB-RETURN statements. It grows backwards. Only when the symbol table and the stack attempt to overlap must the system announce that memory is exhausted.

In the following we shall concentrate on the Type 3 (see Fig. 12-1) stack, since this is the type often implemented in computer hardware.

We reserve space for a stack as follows:

```
DECLARE STACK_SIZE LITERALLY '256',
        STACK (STACK_SIZE) BYTE;
```

We use the LITERALLY declaration to make the rest of our work independent of a particular value for STACK_SIZE. When expressions occur containing only constants known at translation time—such as @STACK + STACK_SIZE—we assume that they are worked out at translation time, so that only their numerical values occur in the translated code.

Or to put it another way, if it happens that @STACK = 1000, and STACK_SIZE is declared as above, then @STACK + STACK_SIZE is just another way of writing 1256, and would be replaced by 1256 at translation time.

Since our stack is to grow backwards, its *bottom* has the highest possible address:

@STACK + STACK_SIZE − 1

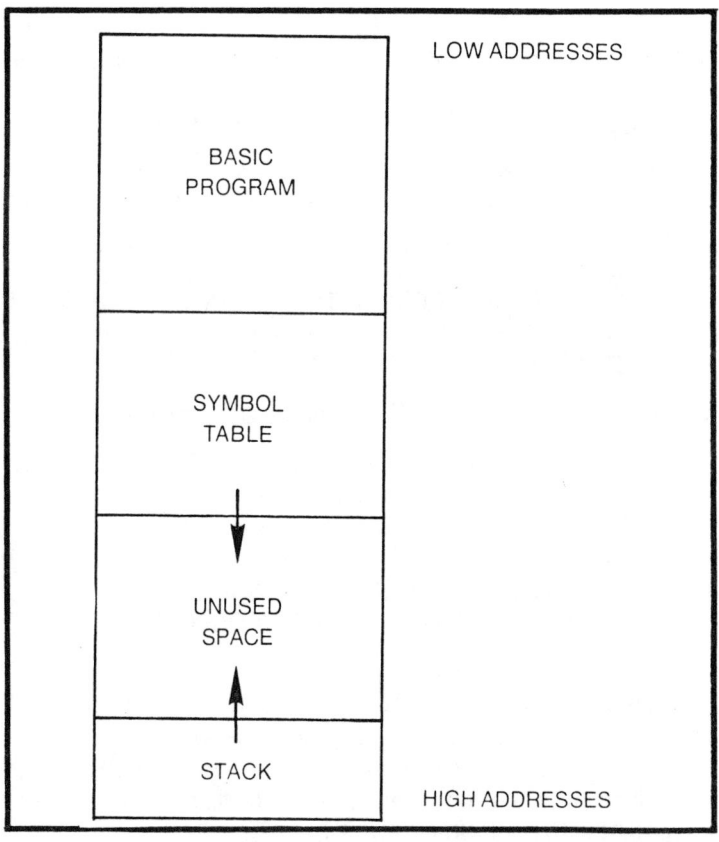

Fig. 12-2. Layout of user's workspace for typical BASIC interpreter.

187

```
PUSH: PROCEDURE (VALUE);
    DECLARE VALUE BYTE;
    IF TOP_POINTER = @STACK THEN
        CALL ERROR (14, @' STACK OVERFLOW');
    ELSE
        DO;
            TOP_POINTER = TOP_POINTER - 1;
            TOP = VALUE;
        END;
END PUSH:
```

Program 12-1. PUSH pushes its argument onto a stack.

We initialize TOP_POINTER by:

TOP_POINTER = @STACK + STACK_SIZE;

This value for TOP_POINTER, one location higher than the bottom of the stack, will be taken as an indication that the stack is empty.

To push the contents of VALUE onto the stack we use:

```
IF TOP_POINTER = @STACK THEN
    CALL ERROR (14, @ 'STACK OVERFLOW');
ELSE
    DO;
        TOP_POINTER = TOP_POINTER - 1;
        TOP = VALUE;
    END;
```

To pop the contents of VALUE off of the stack we use:

```
IF TOP_POINTER = @STACK + STACK_SIZE THEN
    CALL ERROR (15, @ 'STACK UNDERFLOW');
ELSE
    DO;
        VALUE = TOP;
        TOP_POINTER = TOP_POINTER + 1;
    END;
```

Programs 12-1 and 12-2 show the PUSH and POP procedures constructed around these statements.

*An Application: Procedure Calls and Returns.* When one procedure calls another, the calling procedure must supply the one called with the following:

1) The values of the arguments.
2) The return address—the address in the calling procedure that the called one is to branch to when it is finished.

In addition, the calling procedure must save the contents of any processor registers that it does not wish to be changed by the called procedure, and restore these after the called procedure has returned.

Thus a procedure CALL might do the following:

1) Push onto the stack the contents of any registers that are to be saved.
2) Push onto the stack the values of all the arguments that are to be transmitted to the called procedure.
3) Push onto the stack the address of the next instruction in the calling procedure, and branch to the first instruction of the called procedure. Often there is a single "Jump to Subroutine" instruction which does both these things.

Figure 12-3 shows what the stack looks like as the called procedure commences. The called procedure can access its arguments by treating the stack as a linear array. Thus if the arguments are 1 byte each, and the return address takes up 2 bytes, then STACK(TOP_POINTER + 2) is the last argument pushed on, STACK(TOP_POINTER + 3) is the next-to-last argument pushed on, and so on.

The called procedure terminates itself with a "return" instruction, which pops the return address off the stack and

```
POP: PROCEDURE (P);
    DECLARE P WORD, /* POINTER TO VALUE */
            VALUE BASED P BYTE;
    IF TOP_POINTER = @STACK + STACK_SIZE THEN
        CALL ERROR(15, @'STACK UNDERFLOW');
    ELSE
        DO;
            VALUE = TOP;
            TOP_POINTER = TOP_POINTER + 1;
        END;
END POP;
```

Program 12-2. POP pops the top value from a stack and stores it at the location pointed to by the argument.

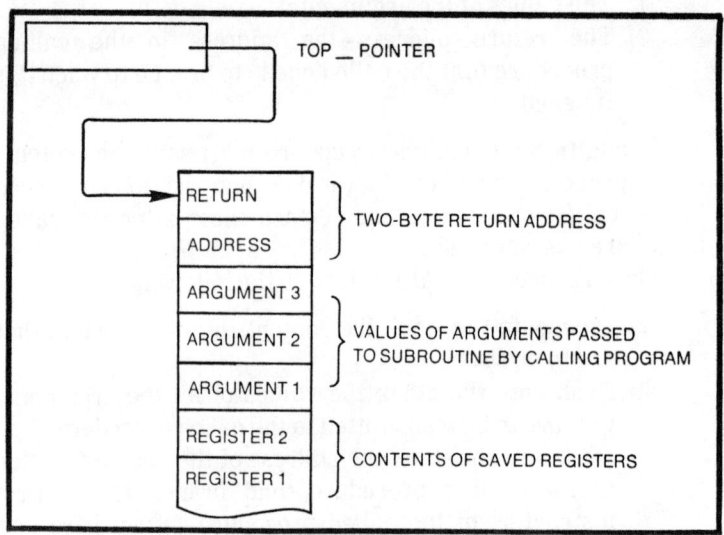

Fig. 12-3. "Snapshot" of stack as called procedure commences.

branches to that address. At that address the calling procedure continues as follows:

4) Increment TOP_POINTER by the number of bytes occupied by the arguments, thus removing them from the stack.
5) Pop the register contents that were saved and restore them to their proper registers.

The calling procedure then continues with the statement following the CALL statement.

If the procedure is a function—it returns a value—then a place may be reserved on the stack for the value to be returned, and the called procedure will store that value in the reserved location. Alternately, the value may be returned in a processor register.

A procedure that has been called may in turn call another procedure. The saved registers, arguments, and return address for the new procedure are simply stacked up on top of those for the procedure which called it. As long as the stack space is not exhausted, any number of nested procedure calls—calls from inside procedures that were themselves called—may take place.

In general, stacks are most frequently used in computer programming for processing nested objects, where we must interrupt the processing of one object to process a similar object contained inside the first one. The stack is used to save information about the first object so that processing of it may be resumed after the object nested inside it has been processed. Nested procedure calls are an example of this use.

Sometimes it is convenient to let a procedure call itself—either directly or through a series of intervening calls. Such a procedure is said to be *recursive*. When a recursive procedure executes a CALL statement, it must save the values of all its local variables on the stack. Otherwise, if the procedure is called again before its first call is complete, then the values of the local variables needed to complete the first call will be changed during the second call.

Thus a recursive procedure has to push the values of all local variables onto the stack before branching to the called procedure, and pop them off after the called procedure returns.

Another possibility is to keep the local variables in a procedure on the stack all the time, and access them like arguments by treating the stack as a linear array. Algol and PL/I use this technique. Efficiency demands that the computer have powerful facilities for array access. Of currently available microprocessors, only the LSI-11 has the appropriate facilities for array access to make efficient use of this method.

## CIRCULAR ARRAYS

Our next two data structures—queues and deques—will make use of *circular lists* or *circular arrays*. These are arrays in which the last location is assumed to be adjacent to the first, forming a ring. If we move off the end of the array we will come back on at the beginning, and vice versa.

Let us define:

DECLARE CIRCULAR_LIST(LIST_SIZE) BYTE,
 ELEMENT_POINTER WORD;

where LIST_SIZE has been declared as being LITERALLY some number.

To move ELEMENT_POINTER to the next element on the list, we do the following:

```
IF
ELEMENT_POINTER = @CIRCULAR_LIST + LIST_
    SIZE - 1
THEN
    ELEMENT_POINTER = @CIRCULAR_LIST;
ELSE
    ELEMENT_POINTER = ELEMENT_POINTER + 1:
```

Here @CIRCULAR_LIST is the address of the *first* element of the array CIRCULAR_LIST, and @CIRCULAR_LIST + LIST_SIZE − 1 is the address of the *last* element. Thus if ELEMENT_POINTER points to the last element, we set it back to the first one; otherwise, we increment it by 1.

To move ELEMENT_POINTER back to the previous element, we use:

```
IF
ELEMENT_POINTER = @CIRCULAR_LIST THEN
    ELEMENT_POINTER     = @CIRCULAR_LIST +
    LIST_SIZE - 1:
ELSE
    ELEMENT_POINTER = ELEMENT_POINTER - 1:
```

If ELEMENT_POINTER points to the first element in CIRCULAR_LIST, then we set it to point to the last element. Otherwise, we decrement it by 1.

Figure 12-4 illustrates a circular list.

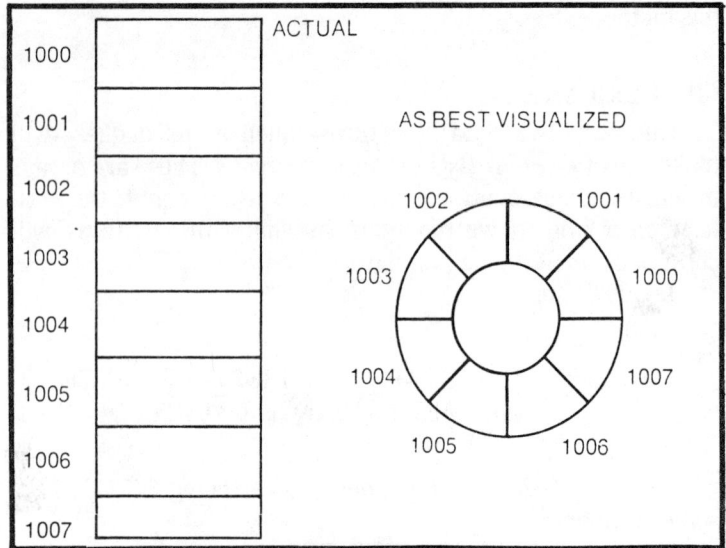

Fig. 12-4. Circular list.

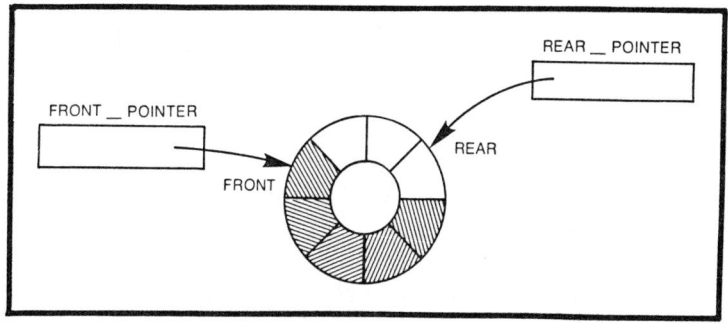

Fig. 12-5. A queue. Occupied locations are shaded.

## QUEUES

A queue is simply a waiting line. In England the word "queue" is the everyday term for a waiting line; in America it is the technical term.

In computer science, a queue is a linear list whose ends are labeled *front* and *rear*. We insert items at the rear of the queue and remove them at the front. A queue satisfies a First In First Out (FIFO) or a First Come First Served discipline: The first item inserted in the queue is the first one deleted.

A queue is implemented using a circular array as shown in Fig. 12-5. The circular array is necessary so that memory locations abandoned at the front of the queue when items are deleted can be reused at the rear when items are inserted.

The needed declarations are as follows:

```
DECLARE QUEUE_SIZE LITERALLY '32',
        QUEUE(QUEUE_SIZE) BYTE,
        FRONT_POINTER WORD,
        REAR_POINTER WORD
        FRONT BASED FRONT_POINTER BYTE,
        REAR BASED REAR_POINTER BYTE;
```

As before, we use QUEUE_SIZE to stand for the size of QUEUE, thus making our work independent of a particular queue size.

FRONT is the currently occupied element at the front of the queue. REAR is the currently unoccupied element at the rear of the queue. That is, REAR is the location in which the next data item to be inserted will be placed. FRONT_POINTER and REAR_POINTER point to FRONT and REAR, respectively.

When FRONT_POINTER = REAR_POINTER, so FRONT and REAR are the same location, the queue is empty. We do not allow the two pointers to be equal when the queue is full, since if we did there would be no way to distinguish the full condition from the empty condition. It follows that at least one location must always be unused. In particular, REAR must always be empty.

(We shall see presently one way to get around the requirement that one location remain unused, but the method is not always applicable.)

Since the two pointers being equal signifies the queue is empty, we initialize them as follows:

FRONT_POINTER = @QUEUE;
REAR_POINTER = @QUEUE;

To insert the contents of VALUE at the rear of the queue, we use:
REAR = VALUE;
IF REAR_POINTER = @QUEUE + QUEUE_SIZE − 1 THEN
    REAR_POINTER = @QUEUE;
ELSE
    REAR_POINTER = REAR_POINTER + 1;
IF REAR_POINTER = FRONT_POINTER THEN
    CALL ERROR (14, @'QUEUE OVERFLOW');

Here @QUEUE is the address of the first element of the array QUEUE, and @QUEUE + QUEUE_SIZE − 1 is the address of the last element.

```
INSERT_REAR: PROCEDURE (VALUE);
    DECLARE VALUE BYTE;
    /* INSERT VALUE */
        REAR = VALUE;
    /* UPDATE REAR_POINTER */
        IF REAR_POINTER = @QUEUE + QUEUE_SIZE − 1 THEN
            REAR_POINTER = @QUEUE;
        ELSE
            REAR_POINTER = REAR_POINTER + 1;
    /* CHECK FOR OVERFLOW */
        IF REAR_POINTER = FRONT_POINTER THEN
            CALL ERROR (14, @'QUEUE OVERFLOW');
    END INSERT_REAR;
```

Program 12-3. INSERT_REAR inserts its argument at the rear of a queue.

Since the location REAR is always empty, we can begin by setting it equal to VALUE. On the other hand, if the insertion causes REAR_POINTER to equal FRONT_POINTER, then overflow is announced, because equality of the pointers is legal only when the queue is empty.

To delete the element at the front of the queue, and assign its contents to VALUE, we use:

```
IF FRONT_POINTER = REAR_POINTER THEN
    CALL ERROR (15, @'QUEUE UNDERFLOW');
ELSE
   DO;
       VALUE = FRONT;
       IF FRONT_POINTER =
       @QUEUE + QUEUE_SIZE − 1 THEN
           FRONT_POINTER = @QUEUE;
       ELSE
           FRONT_POINTER=FRONT_POINTER +1;
   END;
```

If FRONT_POINTER = REAR_POINTER, then the queue is empty, and the attempt to delete an element is in error.

Programs 12-3 and 12-4 show the procedures INSERT_REAR and DELETE_FRONT. Figure 12-6 illustrates the insertion and deletion operations.

```
DELETE_FRONT: PROCEDURE (P);
    DECLARE P WORD,   /* POINTER TO VALUE */
            VALUE BASED P BYTE;
    /* CHECK FOR UNDERFLOW */
            IF FRONT_POINTER = REAR_POINTER THEN
            CALL ERROR (15, @'QUEUE UNDERFLOW');
    ELSE
            DO;
                /* GET VALUE */
                    VALUE = FRONT;
                /* UPDATE FRONT_POINTER */
                    IF FRONT_POINTER = @QUEUE + QUEUE_SIZE − 1 THEN
                        FRONT_POINTER = @QUEUE;
                    ELSE
                        FRONT_POINTER=FRONT_POINTER + 1;
            END;
END DELETE_FRONT;
```

Program 12-4. DELETE_FRONT removes the front item from a queue and stores it at the address pointed to by the argument.

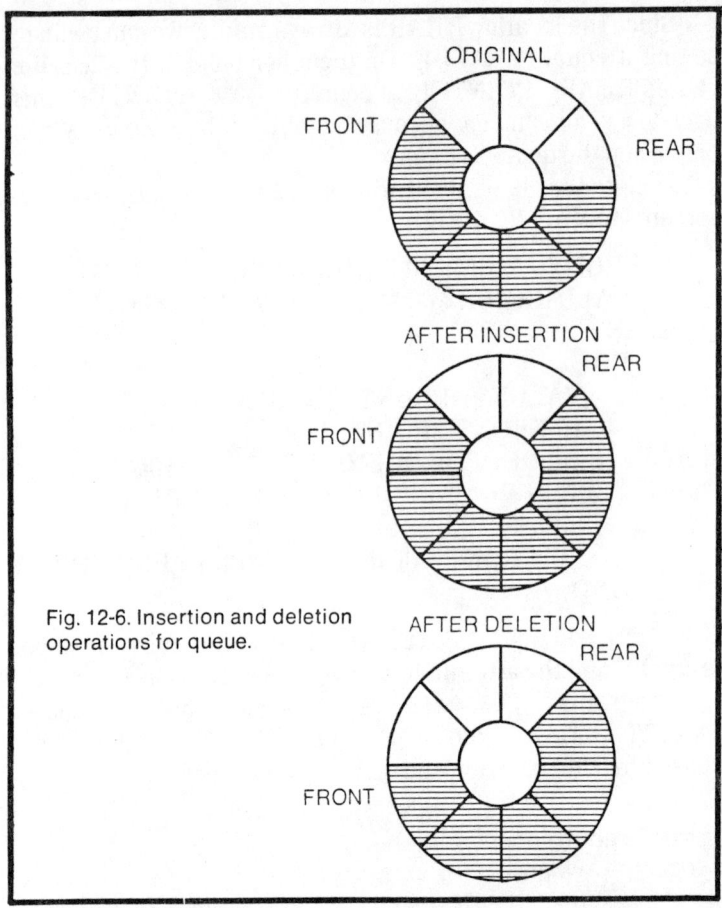

Fig. 12-6. Insertion and deletion operations for queue.

*An Application: Input Buffering.* Consider the problem of servicing an input device such as a keyboard or tape reader. When the input device has a character to transmit, it requests an interrupt from the computer. The computer responds by executing an interrupt service routine which reads the character, and then returns to the program that was executing when the interrupt occurred.

Two procedures are needed: KEYBOARD_INTERRUPT, which the input device calls (via the computer's interrupt mechanism) when it has a character to transmit; and READ_CHAR, which a program calls when it wishes to read a character.

KEYBOARD_INTERRUPT places characters at the rear of a queue, and READ_CHAR removes them from the front.

The queue is called the *input buffer*. If KEYBOARD_INTERRUPT finds the queue full, it announces "input buffer overflow." If READ_CHAR finds the queue empty, it waits until an interrupt causes another character to be placed in the queue.

In the ASCII code the character with code 0 is a null character, such as comes from reading blank tape. If we are careful that no null character is accidentally inserted in the queue, then we can use the value 0 to indicate that a location is empty. The input buffer—our queue—is initially set to zeros, indicating that it is completely empty.

This method of indicating empty locations has the advantage that every location in QUEUE can be filled; REAR is not always required to be empty (though it must be empty before an insertion can be made). The disadvantage of this method is that it requires that one bit pattern be reserved for designating empty locations; this is not always possible or desirable.

Program 12-5 shows the procedure KEYBOARD_INTERRUPT. The word INTERRUPT, following PROCEDURE, indicates that this is an interrupt procedure,

```
KEYBOARD _ INTERRUPT: PROCEDURE INTERRUPT;
    DECLARE INPUT _ CHAR BYTE;
    /* ACCEPT CHARACTER FROM KEYBOARD AND PLACE IN
        INPUT _ CHAR */
    /* IGNORE NULL CHARACTER */
        IF INPUT _ CHAR = 0 THEN RETURN;
    /* IF REAR IS EMPTY, INSERT THE CHARACTER JUST READ
        AND UPDATE REAR _ POINTER. OTHERWISE, ANNOUNCE
        OVERFLOW */
    IF REAR = 0 THEN
        DO;
            REAR = INPUT _ CHAR;
            IF REAR _ POINTER = @QUEUE + QUEUE _ SIZE - 1 THEN
                REAR _ POINTER = @QUEUE;
            ELSE
                REAR _ POINTER = REAR _ POINTER + 1;
        END;
    ELSE
        CALL ERROR (21, @'INPUT BUFFER OVERFLOW');
END KEYBOARD _ INTERRUPT;
```

Program 12-5. KEYBOARD__INTERRUPT accepts a character from the keyboard and places it at the rear of a queue.

```
READ_CHAR: PROCEDURE;
    /* IF QUEUE IS EMPTY THEN WAIT */
        DO WHILE FRONT = 0;
            /* DO NOTHING */
        END;
    /* GET CHARACTER, CLEAR FRONT, AND UPDATE FRONT_POINTER */
        CHAR = FRONT;
        FRONT = 0;
        IF FRONT_POINTER = @QUEUE + QUEUE_SIZE - 1 THEN
            FRONT_POINTER = @QUEUE;
        ELSE
            FRONT_POINTER = FRONT_POINTER + 1;
END READ_CHAR;
```

Program 12-6. READ_CHAR obtains a character from the queue filled by KEYBOARD_INTERRUPT.

---

one that will be called via the computer's interrupt mechanism. This mechanism is disabled at the beginning of the interrupt procedure, and enabled after its return, so that the interrupt procedure cannot itself be interrupted. All the processor registers and status indicators (carry bit, overflow bit, and so on) must be saved before the interrupt procedure is activated, and restored after its return, since any of these could be in use when the interrupt occurred.

Program 12-5 begins by accepting a character from the keyboard and placing it in INPUT_CHAR. Since the technique for accepting a character from an external device varies widely from one system to another, we indicate this operation by a comment. If the character just read is null, it is ignored, and the procedure returns immediately. Otherwise, if REAR is null, then it is empty, and the character just read is inserted. If REAR is not null, then there is no room in the buffer, and "input buffer overflow" is announced.

Program 12-6 shows the procedure READ_CHAR. This procedure first checks to see if the queue is empty; if so, READ_CHAR goes into a waiting loop until something is put in the queue. The character to be read is deleted from the queue and placed in CHAR. The location it occupied in the queue is zeroed, so that KEYBOARD_INTERRUPT can recognize this as an empty location.

In a time sharing system, READ_CHAR, instead of going into a waiting loop when the queue is empty, would cause the program currently being executed to be temporarily dismissed, and another user's program to be activated. The program that was dismissed would continue to lose its turn at the computer as long as its input buffer remained empty.

## DEQUES

A deque (pronounced "deck") is a *double ended queue*. It is a queue in which insertions and deletions can be made at either the front or the rear.

For a deque we have four procedures:

   INSERT_FRONT   DELETE_FRONT
   INSERT_REAR    DELETE_REAR

INSERT_REAR and DELETE_FRONT are the same as the corresponding procedures for a queue, Programs 12-3 and 12-4, and need no further discussion. INSERT_FRONT and DELETE_REAR are similar, except that the pointers are moved backwards instead of forwards. Programs 12-7 and 12-8 show these procedures.

*An Application: A "Bottomless" Stack.* We can use a deque to implement a stack that can overflow onto auxiliary storage—tape or disk. We manipulate the front of the deque exactly like a stack: we use INSERT_FRONT to push items on and DELETE_FRONT to pop items off. Everything is as with a stack until an overflow or underflow occurs.

```
INSERT_FRONT: PROCEDURE (VALUE);
   DECLARE VALUE BYTE;
   /* UPDATE FRONT_POINTER */
      IF FRONT_POINTER = @QUEUE THEN
         FRONT_POINTER = @QUEUE + QUEUE_SIZE - 1;
      ELSE
         FRONT_POINTER = FRONT_POINTER - 1;
   /* CHECK FOR OVERFLOW */
      IF FRONT_POINTER = REAR_POINTER THEN
         CALL ERROR (14, @'DEQUE OVERFLOW');
      ELSE
         /* INSERT VALUE */
            FRONT = VALUE;
   END INSERT_FRONT;
```

Program 12-7. INSERT_FRONT inserts its argument at the front of a deque.

```
DELETE__REAR: PROCEDURE (P);
    DECLARE P WORD; /* POINTER TO VALUE*/
            VALUE BASED P BYTE;
    /* CHECK FOR UNDERFLOW */
        IF REAR__POINTER = FRONT__POINTER THEN
            CALL ERROR (15, @ 'DEQUE UNDERFLOW');
        ELSE
            DO;
                /* UPDATE REAR__POINTER*/
                    IF REAR__POINTER = @QUEUE THEN
                        REAR__POINTER = @QUEUE + QUEUE__SIZE - 1;
                    ELSE
                        REAR__POINTER = REAR__POINTER - 1;
                /* GET VALUE */
                    VALUE = REAR;
            END;
END DELETE__REAR;
```

Program 12-8. DELETE__REAR removes the rear item from a deque and stores it at the address pointed to by the argument.

When an overflow occurs, we remove a block of elements from the rear of the deque and transfer them to auxiliary storage. When an underflow occurs, we retrieve the last block that was sent to auxiliary storage, and insert it at the rear of the deque.

We thus have a stack which resides partly in main memory and partly on auxiliary storage. The part that resides in main memory is the deque. Items which have just been pushed on, and may soon be popped off, reside here for quick access. Items further down in the stack, which were pushed on some time ago, and will probably not be needed again for awhile, reside on auxiliary storage.

# Chapter 13
# Strings

A string is a sequence of characters. Inside the computer it is stored as a linear array of character codes.

We could declare a separate linear array for each string. But, for the sake of flexibility, it is often desirable to use one large array for all the strings in a program. We leave it up to the computer system to allocate space from this array for newly formed strings and—just as importantly—to recover the space occupied by strings that are no longer being used.

This chapter describes a set of string manipulation routines that work in this way.

## DESCRIPTORS

Since space for a string is allocated at run time, the address of the string is not known until then. Therefore we must access the string via a pointer. Also, the routines that manipulate strings need to know their lengths. So we describe a string by two things: its length and the address of its leftmost byte.

This combination is known as a *descriptor*. In programming string operations, we use descriptors just as we would numbers or characters or any other data item. We can assign descriptors to variables, for instance, or use them as elements of arrays or components of structures, or pass them as arguments to subroutines and functions and return them as values of functions.

We define the prototype of all descriptors as follows:

DECLARE 1 STRING,
    2 SIZE BYTE,
    2 ADDRESS WORD;

Every descriptor will be declared as being LIKE STRING and therefore having the above structure. By limiting SIZE to one byte, we limit the lengths of our strings to the range 0–255. A string of length 0, the "null string", is sometimes useful. A maximum length of 255 is sufficient for most purposes, and using a not-too-large maximum length gives us a simple way of knowing when a "garbage collection", or recovery of unused space, is needed.

In order to talk about descriptors conveniently, we will adopt the following informal notation. It is not part of any programming language.

We shall denote by "ABCDE" the *descriptor* of a string consisting of the characters A, B, C, D, and E. We must not confuse this with "ABCDE", which denotes a 5 character array containing the codes for A, B, C, D, and E. We may define "ABCDE" as the descriptor D such that

$$D.SIZE = 5$$
$$D.ADDRESS = @\text{"ABCDE"}$$

We shall consider two strings to be "equal" if they consist of the same characters in the same order. Since strings containing the same characters may occur in different parts of memory, it is possible for two strings to be equal even if their descriptors are not.

If X and Y are descriptors, then the notation

$$X \approx Y$$

means that the strings described by the values of X and Y are equal in the sense described above—they contain the same characters in the same order—even though they may be located in different parts of memory, and hence their descriptors may be different. (The SIZE component of the descriptors would be the same, but the address component would differ.)

## DECLARATIONS

The garbage collector routine, which will recover the space occupied by unused strings, needs a table of the addresses of all the descriptors used in the program. The descriptors may be declared anywhere, as long as a table of their address is supplied to the garbage collector. Consider a program which is to use 4 string descriptors: STRING_A, STRING_B, STRING_C, and STRING_D. It would contain the following declarations:

```
DECLARE DESCRIPTOR_COUNT LITERALLY '4',
    1 STRING_A LIKE STRING,
    1 STRING_B LIKE STRING,
    1 STRING_C LIKE STRING,
    1 STRING_D LIKE STRING,
    DESCRIPTORS(DESCRIPTOR_COUNT) WORD
    INITIAL(@STRING_A,@STRING_B,
      @STRING_C,@STRING_D);
```

DESCRIPTORS is the table of addresses that will be used by the garbage collector.

(Note that the descriptors declared inside our string manipulating procedures *do not* have their addresses included in DESCRIPTORS. Only the addresses of descriptors declared in the program that calls the string manipulating procedures are included.)

Finally, we must declare the large array that is to hold all our strings, as well as some useful abbreviations associated with it:

```
DECLARE SPACE_SIZE LITERALLY '1000',
    SPACE(SPACE_SIZE) BYTE,
    SPACE_BEGIN LITERALLY '@SPACE',
    SPACE_END LITERALLY
      '@SPACE + SPACE_SIZE';
```

We also need a pointer to the first unused byte of SPACE. We designate the pointer FREE_POINTER and the byte it points to, FREE:

```
DECLARE FREE_POINTER WORD,
    FREE BASED FREE_POINTER BYTE;
```

Note that SPACE_END − FREE_POINTER is the number of unused bytes remaining. When this number falls below 255, then there may be insufficient space for the next new string to be created, and so a garbage collection must be done to recover space occupied by strings that the program is no longer using.

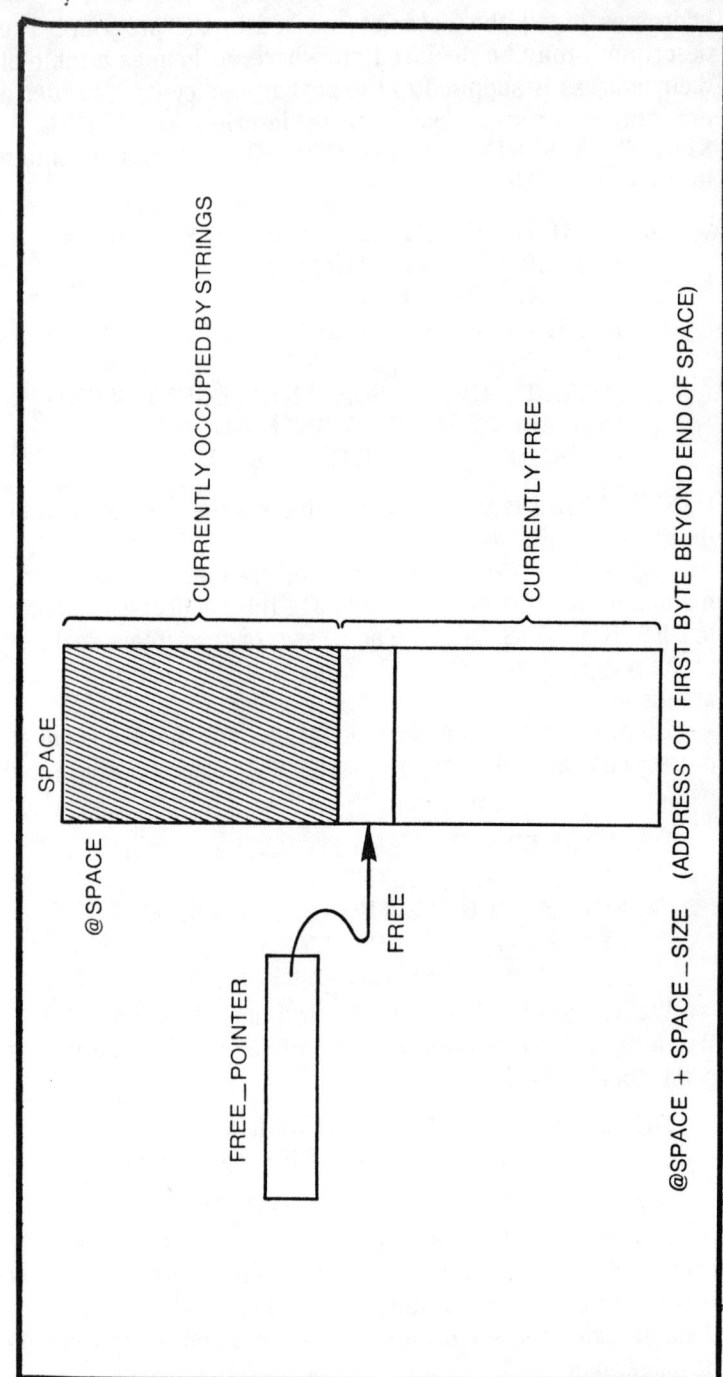

Fig. 13-1. Layout of SPACE.

Fig. 13-1 shows the layout of SPACE. Fig. 13-2 shows some examples of strings and their descriptors. Note that strings may overlap one another.

## STRING INPUT AND OUTPUT

READ_STRING is a function whose one argument is a character which will terminate the string to be read, and which returns as a value the descriptor of the string just read in. Thus.

STRING_A = READ_STRING ('.');

would cause characters to be read until a period was encountered. The characters read—not including the terminating period—would be made into a string, and the descriptor of that string would be returned as a value by READ_STRING and hence assigned to STRING_A.

As before, we use READ_CHAR to get a character from the input device, and we assume that when READ_STRING is called, CHAR already contains the first character of the string to be read.

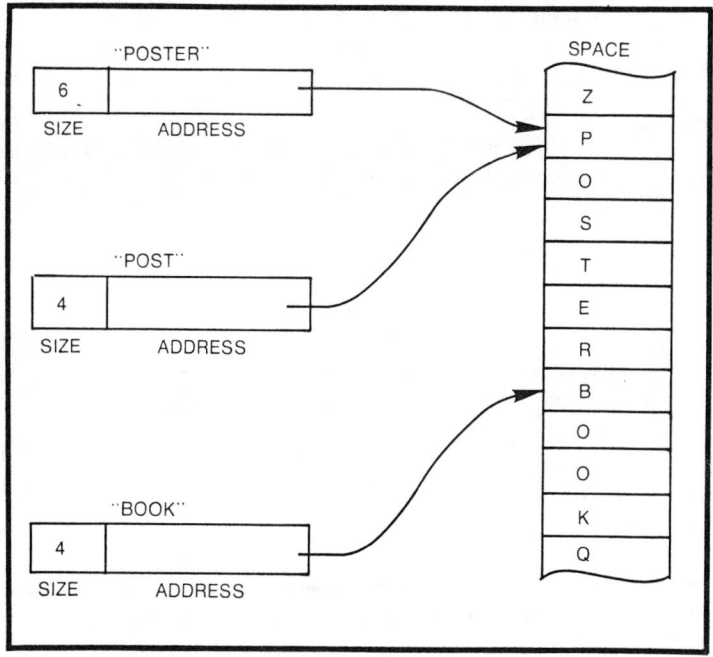

Fig. 13-2. Strings and their descriptors.

205

We start by checking to see if there is room for a string of maximum size, or if a garbage collection must first be performed:

```
IF SPACE_END – FREE_POINTER < 255 THEN
    CALL GARBAGE_COLLECTOR;
```

Let STR be the descriptor of the string that is to be formed. We initialize the components of STR:

```
READ_STRING: PROCEDURE (TERMINATOR) LIKE STRING;
    DECLARE TERMINATOR BYTE,
            1 STR LIKE STRING;
    /* CHECK THAT THERE IS ROOM ENOUGH FOR A STRING OF
        MAXIMUM SIZE (255 BYTES) */
        IF SPACE_END – FREE_POINTER < 255 THEN
            CALL GARBAGE_COLLECTOR;
    /* INITIALIZE THE DESCRIPTOR STR */
        STR.SIZE = 0;
        STR.ADDRESS = FREE_POINTER;
    /* READ IN STRING UNTIL TERMINATOR ENCOUNTERED OR
        MAXIMUM LENGTH REACHED */
        DO WHILE CHAR <> TERMINATOR;
            IF STR.SIZE = 255 THEN
                DO;
                    CALL ERROR (21, @'INPUT STRING TOO LONG');
                    RETURN STR;
                END;
            FREE = CHAR;
            FREE_POINTER = FREE_POINTER + 1;
            STR.SIZE = STR.SIZE + 1;
            CALL READ_CHAR;
        END;
    /* PASS OVER TERMINATOR AND RETURN DESCRIPTOR OF
        STRING READ IN*/
        CALL READ_CHAR;
        RETURN STR;
END READ_STRING;
```

Program 13-1. READ__STRING reads characters until the terminator given as its argument is encountered. The procedure returns the descriptor of the string read in.

STR.SIZE = 0;
STR.ADDRESS = FREE_POINTER;

Now we read in the string, storing the characters in SPACE starting at the position designated by FREE_POINTER (and FREE_POINTER is used throughout the read-in to point to the byte in which the next character will be stored). If STR.SIZE threatens to exceed 255, we announce an error and return. Otherwise, the read in continues until the terminating character is encountered. The terminator is not included in the string being built, but it is passed over, so that when READ_STRING returns, CHAR contains the character following the terminating character.

Program 13-1 shows the complete READ_STRING function.

PRINT_STRING has a single argument, STR, the descriptor of the string to be printed. We use PRINT_CHAR to print the individual characters; we assume that PRINT_CHAR will supply any necessary carriage returns if the string takes up more than one line. Program 13-2 shows the PRINT_STRING procedure.

## OPERATIONS ON STRINGS

We now consider procedures to carry out three operations on strings: concatenation, extraction of a substring, and pattern matching.

```
PRINT_STRING: PROCEDURE (STR);
    DECLARE 1 STR LIKE STRING,
              POINTER WORD,
              VALUE BASED POINTER BYTE;
/*INITIALIZE POINTER */
    POINTER = STR.ADDRESS;
/* PRINT THE CHARACTERS OF THE STRING */
    DO I = 1 TO STR. SIZE;
        CALL PRINT_CHAR(VALUE);
        POINTER = POINTER + 1;
    END;
END PRINT_STRING;
```

Program 13-2. PRINT___STRING prints the string whose descriptor is the argument STR.

*Concatenation.* When we concatenate two strings, we create a new string which consists of the other two joined together, the right end of the first joined to the left end of the second.

Program 13-3 shows the concatenation procedure CAT. Here are some examples of its use:

 CAT ("ABC", "DEF") ≈ "ABCDEF"
 CAT ("BOOK", "S") ≈ "BOOKS"
 CAT ("GOOD", "MORNING") ≈ "GOOD MORNING"

Let STR1 and STR2 be the descriptors of the two strings that are to be joined together, and STR the descriptor of the result. (STR1 and STR2 are the arguments of CAT; STR contains the value CAT will return.)

The size of STR will be the sum of the sizes of STR1 and STR2. We wish to find this sum using *word* arithmetic, so we can detect whether it exceeds the allowed limit of 255. If L is declared to be a word, then:

$$L = STR1.SIZE;$$
$$L = L + STR2.SIZE;$$

If L does not exceed 255, then its value becomes STR.SIZE, the size of the result:

$$STR.SIZE = L;$$

Otherwise, an error is announced and the null string is returned.

If there is insufficient room for the concatenated strings in SPACE, we call the garbage collector to make rooms:

 IF SPACE_END − FREE_POINTER < L THEN
  CALL GARBAGE_COLLECTOR;

The newly created string, consisting of the concatenation of STR1 and STR2, will be built starting at the address contained in FREE_POINTER. Thus

$$STR.ADDRESS = FREE\_POINTER;$$

All that remains is to copy the two strings, one after another, starting at the address contained in FREE_POINTER, and return the already created descriptor of the result, STR.

```
CAT: PROCEDURE (STR1, STR2) LIKE STRING;
    DECLARE 1 STR1 LIKE STRING,      /* FIRST OPERAND */
            1 STR2 LIKE STRING,      /* SECOND OPERAND */
            1 STR LIKE STRING,       /* RESULT */
            (L, POINTER) WORD,
            (VALUE BASED POINTER, I) BYTE
    /* COMPUTE THE LENGTH, L, OF THE RESULT STRING */
        L = STR1.SIZE;
        L = L + STR2.SIZE;
    /* IF LENGTH OF RESULT STRING EXCEEDS MAXIMUM LENGTH,
        ANNOUNCE ERROR AND RETURN NULL STRING. OTHERWISE,
        SET SIZE FIELD OF RESULT STRING */
        IF L > 255 THEN
            DO;
                CALL ERROR (32, @ 'RESULT OF CONCATENATION TOO LONG');
                STR.SIZE = 0;
                RETURN STR;
            END;
        ELSE
            STR.SIZE = L;
    /* CHECK IF THERE IS ENOUGH ROOM FOR RESULT */
        IF SPACE_END - FREE_POINTER < L THEN
            CALL GARBAGE_COLLECTOR;
    /* CONSTRUCT RESULT STRING AND RETURN ITS DESCRIPTOR */
        STR.ADDRESS = FREE_POINTER;
        POINTER = STR1.ADDRESS;
        DO I = 1 TO STR1.SIZE;
            FREE = VALUE;
            POINTER = POINTER + 1;
            FREE_POINTER = FREE_POINTER + 1;
        END;
        POINTER = STR2.ADDRESS;
        DO I = 1 TO STR2.SIZE;
            FREE = VALUE;
            POINTER = POINTER + 1;
            FREE_POINTER = FREE_POINTER + 1;
        END;
        RETURN STR;
END CAT;
```

Program 13-3. CAT concatenates the strings described by its arguments, STR1 and STR2, and returns a descriptor of the result.

```
SUBSTR: PROCEDURE (STR, POSITION, COUNT) LIKE STRING;
    DECLARE 1 STR LIKE STRING,
            1 STR1 LIKE STRING,
            (POSITION, COUNT) BYTE,
            L WORD;
    /* ADJUST POSITION SO THAT LEFTMOST BYTE WILL BE IN
        POSITION ZERO */
        POSITION = POSITION - 1;
    /* CHECK IF SUBSTRING EXTENDS BEYOND STRING */
        L = POSITION;
        L = L + COUNT;
        IF L > STR.SIZE THEN
            DO;
                CALL ERROR (28, @'IMPROPER SUBSTRING SPECIFIED');
                STR1.SIZE = 0; /* NULL STRING */
                STR1.ADDRESS = STR.ADDRESS;
                RETURN STR1;
            END;
    /* CONSTRUCT DESCRIPTOR FOR SUBSTRING AND RETURN IT */
        STR1.SIZE = COUNT;
        STR1.ADDRESS = STR.ADDRESS + POSITION;
        RETURN STR1;
END SUBSTR;
```

Program 13-4. SUBSTR returns a descriptor of the substring of STR specified by POSITION and COUNT

---

*Substrings.* Sometimes we wish to work with only part of a string—a substring. Program 13-4 shows a function SUBSTR which creates a descriptor for a substring and returns that descriptor as a value. No characters are actually manipulated, the characters stored for the string serve for the substring as well. Only the new descriptor need be created.

SUBSTR is passed three arguments: STR, the string from which the substring is to be extracted; POSITION, the position in STR where the substring is to begin; and COUNT, the number of characters in the substring. STR is a descriptor; POSITION and COUNT are bytes. Character positions are numbered from left to right starting with 1 (*not 0*) for the leftmost character in the string.

Here are some examples of the use of SUBSTR:

$$\text{SUBSTR (``CONCATENATION'', 1, 3)} \approx \text{``CON''}$$
$$\text{SUBSTR (``CONCATENATION'', 4, 3)} \approx \text{``CAT''}$$

SUBSTR ("CONCATENATION", 5, 3) ≈ "ATE"
SUBSTR ("CONCATENATION" 8, 6) ≈ "NATION"

Program 13-4 starts subtracting 1 from POSITION to convert it to a more convenient form where the leftmost character is in position 0 rather than position 1. (The reason for numbering from 1 rather than 0 in the first place will be clear when we take up the INDEX function.)

IF POSITION + COUNT exceeds STR.SIZE, then the substring would extend beyond the end of the string, an error. When this condition is detected the error is announced and the null string returned.

With error checking out of the way, we easily construct the substring descriptor:

STR1.SIZE = COUNT;
STR1.ADDRESS = STR.ADDRESS + POSITION;
RETURN STR1;

No new string has been created, only a new descriptor, since the characters for the substring are already present in the string itself. Fig. 13-3 illustrates a string, a substring, and their descriptors.

*Pattern Matching.* Sometimes we wish to locate a substring inside another string, or be informed that no such substring exists. For instance, we might want to know the position of "CAT" inside "CONCATENATION".

This is a special case of what is known as pattern matching. The substring we are searching for is the pattern; we want to see if it matches some substring of a given string, and if so, which substring. String manipulation languages, such as SNOBOL, allow **far** more complex pattern matching than this. But we will stick to the simpler case of matching one string against substrings of another string.

We implement pattern matching with a function INDEX which takes two descriptors, STR1 and STR2, as arguments. If STR2 is a substring of STR1, then the value of INDEX is the position of the first character of STR2 and STR1. If STR2 is not a substring of STR1, then INDEX returns a value of 0.

(And this is why we chose to number character positions starting at 1 instead of 0. We wanted to reverse 0 for the value INDEX returns when its second argument is not a substring of its first.)

Some examples of INDEX:

>INDEX ("CONCATENATION", "CON") = 1
>INDEX ("CONCATENATION", "CAT") = 4
>INDEX ("CONCATENATION", "TEN") = 6
>INDEX ("CONCATENATION", "NATION") = 8
>INDEX ("CONCATENATION", "CATS") = 0

We attempt to match STR2 to a substring of STR1 as follows: Imagine the two strings placed one above the other, and aligned on the left. We match the characters of STR2 against the corresponding characters of STR1. If they are the same, we have a match. Otherwise, we shift STR2 one position to the right, and try again. We repeat the process until either a match is found or until further shifting of STR2 would cause it to extend beyond the right end of STR1.

For instance, INDEX would discover that "TEN" is a substring of "CONCATENATION" as follows:

| | |
|---|---|
| CONCATENATION<br>TEN | No Match |
| CONCATENATION<br> TEN | No Match |
| CONCATENATION<br>  TEN | No Match |
| CONCATENATION<br>   TEN | No Match |
| CONCATENATION<br>    TEN | No Match |
| CONCATENATION<br>     TEN | Match |

INDEX starts by checking to see if STR2 is longer than STR1; if STR2 is longer, it could not possible by a substring of STR1. Hence.

>IF STR2.SIZE > STR1.SIZE THEN RETURN 0;

Let COUNT be the number of different positions in which we place STR2 against STR1 in attempting a match. Let R be a pointer to STR2, and S a pointer to the character in STR1

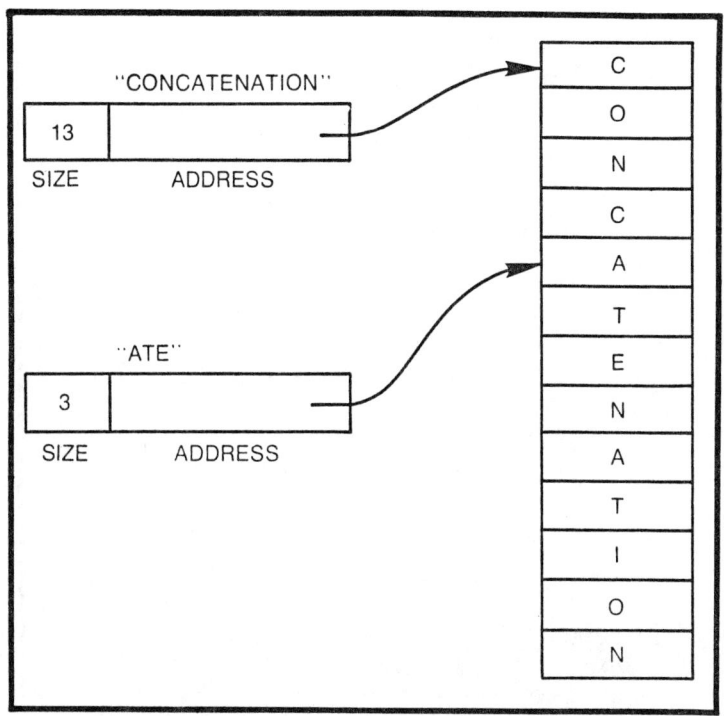

Fig. 13-3. Descriptors for string and substring.

"opposite" the leftmost character of STR2. Then the code for INDEX is:

```
COUNT = STR1.SIZE - STR2.SIZE + 1;
R = STR2.ADDRESS;
DO I = 1 TO COUNT;
    S = STR1.ADDRESS + I - 1;
    IF MATCH (R, S, STR2.SIZE) THEN RETURN I;
END;
RETURN 0;
```

The procedure MATCH (P, Q, N) compares the N-character string pointed to by P with the N-character string pointed to by Q. It returns TRUE if they match, and FALSE if they do not.

The code for MATCH is straightforward. If P_VALUE and Q_VALUE are the bytes pointed to by P and Q, we have:

```
DO J = 1 TO N;
    IF P_VALUE < > Q_VALUE THEN RETURN
```

```
INDEX: PROCEDURE (STR1, STR2) BYTE;
    DECLARE 1 STR1 LIKE STRING,
            1 STR2 LIKE STRING,
            (I, COUNT) BYTE,
            (R, S) WORD;
    /* THE FOLLOWING PROCEDURE MATCHES THE N CHARACTER
        STRING STARTING AT P WITH THE N CHARACTOR STRING
        STARTING AT Q. IT RETURNS TRUE IF THE STRINGS MATCH,
        AND FALSE OTHERWISE */
    MATCH: PROCEDURE (P, Q, N) BYTE;
        DECLARE (P, Q) WORD,
                (P __ VALUE BASED P, Q __ VALUE BASED Q) BYTE,
                (J, N) BYTE;
        DO J = 1 TO N;
            IF P __ VALUE <> Q __ VALUE THEN RETURN FALSE;
            P = P + 1;
            Q = Q + 1;
        END;
        RETURN TRUE;
    END MATCH;
    /* EXECUTION OF INDEX BEGINS HERE */
    /* ELIMINATE TWO SPECIAL CASES */
    IF STR2.SIZE = 0 THEN RETURN 0;
    IF STR2.SIZE > STR1.SIZE THEN RETURN 0;
    /* MATCH STR2 AGAINST STR1 IN ALL POSSIBLE POSITIONS */
    COUNT = STR1.SIZE - STR2.SIZE + 1;
    R = STR2.ADDRESS;
    DO I = 1 TO COUNT;
        S = STR1.ADDRESS + I - 1;
        IF MATCH (R, S, STR2.SIZE) THEN RETURN I;
    END;
    RETURN 0;
END INDEX;
```

Program 13-5. INDEX returns the position of STR2 in STR1, or 0 if STR2 is not a substring of STR1.

```
        FALSE;
        P = P + 1;
        Q = Q + 1;
    END;
    RETURN TRUE;
```

If we reach the last statement, then all characters compared have matched. If any fail to match, return is via the RETURN FALSE statement inside the DO group. Notice that a single failure is enough to assure that the strings do not match.

Program 13-5 shows the complete procedure INDEX. The auxiliary function MATCH is defined inside INDEX, and thus is another example of one procedure defined inside another.

## GARBAGE COLLECTION

During the execution of a program, some of the strings stored in SPACE are abandoned.

For instance, suppose a certain string is referred to by the descriptor STRING_A. If we perform the assignment

$$STRING\_A = STRING\_B;$$

then the former contents of STRING_A is, of course, lost. If no other descriptor referred to the characters in SPACE that STRING_A did, or to some string including them as a substring, then those characters are abandoned: they can never be referred to by the program again.

We would like to recover the space occupied by these abandoned strings. A procedure which accomplishes this is usually referred to as a "garbage collector".

The situation is as shown in the BEFORE part of Fig. 13-4. The shaded areas represent the strings that are currently pointed to by descriptors. The unshaded areas are currently

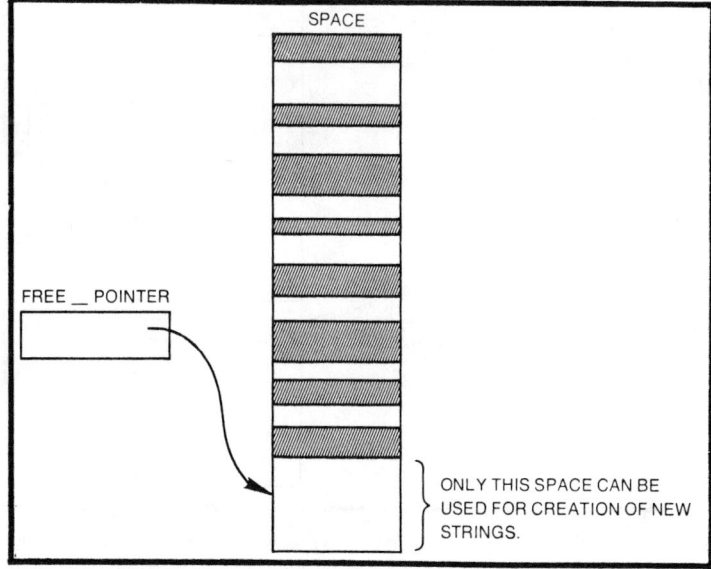

Fig. 13-4. Situation prior to garbage collection. Shaded areas are currently in use. Unshaded areas are not.

unused. The only unshaded area that can be used for new strings is the area at the end of SPACE pointed to by FREE_POINTER.

What we wish to do is to "squeeze" all the currently used strings into a continuous block of storage at the low address end of SPACE. This will leave a continuous block of unused space at the high end of SPACE. Space for new strings can be obtained from this area. The AFTER part of Fig. 13-4 shows the desired situation.

We accomplish our goal by working through SPACE from low address end to high address end, moving each string in use downward—toward the low address end of SPACE—as far as possible.

To know which blocks of bytes in SPACE constitute "strings in use", the garbage collector needs access to all the descriptors used in the program. The table DESCRIPTORS, which contains pointers to all the descriptors declared in the

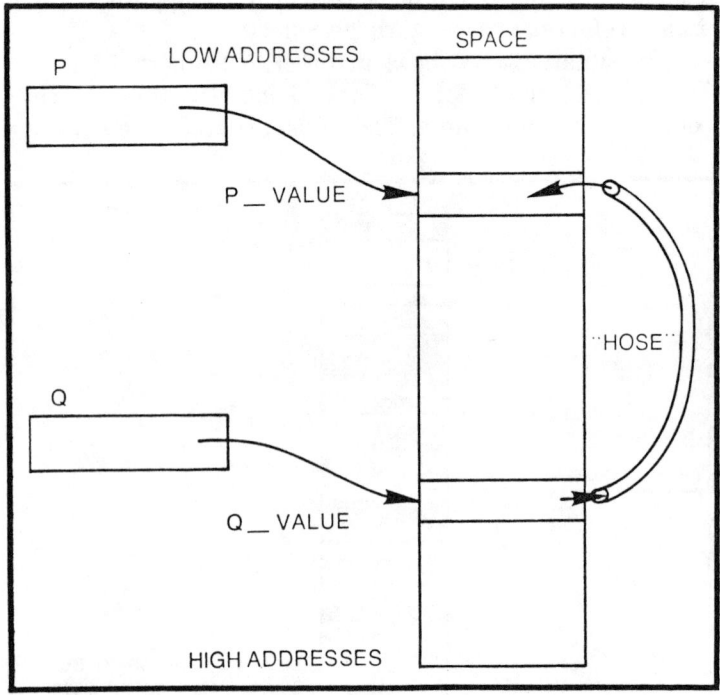

Fig. 13-5. Imaginary hose through which characters are relocated. The distance between the ends of the hose remains fixed as the Q___VALUE end sweeps over the string to be relocated.

program (except those used inside the string manipulation routines themselves) provides this access.

Since we are going to work through SPACE from low address end to high address end, we must process the descriptors in order of increasing ADDRESS components. This means that DESCRIPTORS must be sorted so that DESCRIPTORS(0) points to the descriptor having the lowest ADDRESS component, DESCRIPTORS(1) points to the descriptor having the next highest ADDRESS COMPONENT, and so on.

Since the number of descriptors to be sorted should be small, we can use the so-called *bubble sort* (See Chapter 23). The bubble sort puts a list in order by making repeated passes over it, comparing adjacent items, and exchanging them if they are out of order. The sort terminates when a pass can be made without finding any adjacent items out of order.

Let DP and DQ be *pointers to descriptors*, and let DP_VALUE and DQ_VALUE be the descriptors pointed to. After each pass NO_EXCHANGES will have the value TRUE if no exchanges were made during that pass, and the value FALSE otherwise. LAST (DESCRIPTORS) is the subscript of the last entry in DESCRIPTORS. We have:

```
DO UNTIL NO_EXCHANGES;
   NO_EXCHANGES = TRUE;
   DO I = 0 TO LAST (DESCRIPTORS) − 1;
      DP = DESCRIPTORS(I);
      DQ = DESCRIPTORS(I + 1);
      IF DP_VALUE.ADDRESS > DQ_VALUE.
      ADDRESS   THEN
         DO;
            DESCRIPTORS(I) = DQ;
            DESCRIPTORS(I + 1) = DP;
            NO_EXCHANGES = FALSE;
         END;
   END;
END;
```

We do the actual relocation of strings using two pointers P and Q. Q points to the byte which is about to be relocated, and P points to the position it will be moved to. We can imagine a "hose" extending from Q_VALUE to P_VALUE, with bytes going in to the Q end of the hose and coming out the P end. See Fig. 13-5. We have:

```
P, Q = SPACE_BEGIN;
DO I = 0 TO LAST (DESCRIPTORS);
   DP = DESCRIPTOR(I);
   /* RELOCATE STRING DESCRIBED BY DP_VALUE
END;
```

To relocate the string described by DP_VALUE, we first set Q to the address part of DP_VALUE if it is not already beyond that point:

```
IF DP_VALUE.ADDRESS > Q THEN Q =
         DP_VALUE.ADDRESS;
```

If DP_VALUE.ADDRESS was greater than Q, then Q has skipped over some unused space. DP_VALUE.ADDRESS could be less than or equal to Q, since the corresponding string might be a substring of a string already relocated. Any part of the string whose address falls below Q has already been relocated. Any part whose address is not less than the value of Q needs to be relocated:

```
LIMIT = DP_VALUE.ADDRESS + DP_VALUE.SIZE;
DO WHILE Q < LIMIT;
   P_VALUE = Q_VALUE;
   P = P + 1;
   Q = Q + 1;
END;
```

The amount by which the string described by DP_VALUE was shifted during relocation is Q − P. Thus we adjust DP_VALUE.ADDRESS to point to the new location of the string:

DP_VALUE.ADDRESS = DP_VALUE.ADDRESS − (Q − P)

This completes the relocation process.

We finish up the garbage collector by setting FREE_POINTER to the beginning of the newly collected free space area, and checking to see if enough free space has been collected:

```
FREE_POINTER = P;
IF SPACE_END − FREE_POINTER < 255 THEN
   DO;
      CALL ERROR (22, @'STRING  SPACE
      EXHAUSTED');
      HALT;
   END;
```

```
GARBAGE__COLLECTOR: PROCEDURE;
    DECLARE (P, Q, DP, DQ, LIMIT) WORD;
                (P__VALUE BASED P, Q__VALUE BASED Q) BYTE,
                1 DP__VALUE BASED DP LIKE STRING,
                1 DQ__VALUE BASED DQ LIKE STRING,
                (I, NO__EXCHANGES) BYTE;
        /* SORT POINTERS TO DESCRIPTORS IN ASCENDING ORDER
           ON THE ADDRESS FIELDS OF THE DESCRIPTORS POINTED TO */
            DO UNTIL NO__EXCHANGES;
                NO__EXCHANGES = TRUE;
                DO I = 0 TO LAST (DESCRIPTORS) - 1;
                    DP = DESCRIPTORS (I);
                    DQ = DESCRIPTORS (I + 1);
                    IF DP__VALUE.ADDRESS > DQ__VALUE.ADDRESS THEN
                        DO;
                            DESCRIPTORS (I) = DQ;
                            DESCRIPTORS (I + 1) = DP;
                            NO__EXCHANGES = FALSE;
                        END;
                END;
            END;

        /* RELOCATE STRINGS */
            P, Q = SPACE__BEGIN;
            DO I = 0 TO LAST (DESCRIPTORS);
                DP = DESCRIPTORS|(I);
                /* RELOCATE STRING WHOSE DESCRIPTOR IS DP__VALUE */
                IF DP__VALUE.ADDRESS > Q THEN
                    Q = DP__VALUE.ADDRESS;
                LIMIT = DP__VALUE.ADDRESS + DP__VALUE.SIZE;
                DO WHILE Q < LIMIT;
                    P__VALUE = Q__VALUE;
                    P = P + 1;
                    Q = Q + 1;
                END;
                DP__VALUE.ADDRESS = DP__VALUE.ADDRESS - (Q - P);
            END;
        /* SET FREE__POINTER AND CHECK TO SEE THAT ENOUGH SPACE
           HAS BEEN RECOVERED */
            FREE__POINTER = P;
            IF SPACE__END - FREE__POINTER < 255 THEN
                DO;
                    CALL ERROR (22, @ 'STRING SPACE EXHAUSTED');
                    HALT;
                END;
    END GARBAGE__COLLECTOR;
```

Program 13-6. GARBAGE____COLLECTOR recovers currently unused string space.

The statement HALT indicates that the program is to be terminated, either by stopping the computer or returning control to the operating system. Running out of string space is a "fatal" error: program execution cannot continue.

Program 13-6 shows the complete GARBAGE__COLLECTOR procedure.

# Chapter 14
# Chains

**PLEXES**

A *plex* is a set of blocks of memory such that each block contains one or more pointers to other blocks. The pointers serve to link the blocks together, as shown in Fig. 14-1. The links can represent relations between the objects represented by the memory blocks.

The memory blocks that make up a plex are called *nodes*. In our programming language we use structures to describe blocks of memory. Therefore, a node is defined by means of a structure declaration. Most commonly, all the nodes of a plex have the same structure, and hence one structure declaration will serve for all. However, plexes made up of nodes having different structures are also possible.

At least one component of a structure that defines a node will always be a pointer to another node.

In later chapters we will see how to use plexes to implement branching structures (trees) and network-like structures (graphs). But for the present, we will see how to use plexes to implement lists. This might seem unnecessary, since we already know how to implement lists using linear arrays. But in fact there are several advantages to implementing lists as plexes:

1) We can insert or delete an element at some point other than the ends of the list.

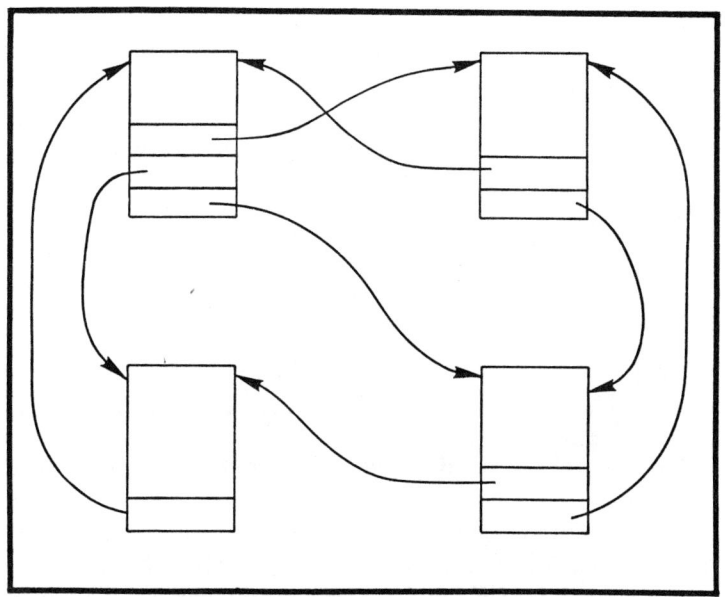

Fig. 14-1. A plex. Each pointer occupies one word.

2) We can join items into a list without regard to their actual location in memory.

3) We can arrange for an item to be on several different lists at the same time, without duplicating it.

Lists implemented as plexes are called *linked lists* or *chains*. Closely related to these are *rings*, where the last element of the list is linked back to the first.

## CHAINS AND RINGS

*Singly Linked Chains.* A singly linked chain—or simply a chain—is the simplest kind of linked list. Each node of the chain has the following structure:

DECLARE 1 NODE,
        2 DATA,
           /* SUBDIVISIONS OF DATA */
        2 LINK WORD;

The DATA component of a node contains all the useful information. It may consist of a single byte or word or—as implied above—it may be subdivided into smaller structures.

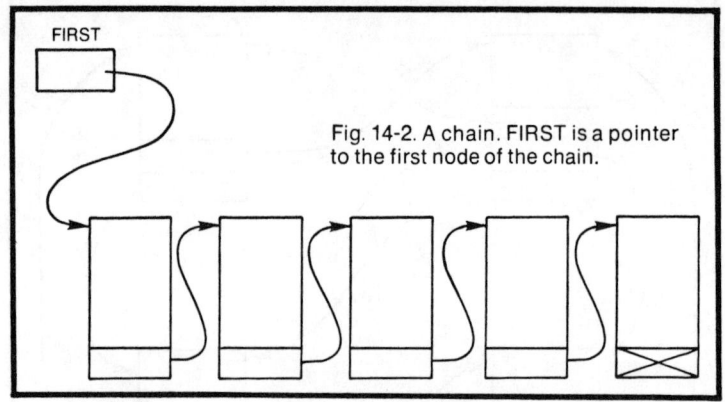

Fig. 14-2. A chain. FIRST is a pointer to the first node of the chain.

The details of the subdivision will, of course, depend on the application.

The LINK component of node contains the pointer to the next node on the chain. The LINK component of the last node contains in its LINK field a special value called a *sentinel*, which indicates the end of the chain. Often this value is chosen to be 0, since address 0 is rarely an appropriate location for a node. This sentinel value is often given the name NIL:

DECLARE NIL LITERALLY '0';

Figure 14-2 illustrates a chain. The chain is accessed through a pointer to its first node—FIRST in Fig. 14-2. Pointers to the first nodes play much the same role for chains as the descriptors in the last chapter did for strings.

An arrow connects each LINK component to the node that it points to. A cross mark in the LINK component of a node indicates that the value of the LINK component for that node is NIL.

Operations on the nodes of chains—such as deletion—usually have to treat the first node as a special case. It is therefore convenient to begin each chain with a *header* node, which is never deleted and never has anything inserted in front of it. Such operations are carried out only on the remaining nodes, none of which must be treated as a special case.

Figure 14-3 shows a singly linked chain with a header. The DATA component of the header—which is shown shaded here—can contain useful information about the entire chain, such as a name for it, the number of nodes on it, or a pointer to its last node.

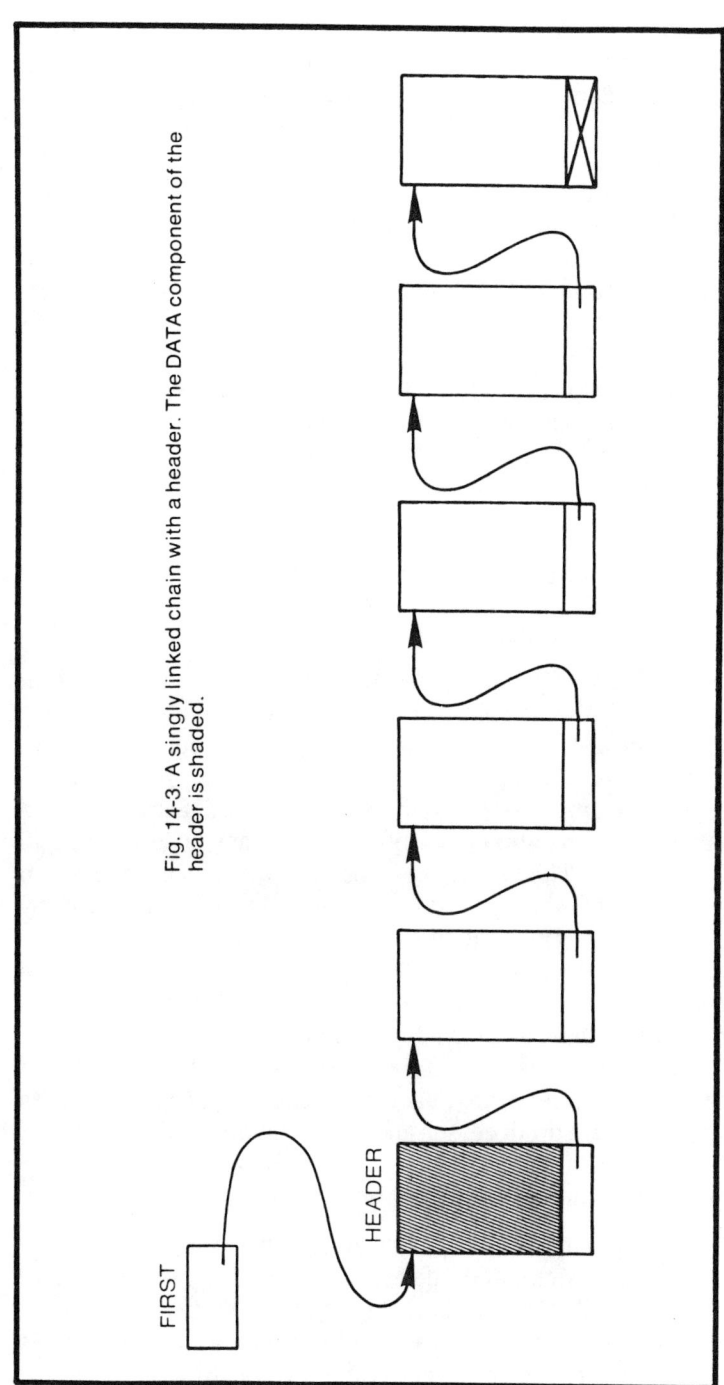

Fig. 14-3. A singly linked chain with a header. The DATA component of the header is shaded.

*Rings.* In a singly linked chain the links allow us to work through the chain from beginning to end, but not in the reverse direction. Sometimes we wish to get back to the beginning of a chain—particularly to the header—from somewhere inside it. One way to provide this capability is to join the last node to the header node, as shown in Fig. 14-4. The resulting data structure is known as a ring.

Notice that the last node of a ring does not contain the sentinel NIL in its LINK, but just a pointer back to the header. Thus it is essential that the header node be distinguishable from the others, lest a program working through the chain circulate forever. In short, the header must act as the sentinel.

For instance, we might reserve a component of each node to indicate whether or not it is the header:

DECLARE 1 NODE,
    2 DATA,
        /* SUBDIVISIONS OF DATA */
    2 HEADER BYTE,
    2 LINK WORD;

NODE.HEADER could have the value TRUE if the node in question is the header node, and FALSE otherwise. Often a spare *bit*—rather than a whole byte—can be found to perform this service.

*Rings with Pointers to the Header Record.* Sometimes it is important to be able to get quickly from any node of a ring to the header. This sometimes occurs when one node is an element of several rings. We may access the node by searching one ring, and then need to access the header of some other ring containing it. We can assure quick access to the header from any node by providing each node with a pointer to the header node, as shown in Fig. 14-5.

*Doubly Linked Chains.* In a doubly linked—or two-way—chain or ring, each node contains two links: one to its immediate predecessor and one to its immediate successor. Figure 14-6 illustrates a doubly linked chain.

Double linking is used for three reasons:

1) We can move both forward and backward in the chain.
2) Insertion and deletion operations become more flexible, as we shall see in the next section.
3) A chain is only as strong as its weakest link. If a link is given an incorrect value, through a program or

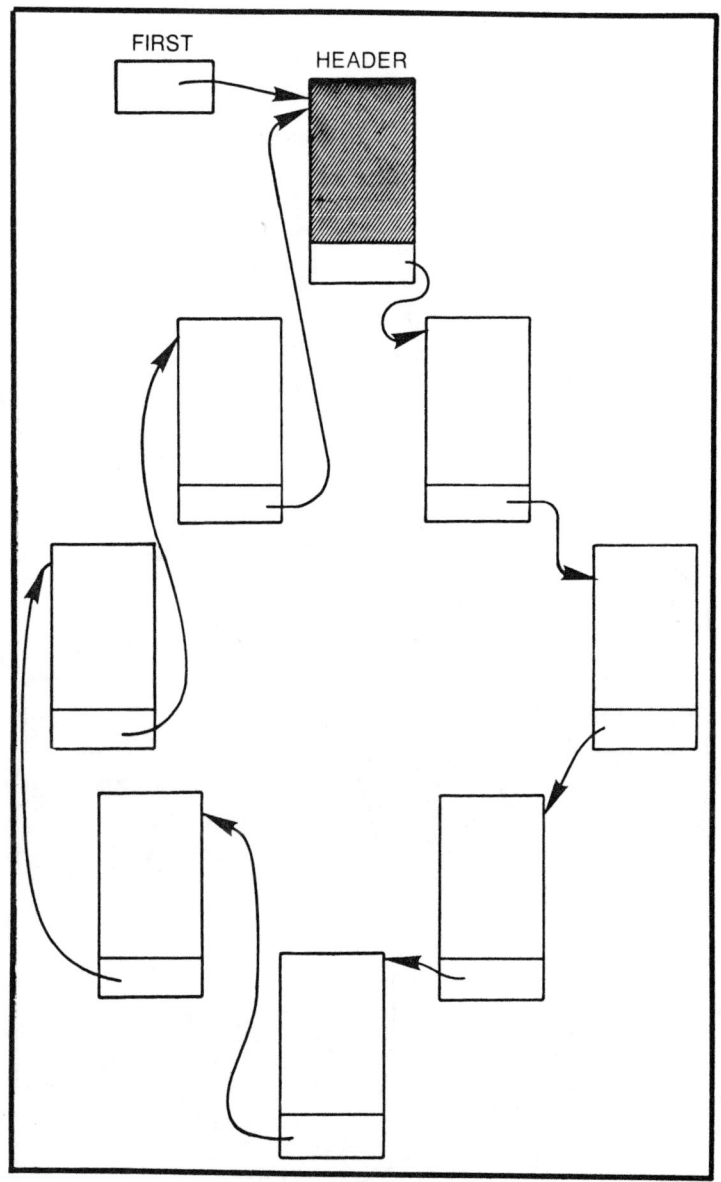

Fig. 14-4. A ring.

machine error, then much data could be lost. Also the program could "go wild" by trying to follow an erroneous link. With double linking we can check the correctness of links. After following the forward link

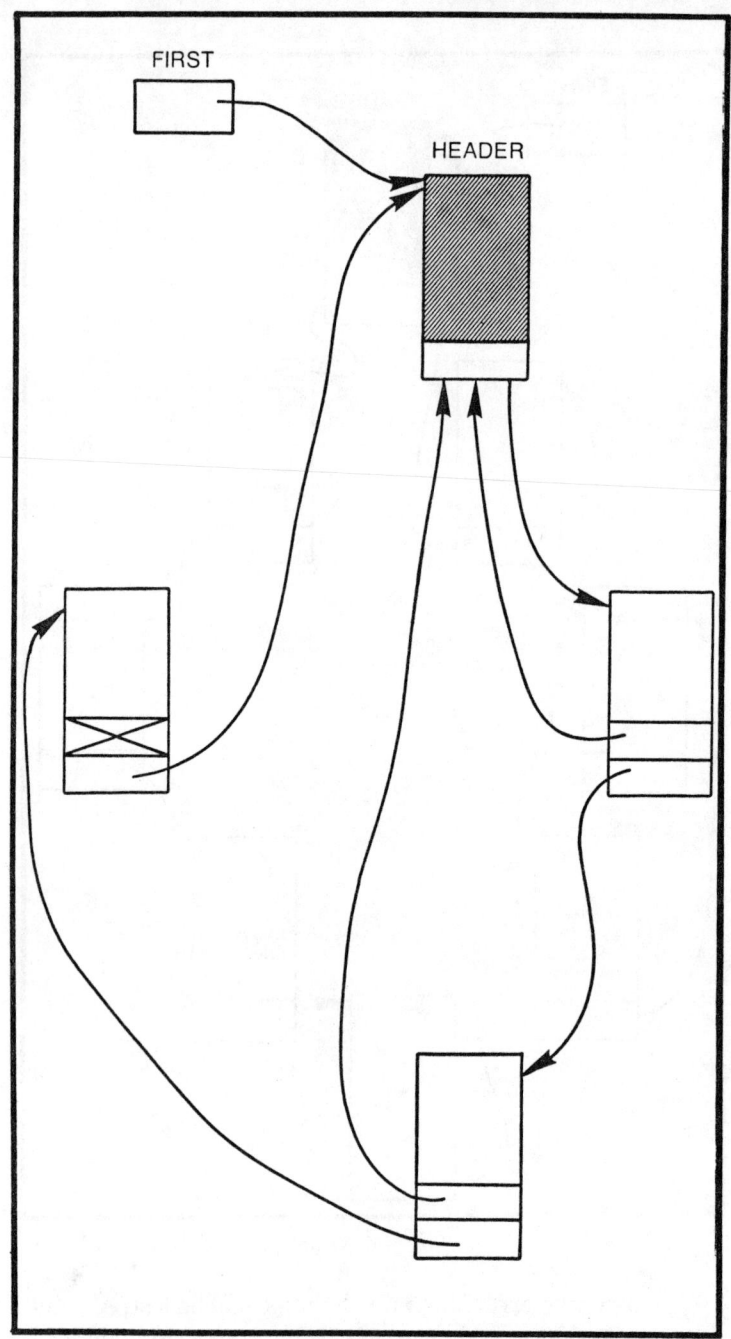

Fig. 14-5. A ring with pointers to the header.

in one record we can check to see if the backward link in the next record points back to the record we just left. If it does not, then something is amiss. But if the backward links are all correct, then the chain is still intact, and the forward links can be corrected. Obviously the same argument holds with "forward" and "backward" interchanged.

## INSERTION AND DELETION

*The Free Space List.* When a program that processes chains or rings first begins to execute, it links together all the nodes in the memory area reserved for chains into a *free space list*. When we wish to insert a new node into a chain, we obtain the node to be inserted from the free space list. When we delete a node from a chain, we return it to the free space list. The free space list actually functions as a *stack*, since we *push* deleted nodes onto it and *pop* off nodes to be used for insertions.

Let FREE be the pointer to the first nod on the free space list. When we need a new node we first check to see if FREE is NIL; if it is, then "free space exhausted" is announced. Otherwise, we set a pointer P to point to the first node on the free space list

$$P = FREE;$$

and set FREE to point to the next node

$$FREE = FREE - > NODE.LINK;$$

thus removing the first node from the free space list. (See Fig. 14-7.) P now points to the node which was removed, and which may be used for an insertion.

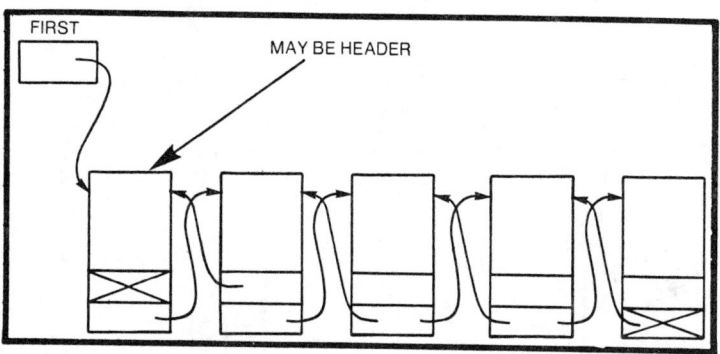

Fig. 14-6. A doubly linked chain.

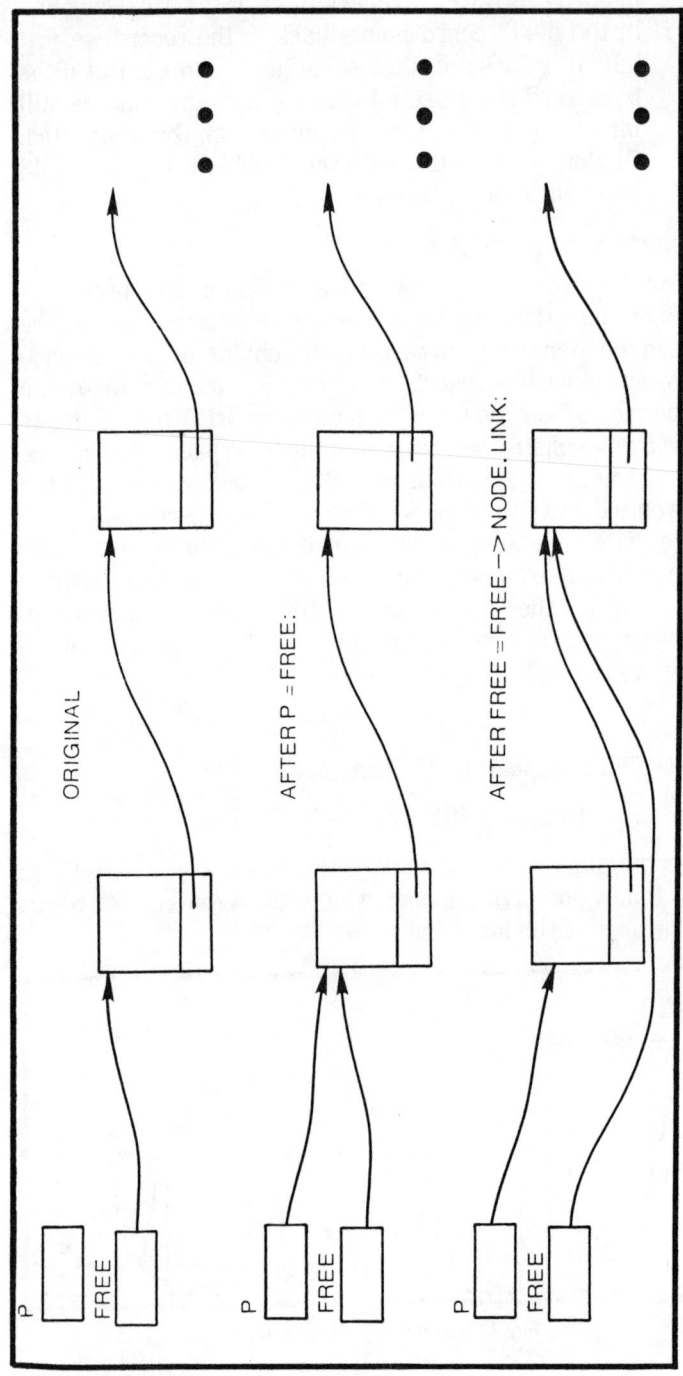

Fig. 14-7. Obtaining a new node from the free space list.

Suppose P now points to a node which has just been deleted from a chain, and which we wish to restore to the free space list. We first set the link of that node to point to the current first node on the free space list

P − > NODE.LINK = FREE;

and then set FREE to point to the new node, which now becomes the first node on the free space list:

FREE = P;

(See Fig. 14-8.)

These statements are the basis of Program 14-1, NEW_NODE, and Program 14-2, DISPOSE_OF.

NEW_NODE is a function with no arguments. It removes the first node on the free space list, as described above, and returns a pointer to that node as its value. Thus

P = NEW_NODE;

will set P to point to a new node obtained from the free space list.

DISPOSE_OF is a subroutine which takes one argument, a pointer to a node to be returned to the free space list.

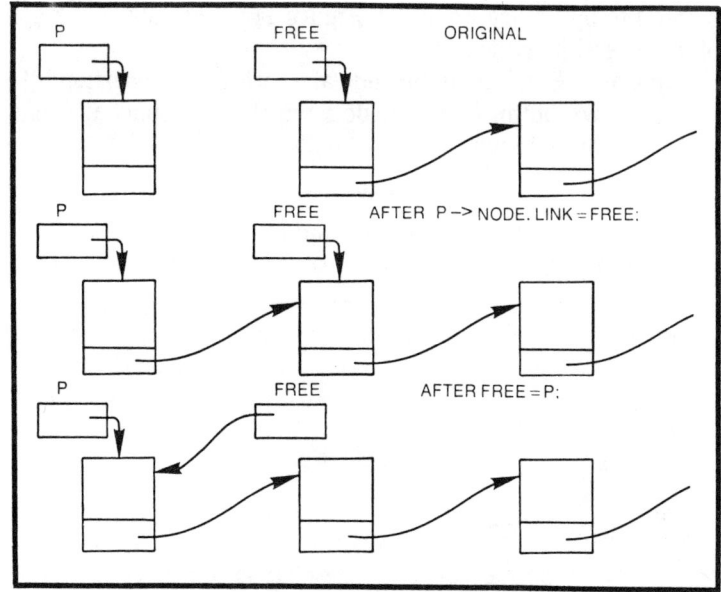

Fig. 14-8. Returning a deleted node to the free space list.

```
NEW_NODE: PROCEDURE WORD;
    DECLARE P WORD;
    /* CHECK IF FREE SPACE IS EXHAUSTED */
        IF FREE = NIL THEN
            CALL ERROR (20, @'FREE SPACE EXHAUSTED');
    /* SET P TO POINT TO FIRST NODE ON FREE SPACE LIST */
        P = FREE;
    /* THE FREE SPACE LIST NOW BEGINS WITH THE NODE FOLLOWING
       FREE -> NODE LINK */
       FREE = FREE -> NODE.LINK;
    /* RETURN POINTER TO NODE OBTAINED */
       RETURN P;
END NEW_NODE;
```

Program 14-1. NEW_NODE obtains a node from the free space list, and returns a pointer to it.

---

DISPOSE_OF adds the node to the beginning of the free space list as described above. Thus

$$\text{CALL DISPOSE\_OF (P)};$$

will return the node pointed to by P to the free space list.

*Singly Linked Chains.* Program 14-3 shows the procedure INSERT_AFTER (P), which inserts a new node after the one pointed to by its argument, P. Figure 14-9 illustrates the steps of the insertion with diagrams.

Initially, P points to the node after which the insertion is to be made. We obtain a new node from the free space list, and set Q to point to it, with:

$$Q = \text{NEW\_NODE};$$

Q -> NODE (the node pointed to by Q) is the node to be inserted. We must link it in between P -> NODE and the

---

```
DISPOSE_OF: PROCEDURE (P);
    DECLARE P WORD;
    /* INSERT P -> NODE AT THE BEGINNING OF THE FREE SPACE
       LIST */
        P -> NODE.LINK = FREE;
        FREE = P;
END DISPOSE_OF;
```

Program 14-2. DISPOSE_OF returns the node pointed to by its argument to the free space list.

```
INSERT_AFTER: PROCEDURE (P) WORD;
   DECLARE (P, Q) WORD;
   /* GET A NEW NODE */
      Q = NEW_NODE;
   /* LINK Q -> NODE INTO CHAIN FOLLOWING P -> NODE */
      Q -> NODE.LINK = P -> NODE.LINK;
      P -> NODE.LINK = Q;
   /* RETURN POINTER TO NEWLY INSERTED NODE */
      RETURN Q;
END INSERT_AFTER;
```

Program 14-3. INSERT_AFTER inserts a new node following the one pointed to by its argument, and returns a pointer to the inserted node.

present successor of $P -> NODE$. We first set the LINK of $Q -> NODE$ to point to the present successor of $P -> NODE$:

$$Q -> NODE.LINK = P -> NODE.LINK;$$

Next we set the LINK of $P -> NODE$ to point to $Q -> NODE$:

$$P -> NODE.LINK = Q;$$

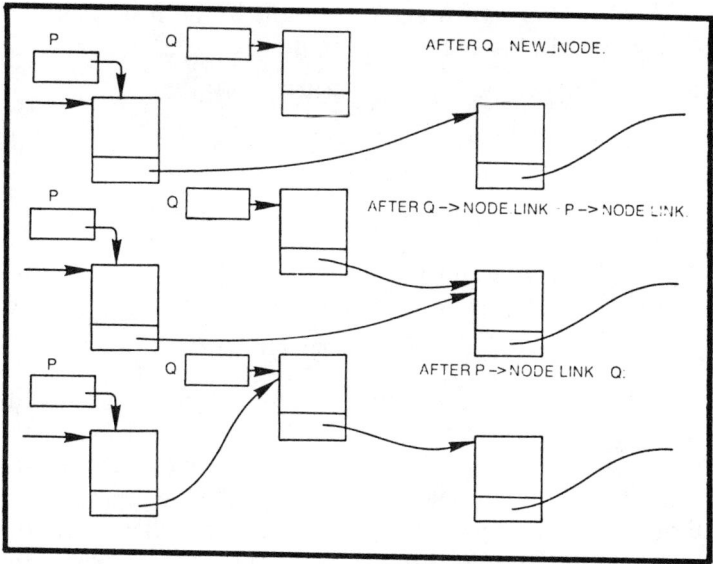

Fig. 14-9. Insertion in a singly linked chain.

```
DELETE__AFTER: PROCEDURE (P);
   DECLARE P WORD;
   /* SET Q TO POINT TO THE NODE TO BE DELETED */
      Q = P -> NODE.LINK;
   /* CHECK THAT WE ARE NOT TRYING TO DELETE BEYOND
      THE END OF THE CHAIN */
      IF Q = NIL THEN RETURN;
   /* ROUTE THE POINTER FROM P -> NODE AROUND Q -> NODE
      TO THE FOLLOWING NODE */
      P -> NODE.LINK = Q -> NODE.LINK;
   /*RETURN Q -> NODE TO THE FREE SPACE LIST */
      CALL DISPOSE__OF (Q);
END DELETE__AFTER;
```

Program 14-4. DELETE__AFTER deletes the node following the one pointed to by its argument.

---

Q -> NODE is now linked in place; we return the pointer to it, Q, as the value of INSERT__AFTER (P).

The deletion routine DELETE__AFTER (P) is shown in Program 14-4. Figure 14-10 illustrates the steps of the deletion procedure.

We are to delete the node following P -> NODE. We first check that such a node exists (P -> NODE.LINK < > NIL). We then set Q to point to the node following P -> NODE, the one to be deleted:

$$Q = P -> NODE.LINK;$$

The LINK of P -> NODE is now "routed around" Q -> NODE to the following node:

$$P -> NODE.LINK = Q -> NODE.LINK;$$

Q -> NODE has now been bypassed; all that remains to be done is to return it to the free space list:

$$CALL\ DISPOSE\_OF\ (Q);$$

With a singly linked chain we can only insert a new node *after* the one pointed to be P, or delete the node *following* the one pointed to by P. This is seldom convenient. In working through a chain, we usually want to delete the current node, the one we have a pointer to, and not the one following it. And for insertion, we must usually pass the position where a node should go before realizing the need for its insertion.

One solution is to work through the chain using two pointers, one of which is always one node ahead of the other. When examining a node, for whatever purpose is at hand, we use the leading pointer. When doing an insertion or deletion, we use the trailing pointer as the argument of the insertion or deletion routine.

*Doubly Linked Chains.* The problem mentioned above may be resolved by using a doubly linked chain, which allows us to delete a designated record, or insert a new record either before or after it.

For doubly linked chains we redefine NODE by:

```
DECLARE 1 NODE,
          2 DATA,
            /* SUBDIVISIONS OF DATA */
          2 LLINK WORD,
          2 RLINK WORD;
```

NODE.LLINK points to the predecessor of NODE; NODE.RLINK points to its successor.

As before, we assume the existence of a free space list containing a supply of nodes of the type just defined. We also

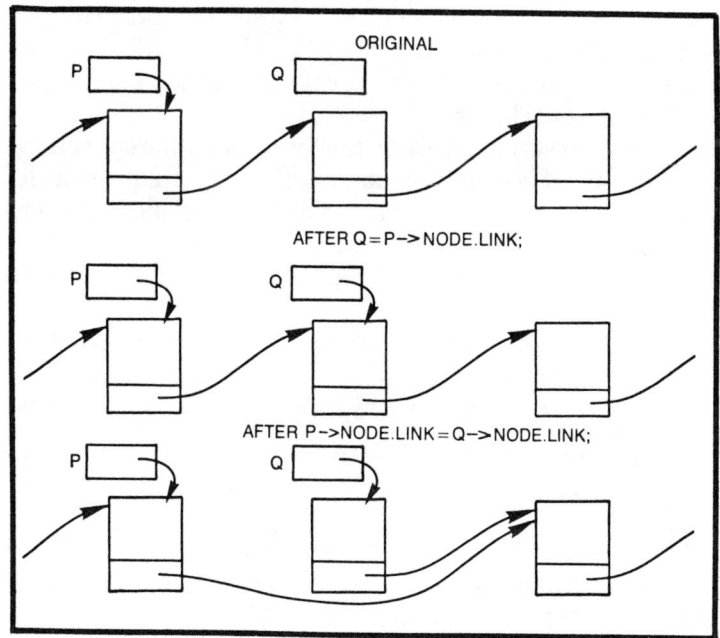

Fig. 14-10. Deletion from a singly linked chain.

```
INSERT_BEFORE: PROCEDURE (P) WORD;
    DECLARE (P, Q, R) WORD;
    /* GET A NEW NODE */
        Q = NEW_NODE;
    /* SET R TO POINT TO THE NODE PRECEEDING P -> NODE */
        R = P -> NODE.LLINK;
    /* INSERT Q -> NODE BETWEEN R -> NODE AND P -> NODE */
        /* SET LEFT LINKS */
            P -> NODE.LLINK = Q;
            Q -> NODE.RLINK = Q;
        /* SET RIGHT LINKS */
            R -> NODELRLINK = Q;
            Q -> NODE.RLINK = P;
    /* RETURN POINTER TO INSERTED NODE */
        RETURN Q;
END INSERT_BEFORE;
```

Program 14-5. INSERT_BEFORE inserts a node before the one pointed to by its argument, and returns a pointer to the inserted node.

---

assume routines NEW_NODE and DISPOSE_OF (P) which function the same as for singly linked chains. (Often the free space list is only singly linked, using just one of the links, say RLINK. In that case NEW_NODE and DISPOSE_OF (P) are, except for minor changes in notation, exactly the same as for singly linked chains.)

We may insert a node either before or after the one pointed to by P. Let us concentrate on insertion *before* a given node, since this is the operation that doubly linked chains offer and singly linked ones do not. Program 14-5 shows the procedure INSERT_BEFORE (P), and Fig. 14-11 illustrates the details of the insertion.

As before, we obtain a new node from the free space list and set Q to point to it:
$$Q = NEW\_NODE;$$

It is also convenient to have a pointer, R, to the node *preceding* P -> NODE:
$$R = P -> NODE.LLINK;$$

Q -> NODE is to be inserted between R -> NODE and P -> NODE. First, we set the left links
$$P -> NODE.LLINK = Q;$$
$$Q -> NODE.LLINK = R;$$

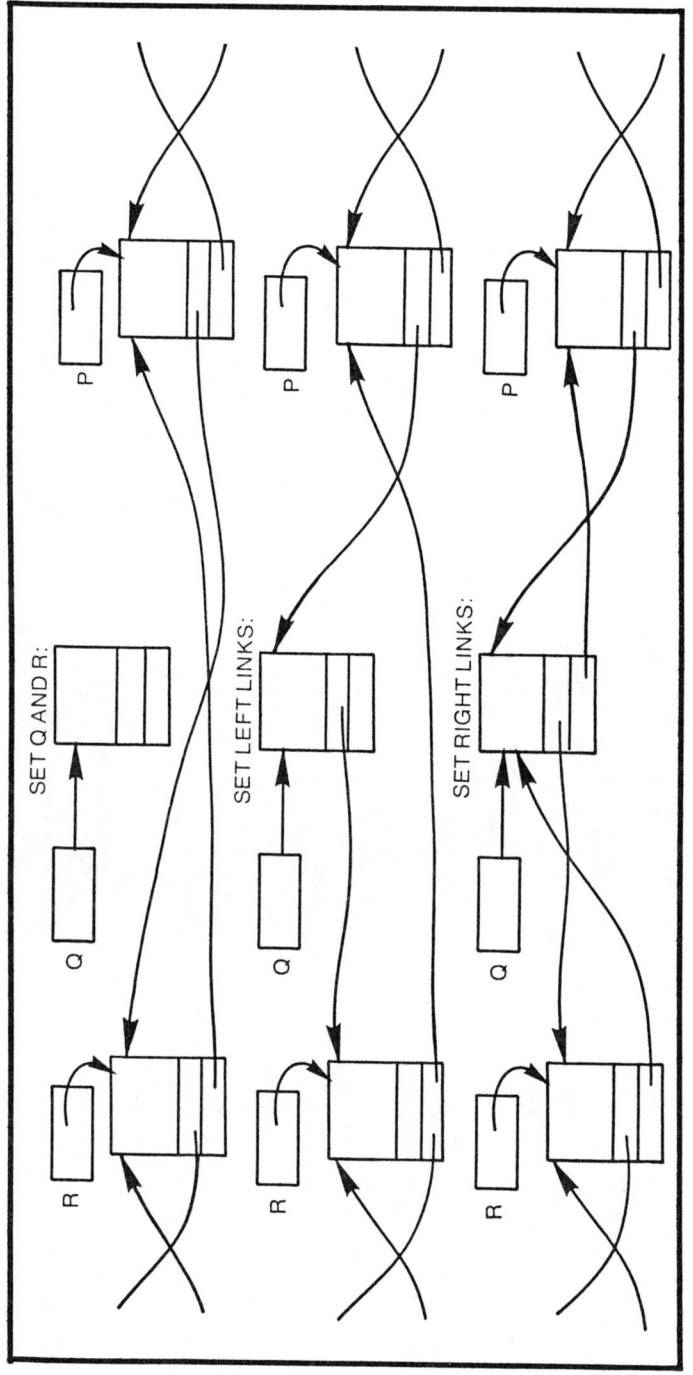

Fig. 14-11. Insertion in a doubly linked chain.

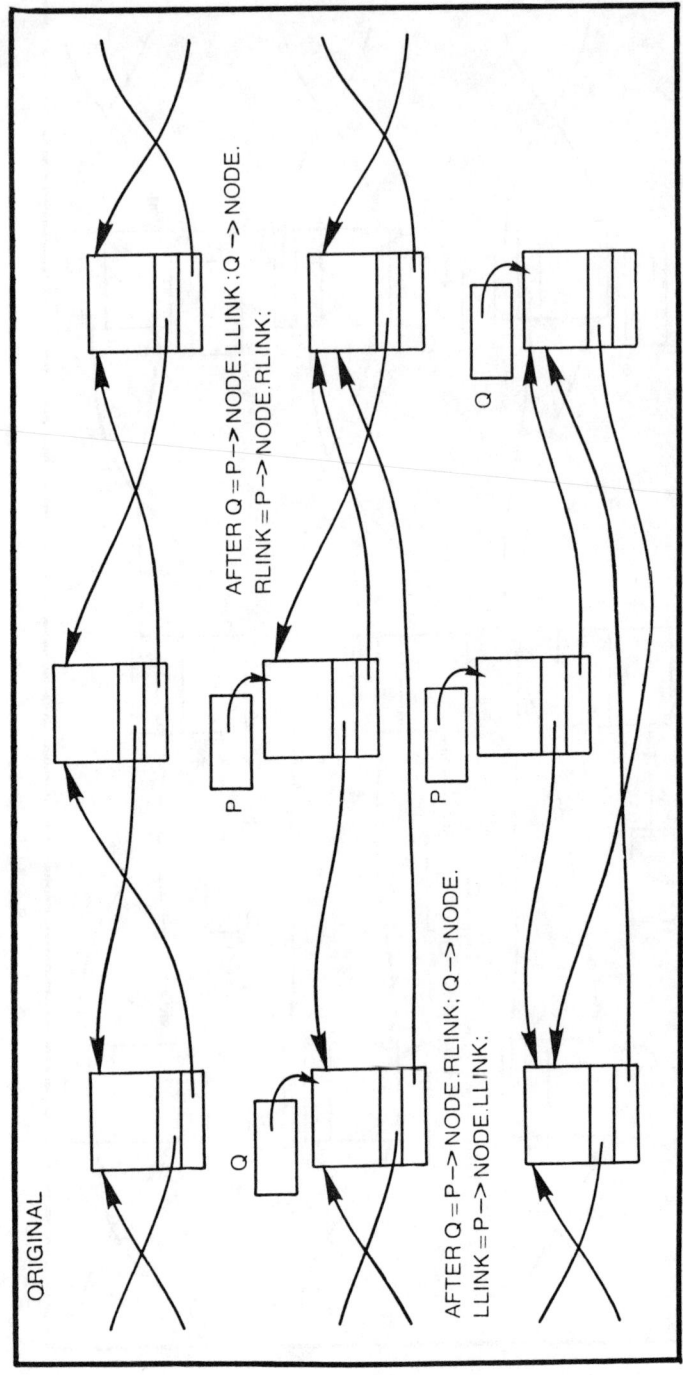

Fig. 14-12. Deletion from a doubly linked chain.

```
DELETE: PROCEDURE (P);
    DECLARE (P, Q) WORD;
    /* SET THE RIGHT LINK OF THE NODE PRECEDING P -> NODE
        TO BYPASS P -> NODE */
        Q = P -> NODE.LLINK;
        Q -> NODE.RLINK = P -> NODE.RLINK;
    /* SET THE LEFT LINK OF THE NODE FOLLOWING P -> NODE
        TO BYPASS P -> NODE. SINCE P -> NODE MAY BE THE LAST
        NODE ON THE CHAIN, WE MUST CHECK TO SEE IF FOLLOWING
        NODE EXISTS */
        Q = P -> NODE.RLINK;
        IF Q <> NIL THEN
            Q -> NODE.LLINK = P -> NODE.LLINK;
    /* RETURN P -> NODE TO FREE SPACE LIST */
        CALL DISPOSE _ OF (P);
END DELETE;
```

Program 14-6. DELETE deletes the node pointed to by its argument.

and then the right links:

$$R -> NODE.RLINK = Q;$$
$$Q -> NODE.RLINK = P;$$

The routine returns with the value of Q, the pointer to the node just inserted.

The deletion procedure for doubly linked chains is DELETE (P), which deletes the node pointed to by P, not the one before or after it. Program 14-6 shows the procedure, and Fig. 14-12 illustrates the steps of the deletion.

P points to the node to be deleted. We first set the right link of the preceding node to bypass P -> NODE:

$$Q = P -> NODE.LLINK;$$
$$Q -> NODE.RLINK = P -> NODE.RLINK;$$

Next we set the left link of the following node to bypass P -> NODE. If we are deleting the last node on a chain, the following node may not exist, a situation we must check for:

$$Q = P -> NODE.RLINK;$$
IF Q <> NIL THEN
$$Q -> NODE.LLINK = P -> NODE.LLINK;$$

P -> NODE has now been bypassed and we are free to return it to the free space list:

$$CALL\ DISPOSE\_OF\ (P);$$

# Chapter 15
# Trees

After linear arrays, trees are the most widely used data structures in computer science. Trees can be used to represent:

1) hierarchical structures
2) nested structures
3) branching structures
4) converging structures

**DEFINITIONS**

Fig. 15-1 illustrates a tree. Notice that it is drawn upside downwards as compared to trees in nature. Natural trees branch upward; computer peoples' trees branch downward.

The circles in Fig. 15-1 are called *nodes*. Beyond this, we draw on two sources for metaphors with which to talk about trees.

From natural trees we appropriate the terms *root* (the topmost node), *leaves* (the bottommost nodes), and *branches* (the lines connecting the nodes).

From family trees we take the terms *parent, child, twin* and *descendant*. The family trees referred to are *lineal charts*, which show all the descendants of a single person, rather than the more familiar *pedigrees*, which show a single person's ancestors.

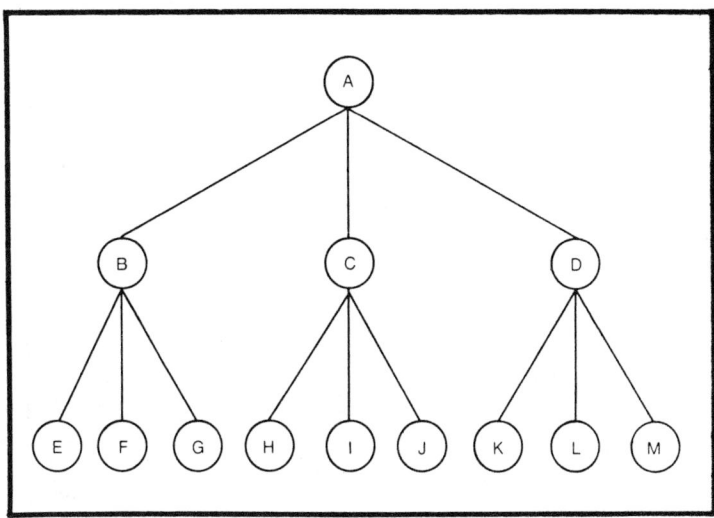

Fig. 15-1. A tree. The "root" of the tree is at the top, and its "leaves" are at the bottom.

In Fig. 15-1, A is the root of the tree, and E, F, G, H, I, J, K, L, and M are its leaves. A is the parent of B, C, and D; consequently, B, C, and D are the children of A. Similarly, E, F, and G are children of B, and so on. All the nodes other than A are descendants of A.

All the children of a given parent are *twins*. Thus B, C, and D are twins, E, F, and G are twins, and so on.

In the older literature the words *father, son* and *brother* are used in place of parent, child, and twin. Modern writers—fearful of being branded sexists, no doubt—use *parent, child,* and *twin* or *parent, descendant,* and *sibling,* and *descendant* serves best when it includes remote as well as immediate descendants.

Each node in a tree occurs on a certain *level*. Level 1 is the level of the root; level 2 is the level of the root's children, level 3 is the level of the root's children's children, and so on. We define the level of every node with the following two statements:

1) The level of the root is 1.
2) The level of any node is the level of its parent plus 1.

If we take a node from a tree, together with all its descendants, we have a *subtree* of the original tree. Fig. 15-2 shows all the subtrees of a tree.

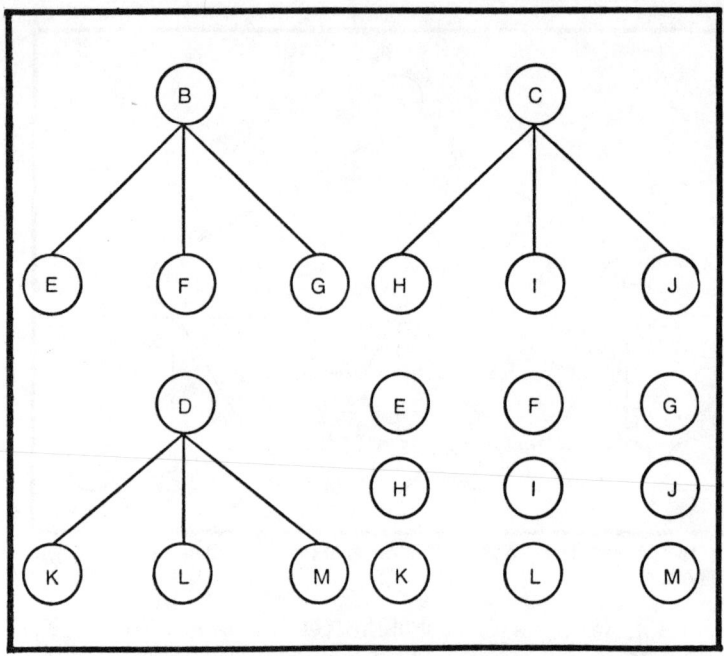

Fig. 15-2. The subtrees of the tree shown in Fig. 15-1.

A collection of trees is called a *forest* (back to nature again!).

A tree in which each node has exactly two children is called a *binary tree*. We label the children of each node the *left child* and the *right child*, depending on their left-to-right order in a diagram of the tree. The *left child* and all its descendants constitutes the *left subtree* of the node in question; the *right subtree* is defined similarly. Figure 15-3 illustrates a binary tree.

## LINEAR REPRESENTATIONS OF TREES

Trees may be represented in memory either as linear arrays or as plexes. The plexes are more flexible and generally useful, but the linear representations are particularly well suited for some applications.

*The Complete Binary Tree.* A binary tree is complete if no nodes are missing, if every node that is not a leaf has both a left child and a right child.

Now consider the complete binary tree shown in Fig. 15-4. Notice how the nodes are numbered: The root is node 1; its children are numbered, from left to right, 2 and 3; on the next

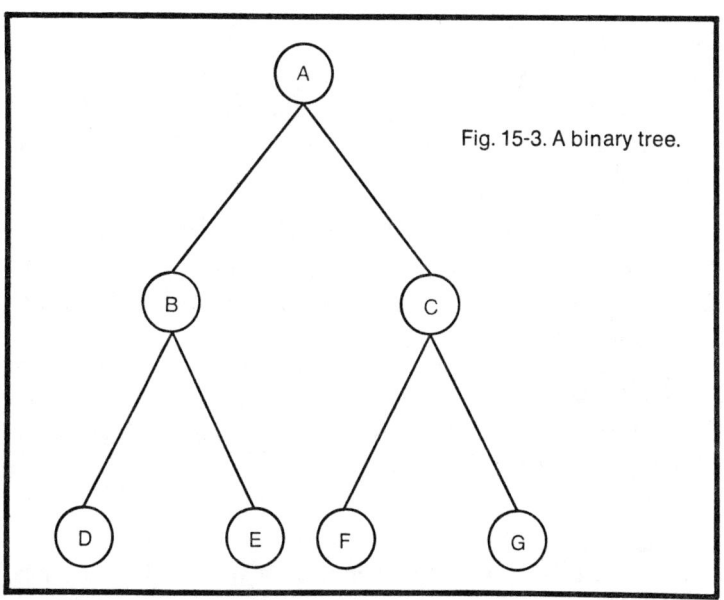

Fig. 15-3. A binary tree.

level the nodes are numbered 4, 5, 6, and 7. Clearly this scheme could be extended to any number of nodes.

Notice further, that the number of a left node is exactly twice that of its parent, and the number of a right node is one

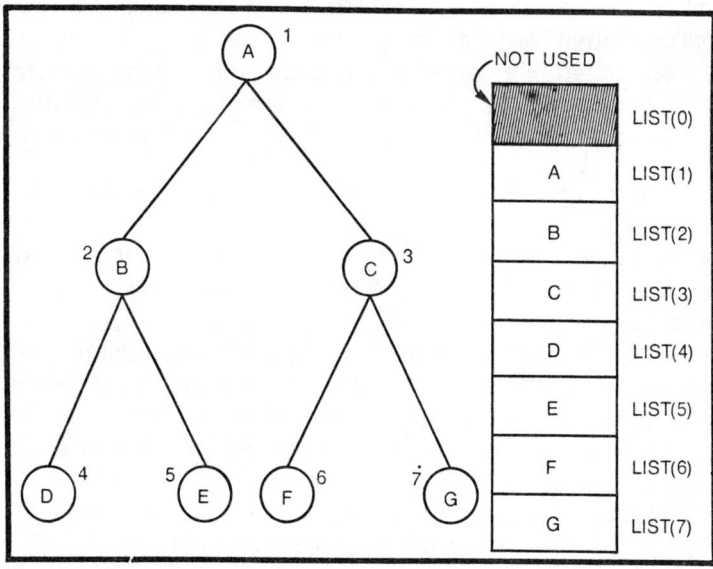

Fig. 15-4. The complete binary tree with 7 nodes and its linear representation.

more than twice the number of its parent. The left child of node 3, for instance, is node 6; the right child of node 3 is node 7.

This suggests that we represent the complete binary tree as a linear array, as shown in Fig. 15-4. If we assume the nodes to be words, we can define:

DECLARE BINARY_TREE(8) WORD;

Then BINARY_TREE(1) is the root of the tree, BINARY_TREE(2) is its left child, BINARY_TREE(3) is its right child, and so on.

In general, BINARY_TREE(I) is the node numbered with the value of I in Fig. 15-4. BINARY_TREE(2*I) is its left child; BINARY_TREE(2*I + 1) is its right child; and BINARY_TREE(I/2) is its parent.

Notice that BINARY_TREE(0) is not used.

*Preorder and Postorder Representations.* We *traverse* a tree when we work through it in such a way as to visit each node exactly once. There are many different ways to traverse a tree, depending on the order in which we visit the nodes.

There is a one-to-one correspondence between ways of traversing a tree and linear representations of the tree. Once we settle on a way of traversing the tree, we can enter each node in a linear array as it is visited, and thus obtain a linear representation of the tree. And if we have the linear representation, we can visit the nodes in the order of their appearance in the linear array, and so obtain the corresponding traversal.

The correspondence between linear representations and traversals is useful, since if we plan to traverse a tree in one particular way, and no other, then the corresponding linear representation will be the most natural way to store the tree inside the computer.

Two important ways of traversing a tree are *preorder* and *postorder* traversals. In a preorder traversal, the descendants of a node are visited immediately after the node itself is visited. In a postorder traversal, the descendants of a node are visited immediately before the node itself is visited. In each case, nodes on the same level are visited in left to right order. Figure 15-5 illustrates a preorder and a postorder traversal.

In the linear representation, we must indicate where we passed from one level to another in the traversal, otherwise the structure of the tree will be lost. There are three ways of doing this:

1) Insert a left parenthesis when we move down from one level to the next, and a right parenthesis when we move p from one level to the previous one. With this method the tree of Fig. 15-5 becomes:

| | |
|---|---|
| A(B(E F) C D(G H)) | preorder |
| ((E F)B C (G H)D)A | postorder |

2) We may indicate what level each node is on:

| | |
|---|---|
| A1 B2 E3 F3 C2 D2 G3 H3 | preorder |
| E3 F3 B2 C2 G3 H3 D2 A1 | postorder |

3) We may indicate the number of children each node has:

| | |
|---|---|
| A3 B2 E0 F0 C0 D2 G0 H0 | preorder |
| E0 F0 B2 C0 G0 H0 D2 A3 | postorder |

Method 1 is useful notation for people; it is not so useful for computers since the left and right parentheses (or their equivalents) must be stored along with the nodes of the tree.

For human use, the parentheses may be replaced by indentation:

```
A
   B
      E
      F
   C
   D
      G
      H
```

PL/I structures, which are trees, are written using both indentation and level numbers (method 2). The indentation is for the human programmer; the level numbers are for the computer.

Method 2 is often the most useful for computers; the nodes will probably be structures, anyway, and it is easy to include a component of each node which gives its level number.

Method 3 is particularly useful in connection with algebraic expressions. Fig. 15-6 shows how an algebraic expression may be represented as a tree. The nodes of the tree

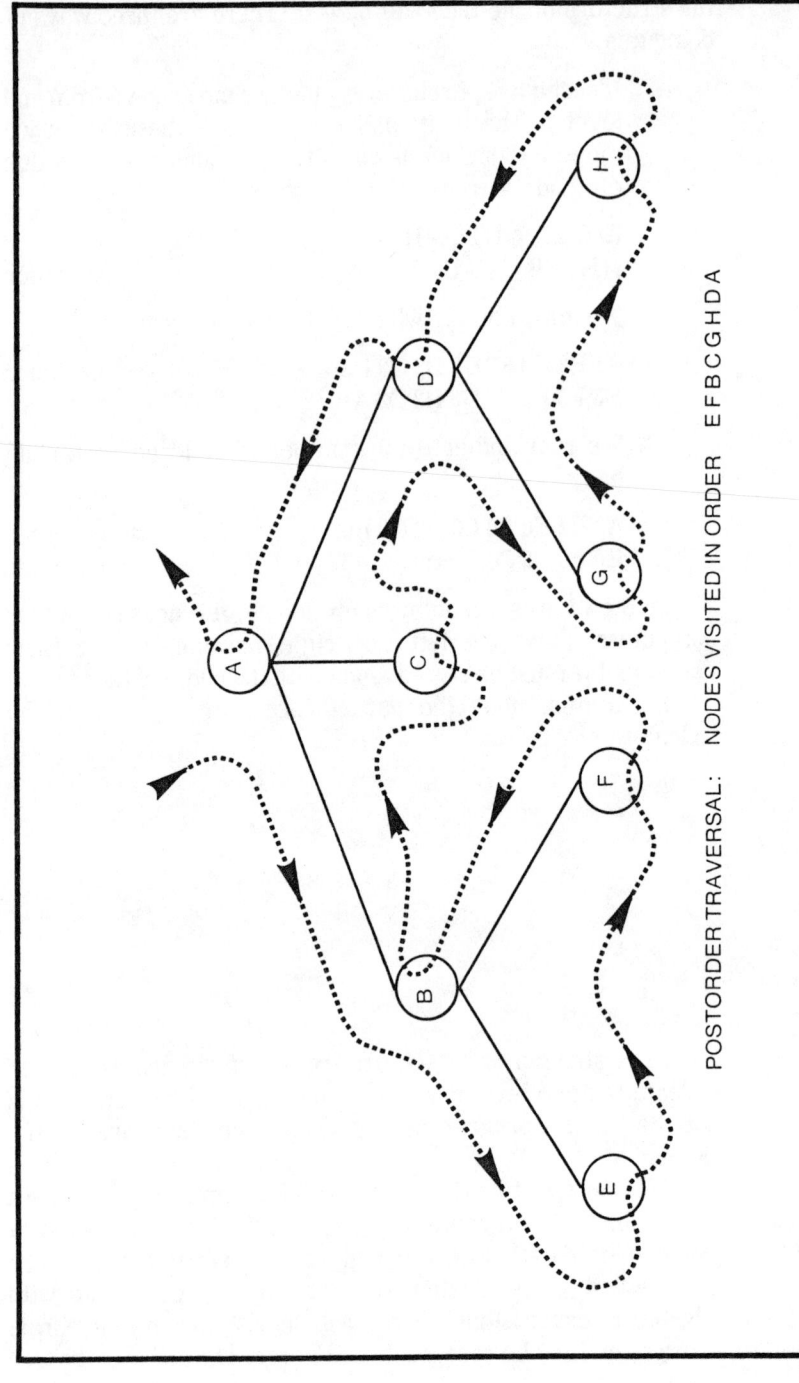

POSTORDER TRAVERSAL: NODES VISITED IN ORDER   E F B C G H D A

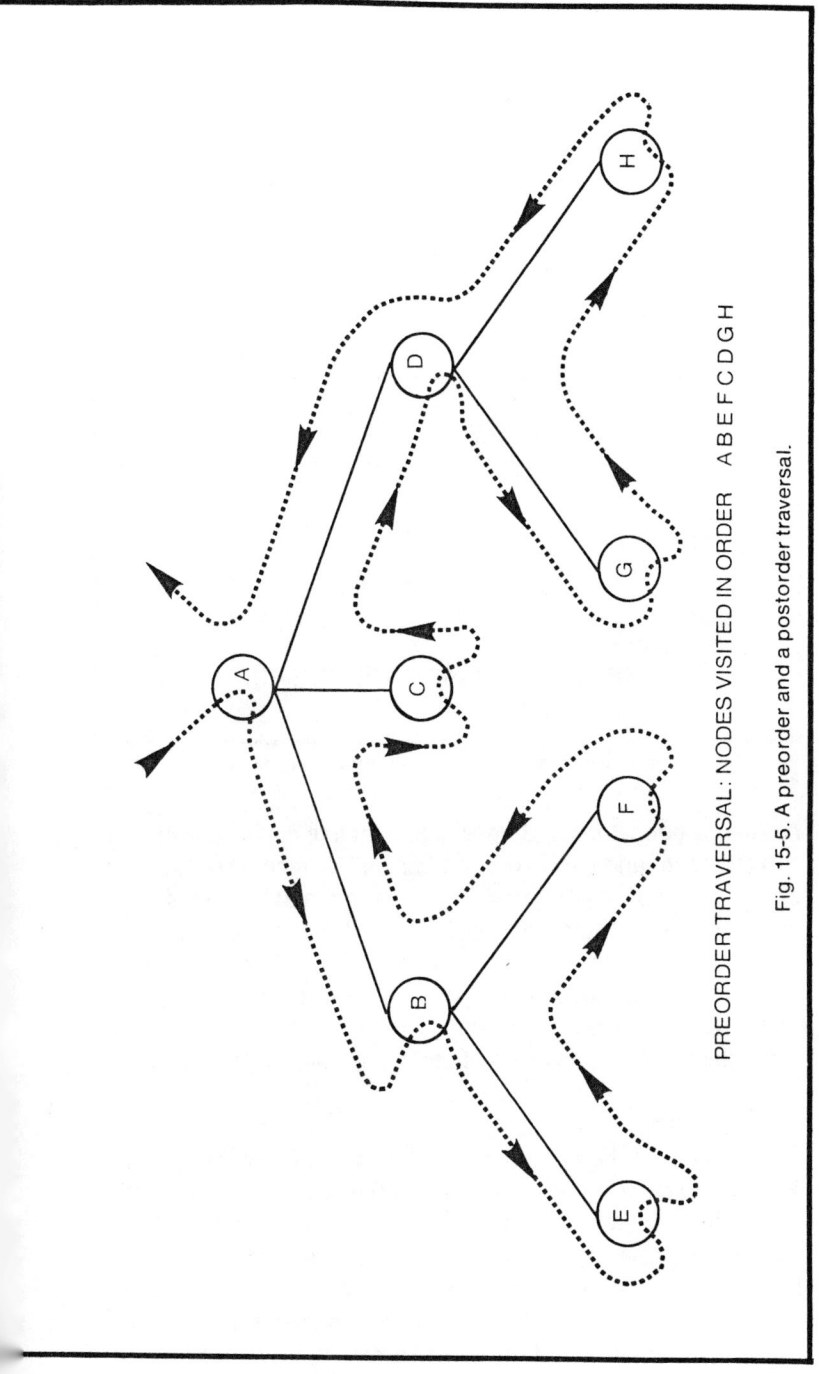

PREORDER TRAVERSAL: NODES VISITED IN ORDER   A B E F C D G H

Fig. 15-5. A preorder and a postorder traversal.

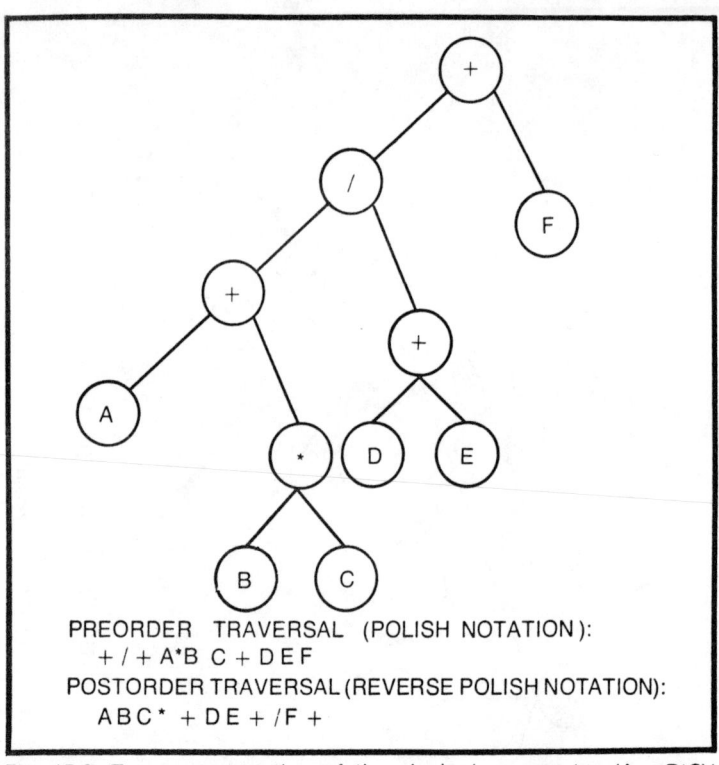

Fig. 15-6. Tree representation of the algebraic expression (A + B*C)/(D + E) + F.

consist of operators and operands. Each operator has exactly two children, and each operand has none. Since these facts are known, we may merely list the operators and operands in the order in which they were encountered during the traversal. The resulting preorder form is commonly known as "Polish notation" and the postorder form as "reverse Polish notation" or RPN. These representations are well known to computer enthusiasts as well as users of certain brands of calculators.

## BIT TABLES

A tree may be represented as a table of bits, as shown in Fig. 15-7. The rows and columns of the table are labeled with the nodes of the tree. An 1 entry indicates that the node labeling the row containing that entry is the parent of the node labeling the column containing the entry. A 0 entry indicates that no parent-child relationship exists between the nodes labeling the row and column of the entry.

Bit tables may be stored compactly, since only a single bit is required for each entry. On the other hand, complicated programming, involving shifting and masking operations, is required to extract the desired bits from the bytes or words in which they are stored.

## PLEX REPRESENTATIONS

With the exception of the array representation of the complete binary tree, linear representations of trees lack flexibility. It is difficult to insert new nodes, or delete old ones. And the tree is easily traversed only in the order corresponding to the representation. Linear representations are best when the tree is static—insertions and deletions are not to be made, at least not often—and the tree is always to be traversed in a particular order.

For more flexible representations we turn to plexes.

*Multiple Child Pointers.* We may place in each node of the tree a pointer to each of its children, as illustrated in Fig. 15-8. This technique is best when each node has the same number of children, as in a binary tree.

Suppose, for instance, that each node has 5 children. Then we may structure each node as follows:

DECLARE 1 NODE,
    2 DATA,
        /* SUBDIVISIONS OF DATA */
    2 CHILDREN(5) WORD;

|        |   | A | B | C | D | E | F | G | H | I | J | K | L | M |
|--------|---|---|---|---|---|---|---|---|---|---|---|---|---|---|
|        | A | 0 | 1 | 1 | 1 | 0 | 0 | 0 | 0 | 0 | 0 | 0 | 0 | 0 |
|        | B | 0 | 0 | 0 | 0 | 1 | 1 | 1 | 0 | 0 | 0 | 0 | 0 | 0 |
|        | C | 0 | 0 | 0 | 0 | 0 | 0 | 0 | 1 | 1 | 1 | 0 | 0 | 0 |
|        | D | 0 | 0 | 0 | 0 | 0 | 0 | 0 | 0 | 0 | 0 | 1 | 1 | 1 |
|        | E | 0 | 0 | 0 | 0 | 0 | 0 | 0 | 0 | 0 | 0 | 0 | 0 | 0 |
| PARENT | F | 0 | 0 | 0 | 0 | 0 | 0 | 0 | 0 | 0 | 0 | 0 | 0 | 0 |
|        | G | 0 | 0 | 0 | 0 | 0 | 0 | 0 | 0 | 0 | 0 | 0 | 0 | 0 |
|        | H | 0 | 0 | 0 | 0 | 0 | 0 | 0 | 0 | 0 | 0 | 0 | 0 | 0 |
|        | I | 0 | 0 | 0 | 0 | 0 | 0 | 0 | 0 | 0 | 0 | 0 | 0 | 0 |
|        | J | 0 | 0 | 0 | 0 | 0 | 0 | 0 | 0 | 0 | 0 | 0 | 0 | 0 |
|        | K | 0 | 0 | 0 | 0 | 0 | 0 | 0 | 0 | 0 | 0 | 0 | 0 | 0 |
|        | L | 0 | 0 | 0 | 0 | 0 | 0 | 0 | 0 | 0 | 0 | 0 | 0 | 0 |
|        | M | 0 | 0 | 0 | 0 | 0 | 0 | 0 | 0 | 0 | 0 | 0 | 0 | 0 |

(CHILD across top)

Fig. 15-7. Representation of the tree of Fig. 15-1 as a bit table.

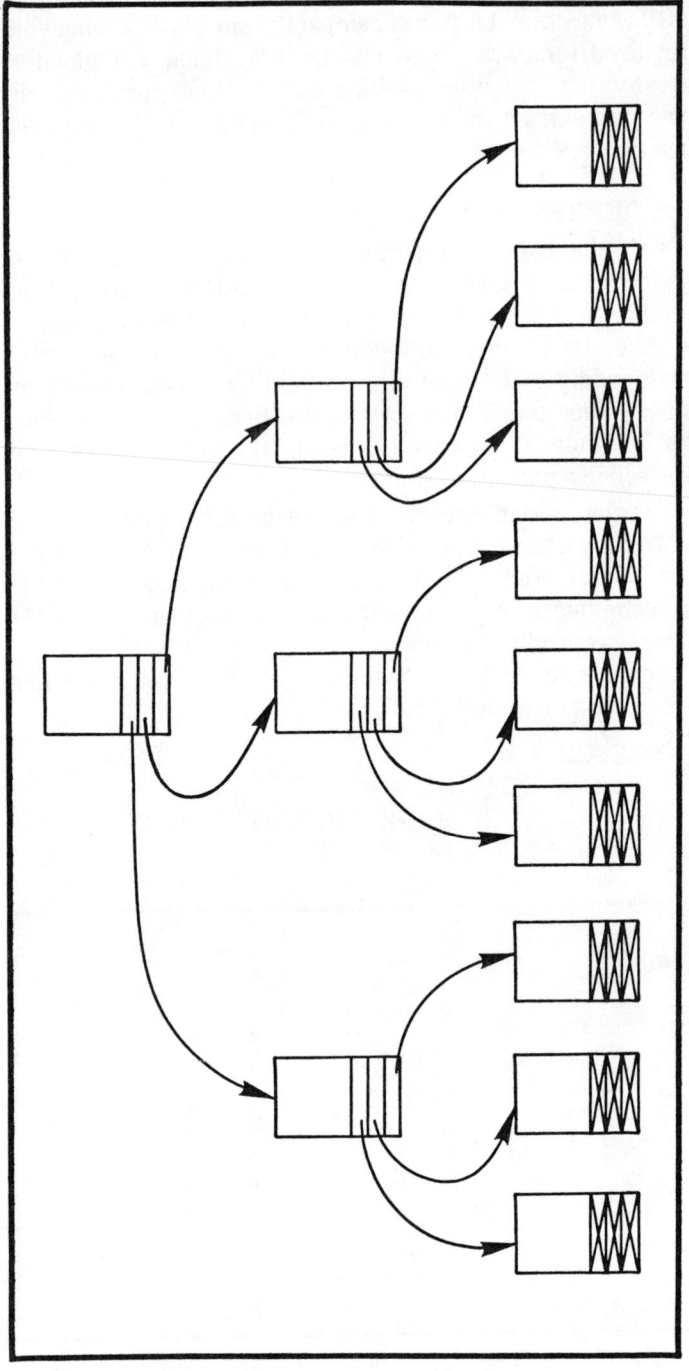

Fig. 15-8. Representing a tree with multiple child pointers.

NODE.CHILDREN(0) would be a pointer to the leftmost child of NODE, NODE.CHILDREN(1) a pointer to its next-to-leftmost child, and so on.

If P points to a node, then we can move P to the leftmost child of that node with

$$P = P -> NODE.CHILDREN(0)$$

and similarly for moving from the parent to any of its children.

If the number of children vary from node to node, then we have two choices. We can allocate enough space in each node for the *maximum* number of children it can have (setting unused pointers to NIL), or we can allow the sizes of the nodes to vary. The first choice wastes memory space; the second increases the complexity of the bookkeeping chores the program must perform, particularly if we wish to use some method of recovering unused space.

*Child and Twin Pointers.* We may represent a tree using two pointers per node. One of these points to the leftmost child of the node; the other points to its right twin.

Fig. 15-9 illustrates this method. We may define a node as follows:

```
DECLARE 1 NODE,
       2 DATA,
          /* SUBDIVISIONS OF DATA */
       2 LEFT_CHILD WORD,
       2 RIGHT_TWIN WORD;
```

If P points to a node, then we can move P to the leftmost child of that node using

$$P = P -> NODE.LEFT\_CHILD;$$

and to the twin just to the right of that node with

$$P = P -> NODE.RIGHT\_TWIN;$$

Child and twin pointers have the advantage that one can move from one twin to another; multiple child pointers do not allow this. On the other hand, with multiple child pointers one can move from a parent to a particular child. With child and twin pointers one must always move to the leftmost child, and then move to the right using the twin pointers until the desired child is found.

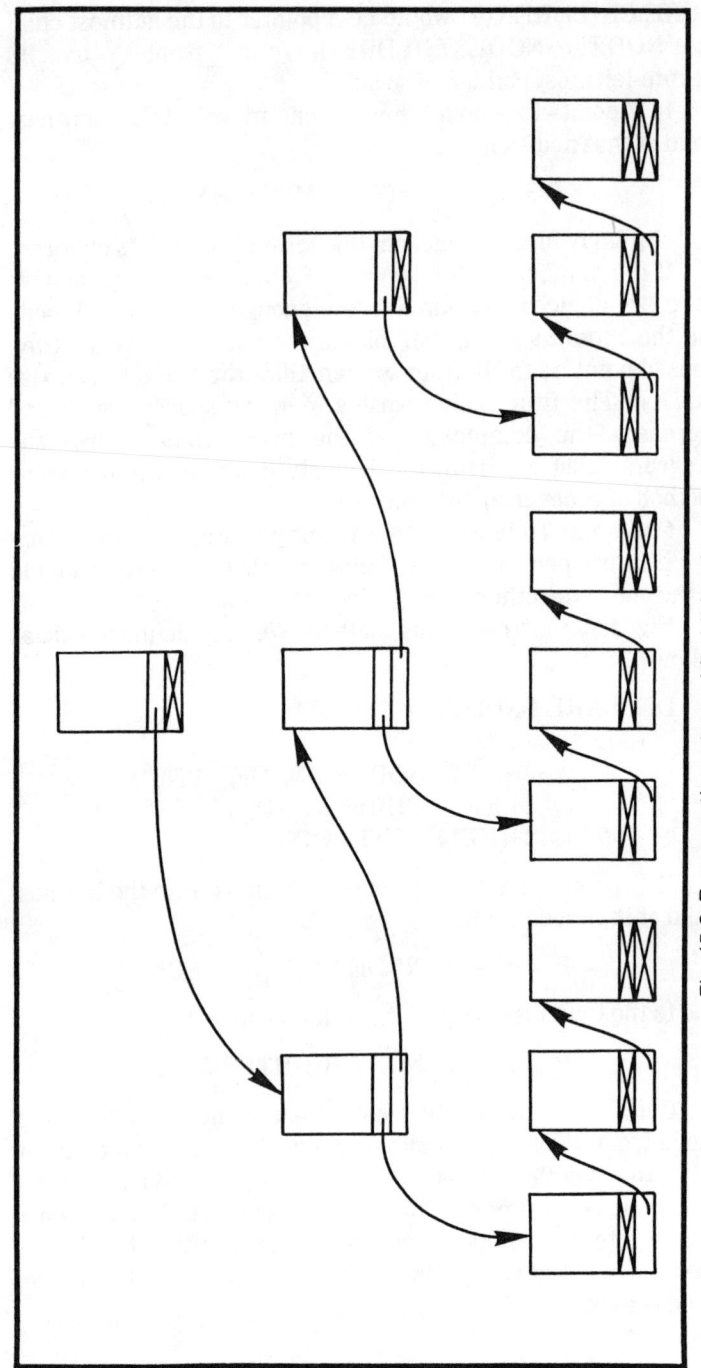

Fig. 15-9. Representing a tree with child and twin pointers.

But the overwhelming advantage of child and twin pointers is that only two pointers per node are required.

*Additional Pointers.* At the expense of using more memory space for each node, we can include additional pointers to simplify tree traversal:

1) Parent Pointers. Each node contains a pointer to its parent.
2) Left and Right Twin Pointers. Each node may contain a pointer to its left twin as well as one to its right twin, thus allowing one to move either to the left or the right among the children of a node. The advantages here are similar to those for doubly linked lists.
3) Root Pointers. Each node may contain a pointer to the root, allowing immediate access to the root from any part of the tree.

Fig. 15-10 illustrates the possibilities.

It is often convenient to think of a parent as being the header of a list of all its children. Then all the possibilities of the last chapter may occur: the list may be a chain or a ring. It may be singly or doubly linked. Each node may contain a pointer to the header (parent pointers). Doubly linked rings with parent pointers offer maximum flexibility.

## RECURSIVE DEFINITION OF TREES

An object is defined *recursively* when it is defined in terms of parts, some of which have the same structure as the object being defined. For instance, we may define a tree recursively:

*Definition.* A tree consists of a root and zero or more subtrees. Each subtree is itself a tree.

Fig. 15-11 illustrates how this definition may be applied. We start with the square box labeled "tree". Using the definition, we replace this by a root and its subtrees. Each subtree is also a tree, and so is also represented by a box labeled "tree".

Now we apply the definition to each of the "tree" boxes representing subtrees, and expand each of those in to a root and a set of subtrees. This creates more "tree" boxes to which the definition can again be applied, creating still more "tree" boxes, and so on.

Obviously we have a case of repetition here. The definition of a tree is being used repeatedly to define a single tree. As

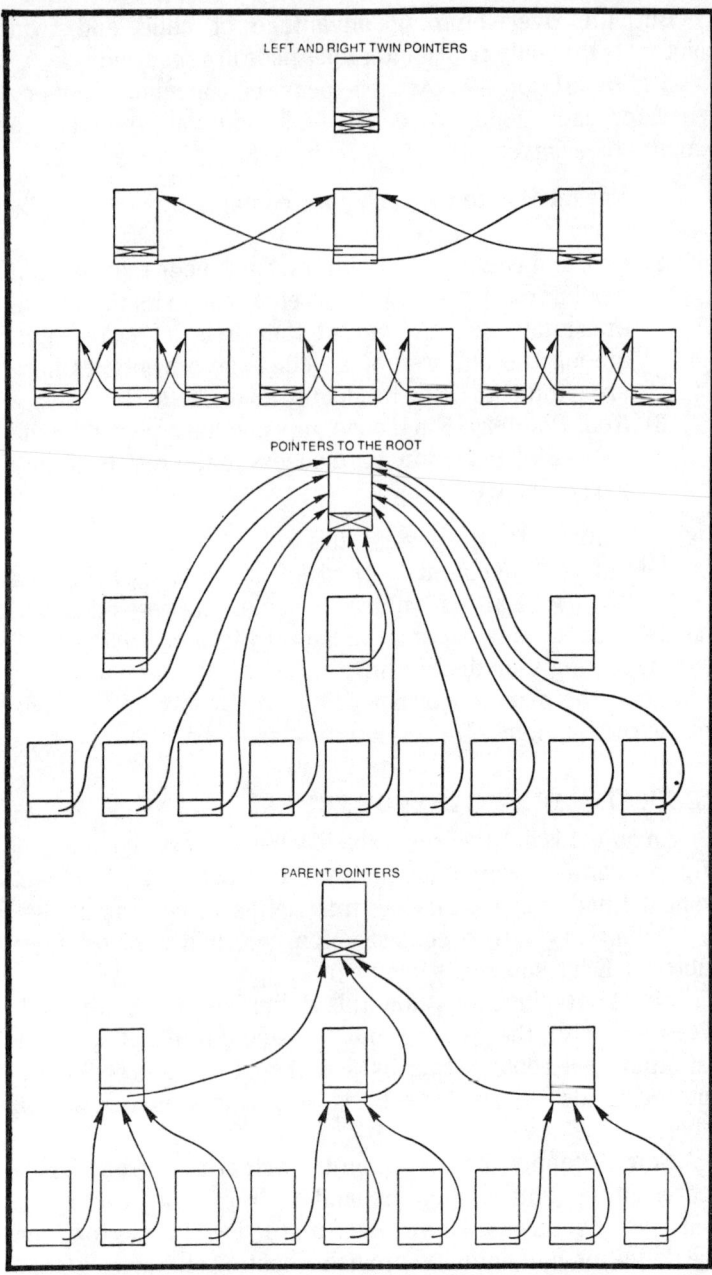

Fig. 15-10. Use of parent pointers, left and right twin pointers, and pointers to the root. Although each technique is illustrated separately, any combination of them may be used. In each drawing the pointers not illustrated are omitted for clarity.

with any other repetition, we want to make sure that this one does not go on forever. What is the terminating condition which will cause the repetition to cease?

The repetition terminates—at least along a given branch of the tree—when a leaf is created. A leaf is a subtree which consists only of a root, and no subtrees. Since a leaf has no further subtrees, the definition is not invoked again, and the repetition stops.

Notice that it is the phrase "zero or more" in the definition which allows for termination. If every tree contained "one or more" subtrees, then we could never stop applying the definition, and a tree would be an infinite structure. It is the fact that a tree may have no subtrees which allows us to define leaves.

## RECURSIVE PROGRAMMING

*Recursive algorithms.* Algorithms may also be defined recursively. Such algorithms are particularly appropriate when the data structure being manipulated is itself recursively defined.

For instance, we may give algorithms for preorder and postorder traversal of a tree in recursive form:

Preorder Traversal:

1) Visit the root.
2) Taking the subtrees (if any) in left-to-right order, do a preorder traversal of each subtree.

Postorder Traversal:

1) Taking the subtrees (if any) in left-to-right order, do a postorder traversal of each subtree.
2) Visit the root.

Each of these algorithms is recursive since the phrases "do a preorder traversal" and "do a postorder traversal" call upon the algorithm being defined.

*Recursive Procedures.* Each of the above algorithms is easily translated into a procedure. Suppose we have a plex representation of a tree using child and twin pointers. Let VISIT (P) be a subroutine which carries out whatever processing is desired on the node pointed to by P. Let PREORDER_TRAVERSAL (P) and POSTORDER_ TRAVERSAL (P) apply VISIT to each node of the tree whose

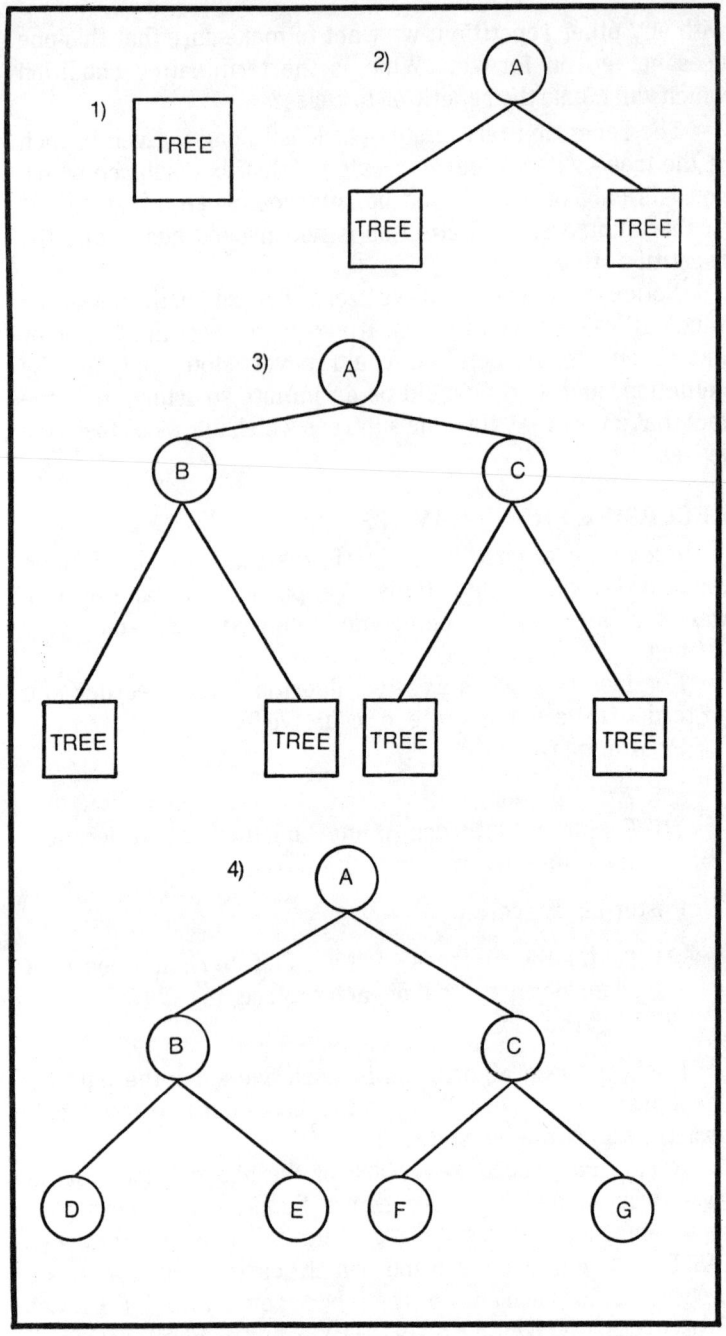

Fig. 15-11. Constructing a tree from the recursive definition.

root is pointed to by P, the nodes being processed in the designated order. We have:

```
PREORDER_TRAVERSAL: PROCEDURE (P) RECURSIVE;
DECLARE P WORD;
    CALL VISIT (P);
    P = P - > NODE.LEFT_CHILD;
    DO WHILE P < > NIL;
        CALL PREORDER_TRAVERSAL (P);
        P = P - > NODE.RIGHT_TWIN;
    END;
END PREORDER_TRAVERSAL;
```

and

```
POSTORDER_TRAVERSAL: PROCEDURE (P) RECURSIVE;
DECLARE (P, Q) WORD;
    Q = P - > NODE.LEFT_CHILD;
    DO WHILE Q < > NIL;
        CALL POSTORDER_TRAVERSAL (Q);
        Q = Q - > NODE.RIGHT_TWIN;
    END;
    CALL VISIT (P);
END POSTORDER_TRAVERSAL;
```

We see that the traversal procedures follow the recursive algorithms almost exactly, the DO WHILE loop being used to process the subtrees of a node. Notice that if P points to a leaf, then P − > NODE.LEFT_CHILD will be NIL, and thus no repetitions of the DO WHILE loop and no recursive calls take place. Thus termination is achieved.

The values of all local variables in a recursive subroutine must be saved before the subroutine calls itself, and restored afterwards, since otherwise the new call would change the values of variables that are being used by the current call. The word RECURSIVE in the first line of the subroutine warns the translator—human or automatic—that this save and restore must be done.

As mentioned in Chapter 12, the local variables are saved on a stack. We can give a "physical interpretation" to these saved values.

For instance, in PREORDER_TRAVERSAL, when we make a recursive call we are working through a set of twins, the children of the parent originally pointed to by P. The pointer P keeps our place in this twin list. When we move down to the next level, through a recursive call, then the saved value of P keeps our place on the level above. When we come back to that level, through a return, then P is restored to its previous value and we can pick up in the twin list where we left off.

More generally, when a node on a given level is being processed, then the stack will contain pointers into twin lists on each level above, simultaneously keeping the routine's place in each of these not-yet-finished-with lists.

In POSTORDER_TRAVERSAL there are two local variables to be saved. Q serves to keep the place in the twin list being processed. P keeps track of the parent of the twins being processed, since the parent must be visited *after* all its subtrees have been traversed.

Programs 15-1 and 15-2, PRINT_PREORDER (P) and PRINT_POSTORDER (P), are practical applications of the traversal routines. These print out the tree pointed to by P in

```
PRINT__PREORDER: PROCEDURE (P) RECURSIVE;
    DECLARE P WORD;
    /* PRINT ROOT */
        CALL PRINT__NODE(P);
    /* PRINT SUBTREES */
        P = P -> NODE.LEFT__CHILD;
        IF P <> NIL THEN
            DO;
                CALL PRINT__CHAR('(');
                CALL PRINT__PREORDER(P);
                P = P -> NODE.RIGHT__TWIN;
                DO WHILE P <> NIL;
                    CALL PRINT__CHAR(' ');
                    CALL PRINT__PREORDER(P);
                    P = P -> NODE.RIGHT__TWIN;
                END;
                CALL PRINT__CHAR(')');
            END;
    END PRINT__PREORDER;
```

Program 15-1. PRINT__PREORDER prints the tree pointed to by its argument in preorder form and using the "method 1" format described in the text.

```
PRINT__POSTORDER: PROCEDURE (P) RECURSIVE;
    DECLARE (P, Q) WORD;
    /* PRINT SUBTREES */
        Q = P -> NODE.LEFT__CHILD;
        IF Q <> NIL THEN
            DO;
                CALL PRINT__CHAR('(');
                CALL PRINT__POSTORDER(Q);
                Q = Q -> NODE.RIGHT__TWIN;
                DO WHILE Q <> NIL;
                    CALL PRINT__CHAR(' ');
                    CALL PRINT__POSTORDER(Q);
                    Q = Q -> NODE.RIGHT__TWIN;
                END;
                CALL PRINT__CHAR(')');
            END;
    /* PRINT ROOT */
        CALL PRINT__NODE(P);
    END PRINT__POSTORDER;
```

Program 15-2. PRINT__POSTORDER prints the tree pointed to by its argument in postorder form and using the "method 1" format described in the text.

the appropriate order using the "method 1" format discussed previously: the subtrees of each node follow it, enclosed in parentheses. We assume the existence of a routine PRINT_NODE (P) which will print a symbolic name for the node pointed to by P.

The leftmost subtree is treated as a special case and is not included in the DO WHILE loop. The reason is that it is not preceded by a space, while every other subtree is preceded by a space, to separate it from the one before.

Recursive routines such as these are well suited to assembly language implementation. The assembly language programmer always knows precisely which variables need to be saved before a recursive call and restored after its return, and so can save and restore these and no others. High level languages that allow recursion often do much unnecessary saving and restoring, and thus are much less efficient than languages which prohibit recursion.

# Chapter 16
# Graphs

The data structures that we shall study in this chapter may be found under diverse names: maps, networks, mazes, flowcharts, schematic diagrams, state transition diagrams, syntax diagrams, and others. To the mathematician all such structures are known as *graphs*.

As shown in Fig. 16-1, a graph consists of points connected by lines. The points are called *nodes*; the lines, *arcs*. The arcs may or may not have arrowheads on them; if they do, then the graph is a *directed graph*. In computer science directed graphs are usually more common than undirected ones, and so we will concentrate our attention on them.

If two nodes, A and B, of a directed graph are joined by an arc, such that the arrow points from A to B, then A is the *initial node* of the arc and B is its *terminal node*. Also, A is the *immediate predecessor* of B and B is the *immediate successor* of A.

A *path* is a sequence of arcs such that the terminal node of any arc is the same as the initial node of the following one. A path is *simple* if it does not contain any arc more than once. A *cycle* is a path that begins and ends on the same node.

Figure 16-2 illustrates the definitions of *initial node, terminal node, immediate predecessor, immediate successor, path, simple path,* and *cycle*.

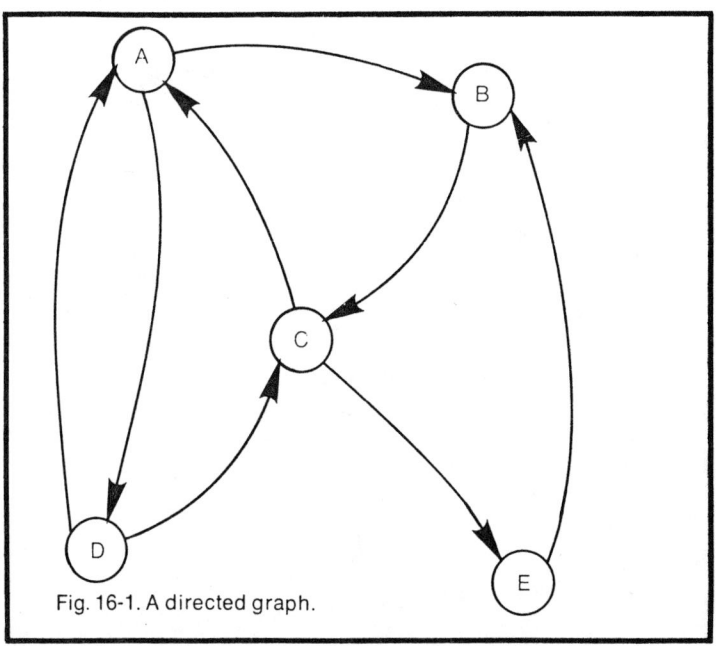

Fig. 16-1. A directed graph.

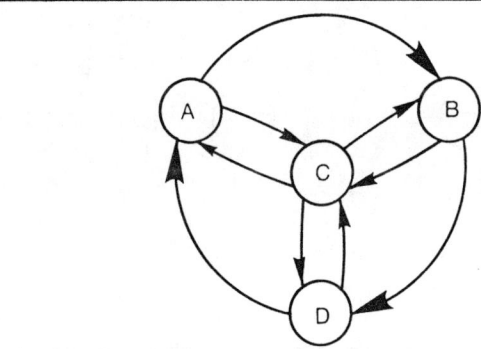

1) A is the **initial node** of the arc AB.
2) B is the **terminal node** of the arc AB.
3) A is an **immediate predecessor** of B (C is the other immediate predecessor of B in this graph).
4) B is an **immediate successor** of A (C is the other immediate successor of A in this graph).
5) ABDC is a **simple path**. ABDCBD is not a simple path, since it contains the arc BD twice.
6) ABDA is a **cycle**.

Fig. 16-2. Illustrations of the definitions of initial node, terminal node, immediate prdecessor, immediate successor, simple path, and cycle.

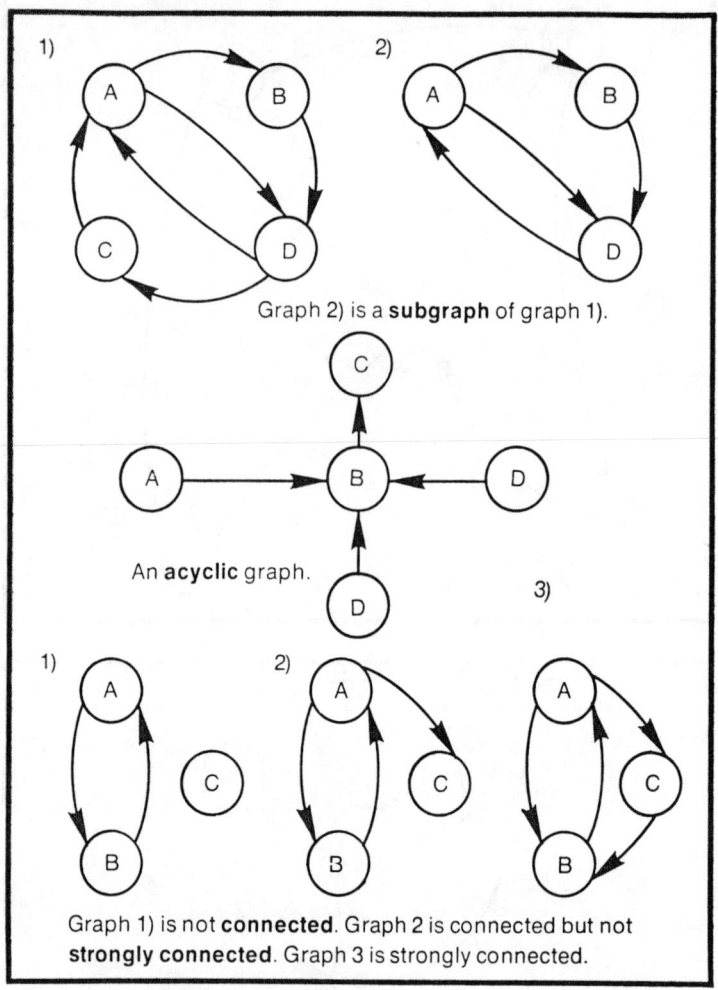

Fig. 16-3. Illustrations of the definitions of subgraph, acyclic graph, connected graph, and strongly connected graph.

A *subgraph* of a graph is a subset of the nodes of the graph, together with all the arcs that joined those nodes in the original graph. A graph is *acyclic* if it contains no cycles. A graph is *connected* if there is a path connecting each pair of nodes. It is *strongly connected* if there are paths connecting each pair of nodes *in either direction*. Figure 16-3 illustrates these definitions.

So far the arcs of our graphs have not been named or *labeled*. When the arcs are unlabeled, then each arc is uniquely determined by its initial and terminal nodes. We can have at most one arc with the same initial and terminal node; to have more would be superfluous, since two arcs with the same initial and terminal nodes would be indistinguishable.

If the arcs are labeled, however, then we may have any number of arcs (with distinct labels) connecting the same initial and terminal nodes.

It is sometimes convenient to think of a graph with labeled arcs as a *state transition graph*. The nodes of the graph are taken to represent the *internal states* of some machine—a computer, for instance. The arc labels are *inputs* to the machine. If the machine is in the state represented by a certain node, and an input is received, then the machine will follow the arc leaving that node and labeled by the input received. (If no such arc exists, then the input was illegal, and an error condition exists.) The terminal node of the arc followed will be the next state of the machine.

As an example, consider a computer component called a JK flip-flop. The JK flip-flop has two internal states, denoted 0 and 1. Hence its state transition graph, Fig. 16-4, has two nodes, Node 0 and Node 1.

The JK flip-flop has two 1-bit inputs, J and K. We will take these together as constituting a 2-bit input. Thus if $J = 1$ and $K = 0$, we will call the input 10; if $J = 0$ and $K = 1$, we will call

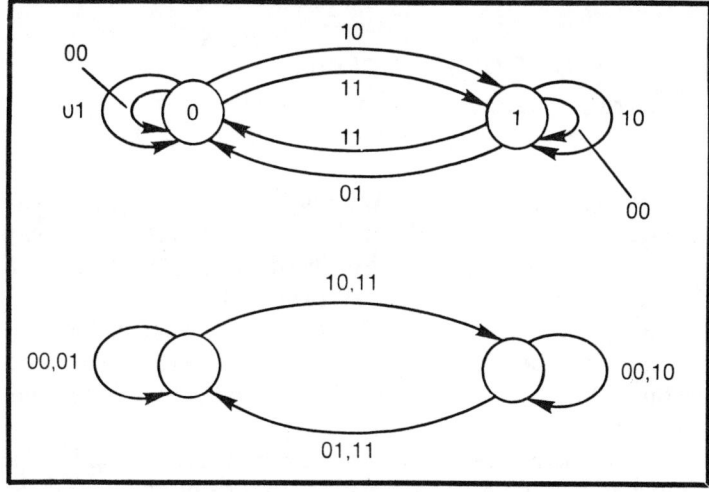

Fig. 16-4. The state transition graph of a JK flip-flop. Each arc in the bottom graph has two labels, and so represents two arcs in the top graph.

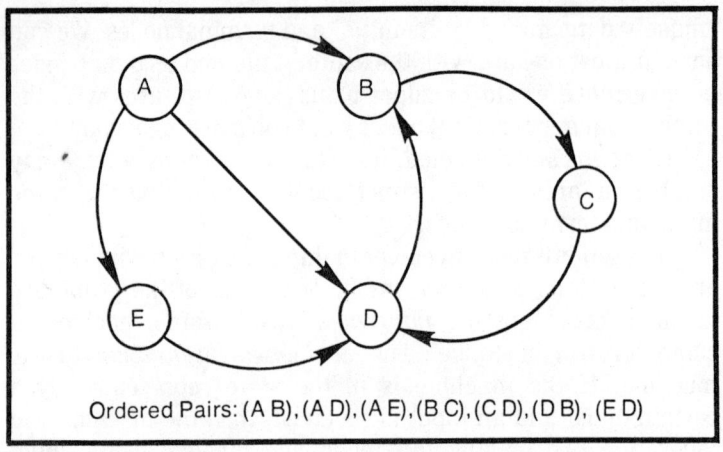

Fig. 16-5. Representation of a graph as a list of ordered pairs.

the input 01; and so on. Each arc in Fig. 16-4 is labeled with a possible input.

Thus we can see from Fig. 16-4 that if the flip-flop were in State 0, and the input was 10, then the next state would be State 1. On the other hand, if the input had been 01, then the JK flip-flop would have remained in State 0.

In drawing a graph with labeled arcs, one often only draws one arc in each direction between two nodes, and places more than one label on it. Thus in the bottom graph in Fig. 16-4, each arc actually stands for two.

## REPRESENTATIONS OF GRAPHS

There are several ways to represent graphs using lists or tables. These lists or tables may be stored inside the computer in whatever way is convenient.

*List of Ordered Pairs.* We may represent a graph with unlabeled arcs by a list of ordered pairs of nodes, as shown in Fig. 16-5. The list contains the ordered pair (A B) if and only if there is an arc connecting node A to node B.

*List of Ordered Triples.* If the arcs are labeled, then the ordered pairs become ordered triples, as in Fig. 16-6. The list contains the ordered triple (A B C) if and only if arc B goes from node A to node C.

*Lists of Immediate Successors.* For graphs with unlabeled arcs, we can give for each node a list of its immediate successors. Thus the entry A: B C D would mean that there

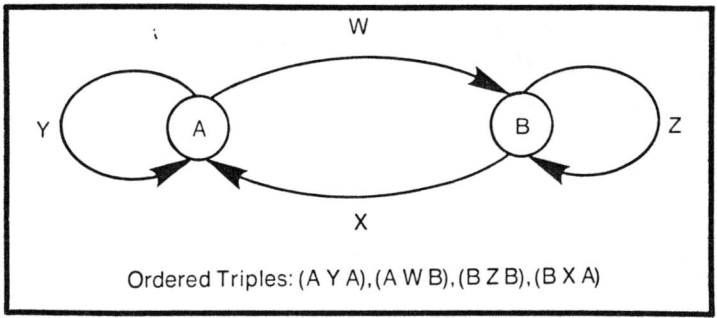

Fig. 16-6. Representation of a graph with labeled arcs as a list of ordered triples.

were arcs joining node A to nodes B, C, and D, and to no other nodes. See Fig. 16-7. The main difficulty with this method is that the successor lists will often differ in length for each node. Either we reserve the same amount of space for each node, and thus waste space for some nodes, or we deal with variable length lists, which makes our programming more complicated.

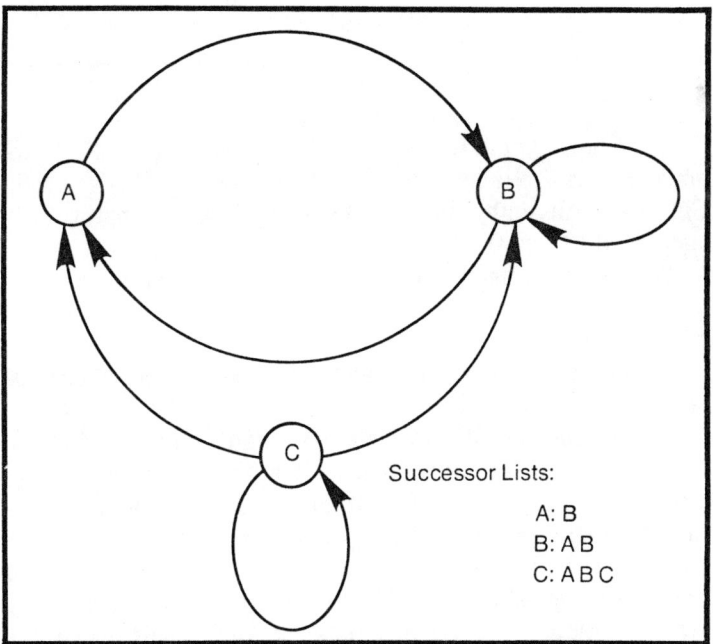

Fig. 16-7. Representing a graph by giving the list of immediate successors for each node.

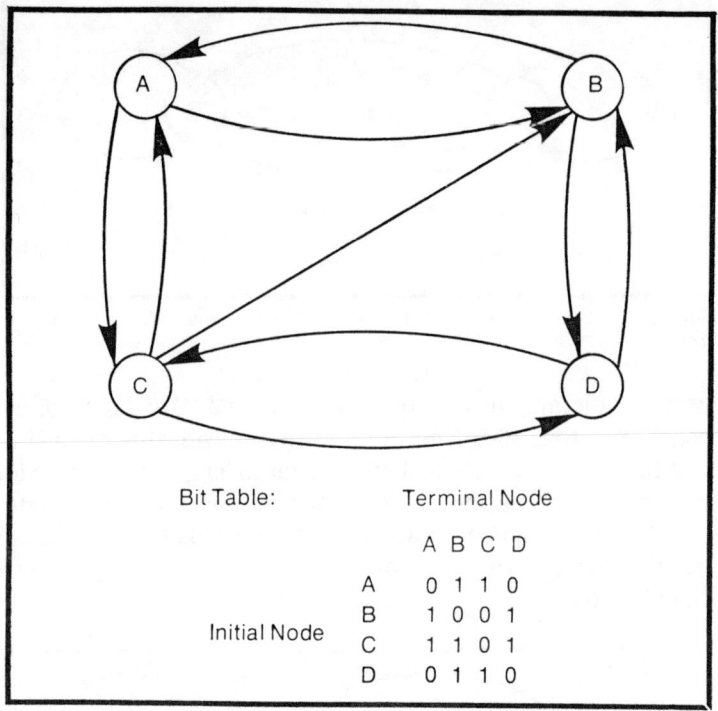

Fig. 16-8. Bit table representation of a graph.

*Bit Table.* Again for graphs with unlabeled arcs. The rows and columns are labeled with the names of nodes, as shown in Fig. 16-8. An entry is 1 if the node labeling that row is connected by an arc to the node labeling that column, and 0 otherwise. As was mentioned in connection with trees, bit tables may be stored compactly but getting to the individual bits may be troublesome.

*Transition Table.* A graph with labeled arcs can be represented by a table as shown in Fig. 16-9. The rows of the table are labeled with node names; the columns are labeled with arc names. An entry is the node reached by starting from the node labeling the row containing the entry, and following the arc labeling the column containing the entry. A "−" entry indicates that there is no arc with that particular label leaving the node in question. In practice "−" entries often indicate error conditions: certain inputs are erroneous when the machine is in certain states. Transition tables are often used in compilers, where the states are internal states of the compiler, and the input is the program to be compiled.

*Plex Representation.* A graph may be represented by a plex, the nodes of the graph being represented by the nodes of the plex, and the arcs being represented by pointers linking the nodes of the plex. Clearly there is a close correspondence between graphs and plexes, and in fact some authors use the two words interchangeably. We, however, will retain "plex" to mean linked blocks of memory, and note that graphs may be represented in other ways than by plexes.

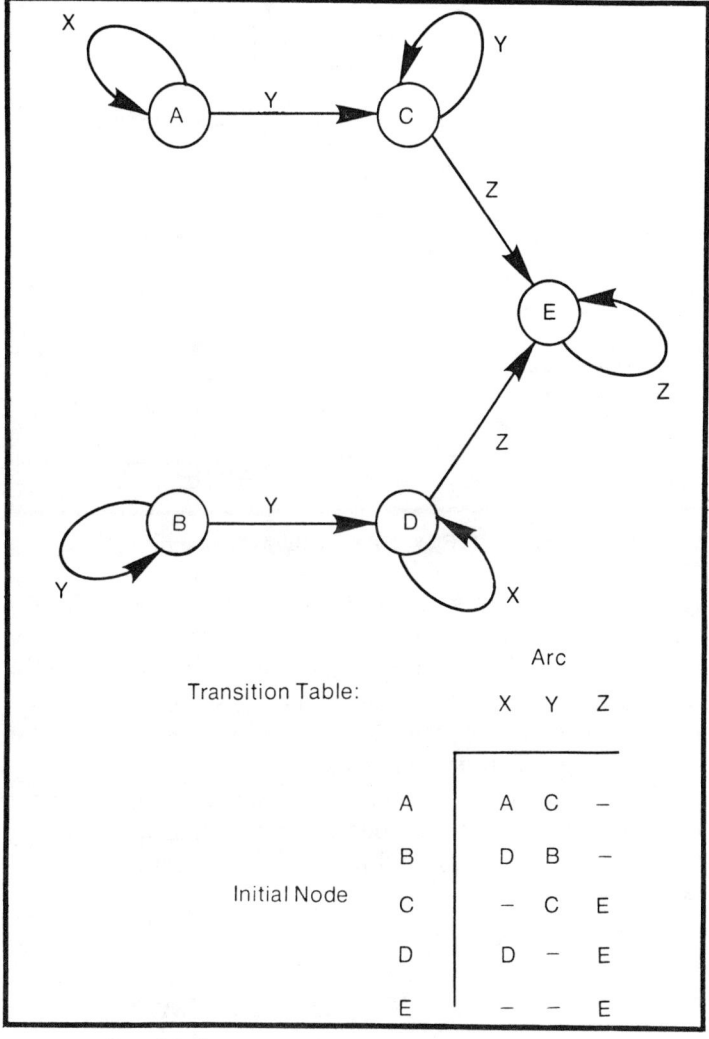

Fig. 16-9. Transition table representation of a graph.

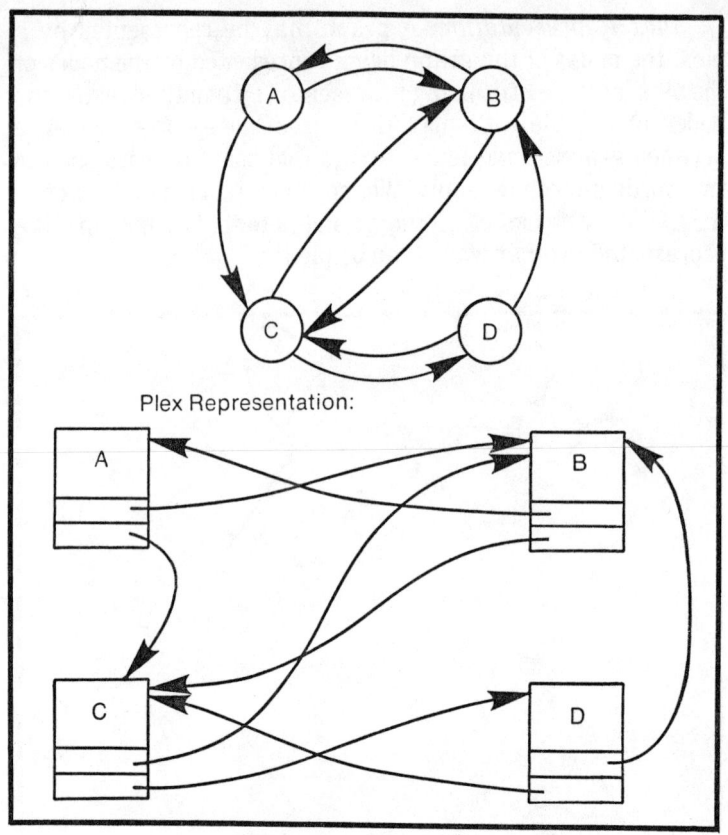

Fig. 16-10. Plex representation of a graph.

The plex representation of graphs is the same as the multiple-child-pointers representation of trees. It is also equivalent to the List of Immediate Successors representation just described, except the successor lists are stored in the nodes themselves instead of a separate table. Figure 16-10 illustrates a graph represented as a plex.

If the arcs are unlabeled, then the order in which the pointers are stored in a node is immaterial, and we may simply use an array to hold all the pointers leaving a given node:

DECLARE 1 NODE,
        2 DATA,
           /* SUBDIVISIONS OF DATA */
        2 SUCCESSORS (5) WORD;

Here each node may have up to 5 immediate successors, which may be stored in SUCCESSORS in any order. Unused entries in successors are set to NIL.

If the arcs are labeled, then each pointer position corresponds to a particular arc label, and the order in which the pointers are stored is important. We might have:

```
DECLARE 1 NODE,
        2 DATA,
              /* SUBDIVISIONS OF DATA */
        2 SUCCESSORS,
              3 ARC_LABEL_A WORD,
              3 ARC_LABEL_B WORD,
              3 ARC_LABEL_C WORD,
              3 ARC_LABEL_D WORD,
              3 ARC_LABEL_E WORD;
```

Each pointer is stored in one of the named locations depending on which label appears on the arc it represents.

(In practice, of course, we could still use an array, in which case the arc labels would be represented by different subscript values.)

## LISTS

We will now turn to a data structure called a List. We follow Knuth in using an initial capital to distinguish Lists from the lists which we have discussed previously. Although Lists are basically binary trees, they can be used to represent graphs. Lists are the basic data structure of LISP (List Processor), the most widely used programming language in artificial intelligence research.

Lists are built up from atoms. An atom is an arbitrary sequence of letters or numbers that begins with a letter. Thus

DOG
CAT
VERYLONGSEQUENCEOFLETTERS
Z5

are all atoms.

A List is defined recursively as a sequence of Lists or atoms, separated by spaces and enclosed in parentheses. Thus

(DOG CAT)
(A B C)
(A (B C) D)
(((A B) (C D) (E F)) G H)

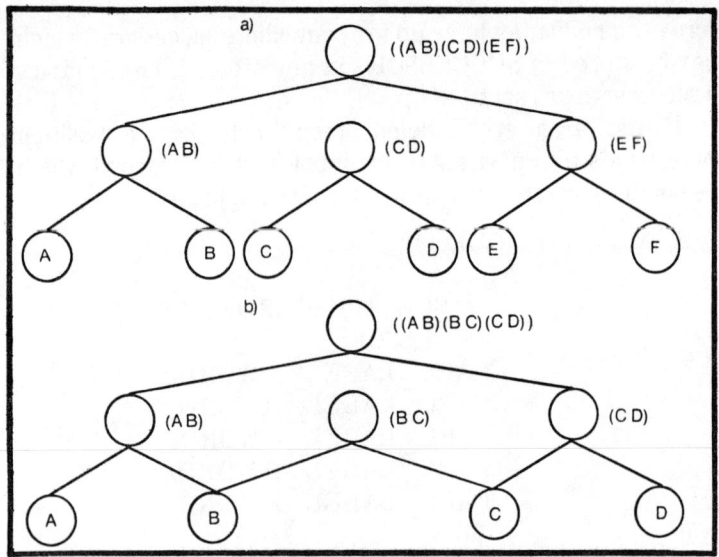

Fig. 16-11. Lists which form (a) a tree and (b) a graph.

are all Lists. Note that the third List contains three elements: A, (B C), and D. The second element is itself a list. The fourth list also contains three elements: ((A B) (C D) (E F)), G, and H. The first of these is itself a list; the remaining two are atoms.

A List is basically a tree, as shown in Fig. 16-11a. The root of the tree is the List; the leaves are the atoms. The other nodes are List elements that are themselves Lists.

Actually, a List is slightly more general than a tree. The same atom may occur more than once in a List, whereas the leaves of a tree are required to be distinct. Thus the List ((A B) (B C) (C D)) forms a graph rather than a tree, as shown in Fig. 16-11b.

Graphs are easily represented using Lists. Thus, using ordered pairs, we can represent the graph of Fig. 16-1 as:

((A B) (A D) (B C) (C A) (C E) (D A) (D C) (E B))

If we wished to use successor lists, then the representation would be:

((A (B D)) (B (C)) (C (A E)) (D (A C)) (E (B)))

Obviously, graphs with labeled nodes can be represented in the same way using ordered triples. Also, whereas we have shown the nodes of the graph as atoms, they could be more complex objects, themselves List structures.

Artificial intelligence researchers have used Lists to represent such diverse structures as chemical molecules, English sentences, logical propositions, and geometrical diagrams.

*Representing Lists.* To represent both atoms and Lists inside the computer, we use the two word CELL illustrated in Fig. 16-12 and declared as follows:

DECLARE 1 CELL,
        2 CAR WORD,
        2 CDR WORD;

The designations CAR and CDR (pronounced "could-er" ) are tradtional in LISP. They may possibly be the worst mnemonics in computer science since all they bring to mind are obscure hardware features of an obsolete computer (the IBM 7094). Nevertheless, they seem to have worked their way—via LISP—into the terminology of List processing.

A cell may represent either an atom or an element of a List. For an atom we leave the contents of the cell unspecified (except for two bits—see below). We assume, however, that the contents of an atom cell allow access to the name of the atom—called its print-name in LISP. In diagrams we shall simply represent an atom by its name.

If the cell represents a List element, then the CAR part of the cell is a pointer to the item that appears in the corresponding position on the List—either an atom cell or the first cell of another List. The CDR part of the cell points to the next cell on the List, or is NIL if the current cell is the final one. Figure 16-13 shows the internal representations of several Lists.

In each cell—be it atom or List element—two bits are reserved. These are the rightmost bits of the CAR and CDR

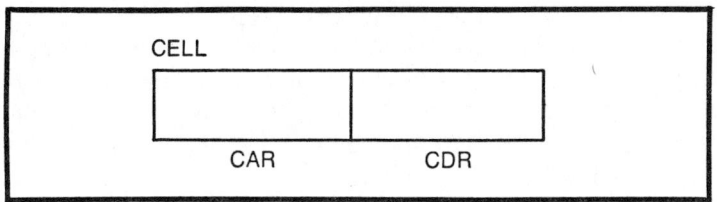

Fig. 16-12. The basic cell from which Lists are constructed.

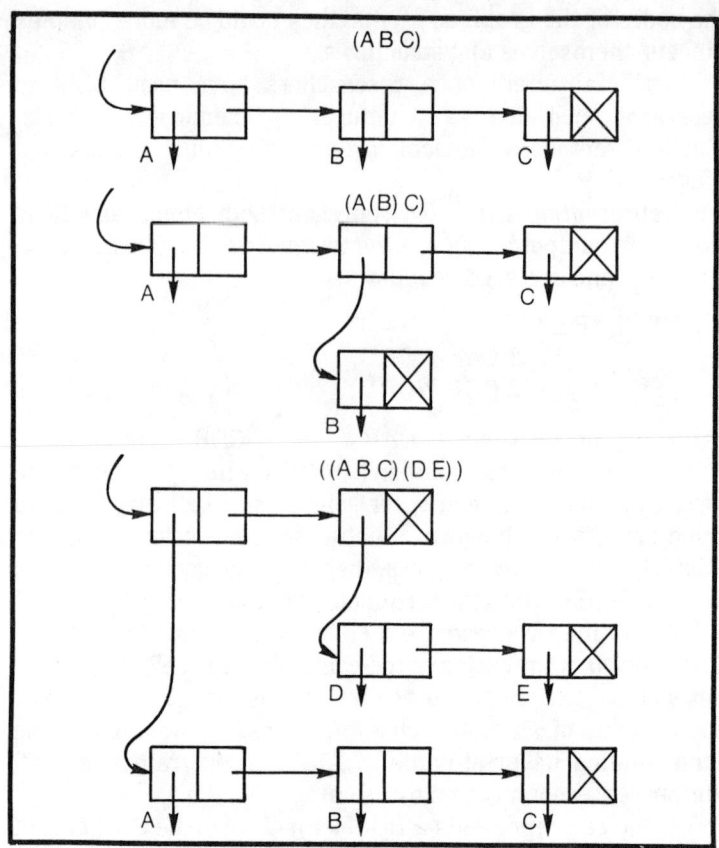

Fig. 16-3. Representations of Lists in terms of cells. Atoms are represented by their names (A, B, C, and so on).

parts. For List cells, at least, we can be sure that these bits are available: a List cell consists of four bytes. We can, then, let the addresses of successive cells start at addresses that are divisible by 4: 1000, 1004, 1008, 1012, and so on, for instance, In binary notation the rightmost two bits of any number divisible by 4 are 0. Since these bits are known—their value must always be 0—we can use these positions in the word for other purposes. We shall use one of these bits in both the CAR and CDR word. We shall also assume that steps have been taken to reserve these bits in atom cells, too, even though a word in an atom cell may contain something other than a pointer to another cell.

The rightmost bit of the CAR of a cell determines whether it is an atom or not. If the bit is 1, the cell is an atom cell; if the bit is 0, it is a List cell. The rightmost bit of the CDR is used by the garbage collector.

*A Garbage Collector for Lists.* LISP features an interesting garbage collector, which recovers unused cells and returns them to the free space list. The garbage collector has two phases: a *marking phase*, in which each cell in use is marked by setting the rightmost bit of its CDR to 1; and a *linear sweep phase*, in which we scan the List storage area and place every unmarked cell on the free space list.

Let us assume a *savelist*, pointed to by P, which contains all the List structures currently in use. More specifically, an atom or List cell will be saved if it can be reached by starting with P − > CEL and following all CAR and CDR pointers until atoms are encountered.

We need a procedure MARK (P) that will mark (by setting the rightmost bit of its CDR to 1) every atom or List cell accessible from P. MARK is shown in Program 16-1. It is recursive, and is similar to the tree traversal routines of the last chapter. If its argument points to an atom, then it marks

---

```
MARK: PROCEDURE (P) RECURSIVE;
    DECLARE P WORD;
    IF P = NIL THEN RETURN;
    /* IF THE LIST OR ATOM POINTED TO BY P HAS NOT ALREADY
        BEEN MARKED, MARK IT */
        IF (P − > CELL.CDR AND 1) = 0 THEN
            DO;
                /* IF P − > CELL IS AN ATOM THEN MARK IT
                    OTHERWISE, MARK A LIST */
                IF (P − > CELL.CAR AND 1) = 1 THEN
                    /* MARK AN ATOM */
                    P − > CELL.CDR = P − > CELL.CDR OR 1;
                ELSE
                    /* MARK A LIST */
                    DO UNTIL P = NIL;
                        CALL MARK (P − > CELL.CAR);
                        P − > CELL.CDR = P − > CELL.CDR OR 1;
                        P = (P − > CELL.CDR) AND OFFFEH;
                    END;
            END;
END MARK;
```

Program 16-1. MARK marks those list cells which are accessible from its argument, P.

```
LIST__GARBAGE__COLLECTOR: PROCEDURE (P);
   DECLARE (P, Q) WORD;
   /* MARKING PHASE: MARK EVERY CELL ACCESSIBLE FROM P*/
      CALL MARK(P);
   /* LINEAR SWEEP PHASE: EXAMINE EACH CELL. IF A CELL
      IS UNMARKED, PUT IT ON THE FREE SPACE LIST. IF
      IF IS MARKED, UNMARK IT */
      FREE = NIL;
      DO Q = @SPACE TO @SPACE + SPACE__SIZE − 4 BY 4;
         IF (Q − > CELL.CDR AND 1) = 0 THEN
            DO;
               Q − > CELL.CAR = NIL;
               Q − > CELL.CDR = FREE;
               FREE = Q;
            END;
         ELSE
            Q − > CELL.CDR = Q − > CELL.CDR AND 0FFFEH;
      END;
END LIST__GARBAGE__COLLECTOR;
```

Program 16-2. LIST__GARBAGE__COLLECTOR returns to the free space list all cells which are not accessible from its argument, P.

the atom and returns. But it calls itself to mark each of the elements of a List. When MARK encounters a cell that has already been marked, then it returns without doing anything further.

Program 16-2 shows the complete garbage collector, LIST__GARBAGE__COLLECTOR (P). P is the pointer to *savelist*; it is passed on to MARK, which marks all the cells to be saved. Then a sweep is made through the List storage area. All unmarked cells go on the free space list. Cells that were marked by MARK are now unmarked.

The following global declarations are assumed:
DECLARE FREE WORD,
  SPACE__SIZE LITERALLY ' /* SIZE OF LIST SPACE */ ',
  SPACE(SPACE__SIZE) BYTE;

The address of the first cell in SPACE is @SPACE, and the address of the last one is @SPACE + SPACE__SIZE − 4. To go from one cell to the next we increment its address by 4, since every cell takes up 4 bytes. Thus the following iterative DO statement will cause Q to point to each cell in turn:

DO Q = @SPACE TO @SPACE + SPACE__SIZE − 4 BY 4;

# Part V
# Searching

# Chapter 17
# Searching Lists

We store information inside a computer in the form of lists and tables, as well as more complicated structures such as trees and graphs. The information may be stored for a short time in main memory, or for a much longer time on auxiliary storage, such as tape or disk. Either way, eventually the time comes when a program must retrieve the stored information. Sometimes we can arrange matters so that the program can go immediately to the memory location that holds the desired data. More commonly, the program has to search for the data it wants (just as we do when using a library or a dictionary). Hence this part of the book, which is devoted to search techniques.

Before turning to the main topic of this chapter, which is methods of searching simple lists, it will help if we think a moment about the way information is stored inside a computer.

## ENTITIES, ATTRIBUTES, VALUES, AND RELATIONS

*Entities.* Often the information we store refers to persons, places, or things we call *entities*. An entity may be an object from the outside world: a person, a business, a book, an inventory item, and so on. Or it may be some purely "internal" object which a program has constructed as an aid to its manipulations. Compilers, for instance, make frequent use of such internal constructs.

We define a *record* as a block of data referring to a single entity. A record will usually be a value of a structure, that is, a block of data that can be stored in the block of memory described by a structure declaration. The components of the structure then define the components, or *fields*, of the record. We may think of a structure as defining a particular *record type*, that is, a particular configuration of fields.

*Attributes.* Each entity has certain properties we wish to record. We call these properties *attributes*. For a person, the attributes of importance for a certain application might be name, address, social security number, marital status, and salary. Of course, a person has many more attributes than these. Almost invariably, we *abstract* objects from the real world by selecting a small number of attributes relevant to a particular application.

Usually we will not choose a separate set of attributes for each entity that we store information about. One set of attributes will apply to a large class of entities. For instance, we would probably be interested in one set of attributes for all the employees, and not a separate set for each employee. On the other hand, we would use a different set of attributes to describe the items in the company's inventory.

Typically, then, we have the following situation. We are interested in a certain type of entity—employee, or student, or inventory item, say. We wish to describe each entity of this type using certain attributes. We will describe each entity with a record, all records will have the same type, and that type will be specified (in our programming language) by a structure declaration. There will be a one-to-one correspondence between the attributes used and the components of the structure.

For instance, we might specify the structure of the records representing the employees of a company as follows:

```
DECLARE 1 PERSONNEL_RECORD,
          2 NAME(40) BYTE,
          2 ADDRESS(40) BYTE,
          2 SOCIAL_SECURITY_NUMBER(9)
              BYTE,
          2 MARITAL_STATUS BYTE,
          2 SALARY(7) BYTE;
```

The correspondence between components and attributes is obvious.

*Values.* For each entity we can assign a value to each attribute. Thus for a certain employee, NAME might have the value 'BILL JACKSON', the value of MARITAL STATUS might be 'S' (for single), and so on. A record, then, simply consists of the values of all attributes specified in the structure which defines the record type.

*Relations.* A relation is a table such as the one shown in Fig. 17-1. Each row of the table corresponds to a particular entity. Each column corresponds to a particular attribute, and the name of that attribute heads the column. The entries in the body of the table are values; in particular, the entry in a particular row and column is the value of the attribute heading the column for the entity described by that row. Since each row gives the values of the attributes for one entity, it constitutes a record. The column heads describe the record type, and are equivalent to a structure declaration.

We can always think of the data stored inside a computer as a set of relations. The advocates of *relational data bases* argue that we should always think of data in this way, regardless of how it is actually stored inside the computer. We can then, for instance, specify all the manipulations we wish to carry out on the data in terms of operations on relations.

A relation must contain at least one attribute whose value will uniquely identify an entity. (It occasionally happens that the values of several attributes must be used together to identify an entity, a situation we will ignore for simplicity.) Social Security Number, as well as various "account numbers" are examples. An attribute that serves this purpose is a *key.* We always select one such attribute as the *primary key*

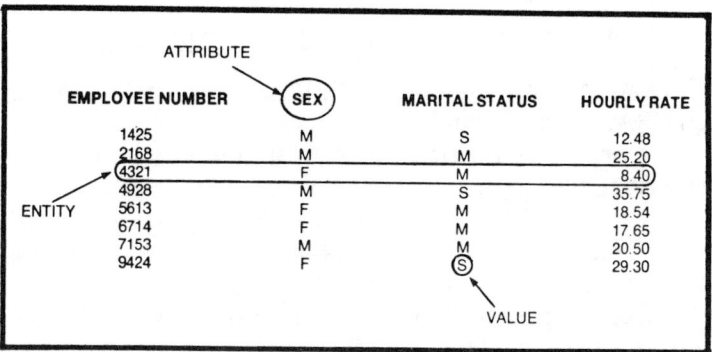

Fig. 17-1. A relation. The rows correspond to entities. The column heads are attributes. Each entry is a value.

275

of the relation. Other attributes, which in a certain context might be useful in specifying an entity, are called *secondary keys*.

Much of our work in this part of the book will be devoted to *key to address transformations*. We wish a routine that, given the value of a primary key, will return the address of the record for that entity. We will also devote a chapter to the more difficult problem of retrieving records described in terms of secondary keys.

## SEQUENTIAL SEARCH: LINEAR ARRAYS

Let us assume that we are working with records with the following structure:

```
DECLARE 1 RECORD,
        2 KEY WORD,
        2 DATA,
            /* SUBDIVISIONS OF DATA */
```

KEY is the primary key, and we assume that it is stored as a single word. This is possible if the key is a small number, such as 1345, 7318, and so on. Actually, a key is often stored as a character string. We avoid this case, however, since it would require that we call a subroutine to compare keys, rather than just use the " = " operator, and therefore would make our programs harder to read. The same principles discussed here hold for character string keys, provided we use an appropriate subroutine to do the comparison (or else write in a language that defines the " = " operator for strings!).

The most obvious way to store a set of records is as a linear array. We define:

```
DECLARE 1 LIST(LIST_SIZE) LIKE RECORD;
```

where we assume that LIST_SIZE has been declared to be LITERALLY some number.

We are given a certain value, V, for the primary key, and we wish to find the subscript of the record whose primary key has this value. Thus we are constructing a key-to-subscript transformation, a slight variation of the key-to-address transformation mentioned earlier.

Also, it is possible that *no* record exists whose key has the desired value, in which case our search routine must return some special indication that this state of affairs holds.

The simplest kind of search is the *sequential search*, in which we start at the beginning of the list and work through it record by record until we find the one we are looking for, or until we reach the end of the list:

```
I = 0;
DO WHILE (I < = LAST(LIST)) AND (LIST(I).KEY
    < > V);
    I = I + 1;
END;
```

When the repetition terminates, one of two conditions can hold. We can have I greater than LAST(LIST), in which case the search terminated because the end of the list had been reached, and the desired record has not been found. Or, we can have I less than or equal to LAST(LIST), in which case LIST(I).KEY = V; the desired record was found and I is its subscript.

We may thus follow the above search with the following IF statement:

```
IF I < = LAST(LIST) THEN
    /* RETRIEVE THE DESIRED INFORMATION
       FROM LIST(I) */;
ELSE
    /* TAKE THE APPROPRIATE ACTION FOR THE
       CASE WHERE THE RECORD BEING
       SEARCHED FOR WAS NOT FOUND */
```

The above search routine makes two tests on each repetition: one to see if it has run off the end of the list, and one to see if it has found the desired record. It is important that the first test be made first, since otherwise we might test a memory location which is not part of the list being searched. On the small computers used by amateurs this would only result in an extra, meaningless test. But on large machines it could cause a program termination, since the program might attempt to refer to a memory location outside the area assigned to it.

Therefore it is important that we assume a "sequential AND": The conditions are tested in left to right order, and if one is found to be FALSE the remaining ones will not be tested at all. The method discussed in Chapter 5 for handling logical expressions in control statements yields the sequential AND.

Another approach, which is more efficient as well, is to eliminate the end-of-list test and use a sentinel as the last record on the list. We will let the last record on the list be a dummy record, and set its key to the value for which we are searching. This value, then, will always be found, even if only in the dummy record at the end of the list. Hence the only test we have to make during the search is whether or not we have found a record having the desired value for its key:

```
LIST(LAST (LIST)).KEY = V;
I = 0;
DO WHILE LIST(I).KEY < > V;
    I = I + 1;
END;
```

After this repetition terminates, we test to see if $I = LAST(LIST)$. If it does, then the search stopped on the sentinel record, and the record we were looking for is not on the list. Otherwise, I is the subscript of the record sought.

The sentinel technique is the most efficient way to search a list, since the search routine has to make only one test per repetition instead of two. Usually this increased efficiency is well worth the record position that has to be reserved for the sentinel.

Usually a sequential search is coded "in line" rather than as a separate procedure. Nevertheless, we can write the search as a procedure if we wish. If we do not choose to use the sentinel technique, then we can make effective use of the RETURN statement to terminate repetition when the desired record has been found:

```
SEQUENTIAL_SEARCH: PROCEDURE (V) WORD;
    DECLARE (I, V) WORD;
        DO I = 0 TO LAST(LIST);
            IF LIST(I).KEY = V THEN RETURN I;
        END;
        RETURN I;
END;
```

The statement

$$X = SEQUENTIAL\_SEARCH (1234);$$

will set X to the subscript of the record whose key is 1234, if such a record exists, or to LAST (LIST) + 1 otherwise. The same test as before—is X less than or equal to LAST (LIST)—can be used to determine whether or not the desired record was found.

Sequential search is appropriate only for small lists. The number of *probes*—the number of list elements we must examine before finding the desired one—is on the average $(N + 1)/2$, where N is the length of the list. Thus if we had a list of 500 entries, we would on the average have to examine 250 of them each time we made a search. And if we had a million records, not at all uncommon in some large governmental and commercial data bases, then we would need an average of 500,000 probes, which would put sequential search out of the question.

Sequential search does have one advantage, though: The records on the list may be in any order whatever. This means that a new record may simply be added to the end of the list; it does not have to be inserted in a particular position. More sophisticated search routines usually do require the records to be in a particular order, and this makes insertions and deletions more difficult.

## SEQUENTIAL SEARCH: CHAINS

Chains may be searched by sequential search. Indeed, unless some more complicated structure is maintained, sequential search is the only available method.

Suppose our records, which are to be the nodes of the chain, are declared as follows:

```
DECLARE 1 RECORD,
          2 KEY WORD,
          2 DATA,
             /* SUBDIVISIONS OF DATA */
          2 LINK WORD;
```

If the link component of the last record on the list contains NIL, then we can use that as a sentinel:

```
P = FIRST;
DO WHILE (P < > NIL) AND (P - > RECORD.KEY < > V);
    P = P - > RECORD.LINK;
END;
```

Here FIRST is the pointer to the first record of the chain.

If we are searching a ring instead of a chain, then we may place a sentinel in the key field of the header record:

```
FIRST - > RECORD.KEY = V;
P = FIRST - > RECORD.LINK;
DO WHILE P - > RECORD.KEY < > V;
    P = P - > RECORD.LINK;
END;
```

When the repetition terminates, if P = FIRST then the desired record was not found. Otherwise, it was.

Since records may be inserted and deleted from any position of a chain, it is easy to maintain the records on the chain in order of increasing key values. Thus a search need only continue until it discovers a record whose key is greater than the key being searched for.

Also, with a singly linked chain, we must always supply the insertion and deletion routines with a pointer to the record *before* the one to be deleted or *before* the position where an insertion is to be made. Thus when our search terminates, either because we found the desired record or found the first one record with a greater key, then we would like to have a pointer to the previous record as well as to the one on which the search stopped.

Assuming that FIRST points to a header record, which is not to be examined, we have:

```
P = FIRST;
Q = FIRST - > RECORD.LINK;
DO WHILE (Q < > NIL) AND (Q - > RECORD.KEY < V);
    P = Q;
    Q = Q - > RECORD.LINK;
END;
```

When the repetition terminates, if Q = NIL or Q - > RECORD.KEY < > V, then the desired record was not found. Otherwise, it was, and Q is a pointer to it.

P is used for insertions and deletions. If we wish to delete the record that was found we call DELETE_AFTER (P). If we wish to insert a new record with key $\overline{V}$, then we call INSERT_AFTER (P). (INSERT_AFTER and DELETE_AFTER are defined in Chapter 14.)

## BLOCK SEARCH

When the records on a list are in no particular order, we have no choice but to examine each record until we find the one we are looking for, or we come to the end of the list. If the records are ordered according to key, however, we *do not* have to examine every record on the list.

Suppose the list has been sorted so that the keys are in ascending order. We may divide the list up into blocks and, starting with the first block, examine the last record in each block. If the key of the record is less than the key being searched for, then the desired record cannot be in that block, and we can move on to the next one. But if the key we are looking for is less than or equal to the key of the last record in a block, then the desired record will be in that block if it is in the list at all. Thus by looking at the last record in each block, we narrow our search down to a single block, which is then searched sequentially. Fig. 17-2 illustrates the process.

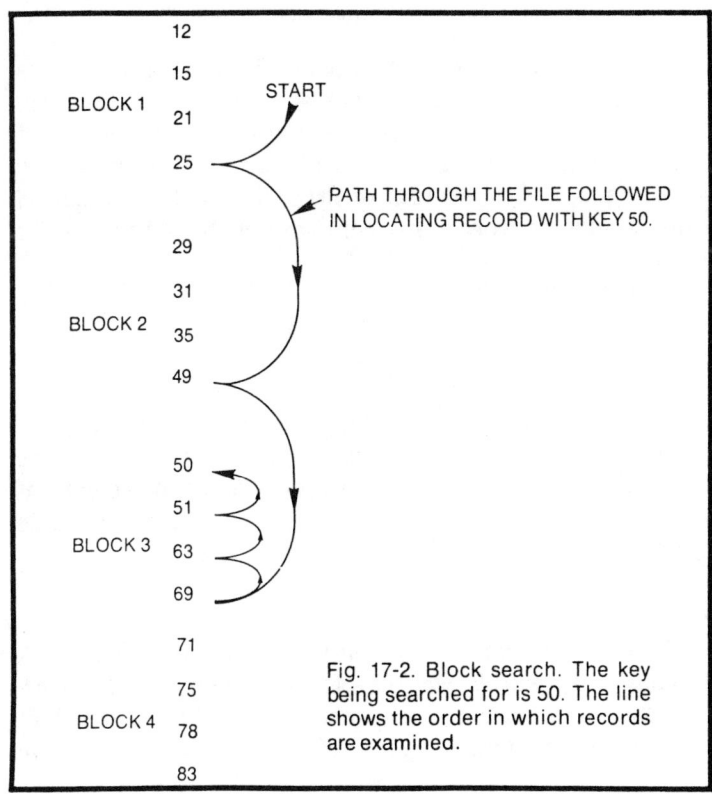

Fig. 17-2. Block search. The key being searched for is 50. The line shows the order in which records are examined.

```
BLOCK__SEARCH: PROCEDURE (V, BLOCK__SIZE) WORD;
    DECLARE (I, J, V, BLOCK__SIZE) WORD;
    /* V IS THE VALUE BEING SEARCHED FOR */
    /* FIND CORRECT BLOCK */
        I = BLOCK__SIZE - 1;
        DO WHILE (I <= LAST (LIST)) AND (LIST (I).KEY < V);
            I = I + BLOCK__SIZE;
        END;
    /*SEARCH BLOCK FOUND */
        IF I <= LAST (LIST) THEN
            DO J = 1 TO BLOCK__SIZE;
                IF LIST (I).KEY = V THEN RETURN I;
                I = I - 1;
            END;
    /* INDICATE DESIRED ITEM NOT FOUND */
        RETURN OFFFFH;
END BLOCK__SEARCH;
```

Program 17-1. BLOCK__SEARCH searches LIST for the record with key V.

It turns out that the optimal block size is $\sqrt{N}$, where N is the length of the list. If the blocks are chosen to be this size, then the average number of probes is also $\sqrt{N}$. Thus if our list contained 10,000 records, we should use 100 blocks of 100 records each, and an average of 100 probes would be required to find a given record. This compares with 5000 probes for sequential search.

Program 17-1 shows the procedure BLOCK_SEARCH. This routine returns the subscript of the desired record, if that record was found, and OFFFFH otherwise, which value serves as a signal that the desired record was not found.

This procedure assumes that the list contains a whole number of blocks; it makes no test for a fractional block at the end of the list. If a fractional block does occur, one can fill it out with dummy records, each containing the largest possible key OFFFFH.

## BINARY SEARCH

With an ordered list we can do much better than block search. *Binary search* requires an averge of $\log_2 N - 1$ probes, and a maximum of $\log_2 N + 1$ probes, where N is the length of the list, and the function $\log_2$ is defined in Chapter 2. Thus we find that for 10,000 records we need an average of 12 probes and a maximum of 14. And for one million records we need an average of 18 probes and a maximum of 20. (Block search would require an average of 1000 probes in this case.)

On the other hand, with block search the records may be read in block by block from an auxiliary storage device. Binary search requires so much jumping around in the list that it is rarely suitable for lists stored on auxiliary storage. It is restricted to lists stored in main memory.

Fig. 17-3 illustrates binary search. We start by examining the *middle* record of the list to be searched. Three cases can occur:

1) The key being searched for equals the key of the middle record.
2) The key being searched for is less than the key of the middle record.
3) The key being searched for is greater than the key of the middle record.

If case 1 occurs, then we have found the record we are looking for. If case 2 occurs, then the record we are looking for must be in the first half of the list; we can eliminate the second

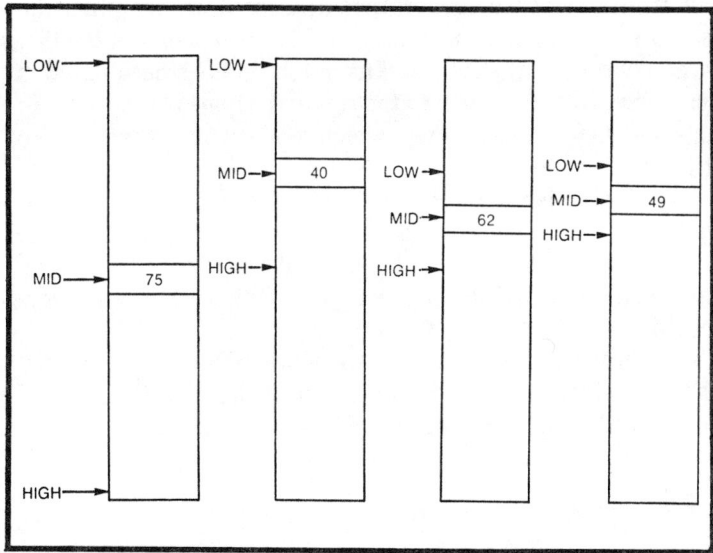

Fig. 17-3. The first few steps of a binary search. The pointers LOW and HIGH delimit the part of the list remaining to be searched. The size of this part is halved at each step. Search is for record with key 50.

```
BINARY_SEARCH: PROCEDURE (V) WORD;
    DECLARE (LOW, MID, HIGH, V) WORD;
    /* V IS THE VALUE BEING SEARCHED FOR */
    /* INITIALIZE LOW AND HIGH */
        LOW = 0;
        HIGH = LAST(LIST);
    /* CARRY OUT BINARY SEARCH */
        DO UNTIL LOW > HIGH;
            MID = (LOW + HIGH)/2;
            IF V = LIST(MID) THEN RETURN MID;
            IF V < LIST(MID) THEN
                HIGH = MID - 1;
            ELSE
                LOW = MID + 1;
        END;
    /* INDICATE DESIRED ITEM NOT FOUND */
        RETURN 0FFFFH;
END BINARY SEARCH;
```

Program 17-2. BINARY_SEARCH searches LIST for the record with key V.

half from further consideration. If case 3 occurs, then the record we're looking for must be in the second half of the list, we can eliminate the first half from further consideration. It is this ability to eliminate half the remaining part of the list from consideration at each step which makes binary search so efficient.

Having selected either the first or second half of the list, we repeat the process with it. We keep repeating the same process until we have found the desired record or until we have narrowed the partition we are searching down to a single record.

Program 17-2 shows the procedure BINARY_SEARCH. The procedure returns the subscript of the record sought, if that record was found, and 0FFFFH otherwise.

# Chapter 18
# Hashing

It would be very helpful if, instead of having to search for the record having a given key, we could carry out some simple calculation on the key that would yield the address of the sought-after record directly.

One simple way to accomplish this is to make the address of the record part of the key. Thus we might assign a customer of a business an account number such as 45-6891-2157, where 2157 is the address of that customer's record in a disk file, and the remaining digits are used for other purposes, as demanded by the application.

Another example: inside a compiler, a *name* in the program being compiled is usually represented internally by a *token*. The token consists of a code indicating the type of object the name refers to, together with the address of that name's symbol table entry. Thus the token for a certain name might be 152C3FH, where 15H indicates that this is the name of a procedure, and 2C3FH is the address of the corresponding symbol table entry.

Unfortunately, the choice of a key is often beyond our control. And when we do not get to choose the key, it is very unlikely that we will be able to discover any simple algorithm that will yield a unique address for each key.

## HASHING

But all is not lost. What we have to give up is the requirement that the algorithm yield a *unique* address for each key. We can easily find a simple algorithm that will convert a key into an address. But it will from time to time convert *different* keys to the *same* address. That is, it will try to assign more than one record to the same location. We accept this, and work out ways to handle the resulting *collisions* when they occur.

The resulting technique goes under the name of *hashing*, since in computing the address we "scramble up" or "make a hash out of" the bits of the original key.

A well designed hashing algorithm provides extremely fast access to a list. In most cases the desired record will be at the first address computed. Where a collision has occurred, a short search will be needed, but rarely will more than two or three records have to be examined.

On the other hand, hashing does have some disadvantages.
1) Hashing becomes very inefficient after the list is about 80% filled. Hence the space reserved for our list must be about 20% more than will actually be used.
2) Hashing stores the records of a list in random order. If the records have to be processed in some other order—say in order of increasing keys—then the list will have to first be sorted.
3) The good performance of hashing is a matter of chance. The chances are very good that the performance will be excellent. Still it is possible, if unlikely, that for a particular set of keys hashing will give poor performance—as poor as sequential search, even. Thus hashing might not be appropriate for some real time applications where an unexpected increase in search time could cause a disaster.

These weaknesses will eliminate hashing in a few applications. But for many others, hashing will prove to be the best method for rapidly accessing stored records.

## HASHING FUNCTIONS

A hashing function converts a key into an address or, more commonly, a subscript.

To avoid collisions as much as possible, the hashing function should distribute the stored records throughout the table, rather than clustering them all in one or two areas. We could obtain such an even distribution if we chose the position each record was to occupy at random, with each position in the table having an equal chance of being chosen. We know from Chapter 10 that there are simple functions that will yield apparently random results. We wish to use such a function as our hashing function.

Many hashing functions have been invented, some of them quite elaborate. But the one that has consistently proved best in performance tests is extremely simple. Let M = LENGTH (LIST) be the size of the list in question. We merely divide the key by M, and take the remainder—which will range from 0 through M − 1—as the desired subscript:

$$I = K \text{ MOD } M;$$

Here K is the key being searched for and I is the subscript of the corresponding record.

There is one requirement for this function to give good results, and that is that M be a *prime number*, a number not evenly divisible by any other number other than 1 and itself. Tables of prime numbers may be found in most mathematical handbooks. There are prime numbers near most commonly used table sizes, such as 97, 251, 509, and 1021.

Interestingly, when the division function fails to be random, it fails in a useful way. In many applications keys which differ by one are frequently encountered. The division function assigns such keys to successive memory locations, a definitely nonrandom choice. But since records whose keys differ by one are never assigned to the *same* location, they can never be the cause of a collision. Thus the division function will often give better performance than one which makes a truly random choice.

In the following sections we will assume that the key is a single word, so we can conveniently express operations on it in our programming language. In practice, however, the key will often be a string of alphabetic characters. In that case the best course is to treat the string as a long, multiple precision, number, and divide it by the list size M and take the remainder just as we would do with a one word key. The key should be right justified: if it was filled out with blanks on the right then it should be shifted to the right until the blanks are eliminated.

The multiple precision division needed to divide a long key by M may be too time consuming for some applications. For those cases, the key may be broken up into words, and the words added or XORed together. Another technique is to add up all the characters of the key, shifting the sum one place to the left after each addition. These techniques are probably not

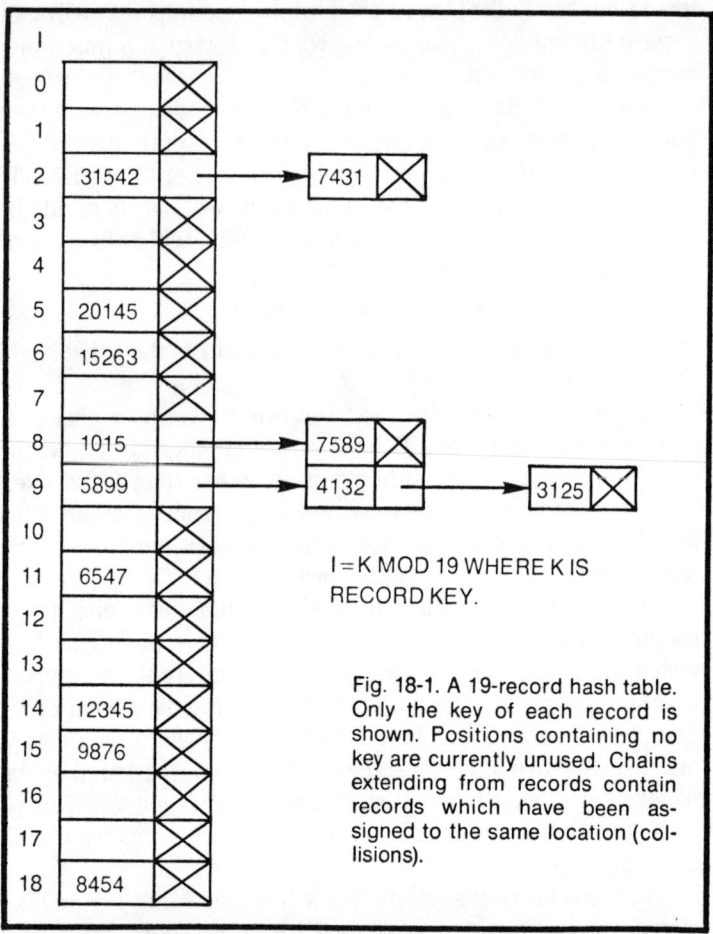

Fig. 18-1. A 19-record hash table. Only the key of each record is shown. Positions containing no key are currently unused. Chains extending from records contain records which have been assigned to the same location (collisions).

I = K MOD 19 WHERE K IS RECORD KEY.

as good as dividing the entire key by M, but will be satisfactory for many applications.

Figure 18-1 illustrates hashing for numerical keys.

## COLLISION HANDLING

Having settled on the division method for our hashing function, the question that remains is how to handle collisions. There are basically two techniques (with many variations on each): chaining and open addressing. In chaining, each entry in the list is the head of a chain which contains all the records assigned to that location. With open addressing, records assigned to a location after it has already been filled are placed in the first available location thereafter.

*Chaining.* Assume that we have a list of records declared as follows:

    DECLARE 1 LIST(/* DESIRED SIZE */),
             2 KEY WORD,
             2 DATA,
                 /* SUBDIVISIONS OF DATA */
             2 LINK WORD:

LINK is the *subscript* (not the machine address) of the next record on a chain. Since 0 is a legitimate subscript, we redefine NIL by:

    DECLARE NIL LITERALLY NOT 'OFFFFH';

We assume that LIST is divided into two parts, as shown in Fig. 18-2. The records with subscripts 0 through $M - 1$ constitute the *prime area*. The remaining records form an *overflow area*, in which we will store records assigned to already filled locations in the prime area. The keys of the records in the prime area are all initialized to 0, indicating that

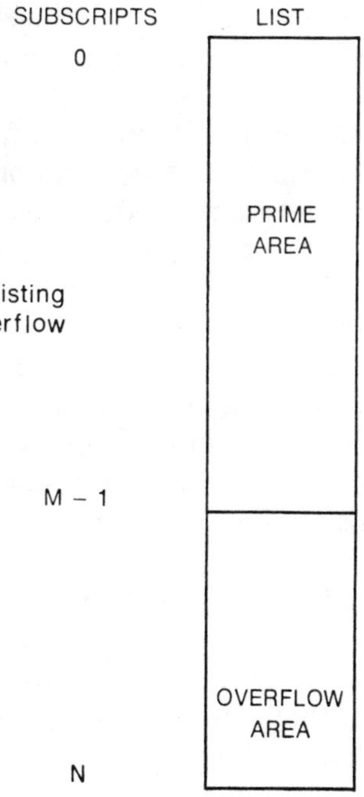

Fig. 18-2. A hash table consisting of a prime area and an overflow area.

```
INSERT: PROCEDURE (K) WORD;
    DECLARE (I, J, K) WORD;
    /* COMPUTE LOCATION USING HASHING FUNCTION */
        I = K MOD M;
    /* IF THIS LOCATION IS FREE, RETURN SUBSCRIPT COMPUTED */
        IF LIST (I).KEY = 0 THEN RETURN I;
    /* OTHERWISE, OBTAIN LOCATION FROM FREE SPACE LIST */
        IF FREE = NIL THEN CALL ERROR (14 @ 'TABLE OVERFLOW');
        J = FREE;
        FREE = LIST(FREE).LINK;
    /* LINK THIS LOCATION INTO THE CHAIN STARTING AT LIST (I) */
        LIST(J).LINK = LIST(I).LINK;
        LIST(I).LINK = J;
    /*RETURN SUBSCRIPT OF NEW LOCATION */
        RETURN J
END INSERT;
```

Program 18-1. INSERT obtains a new location in a hash table (chaining technique).

---

those record positions are currently unused. The records in the overflow area are initially linked together into a free space list. FREE contains the subscript of the first record on the free space list.

Program 18-1 shows the function INSERT (K), which returns the subscript of a location for a record with key K.

The procedure starts by computing the subscript, I, of a record in the prime area using the hashing function:

$$I = K \text{ MOD } M;$$

If LIST(I) .KEY = 0, then the record in position I is currently unused, and so we may make an insertion in that position. The procedure returns the value of I.

If LIST(I) .KEY is not 0, then we have a collision. A record is obtained from the free space list and is inserted into the chain that begins with LIST(I). The new record is inserted immediately after LIST(I), and before any other records that might already be on the chain. The procedure returns the subscript of the inserted record.

Program 18-2 shows the procedure FIND (K), which returns the subscript of the record with key K, or NIL if no such record is found.

FIND computes a subscript I using the hashing function as usual. If LIST(I) .KEY = K, then LIST(I) is the record sought, and the value of I is returned. Otherwise, the procedure searches the chain beginning at LIST(I). If the record sought is found on the chain, its subscript is returned. Otherwise, NIL is returned.

Program 18-3 gives the procedure DELETE (K), which deletes the record with key K. DELETE is much more complicated than INSERT or FIND. This is typical: deletion is often the most complicated operation to perform on a data structure.

Again we begin by applying the hashing function to K to obtain I, the subscript of a record in the prime area. If LIST(I) .KEY = K, then the record to be deleted is in the prime area. Otherwise, if the record is on the list at all, it is on the chain beginning at LIST(I).

If LIST(I) .KEY does equal K then two cases arise. If LIST(I) .LINK = NIL, then there is no overflow chain headed by LIST(I), so we can merely set LIST(I) .KEY to 0, marking LIST(I) as unused, and return.

If LIST(I) .LINK is not NIL, and LIST(I) is at the head of an overflow chain, then we cannot just mark LIST(I) as unused since that would prevent other routines from accessing the overflow chain. Therefore we move the contents of the record following LIST(I) on the chain to LIST(I), and delete

```
FIND: PROCEDURE (K) WORD;
    DECLARE (I, K) WORD;
    /* COMPUTE I USING HASHING FUNCTION */
    I = K MOD M;
    /* IF RECORD WITH KEY K IS PRESENT, IT WILL BE ON
       CHAIN STARTING WITH LIST(I) */
    DO UNTIL I = NIL;
        IF LIST(I).KEY = K THEN RETURN I;
        I = LIST(I).LINK;
    END;
    /* RECORD WITH KEY K NOT FOUND */
    RETURN NIL;
END;
```

Program 18-2. FIND locates the record with key K in a hash table (chaining technique).

```
DELETE: PROCEDURE (K):
    DECLARE (I, J, K) WORD:
    /* COMPUTE I USING HASHING FUNCTION */
        I = K MOD M:
    /*DELETE RECORD WITH KEY K */
        IF LIST(I).LINK = K THEN
            /* RECORD TO BE DELETED IS IN LIST(I) */
                DO:
                    IF LIST(I).LINK = NIL THEN
                        /* NO OVERFLOW CHAIN */
                            DO:
                                LIST(I).KEY = 0:
                                RETURN:
                            END:
                    ELSE
                        /* THERE IS AN OVERFLOW CHAIN */
                            DO:
                                J = LIST(I).LINK:
                                LIST(I) = LIST(J):
                                CALL DISPOSE _ OF (J):
                                RETURN:
                            END:

        ELSE
            /* RECORD TO BE DELETED IS ON OVERFLOW CHAIN */
                DO:
                    /* FIND RECORD */
                        J = LIST(I).LINK:
                        DO WHILE (J < >NIL) AND (LIST(J).KEY < >K):
                            I = J:
                            J = LIST(J).LINK:
                        END:
                    /* DELETE IT */
                        IF J = NIL THEN RETURN:
                        LIST(I).LINK = LIST(J).LINK:
                        CALL DISPOSE _ OF (J):
                END:
END DELETE:
```

Program 18-3. DELETE deletes the record with key K from a hash table (chaining technique).

the following record. We assume that DISPOSE_OF (J) functions like the DISPOSE_OF routine discussed in Chapter 12, and returns LIST(J) to the free space list.

If LIST(I) .KEY does not equal K, then we search the overflow chain beginning at LIST(I) .LINK for the record with key K; if it is found, it is deleted using the methods of Chapter 12.

It is possible to let the prime area and the overflow area overlap, so that when a collision occurs, the overflow record is taken from the prime area. This technique makes deletion even more complicated than it already is. From the point of view of simplicity there is much to recommend the independent overflow area.

*Open Addressing.* In open addressing, when a collision occurs, we simply initiate a sequential search through the hash table starting at the point where the collision took place. We place the record that caused the collision in the first free space found. The hash table is treated as a circular array, so if we run off the bottom during the search we come back on at the top. The hope is that unused space is sufficiently well distributed so that the search will hardly ever be a long one.

We declare our hash table by:

DECLARE 1 LIST(/* DESIRED SIZE */);
        2 KEY WORD,
        2 DATA,
            /* SUBDIVISIONS OF DATA */;

We let $M = \text{LENGTH (LIST)}$. M must be a prime number. LIST(I) .KEY is initialized to 0 for each I, to indicate that LIST(I) is not occupied.

We use N to keep track of the number of unused locations in LIST. N is initially set to M. Every time an insertion is made, N is decreased by 1. Every time a deletion is made, N is increased by 1. We must keep at least one empty position in LIST to prevent search routines from looping indefinitely. Therefore, if an insertion is attempted with $N = 1$, overflow is announced. (Of course N should never be allowed to get anywhere near this small, since hashing gives poor performance if the hash table is more than about 80% full.)

Program 18-4 shows the function INSERT (K) for open addressing. Like the corresponding procedure for chaining, it returns the subscript of the position into which the record with key K is to be inserted.

```
INSERT: PROCEDURE (K) WORD;
    DECLARE (I, K) WORD;
    /* MAKE SURE THERE IS ROOM FOR THE INSERTION */
        N = N - 1;
        IF N = 0 THEN CALL ERROR (14, @'TABLE OVERFLOW');
    /* COMPUTE I USING HASHING FUNCTION */
        I = K MOD M;
    /* SEARCH FOR FREE LOCATION STARTING AT LIST(I) */
        DO WHILE LIST(I).KEY < > 0;
            IF I = 0 THEN I = M - 1;
            ELSE I = I - 1;
        END;
    /* RETURN SUBSCRIPT OF LOCATION FOUND */
        RETURN I;
END INSERT;
```

Program 18-4. INSERT obtains a new location in a hash table (open addressing technique).

INSERT begins by computing the subscript I corresponding to K using the hashing function. If that location is occupied (LIST(I) .KEY not equal to 0) then the routine searches backwards toward the beginning of the table for an unoccupied location. When it reaches the beginning, then it goes to the end and continues searching backwards. The search eventually terminates, since we have assured that there is at least one free location in LIST. When the search does terminate, INSERT returns the subscript of the location found.

A record is always inserted in the first free location encountered in the search. In searching for a particular record, then, if we encounter a free location before finding the record, we can terminate the search, since that free location would not have been passed by in inserting the record. We use free locations as sentinels to terminate searches.

This principle is used by Program 8-5, FIND (K), which starts at the location obtained by applying the hashing function to K. If a record is encountered with LIST(I) .KEY = K, this is the record sought, and I is returned. If a free location is encountered, one with LIST(I) .KEY = 0, then the record sought is not in LIST, and OFFFFH is returned.

Program 8-6 shows DELETE (K), which deletes the record with key K. As usual, DELETE is more complicated than the other routines.

It might seem at first sight that deletion would be very simple. All we have to do is to set the key of the record we wish to delete equal to 0. Its position will thereafter be considered a free location by INSERT and FIND.

Unfortunately, a problem arises. We have assumed that when searching for a record we need only search as far as the first free location, since a search during insertion would not have passed over a free location. If we delete records, creating new free locations, and take no further precautions, we destroy this condition.

Specifically, suppose that the hashing function applied to the key of a record to be inserted yielded the subscript I. Suppose that LIST(I) was already occupied, so a search for a free location was instituted, and as a result the record was actually inserted at LIST(J). Suppose further that a deletion is made between LIST(I) and LIST(J). Then when FIND attempts to locate the record in LIST(J), it will start at LIST(I), but will terminate its search when it reaches the free location, the one where a record had been deleted.

Therefore, when we delete a record at position J, we must examine each record between position J and the next free space, and see if the free location at position J would

---

```
FIND: PROCEDURE (K) WORD;
    DECLARE (I, K) WORD;
    /* COMPUTE I USING HASHING FUNCTION */
        I = K MOD M;
    /* START SEARCH FOR RECORD WITH KEY K AT LIST(I). SEARCH
        TERMINATES WHEN AN EMPTY LOCATION IS ENCOUNTERED */
        DO WHILE LIST(I).KEY <> 0;
            IF LIST(I).KEY = K THEN RETURN I;
            IF I = 0 THEN I = M - 1;
            ELSE I = I - 1;
        END;
    /* DESIRED RECORD NOT FOUND */
        RETURN NIL;
END FIND;
```

Program 18-5. FIND locates the record with key K in a hash table (open addressing technique).

```
DELETE: PROCEDURE (K):
   DECLARE (I, J, K, L) WORD:
   /* SET I TO SUBSCRIPT OF RECORD WITH KEY K. IF NO
      SUCH RECORD EXISTS, RETURN */
      I = FIND (K);
      IF I = NIL THEN RETURN:
   /* KEEP TRACK OF NUMBER OF FREE POSITIONS */
      N = N + 1:
   /* DELETE RECORD IN LIST(I) AND RELOCATE OTHER RECORDS
      AS IS NECESSARY (SEE TEXT) */
      DO WHILE TRUE: /* DO FOREVER */
         LIST(I).KEY = 0;
         J = I:
         DO UNTIL   ((I < J) AND((L < I) OR(L >= J)))
                 OR ((I > J) AND (J <= L) AND (L < I)):
            IF I = 0 THEN I = M - 1;
            ELSE I = I - 1;
            IF LIST(I).KEY = 0 THEN RETURN: /* EXIT HERE */
            L = LIST(I).KEY MOD M:
         END:
         LIST(J) = LIST(I):
      END:
END DELETE:
```

Program 18-6. DELETE deletes the record with key K from a hash table (open addressing technique).

prematurely terminate a search for that record. If such a record is found, then it is placed in position J, replacing the record that was originally deleted. A new free location is created at the position of the record that was moved, J is set to that position, and the process is repeated. Figure 18-3 ilustrates this process.

Now let J be the position where the deletion was made, and I the position currently under examination. Let L = LIST(I).KEY MOD M. L is the position at which a search would begin for the record stored in LIST(I). What we want to discover is whether the deletion at J would prevent a search starting at L from reaching I. This will occur if J lies "between" L and I. But because we allow our subscripts to go from the beginning of the list to its end during a search, the definition of "between" is slightly complicated.

Suppose I < J. (See Fig. 18-4a.) Then the search has not passed from the beginning of the list to its end in going from J to I. If L > = J then J is indeed between L and I, and so the deletion at J could prevent a search starting at L from reaching I.

But the same thing could happen if L < I. The search starting at L would go off the beginning of the list, come back on at the end, and then encounter the free location at J before getting to I.

Thus one set of conditions under which the record at I must be moved to J is:

$$(I < J) \text{ AND } ((L < I) \text{ OR } (L > = J))$$

On the other hand, suppose that I > J. (See Fig. 18-4b.) Then I has run off the beginning of the list and come back on at

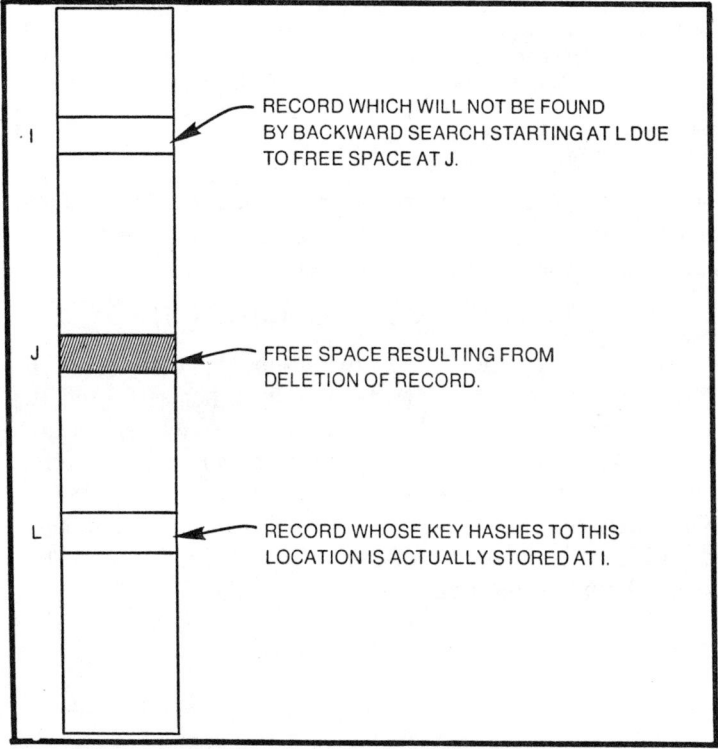

Fig. 18-3. A record has been deleted at position J. The resulting free space could prematurely terminate a search for the record at position I. Therefore the record at I is moved to J. Now position I is free and a check must be made to see if it could prematurely terminate any searches.

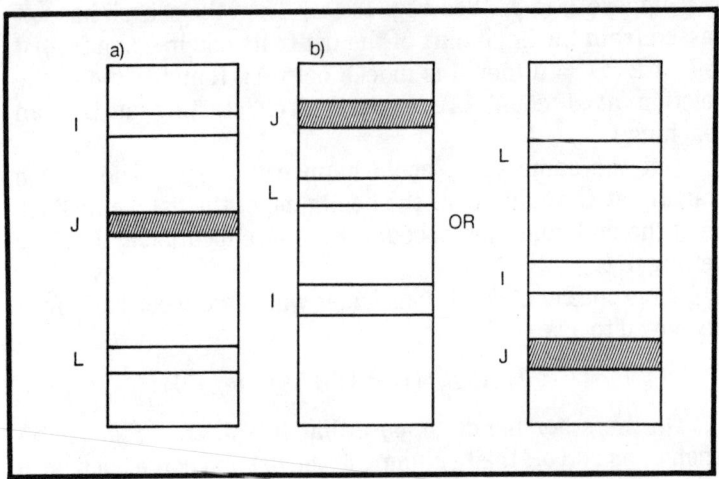

Fig. 18-4. A free space at position J could prematurely terminate a search for the record at position I whose key hashes to position L provided that position J is between position L and position I. Since the hash table is a circular list, there are two situations (a and b in the figure) in which position J is regarded as being between position L and position I. In b) a search starting at position L goes off the beginning of the list and comes back on at the end.

the end during its backward search. Now the locations from which the deletion at J could interrupt a search occur between J and I, including J but not I. Thus our second condition is:

$$(I > J) \text{ AND } (J <= L) \text{ AND } (L < I)$$

Therefore: DELETE sets I to the subscript of the record to be deleted, and sets LIST(I) .KEY = 0. It then sets J to I (to remember where the deleted record was). It then steps I backward examining each LIST(I). If it finds a free location then it returns. If it finds an I such that I, J, and L = LIST(I) .KEY MOD M satisfy one of the conditions just mentioned, then LIST(I) is moved to LIST(J), LIST(I) .KEY is set to 0, J is set to I, and the entire process is repeated.

# Chapter 19
# Searching Binary Trees

Binary trees provide an access technique comparable to hashing in efficiency. Hashing will usually be faster, but binary trees offer more flexible memory management. Also, it is possible to scan the records stored in a binary tree in sequential order, something that is impossible with hashing unless the hash table is first sorted. For some applications this is the deciding factor in favor of binary trees.

**DEFINITIONS**

For the sake of flexibility we use a plex representation of binary trees, although for some applications the linear array representation for complete binary trees might be adequate. Our trees, therefore, will be made up of nodes declared as follows:

```
DECLARE 1 RECORD,
          2 KEY WORD,
          2 DATA,
             /* SUBDIVISIONS OF DATA */
          2 LEFT WORD,
          2 RIGHT WORD;
```

As usual KEY is the primary key of the record. LEFT and RIGHT are pointers to the left and right children of the current record. If a particular child does not exist, then the corresponding pointer will have the value NIL.

When we are working on a given record we may need a pointer to the parent of that record. But actually we need more than that. A record may be pointed to from one of two places inside its parent: RECORD.LEFT or RECORD.RIGHT. We may have to change the appropriate link in the parent as a result of work done on the child, and so we need to know whether it is the LEFT or the RIGHT link of a parent that points to a particular child.

What we need, then, is not a pointer to the parent record, but to the particular word (RECORD.LEFT or RECORD.RIGHT) in the parent which points to the child.

We thus define a global variable P which points to P_WORD:

>     DECLARE P WORD,
>          P_WORD BASED P WORD;

The value of P will be either @RECORD.LEFT or @RECORD.RIGHT for some record, so that P_WORD will be either RECORD.LEFT or RECORD.RIGHT. Hence an assignment to P_WORD will be an assignment to the appropriate pointer.

We declare ROOT to be a word, and let it be the pointer to the root of the tree. If the tree is empty, then ROOT is NIL. We may let P also have the value @ROOT, so that P_WORD can stand in place of ROOT, thus giving us even more flexibility when dealing with the parent of a child. We can even deal with the "parent" of the root.

The fundamental principle of binary search tree organization is this: All the descendants of a record having keys *less than* that of the record occur in its left subtree. All descendants having keys *greater than* the key of the record occur in its right subtree.

When we search for a record in a binary tree, then, we compare the key of the record being searched for with the key of the record being examined. If the keys are the same, we have found the record we were looking for. If the key being searched for is less than the key of the current record, we follow the left link and search the left subtree. Otherwise, we follow the right link and search the right subtree. If the link we attempt to follow is NIL, then the record we are searching for is not in the tree.

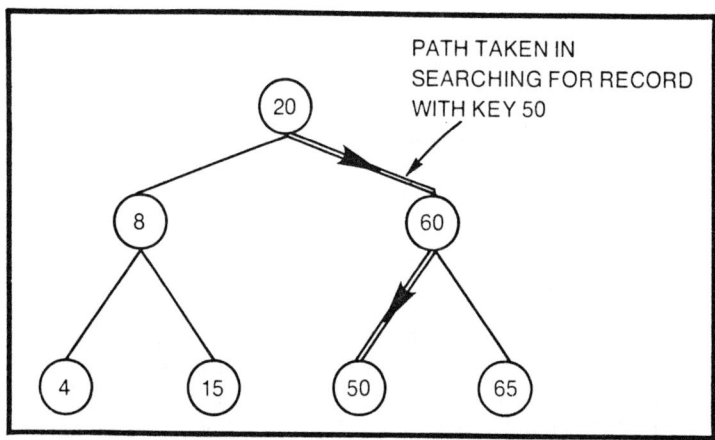

Fig. 19-1. The path taken through the binary tree in searching for the record with key 50.

Figure 19-1 illustrates a binary tree and the search process.

## SEARCHING

Using the technique just described we construct Program 19-1, FIND (K), a function whose argument is the key K being

```
FIND: PROCEDURE (K) WORD;
    DECLARE (Q, K) WORD;
    /* Q POINTS TO A RECORD. P POINTS TO THE LINK WORD
        THAT IN TURN POINTS TO Q -> RECORD. THE LINK WORD
        IS EITHER ROOT OR ELSE RECORD.LEFT OR RECORD.RIGHT
        IN THE PARENT OF Q -> RECORD */
    P = @ROOT;
    Q = ROOT;
    DO WHILE Q <> NIL;
        IF K = Q -> RECORD.KEY THEN RETURN Q;
        IF K < Q -> RECORD.KEY THEN
            P = @Q -> RECORD.LEFT;
        ELSE
            P = @Q -> RECORD.RIGHT;
        Q = P __ WORD;
    END;
    RETURN NIL; /* RECORD WITH KEY K NOT FOUND */
END FIND;
```

Program 19-1. FIND locates the record with key K in a binary tree.

searched for, and whose value is a pointer to the record found, or NIL if no record with the given key was found. As a side effect, FIND sets P to point either to ROOT or to the link word in the parent of the record found which points to that record. If the record was not found, P points to the position at which it could be inserted, that is, to a link word in which a pointer to a record with key K could be placed.

### INSERTIONS

Program 19-2 shows the binary tree insertion routine, INSERT (K). INSERT calls FIND to work through the binary tree as when searching. When FIND encounters a link word (RECORD.LEFT or RECORD.RIGHT) that is NIL, it returns with P pointing to the link word found. A pointer to the inserted record is placed in this link word, as shown in Fig. 19-2. When, subsequently, FIND is called with the same key, its search will lead it to the same link word, which will now contain not NIL but a pointer to the record with the key which was inserted.

The new record is obtained by calling NEW_RECORD, which removes a record from a free space list, and returns a pointer to it. INSERT (K) returns a pointer to the record just inserted. (If a record with key K is already present in the tree, INSERT returns a pointer to it and no new record is inserted.)

### DELETION

As usual, deletion is not nearly so simple as insertion and search.

```
INSERT: PROCEDURE (K) WORD:
    DECLARE (K, Q) WORD;
    /* A CALL TO FIND (K) SETS P TO POINT TO THE LINK WORD
        THAT SHOULD POINT TO A RECORD WITH KEY K. IF SUCH
        A RECORD IS PRESENT FIND RETURNS A POINTER TO IT.
        OTHERWISE FIND RETURNS NIL */
    Q = FIND (K);
    IF Q < > NIL THEN RETURN Q;
    Q, P _ WORD = NEW _ RECORD;
    RETURN Q;
END INSERT;
```

Program 19-2. INSERT locates the position in a binary tree where the record with key K should be inserted.

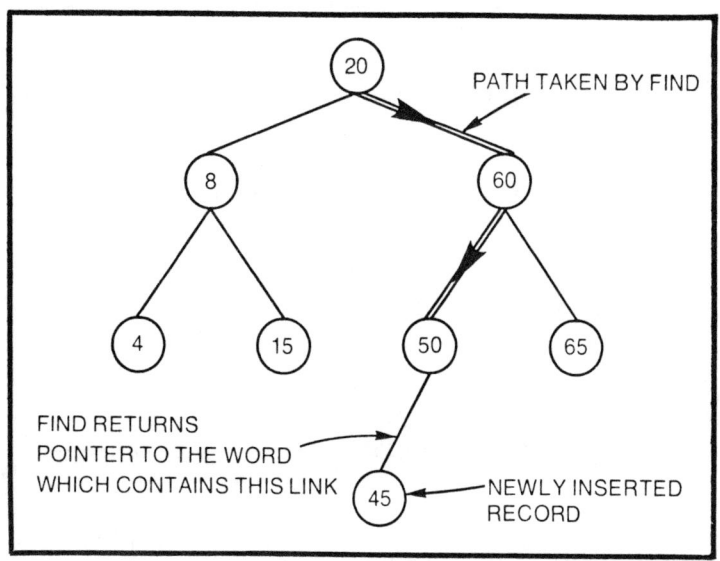

Fig. 19-2. Insertion of record with key 45.

Deleting a leaf, a node with no subtrees, is easy. And so is deleting a node with only one subtree (one link is NIL), since the link in the parent can be set to point to the single subtree, thus "routing it around" the deleted node. The problem arises when we delete a node with two subtrees. The link in the parent can only point to one node, whereas the deleted node had two children. The problem is illustrated in Fig. 19-3

What we do is exchange the node to be deleted with its immediate successor in key order, that is, the one with the next largest key. The left link of the immediate successor must

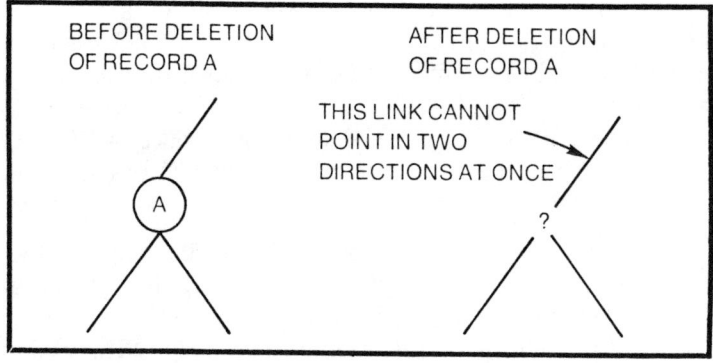

Fig. 19-3. The deletion problem.

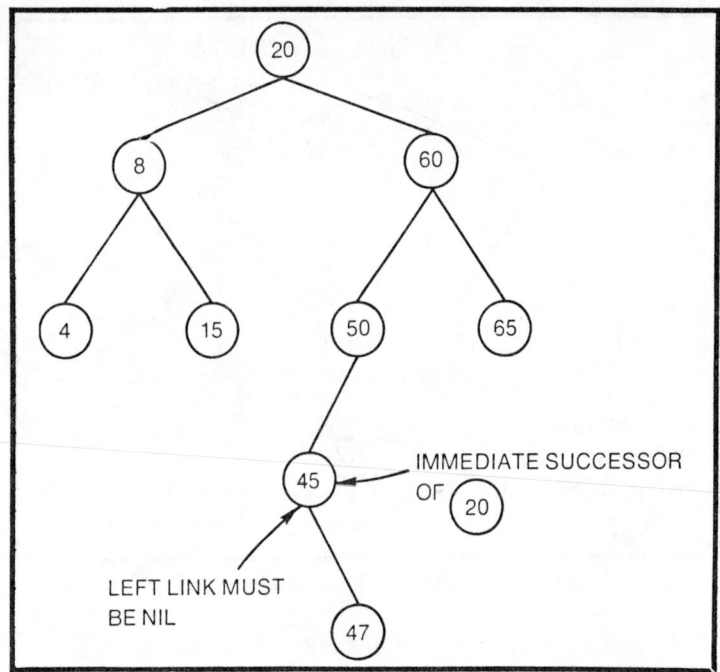

Fig. 19-4. The record with key 45 is the immediate successor of the record with key 20. The left link of the immediate successor must be NIL, since otherwise there would be a record with key between 20 and 45.

be NIL, otherwise it would point to a node whose key lies between that of the record being deleted and the immediate successor. If such a node existed the "immediate successor" would not be an immediate successor! Since the immediate successor does have one link equal to NIL it may be deleted without difficulty. See Fig. 19-4.

We may find the immediate successor of a node by starting from its right child, and following left links until a node is reached whose link is NIL. That node is the immediate successor.

Program 19-3 shows the deletion procedure, DELETE (K). The steps of the procedure are illustrated in Fig. 19-5 and described below:

1) Call FIND to set P to point to the link that points to the node to be deleted. If FIND returns NIL then announce that the node to be deleted does not exist.
2) If the left link in the node to be deleted is NIL, set the link in its parent (P_WORD) to point to its right child.

3) IF the right link in the node to be deleted is NIL, set the link in its parent (P_WORD) to point to its left child.
4) If the left link of the right child of the node to be deleted is NIL, set that left link to point to the left child

```
DELETE : PROCEDURE (K);
   DECLARE (K, Q, R, S) WORD;
   /* SET P TO POINT TO LINK WORD WHICH POINTS TO
      RECORD TO BE DELETED, AND TO POINT TO THE RECORD ITSELF */
      Q = FIND (K);
   /* CHECK THAT RECORD TO BE DELETED EXISTS */
      IF Q = NIL THEN
          CALL ERROR (36, @ 'ATTEMPT TO DELETE NONEXISTENT RECORD');
   /* CASES REFER TO DISCUSSION IN TEXT */
      R = Q -> RECORD.RIGHT;
      IF Q -> RECORD.LEFT = NIL THEN      /*CASE 2*/
          P_WORD = Q -> RECORD.RIGHT;
      ELSE IF Q -> RECORD.RIGHT = NIL THEN   /* CASE 3 */
          P_WORD = Q -> RECORD.LEFT;
      ELSE IF R -> RECORD.LEFT = NIL THEN   /* CASE 4 */
          DO;
              R -> RECORD.LEFT = Q -> RECORD.LEFT;
              P_WORD = Q -> RECORD.RIGHT;
          END;
      ELSE
          DO;
              /* SET S TO POINT TO IMMEDIATE SUCCESSOR OF
                 Q -> RECORD */
              S = R -> RECORD.LEFT;
              DO WHILE S -> RECORD.LEFT <> NIL;
                  R = S;
                  S = S -> RECORD.LEFT;
              END;

              /* REPLACE Q -> RECORD BY S -> RECORD */
                  R -> RECORD.LEFT = S -> RECORD.RIGHT;
                  P_WORD = S;
                  S -> RECORD.LEFT = Q -> RECORD.LEFT;
                  S -> RECORD.RIGHT = Q -> RECORD.RIGHT;
          END;
   /* DELETE Q -> RECORD */
      CALL DISPOSE_OF (Q);
END DELETE;
```

Program 19-3. DELETE deletes the record with key K from a binary tree.

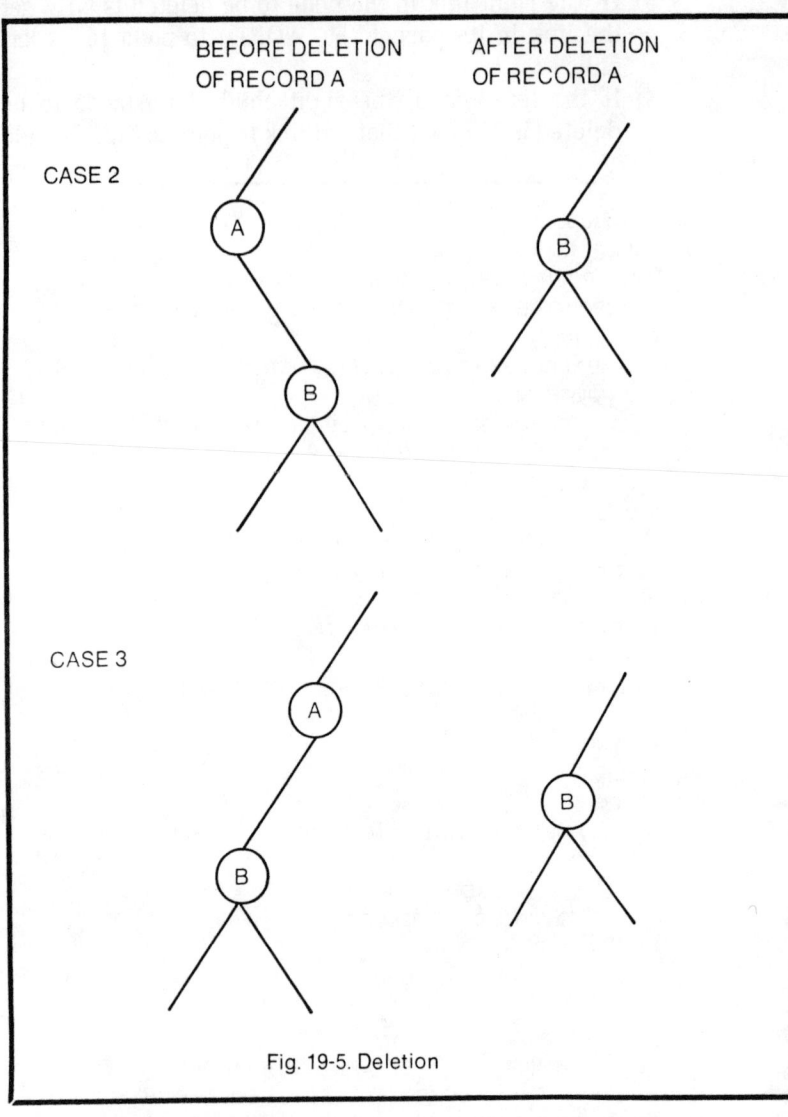

Fig. 19-5. Deletion

of the node to be deleted, and set the link in the parent of the node to be deleted to point to the right child of the node to be deleted.

5) Starting with the right child of the node to be deleted, follow left links until a node is found whose left link is NIL. This is the immediate successor of the node to be deleted. Set its left and right links to point to the children of the node to be deleted, and set the link in

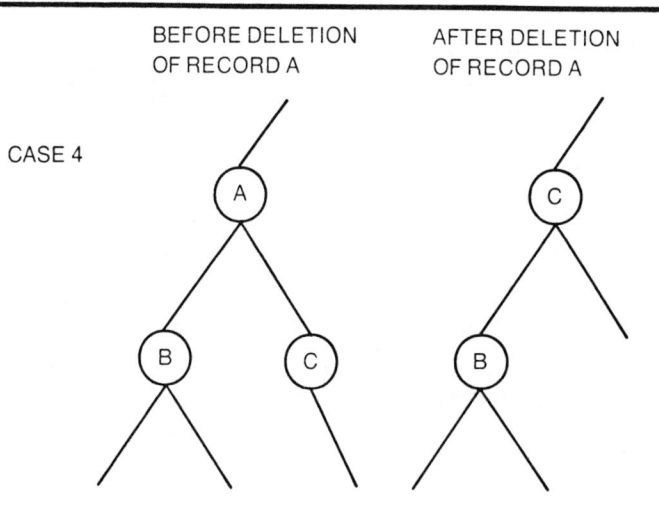

BEFORE DELETION OF RECORD A

AFTER DELETION OF RECORD A

CASE 4

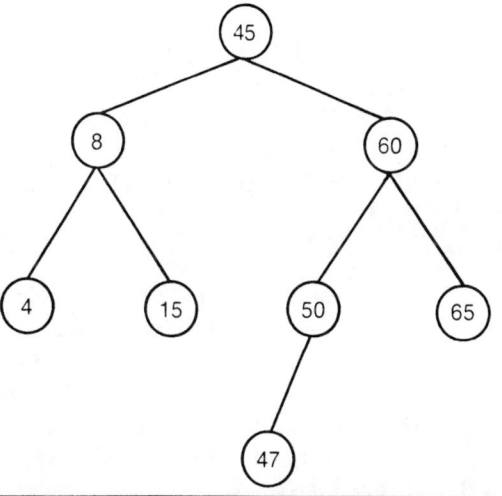

CASE 5: Fig. 19-4 AFTER DELETION OF RECORD 20

the parent of the node to be deleted to point to it. (Thus it replaces the node to be deleted.) Set the left link in the former parent of the immediate successor to point to the former right child of the immediate successor.

6) Regardless of which of the above cases (2, 3, 4, or 5) occurred, the deleted node is returned to the free space list by a call to DISPOSE_OF (Q), where Q points to the node to be returned.

## SEQUENTIAL TRAVERSAL

As was mentioned, an advantage of binary trees over hashing is that we can process the records in key sequence if desired. Suppose we wish to print the records in order of increasing keys. Because of the way the tree was constructed, the following algorithm will accomplish the desired result:

Print Tree:

1. Print out the left subtree in key sequence.
2. Print the root.
3. Print out the right subtree in key sequence.

This leads to a recursive procedure, since we must use the procedure being defined to print out the left and right subtrees. If PRINT_RECORD (Q) prints the record pointed to by Q, then we have:

```
PRINT_TREE: PROCEDURE (Q) RECURSIVE;
    DECLARE Q WORD;
    IF Q < > NIL THEN
        DO;
            CALL PRINT_TREE
              (Q - > RECORD.LEFT);
            CALL PRINT_RECORD (Q);
            CALL PRINT_TREE
              (Q - > RECORD.RIGHT);
        END;
END PRINT_TREE;
```

The second recursive call to PRINT_TREE can be eliminated. Since the record pointed to by Q has already been printed, there is no need to save Q on a stack. Instead of calling PRINT_TREE again we simply loop back to the beginning of the PRINT_TREE routine. In short, we replace a recursion by a repetition. Program 19-4 shows the modified PRINT_TREE procedure.

## PERFORMANCE

The performance of a binary tree search depends on the shape of the binary tree. And that shape depends on the order in which the records were inserted into the tree.

The best performance is for the *balanced* tree shown in Fig. 19-6a, where the leaves of the tree are all on the same level or, at worst, on two adjacent levels. For a balanced tree, the

```
    PRINT _ TREE: PROCEDURE (Q) RECURSIVE;
      DECLARE Q WORD;
      DO WHILE Q < > NIL:
        CALL PRINT _ TREE (Q - > RECORD.LEFT);
        CALL PRINT _ RECORD (Q);
        Q = Q - > RECORD.RIGHT;
      END;
    END PRINT _ TREE;
```

Program 19-4. PRINTTREE prints the records of a binary tree in ascending order according to key.

performance for binary tree search is the same as for binary search: The maximum number of probes required is $\log_2 N + 1$, and the average number is approximately $\log_2 N - 1$, where N is the number of records.

The worst performance is for the trees shown in Fig. 19-6b. Here the tree degenerates to a list, and binary tree switch degenerates to sequential search, the worst kind known. Furthermore, the degenerate tree on the left of Fig. 19-6b is easy to obtain: we get it if we insert the records in order of increasing keys. (Decreasing key order would give a similar tree extending to the left rather than to the right.)

If records are inserted in random order, then the average number of probes will be $1.4*\log_2 N - 1$. Since $\log_2 N$ is a small number—usually in the range 10-20—increasing it by 40% does not represent too much of a degradation in performance. For many applications the randomly built tree is satisfactory.

If the performance of a randomly built tree is not satisfactory, if insertions in sequential order are likely to take place, or if one is simply worried about the possibility of by chance getting a highly degenerate tree, then one can use algorithms that transform a tree after an insertion so as to improve its balance.

To maintain a balanced tree generally requires that the entire tree be restructured after each insertion. The work required is proportional to N, the number of nodes in the tree. This is usually not practical.

Much easier to maintain is a height-balanced tree. We define the height of a tree as its maximum level, that is, the maximum number of nodes along any path from root to leaf. A tree is *height-balanced* if the heights of the left and right

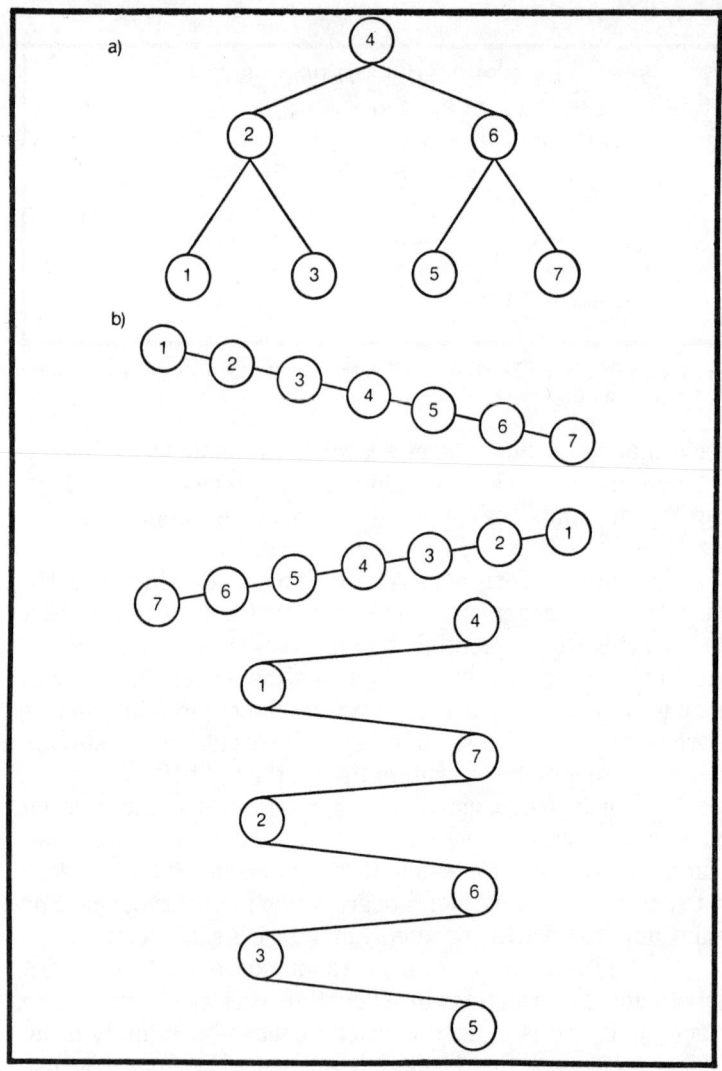

Fig. 19-6. Best performance in a binary tree search is for the balanced tree (a). Worst performance is for the completely unbalanced trees (b).

subtrees of any node differ by at most 1. Height-balance may be maintained by doing only a small amount of work—changing a few pointers—after each insertion. A deletion requires about h/2 times as much work as an insertion, where h is the height of the tree. The average number of probes for a height-balanced tree is $\log_2(N + 1)$, only slightly worse than for the completely balanced tree.

# Chapter 20
# Indexes

So far we have seen how to implement the key-to-address transformation in two ways: By searching through the data structure containing the records, and by using a hashing function (which might involve a search through the records in the event of a collision). A third way is to use an *index*.

An index is an auxiliary table which allows the location of a record to be found from the values of one or more of its attributes. The attribute most commonly used is the primary key. Some familiar examples of indexes are: The index to a book, the card catalog in a library, the thumb index to a large dictionary, and the tags placed on the front of filing cabinet drawers to show the contents of each draw. (The drawers of a card catalog have such tags, which constitute an index to an index.)

To locate a record we search the index instead of the file. (In the following we shall use the term *file* to refer to any collection of records, stored either in main memory or on auxiliary storage.) The index will be easier or faster to search than the file because:

1) The index entries will usually be shorter than the records in the file.
2) There may be many fewer index entries than there are records.
3) The index entries may be in sequential (or some other easily searchable) order, while the file entries are not.
4) The records may vary in length while the index entries are of fixed length.

Because of points 1) and 2), the index, or a large segment of it at least, may often be kept in main memory whereas the file itself must reside on auxiliary storage. A computer can access data in main memory about a thousand times faster then data on auxiliary storage. So even a simple sequential search done in main memory may be faster than a highly sophisticated one done on auxiliary storage.

## ARGUMENTS

When we look something up in an index, we search for the entry containing a certain value, the value we are looking for, and having found that entry obtain from it one or more additional values. The value we search for is called the *argument*; the values we obtain are called *functions*. In the index to a book, for example, the word or phrase we look up is the argument; the page numbers are the functions.

An index is a *primary index* if its argument is the *primary key* of the record being sought, and a *secondary index* if the argument is a *secondary key*. In this chapter we will focus our attention on primary indexes; we will save secondary indexes to the next chapter, where we take up secondary and multiple key retrieval.

The argument may refer to a single value, or to a *range* of values. For instance, the tag on the front of a filing cabinet drawer gives the range of entries stored in the drawer. The use of arguments corresponding to ranges is why the index may contain far fewer entries than there are records in the file. (The number of tags on the front of the filing cabinet drawers is far smaller than the number of records in the drawers.)

As a variation on this theme, if the value of the attribute being indexed can vary continuously, or in very small increments, then it may be *quantized*: we may divide the acceptable range of values into small subranges, or *quanta*, and include one index entry for each *quantum*.

Suppose, for instance, the argument (for a secondary index) is *Salary*. Salaries vary in increments of one cent, but this may be too small for our purposes. Suppose we choose a quantum, or increment, of $10. Then the index entries would go . . . 10250, 10260, 10270, . . . .The entry for 10250 would contain the locations of all records where salary lies in the range 10250.00−10259.99, the entry for 10260 would contain the locations of the records with salaries in the range 10260.00−10269.99, and so on.

## FUNCTIONS

The functions are the values we obtain from an index entry; they give the locations of the records described by the argument. These locations may be specified in several ways.

*Absolute machine addresses.* We may locate a record by giving its machine address. This may be an address in main memory or on auxiliary storage. (The address of a record on disk, for instance, might consist of a track number, the number of a sector on that track, and the number of bytes the record is located beyond the beginning of the sector.) The problem with absolute machine addresses is that if the list in main memory or the file on disk is moved, then the addresses are no longer valid. Such movement is common on large scale computer systems, and may take place without the user being informed.

*Relative Addresses.* A relative address gives the position of a record relative to the beginning of a list or file. The first record in the file has a relative address of 0, the second a relative address of 1, and so on. For lists in main memory the relative address is simply the familiar subscript.

A relative address remains unchanged if the list or file is moved. A relative address may take up less space than a machine address, since the relative address need only refer to the records in one file, whereas the machine address must be large enough to be able to refer to all the addressable locations in main memory or on some auxiliary storage device. And a relative address can be a single number, while a machine address may have several components (track number, sector number, position of record within sector).

*Symbolic Address.* A record may be referred to by a *symbol* or *name* rather than by its location. This symbol must usually be looked up in another index to obtain the location of the record. For instance, secondary indexes may refer to records by their primary keys. Each primary key must then be looked up in the primary index to obtain the location of the record. The advantage of this scheme is that when file maintenance causes records to be repositioned, only the primary index has to be changed. The disadvantage is the extra lookup that must be done for each record.

*Bucket Address.* This is one of the most commonly used methods of locating a record. Its use is motivated by the structure of commonly used auxiliary storage devices, such as disks.

Because of the construction of such devices, their storage areas are naturally divided up into segments called *blocks* or *buckets* (we will use the latter term). A disk surface, for instance, is divided into *tracks*, and each track may be further subdivided into *sectors*. On multisurface disk packs we also have *cylinders*, a cylinder consisting of those tracks on all the surfaces that are at the same distance from the center.

Usually it is much more time consuming to move from bucket to bucket than it is to read in the information in one bucket, and locate a particular record in it. Therefore we use the index to tell us which bucket contains a given record; we read that bucket into main memory and search it at high speed for the desired record. (Some disk drives will automatically search a track for a record with a given primary key during a single revolution of the disk.)

In the examples discussed in detail later in this chapter, we will usually assume that the file is organized into buckets and that the index provides a bucket address rather than a record address.

*Multilist.* As was mentioned in Chapter 17, a chain can only be searched sequentially unless some additional structure is maintained to aid searching. That additional structure may be an index.

If the items on a chain are in sequential order, as they may easily be because of the ease of making insertions and deletions from any part of a chain, then we may divide the chain into segments, as shown in Fig. 20-1, and use an index to narrow the search down to a single segment. A chain segmented in this way is called a *multilist chain* or, simply, a *multilist*.

Each index entry contains the key of the *last* record on a segment (the argument) and a pointer to the *first* record of that segment (the function). To find a record, we search through the index until we find a segment whose final record has a key greater than or equal to the key we are searching for. Then, using the pointer, we go to the beginning of that segment, and search it sequentially.

When the multilist resides on auxiliary storage, we usually arrange matters so that each segment is in a separate hardware bucket. In that case we speak of a *cellular multilist*.

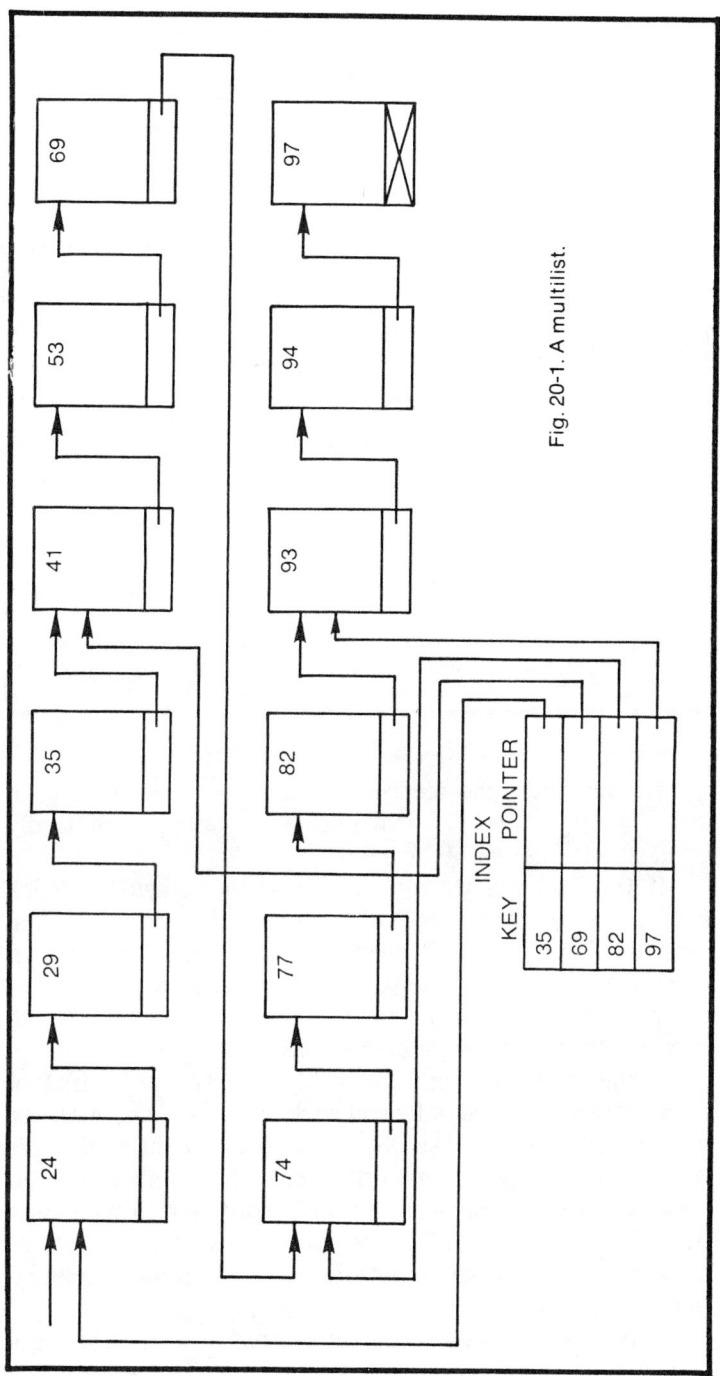

Fig. 20-1. A multilist.

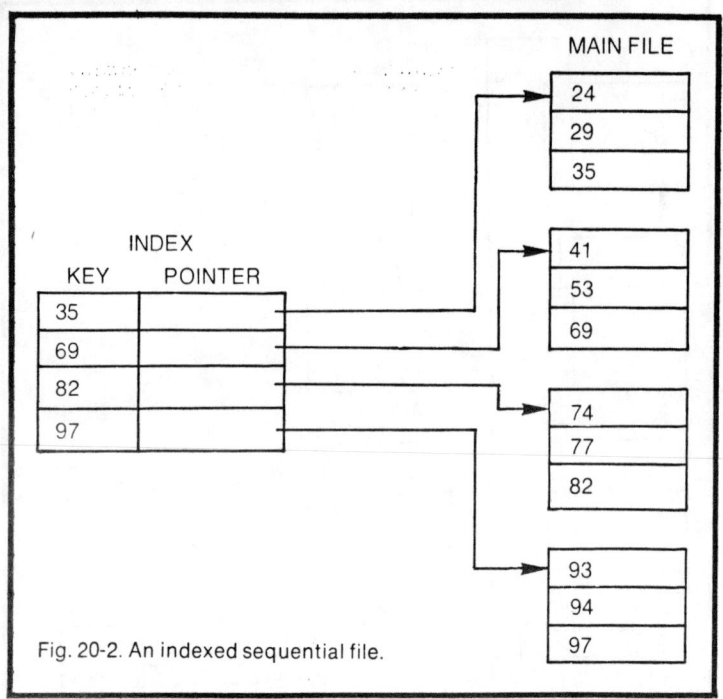

Fig. 20-2. An indexed sequential file.

## SEQUENTIAL AND NONSEQUENTIAL FILES

We may store the records in a file in key sequence, or in some other order. Which choice we make profoundly influences the nature of the index.

If the records are stored in sequence, then the index entries may refer to ranges of records, rather than individual records. Thus there will be many fewer index entries than there are records. Typically, each entry refers to the range of records stored in a bucket, so there is one index entry for each bucket rather than one for each record.

Consider the filing cabinet example. The tag on the front of each drawer will bear a legend such as AA-AE, or DF-DJ, or perhaps BAKER-EDWARDS. It is because we know that the records are in alphabetical order that AA-AE tells us that all the records in that drawer have keys starting with the letters AA, AB, AC, AD, or AE. Also there is exactly one tag per drawer, a drawer being a natural bucket for a file stored in a filing cabinet.

Figure 20-2 shows a sequential file and its index. The file is divided into buckets. Each index entry contains the key of the last record in a bucket, and the address of that bucket. The index entries are in key sequence.

Let us assume that the index is stored in an array, INDEX, declared as follows:

```
DECLARE 1 INDEX (/* DESIRED SIZED */),
          2 LAST_RECORD_KEY WORD,
          2 BUCKET_ADDRESS WORD;
```

We wish to find the first bucket whose last record has a key greater than or equal to the key, K, we are searching for:

```
I = 0;
DO WHILE (I < = LAST (INDEX)) AND (K < INDEX(I).
LAST_RECORD_KEY);
   I = I + 1;
END;
```

When the repetition terminates, if I > LAST (INDEX), then K is greater than the largest key stored in the file. Otherwise, INDEX(I) .BUCKET_ADDRESS is the address of the bucket containing the record whose key equals K, if in fact the file contains such a record.

For a *nonsequential file*, the index must contain one entry for each *record*, rather than one entry for each *bucket*, as is shown in Fig. 20-3. Thus the index is much larger for a nonsequential file. Note, however, that the index entries are in key sequence, even though the records are not. This makes the index easier to search than the file.

It would seem, then, that we would always want to store our records in key sequence. Unfortunately, we can only store the records in key sequence with respect to *one key*. If we are going to use more than one key then, typically, we would store the records in sequence according to the primary key. The file would be nonsequential with respect to the secondary keys. Consequently, the secondary indexes would be much larger than the primary index.

## MAINTENANCE OF INDEXED SEQUENTIAL FILES

When a record is inserted into a sequential file, it must be inserted in the correct position according to the value of its key. For records stored in main memory this is most easily done with a chain or perhaps a binary tree. For records stored

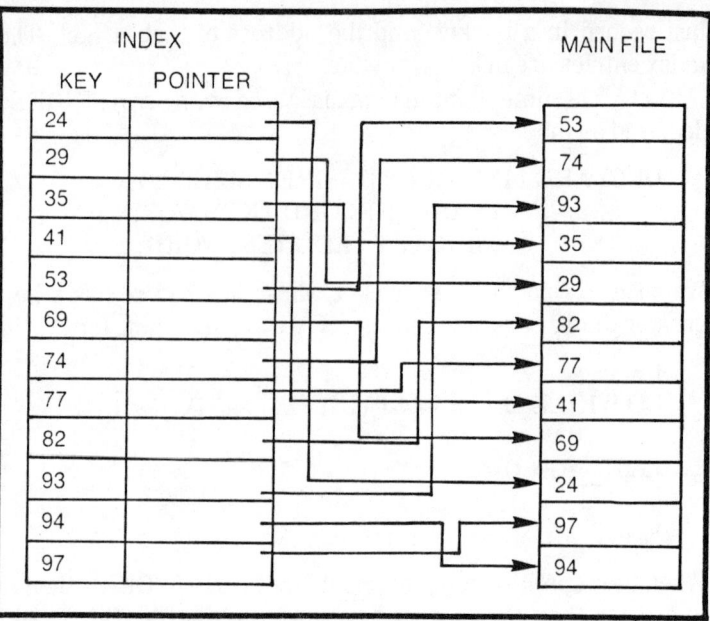

Fig. 20-3. An indexed nonsequential file. Notice that the index is much larger than for the indexed sequential file.

in buckets on auxiliary storage, two methods are in widespread use: *overflow areas* and *distributed free space*.

These techniques are sometimes referred to by their IBM-bestowed names ISAM (overflow areas) and VSAM (distributed free space). ISAM stands for Indexed Sequential Access Method and is self-explanatory. VSAM stands for Virtual Storage Access Method and is not self-explanatory. The only thing VSAM has to do with virtual storage is that it is used in the IBM 370 virtual storage operating system.

Figure 20-4 illustrates an indexed sequential file using an overflow area. The file consists of a prime data area and an overflow area. The prime data area is divided into buckets. The overflow area may also be divided into buckets, but its bucket structure is less important and is not shown.

There are *two* index entries for each bucket. The first contains the key of the last record in the bucket, and the bucket address, as usual. The second entry refers to a chain of records in the overflow area: It contains the key of the last record on the chain and a pointer to the first record on the chain. The records on the chain are the "overflow" from the corresponding bucket.

When the file is initially loaded, the records are stored in the prime data area. The index is built with a prime and overflow entry for each bucket. The prime entries are set up as usual, each containing the key of the last record and the address for the corresponding bucket. Each overflow entry is set with its key component equal to the key component of the preceding prime entry, and with its pointer component equal to NIL, indicating that no overflow chain yet exists for that bucket.

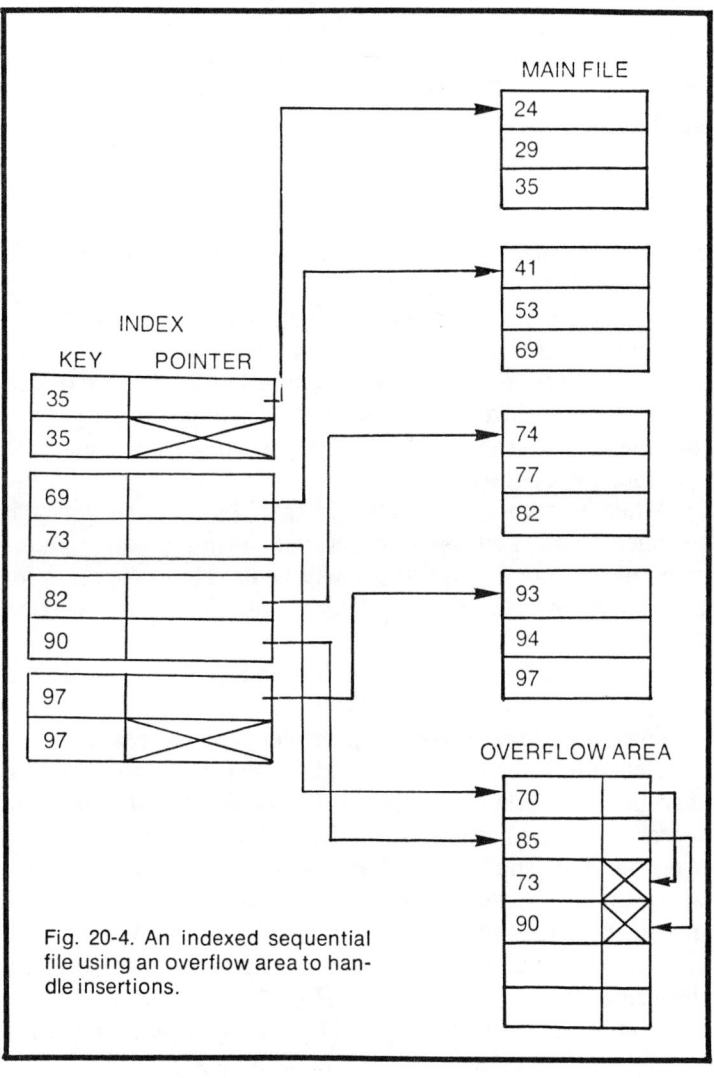

Fig. 20-4. An indexed sequential file using an overflow area to handle insertions.

(Note that setting the key field in the overflow entry equal to the key field in the immediately preceding prime entry assures that no search will stop on the overflow entry. If the key value in question was the one that would terminate a search, then the search would stop on the *first* index entry containing that key value, which would be the prime entry and not the overflow entry.)

When a record is inserted in a bucket in the prime area, then every record in the bucket following the record to be inserted must move up one position to make room for the new record. When the bucket is full, this causes a record to get pushed off the end of the bucket. That record goes into the overflow area.

The overflow record is inserted at the beginning of the overflow chain for that bucket. The pointer in the overflow index entry is updated so that it points to the new head of the overflow chain. The key value in the prime index entry is updated so that it corresponds to the new last record (the old one got pushed off, remember) in the prime area bucket.

Sometimes it is obvious from the index that a new record is to be inserted in an overflow chain rather than a prime area bucket. The record is inserted at the appropriate position in the chain, and the corresponding overflow index entry is updated, if necessary.

When a record is deleted from a bucket, the space it occupied is marked as being unused. If an insertion is later made in that bucket, the space will be used to make room for the new record. No record will get pushed into the overflow area.

Searching is as for any other indexed sequential file, except that we must be prepared to seek the desired record in either a prime area bucket or in an overflow area chain.

Depending somewhat on the details of the hardware used, searching overflow chains will usually be slower than searching prime area buckets. This will certainly be true if an overflow chain spans more than one bucket. Thus performance will gradually be degraded as more and more records are moved into the overflow areas. Eventually, we will have to build a new, larger, file in which all the records are again in the prime area.

Figure 20-5 illustrates an indexed sequential file using distributed free space. When the file is originally built, two

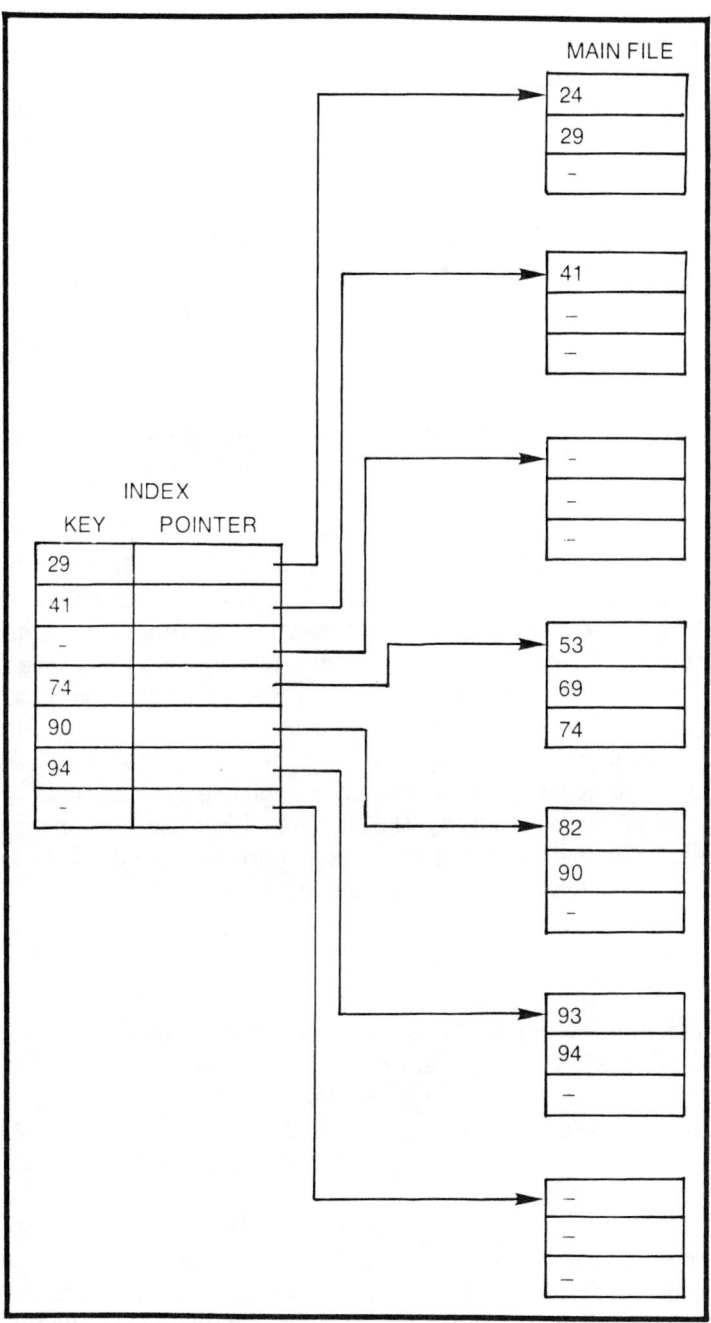

Fig. 20-5. An indexed sequential file using distributed free space to handle insertions.

kinds of free space are included. First, free record positions are included in each bucket. And second, empty buckets are included in the file.

The index contains one entry for each bucket, since no overflow entries are needed. However, a dummy free space entry is inserted for every empty bucket in the file. Thus the index also has distributed free space, so that when the now empty buckets are put to use, there will be room for the corresponding index entries.

When a new record is inserted, two cases arise. Either the bucket into which the record is to be inserted contains a free position, or it does not.

If the bucket still contains free space, then all records in that bucket which should follow the new record are moved up one position to make room for it. Because of the free space, no record gets pushed off the end of the bucket.

If the bucket in which the insertion is to be made has no free space left, then that bucket is split in two. Half of the records remain in the original bucket; the other half are moved to one of the empty buckets. A new index entry is created for the new bucket. Space for this entry has been reserved, but it might not be in the correct position, so some shifting of the index entries may be necessary.

When the last empty bucket has been used, the time is fast approaching when the file must be rebuilt using more space.

It is worth noting that the distributed free space technique is usually used for filing cabinets and library shelves to allow for expansion. Many exotic sounding computer techniques mimic common sense approaches that we all use every day.

## MULTILEVEL INDEXES

When an index becomes sufficiently large, we may need an "index to the index" to locate entries in the index itself. The index tags on the drawers of a library card catalog are an example of this. For very large files we may require an "index to the index to the index," and so on.

The result is a multilevel index having a tree structure, as shown in Fig. 20-6.

The file may be either sequential or nonsequential. Notice, however, only the lowest level index need be for a nonsequential file. Since its entries are in sequence, as are the entires in the higher level indexes, all the indexes above the lowest level are for sequential files.

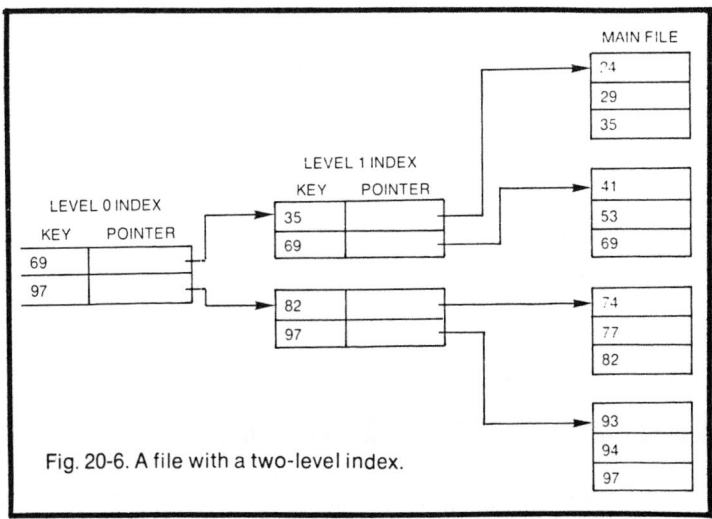

Fig. 20-6. A file with a two-level index.

The leaves of the index tree are called the *sequence set*. They are used when the records in the file are to be processed in key sequence. Even if the file is sequential, the sequence set may be useful, because the processing may skip over many records, but access those that are processed in key sequence. If the buckets of the sequence set are not stored adjacent to one another, then they will usually be linked together into a chain, as shown in Fig. 20-6.

# Chapter 21

# Secondary and Multiple Key Retrieval

The complexity of an information retrieval system, and the indexes that it uses, depends on the kinds of questions that we put to it.

In the simplest case we may ask for the record whose primary key has a particular value. We may state the request by stating the condition the record desired has to satisfy:

$$\text{EMPLOYEE\_NUMBER} = 1435$$

This is the easiest kind of query to answer; a simple indexed sequential file will suffice.

We may base our query on a secondary key. We might ask, for instance, for the records of all employees for which:

$$\text{SALARY} < 10250$$

Now we need a secondary index for each secondary key that may appear in a query.

Finally, we may ask for those records satisfying a condition based on more than one secondary key:

(SALARY < 10250) AND ((DEGREE = 'MS') OR (YEARS_EXPERIENCE > 5))

Now not only must the requisite indexes be available, but the retrieval system must be prepared to merge lists of records satisfying parts of the condition in such a way as to obtain just those records which satisfy the entire condition.

In this chapter we shall examine some ways to retrieve records on one or more secondary keys.

## INVERTED FILES

A file that has secondary indexes associated with it is said to be an *inverted file*. If there is an index for each secondary key, then the file is *completely inverted*. Otherwise, it is *partially inverted*. The secondary indexes are sometimes called *inverted lists*.

What is "inverted", actually, is not the file but the way we use it. With an ordinary file we supply a value for the primary key and obtain the values of one or more secondary keys as results. With an inverted file, we may supply a value for a secondary key and obtain one or more values of the primary key as a result (namely, the primary keys of the records for which the secondary key has the given value).

A library is an example of an inverted file. The card catalog contains three indexes: a title index, an author index, and a subject index. If we consider Title to be the primary key of a book, with Author and Subject secondary keys, then the title cards make up the primary index, while the author and subject cards make up the secondary indexes.

Figure 21-1 shows an inverted file. Each secondary index lists, for every value of the secondary key, the addresses of all records in which the secondary key has that value. The list of record addresses given for a particular value of the secondary key is called an occurrence list. Each occurrence list is usually preceded by an entry giving the length of the list. For clarity, these length entries are omitted in Fig. 21-1.

The occurrence lists vary in length. Rather than use variable length records for the secondary index entries, it is better to store all the occurrence lists as one long list. A secondary index pairs each secondary key value with a pointer to the beginning of the corresponding occurrence list. Figure 21-2 illustrates this. With this scheme the secondary indexes contain fixed length records, simplifying maintenance.

Finally, we may store all the secondary indexes together, and provide a *secondary key dictionary* which pairs the name of each secondary key with a pointer to the appropriate secondary key index. This is illustrated in Fig. 21-3.

To understand the scheme of Fig. 21-3, suppose we were to find all records such that:

$$DEPT\_NO = 105$$

First we would look up DEPT_NO in the secondary key

### MAIN FILE

| BUCKET ADDRESS | RECORD ADDRESS | SECONDARY KEYS | | |
|---|---|---|---|---|
| | | KEY1 | KEY2 | KEY3 |
| 0 | 0 | 3 | 1 | 1 |
| 0 | 1 | 3 | 2 | 1 |
| 0 | 2 | 2 | 3 | 1 |
| 0 | 3 | 2 | 3 | 4 |
| 1 | 4 | 3 | 2 | 3 |
| 1 | 5 | 1 | 1 | 3 |
| 1 | 6 | 4 | 1 | 4 |
| 1 | 7 | 2 | 2 | 2 |
| 2 | 8 | 1 | 1 | 4 |
| 2 | 9 | 3 | 4 | 1 |
| 2 | 10 | 2 | 3 | 3 |
| 2 | 11 | 4 | 4 | 1 |
| 3 | 12 | 4 | 3 | 2 |
| 3 | 13 | 1 | 2 | 3 |
| 3 | 14 | 2 | 2 | 1 |
| 3 | 15 | 1 | 2 | 4 |

### SECONDARY INDEXES

#### KEY1

| KEY VALUES | RECORD ADDRESSES |
|---|---|
| 1 | 5, 8, 13, 15 |
| 2 | 2, 3, 7, 10, 14. |
| 3 | 0, 1, 4, 9 |
| 4 | 6, 11, 12 |

#### KEY2

| KEY VALUES | RECORD ADDRESSES |
|---|---|
| 1 | 0, 5, 6, 8 |
| 2 | 1, 4, 7, 13, 14, 15 |
| 3 | 2, 3, 10, 12 |
| 4 | 9, 11 |

#### KEY3

| KEY VALUES | RECORD ADDRESSES |
|---|---|
| 1 | 0, 1, 2, 9, 11, 14 |
| 2 | 7, 12 |
| 3 | 4, 5, 10, 13 |
| 4 | 3, 6, 8, 15 |

Fig. 21-1. An inverted file.

dictionary and get a pointer to the corresponding secondary key index. We would look up 105 in the secondary key index, and get a pointer to the occurrence list containing the addresses of all records for which the DEPT_NO field contains 105. The occurrence list entries would be used to retrieve the desired records from the main file.

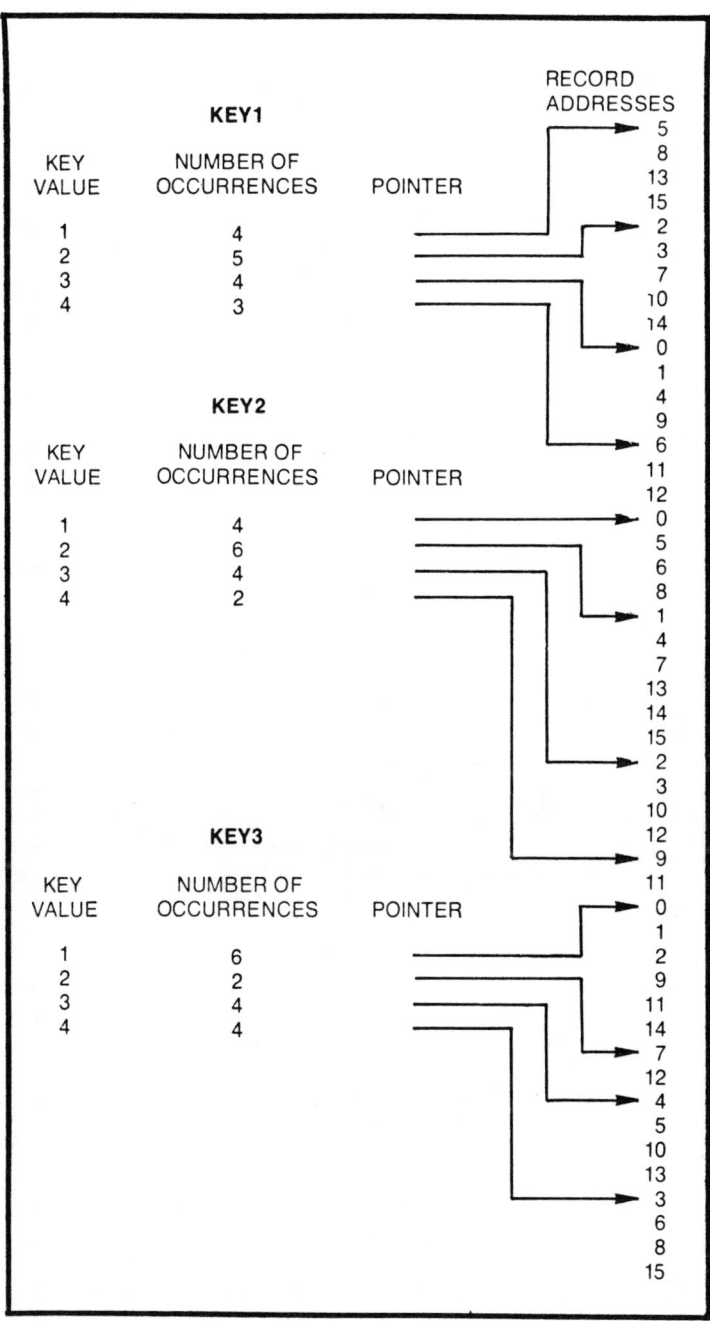

Fig. 21-2. Storing all the occurrence lists in a single area. (Main file same as in Fig. 21-1).

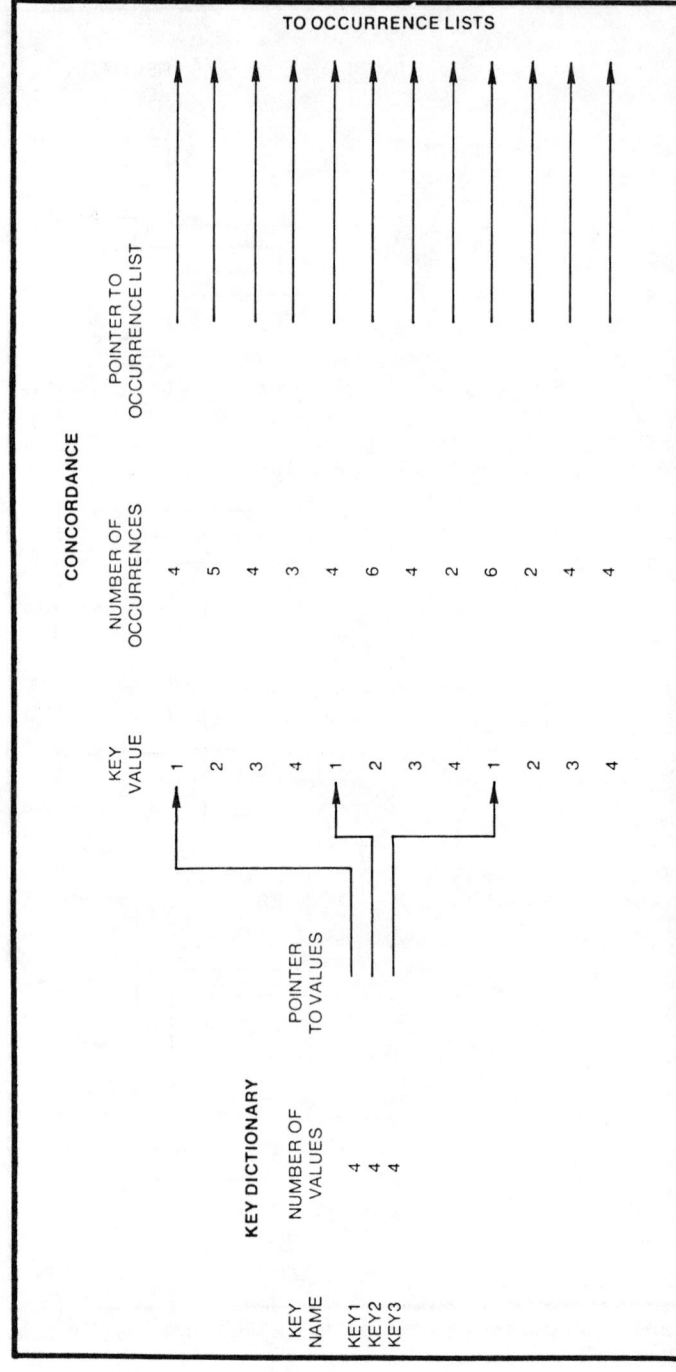

Fig. 21-3. An inverted file with a secondary key dictionary. (Occurrence lists same as in Fig. 21-2).

If a condition refers to more than one secondary key, then we must *merge* two or more occurrence lists to obtain a list of the addresses of just those records which satisfy the condition.

There are basically two kinds of merges, which I shall call an OR-merge and an AND-merge. (They are the same as "union" and "intersection" in set theory.)

An OR-merge would be used to find the records satisfying a condition such as:

(DEPT_NO = 105) OR (DEGREE = 'MS')

Here searching the secondary indexes yields two occurrence lists. One contains the addresses of all records for which DEPT_NO = 105. The other contains the addresses of all records for which DEGREE = 'MS'. The merged list contains the addresses that are on either list, with duplicates resulting from addresses that are on both lists eliminated. Figure 21-4 illustrates an OR-merge.

The AND-merge would be used to find the record satisfying a condition such as:

(DEPT_NO = 105) AND (DEGREE = 'MS')

Now the merged list contains only those records that appear on *both* occurrence lists. Figure 21-5 illustrates an AND-merge.

The lists to be merged must be sorted in order of increasing addresses. Both the AND-merge and the

| C | A AND B | |
|---|---------|---|
|   | 1 3 7 8 9 | |
|   | 1 2 3 5 7 | |
| 1 | 3 7 8 9 | |
|   | 2 3 5 7 | |
| 1 2 | 3 7 8 9 | Fig. 21-4. The OR-merge. |
|   | 3 5 7 | |
| 1 2 3 | 7 8 9 | |
|   | 5 7 | |
| 1 2 3 5 | 7 8 9 | |
|   | 7 | |
| 1 2 3 5 7 | 8 9 | |
| 1 2 3 5 7 8 9 | | |

elimination of duplicates in the OR-merge would be very inefficient if the lists were not in order. And the merged list must also be in order, both because it may have to be merged with still another list, and for efficiency in retrieving the records listed from the main data file.

To illustrate the two merges we will give, for each case, the statements necessary to merge the ordered lists A and B, placing the merged result on list C. We will assume that C is large enough to hold the result, so that we will not have to check for overflow of C.

At each step of the OR-merge, we compare the next entries on A and B. If they are unequal, then the smaller of the two is moved to C. If they are equal, then one, say the one on A, is passed over, thus eliminating the possibility of duplicates on C. When one list is exhausted, the remaining entries on the other list are moved to C:

```
I, J, K = 0;
DO UNTIL (I > LAST (A)) OR (J > LAST (B)):
    IF A(I) < B(J) THEN
        DO;
            C(K) = A(I);
            I = I + 1;
            K = K + 1;
        END;
    ELSE IF A(I) > B(J) THEN
        DO;
            C(K) = B(J);
            J = J + 1;
            K = K + 1;
        END;
    ELSE /* A(I) = B(J) */
        I = I + 1;
END;
DO WHILE I < = LAST (A);
    C(K) = A(I);
    I = I + 1;
    K = K + 1;
END;
DO WHILE J < = LAST (B);
    C(K) = B(J);
    J = J + 1;
    K = K + 1;
END;
```

| C | A AND B |
|---|---|
|  | 1 3 5 7 8 9 |
|  | 1 2 3 5 7 |
| 1 | 3 5 7 8 9 |
|  | 2 3 5 7 |
| 1 | 3 5 7 8 9 |
|  | 3 5 7 |
| 1 3 | 5 7 8 9 |
|  | 5 7 |
| 1 3 5 | 7 8 9 |
|  | 7 |
| 1 3 5 7 | 8 9 |
| 1 3 5 7 |  |

Fig. 21-5. The AND-merge.

At each step of the AND-merge, the next entries on A and B are compared. If they are unequal, then the smaller of the two is passed over. If they are equal then one of them, say the one on A, is moved to C. The merge terminates when one of the lists is exhausted; the entries remaining on the other list are discarded:

```
I, J, K = 0;
DO UNTIL (I > LAST (A)) OR (J > LAST (B));
    IF A(I) < B(J) THEN
        I = I + 1;
    ELSE IF A(I) > B(J) THEN
        J = J + 1;
    ELSE /* A(I) = B(J) */
        DO;
            C(K) = A(I);
            I = I + 1;
            K = K + 1;
        END;
END;
```

The indexes to an inverted file may very well occupy more storage than the main data file. The main offenders are the occurrence lists.

One way to reduce the sizes of the occurrence lists is to use bucket addresses instead of record addresses. Since there are

|  | KEY1 BUCKET ADDRESS | | | | | KEY2 BUCKET ADDRESS | | | |
|---|---|---|---|---|---|---|---|---|---|
|  | 0 | 1 | 2 | 3 |  | 0 | 1 | 2 | 3 |
| KEY VALUES 1 | 0 | 1 | 1 | 1 | KEY VALUES 1 | 1 | 1 | 1 | 0 |
| 2 | 1 | 1 | 1 | 1 | 2 | 1 | 1 | 0 | 1 |
| 3 | 1 | 1 | 1 | 0 | 3 | 1 | 0 | 1 | 1 |
| 4 | 0 | 1 | 1 | 1 | 4 | 0 | 0 | 1 | 0 |

|  | KEY3 BUCKET ADDRESS | | | |
|---|---|---|---|---|
|  | 0 | 1 | 2 | 3 |
| KEY VALUES 1 | 1 | 0 | 1 | 1 |
| 2 | 0 | 1 | 0 | 1 |
| 3 | 0 | 1 | 1 | 1 |
| 4 | 1 | 1 | 1 | 1 |

Fig. 21-6. An inverted file using a bit table as a bucket resolved index. (Main file same as in Fig. 21-1).

many fewer buckets than there are records, the occurrence lists are correspondingly shorter.

With "bucket resolved" occurrence lists, we merge the occurrence lists as before to obtain a list of all buckets which *may posssibly* contain records satisfying the given condition. Each such bucket is read into main memory, and each record in the bucket is examined to see if it does indeed satisfy the required condition.

This examination is done in main memory, and can usually be done in less than the time required to read another bucket. Hence the time required is proportional to the number of buckets read. A bucket resolved index is less efficient than a record resolved one only in that some buckets that are read will turn out not to contain any records satisfying the required condition. With a record resolved index, we know where every record satisfying the condition is, and hence will only read buckets that contain at least one such record.

An interesting form of bucket resolved index uses a *bit table*, as shown in Fig. 21-6. Each row of the table is labeled with a value of the secondary key; each column is labeled with a bucket address. A 1 entry, located at the intersection of a certain row and column, indicates that the bucket labeling that column contains a record with the secondary key value labeling that row.

The interesting thing about bit tables is that the rows can be combined using the logical operators AND, OR, and XOR. The NOT operator can be applied to a single row.

Suppose, for instance, that 11000010 is the row for DEPT_NO = 105, indicating that buckets 1, 2, and 7 contain at least one record satisfying this condition. Suppose further that the row for DEGREE = 'MS' is 10110001. Then the row for

(DEPT_NO = 105) OR (DEGREE = 'MS')

is

11000010 OR 1011001 = 11110011

and the row for

(DEPT_NO = 105) AND (DEGREE = 'MS')

is

11000010 AND 10110001 = 10000000

Thus with bit tables the logical operations replace merging.

Bit tables may be used with record resolved indexes also, but the tables are very large, since they must contain one column for each record.

In a record resolved index, the occurrence lists may contain the primary keys of the records, rather than their addresses. When the time comes to access the actual data records, the primary keys are looked up in the primary index to obtain the record locations. When the file is reorganized, causing the record addresses to change, only the primary index needs to be updated. With this technique an indexed sequential file is often used as the "bottom level" of a data base management system.

Primary keys are often character strings, perhaps of variable length. These take up excessive amounts of storage and are clumsy to manipulate. The solution is to replace each character string with a unique fixed length identifier, an "internal name" for the record. A table records the correspondence between the "external name" and the "internal name" for a record. The external name need be looked up only when it is required to be printed.

**CHAINED FILES**

One way to reduce the size of the indexes is to replace each occurrence list with a chain linking together all records having a given value for a given secondary key. Of course, the records in the main data file become larger, since each must contain a link word for every secondary key indexed. But in terms of file maintenance, it is usually better to have a larger main data file than to have a separate large file of occurrence lists to be maintained. Figure 21-7 illustrates a chained file.

Each secondary index entry contains a value for the secondary key, a pointer to the first record on the chain of records for which the secondary key has that value, and the number of records on the chain.

For a condition such as

(DEPT_NO = 105) OR (DEGREE = 'MS')

we would obtain from the index a pointer to a chain of records for which DEPT_NO = 105, and a pointer to a chain for which DEGREE = "MS". We would then merge the records on those chains, eliminating duplicates, much as the occurrence lists were merged for inverted files.

For a condition such as

(DEPT_NO = 105) AND (DEGREE = 'MS')

we would determine from the index which condition had the shorter chain. We would search the records of that chain, checking each record for the other condition. In general, when any number of conditions are ANDed together, search the shortest chain and check each record on it to see if the other conditions are satisfied.

When the chains become long they become time consuming to search. In that case we can replace each single chain with a multilist (see MULTILISTS in the previous chapter). Each index entry now contains a *short* occurrence list, and each entry on the occurrence list is a pointer to a *short* chain of records. Thus the multilist technique is a combination of the "inverted list" and the "chaining" techniques.

Often the multilists are *cellular multilists*, that is, each chain is confined to a single bucket. Obviously, this is very similar to the bucket resolved inverted file discussed earlier. The only difference is that within a bucket the records having a given value for a given secondary key are chained together.

## MULTIDIMENSIONAL BINARY TREES

This is a recently introduced technique which seems to hold promise for many applications. It may be applied either to an index or to the data records themselves.

An ordinary "one-dimensional" binary tree contains only one key per record, the primary key. In a multidimensional

| MAIN FILE | | | | |
|---|---|---|---|---|
| RECORD ADDRESS | KEY1 | LINK | KEY2 | LINK |
| 0 | 3 | 1 | 1 | 5 |
| 1 | 3 | 4 | 2 | 4 |
| 2 | 2 | 3 | 3 | 3 |
| 3 | 2 | 7 | 3 | 10 |
| 4 | 3 | 9 | 2 | 7 |
| 5 | 1 | 8 | 1 | 6 |
| 6 | 4 | 11 | 1 | 8 |
| 7 | 2 | 10 | 2 | 13 |
| 8 | 1 | 13 | 1 | NIL |
| 9 | 3 | NIL | 4 | 11 |
| 10 | 2 | 14 | 3 | 12 |
| 11 | 4 | 12 | 4 | NIL |
| 12 | 4 | NIL | 3 | NIL |
| 13 | 1 | 15 | 2 | 14 |
| 14 | 2 | NIL | 2 | 15 |
| 15 | 1 | NIL | 2 | NIL |

SECONDARY INDEXES

KEY1

| KEY VALUE | NUMBER OF OCCURRENCES | POINTER TO BEGINNING OF CHAIN |
|---|---|---|
| 1 | 4 | 5 |
| 2 | 5 | 2 |
| 3 | 4 | 0 |
| 4 | 3 | 6 |

KEY2

| KEY VALUE | NUMBER OF OCCURRENCES | POINTER TO BEGINNING OF CHAIN |
|---|---|---|
| 1 | 4 | 0 |
| 2 | 6 | 1 |
| 3 | 4 | 2 |
| 4 | 2 | 9 |

Fig. 21-7. A chained file.

tree, each record contains more than one key—a primary key and one or more secondary keys.

Let us illustrate with the two dimensional tree shown in Fig. 21-8. Each record contains two keys, key 1 and key 2. The value of each key ranges from 1 through 9. Key 1 appears on the left in each node; key 2 appears to the right. (Ignore, for the moment, the bracketed numbers by each branch.)

The root has the keys (3, 4). That is, key 1 = 3 and key 2 = 4. When inserting other records, we use the value of *key 1*

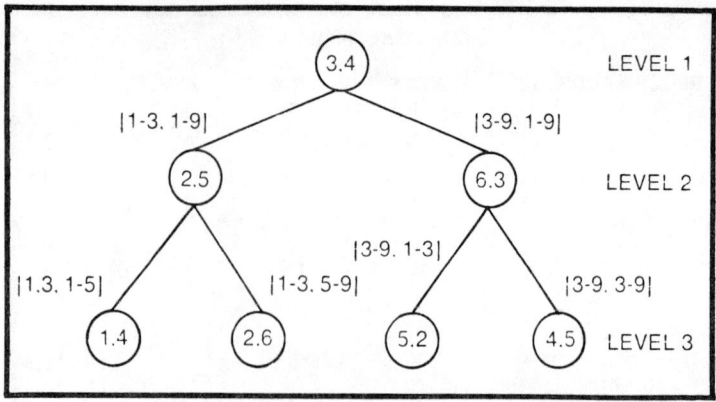

Fig. 21-8. A two-dimensional binary tree.

for the root to determine whether the record goes in the left subtree or the right one. Thus if (2, 5) and (6, 3) are inserted, then (2, 5) becomes the left child of the root, since 2 is less than 3, and (6, 3) becomes the right child, since 6 is greater than 3.

Thus on level 1, the level of the root, key 1 is the discriminating key. It is the key used to determine whether a record being inserted should go in the left subtree or the right subtree.

On level 2 we discriminate on key 2. Consider the insertion of the record (2, 6). On level 1 we take the left branch, since 2 is less than 3. On level 2 we take the right branch, since 6 is greater than 5. Or consider (5, 2). On level 1 we take the right branch, since 5 is greater than 4. On level 2 we take the left branch, since 2 is less than 3.

This scheme repeats itself for levels after the second. Thus on level 3 we would discriminate on key 1, on level 4 we would discriminate on key 2, on level 5 we would use key 1 again, and so on.

If the values of the key we are discriminating on happen to be equal, we then discriminate on the other key. Thus (3, 2) would go into the left subtree of the root, since 2 is less than 4, and (3, 5) would go into the right subtree, since 5 is greater than 4.

In general we will want to find all those records in which the values of key 1 and key 2 lie in particular ranges. Thus we might want to find all records in which key 1 lies in the range 1-2 and key 2 lies in the range 6-8. To do this it is important for us to know the range of values each key can take in a particular subtree, since these ranges will determine whether that subtree has to be traversed on a particular search. This information is included in brackets by each branch.

For the entire tree, each key is, by definition, limited to the range 1-9. We could indicate this with the notation [1-9, 1-9], where the first range is for key 1 and the second is for key 2.

Now at root we are discriminating on key 1, and the discriminating value is 3. Thus for all records in the left subtree of the root, the value of key 1 will be in the range 1-3. For the left subtree, the range is 3-9. In both subtrees the range for key 2 is still 1-9. Thus the ranges for the left subtree of the root are [1-3, 1-9], while those for the right subtree are [3-9, 1-9].

Now let us consider some level 2 record, say (2, 5). We are now discriminating on key 2, and the discriminating value is 5. In the left subtree, then, key 2 will range from 1 through 5; and it the right subtree it will range from 5 through 9. Since the range for key 1 is not changed, the ranges for the subtrees of (2, 5) are [1-3, 1-5] for the left and [1-3, 5-9] for the right.

The same reasoning is applied on the second and higher levels. As the level number gets larger and larger, the ranges become narrower and narrower, and it becomes easier and easier to reject unwanted subtrees.

Now suppose we are searching for all records such that the values of key 1 and key 2 lie in certain ranges. We can use the following recursive algorithm:

Multidimensional Binary Tree Search:

1. If the key values for the root lie in the desired ranges, then process the root.
2. If, *for each key*, the desired range overlaps the range for the left subtree, then search the left subtree.
3. If, *for each key*, the desired range overlaps the range for the right subtree, then search the right subtree.

Note that sometimes we will have to search both the left and the right subtrees of a given node. Therefore the search will not be so fast as for a one-dimensional binary tree, where we can always select one subtree and reject the other. Nevertheless, the claim has been made that a multidimensional binary tree search should be faster than either an inverted file or a multilist search.

# Chapter 22
# Searching Game Trees

In this chapter we turn to a different kind of searching, one more typical of artificial intelligence than data base management. Instead of searching through records stored in files, the computer searches through sequences of actions in an attempt to find a course of action that will lead to a desired result. In particular, we consider the case of a computer playing a game, either against a human opponent or another computer, and searching for the best move to make from a given position.

The computer conducts its search through a *game tree*, such as the one shown in Fig. 22-1. Each node represents a game position, a chess position, for instance. The square nodes are those in which the computer has the next move; the round ones are positions in which the opponent has the next move. Each branch represents the move that leads from the position at its upper end to the position at its lower end. The root of the tree is the position currently facing the computer. The leaves are the positions at which the search will be terminated, either because the game has been won or lost or, more commonly, simply to keep the tree from getting too big.

The computer wishes to find the best move in the position facing it, the one at the root of the tree. If the computer (or a human player) were sufficiently smart, it could determine the best move merely by examining the pattern of men on the board, that is, by examining the root position. But as every

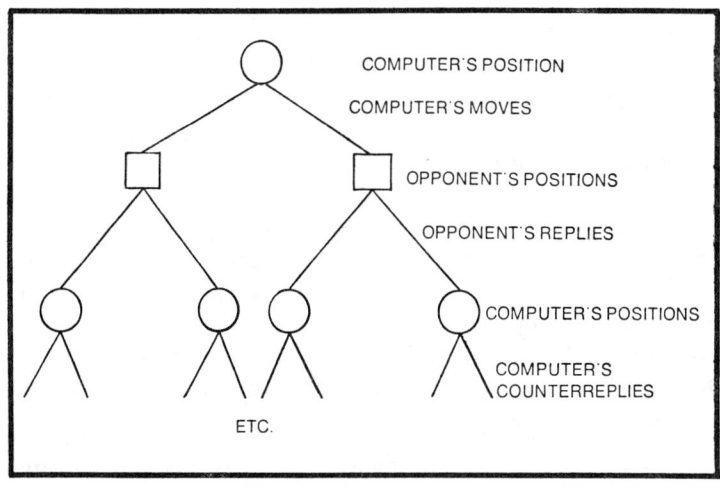

Fig. 22-1. A game tree.

gameplayer knows, to rely purely on such an examination is to court disaster. A seemingly attractive move can lead one into a deadly trap cleverly laid by the opponent. Thus, before making a move, it is wise to explore the consequences of it.

Thus the computer tries out, in its "head", all moves that it is seriously considering. These lead to the positions on the second level. Now in each case the computer imagines the replies its opponent might make to each move. This leads to the third level positions. Now it imagines its own counter replies, and gets the level 4 positions. And so on.

How far should this lookahead go? Ideally it should continue until we reach the true leaves of the game tree, the positions in which the game has been won, drawn, or lost.
But except for trivial games, such as Tic Tac Toe, this is impossible. A game tree for chess, starting with some position near the opening, would contain about $10^{120}$ nodes, an absurdly large number. Some other criteria for terminating a search must be used.

## TERMINATION CRITERIA

As mentioned, the simplest search criterion is "game is over". The end-of-game condition will always terminate a search, since it would be meaningless to explore any positions beyond one in which the game has been decided.

Often there is a *maximum level*, beyond which time and memory space considerations make it impossible or unwise to go. Search is terminated for a position if it is at the maximum level.

Frequently there is a *minimum level* too. Search is never terminated prior to reaching the minimum level unless the end-of-game condition occurs.

Between the minimum and the maximum level the search is terminated if a position is *dead*. A dead position is one in which no move is likely to profoundly affect the position. In human terms, nothing *interesting* is about to happen. In checkers, a dead position might be one in which no jumps are possible. In chess, it could be one in which neither king is in check, and no other capture is immediately possible.

**STATIC EVALUATION**

Each leaf of the game tree must be evaluated as to its desirability for the computer or its undesirability for the opponent. If the position is one in which the computer has won, then it is maximally desirable to the computer. If it is one in which the opponent has won, it is minimally desirable to the computer. But, as we have seen, terminal positions are rarely those in which the game has been lost or won. We must devise some way of estimating the worth of a terminal position, based on the patterns formed by the pieces on the board. The procedure for doing this is called a *static evaluation function*.

It is convenient to make the static evaluation function symmetrical with respect to the two players. That is, a value of 0 indicates a position that favors neither player. If a position has a value of 100 for the computer, it will have a value of $-100$ for the opponent. This position favors the computer. A position which has a value of $-50$ for the computer will have a value of 50 for the opponent, and so favors the opponent.

We may illustrate a static evaluation function using the game of checkers. In checkers, as in many games, a rough measure of advantage can be had from the number of men each side has on the board. We define:

MEN = COMPUTERS_MEN - OPPONENTS_MEN;
KINGS = COMPUTERS_KINGS - OPPONENTS_KINGS;

Notice that MEN and KINGS exhibit the desired symmetry: they will merely change sign if we interchange the roles of the computer and its opponent. In checkers it is generally accepted that 3 kings are worth 2 men. To maintain this ratio we define the static value, TERMINAL_VALUE, by:

TERMINAL_VALUE = 3*KINGS + 2*MEN;

Piece advantage is only a rough measure of the value of a position, since often the computer cannot look far enough ahead to a point where piece advantage is decisive. Many other terms could be added. For instance, we might define the mobility of a player as the number of positions one of his men could move to without getting jumped. Let:

MOBILITY = COMPUTERS_ MOBILITY − OPPONENTS_MOBILITY;

Now we must decide the relative importance of mobility versus piece advantage, and here checkers lore is of no help. If we decided that two squares of mobility were worth one man, we could write

TERMINAL_VALUE = 3*KINGS + 2*MEN + MOBILITY;

whereas if we wished to count 1 man as being worth 4 squares of mobility, we would write

TERMINAL_VALUE = 6*KINGS + 4*MEN + MOBILITY;

and so on. Ultimately, the coefficients can only be determined by experiment.

For an actual checkers-playing program, the static evaluation function would contain many more terms. For more sophisticated games such as chess, advanced pattern recognition techniques might be brought to bear on the static evaluation. For instance, a position might be credited with points because of certain patterns that appear on the board. Also the value of a position might depend on its relevance to some overall plan of attack being pursued by the computer.

**THE MINIMAX METHOD**

Assume that the static evaluation function has assigned values to the leaves of the game tree. We now wish to pass these values up the tree and so assign values to the other positions as well. In particular, we want to assign values to the children of the root position, so the computer can determine which move at its disposal will give it the greatest advantage.

Suppose, for the moment, that the value of each position is its value *to the computer*. In any position where the computer has the move, it will choose the move leading to the child having the greatest value. We define the value of a position in which the computer has the move, then, as the *maximum* of the values of all its children.

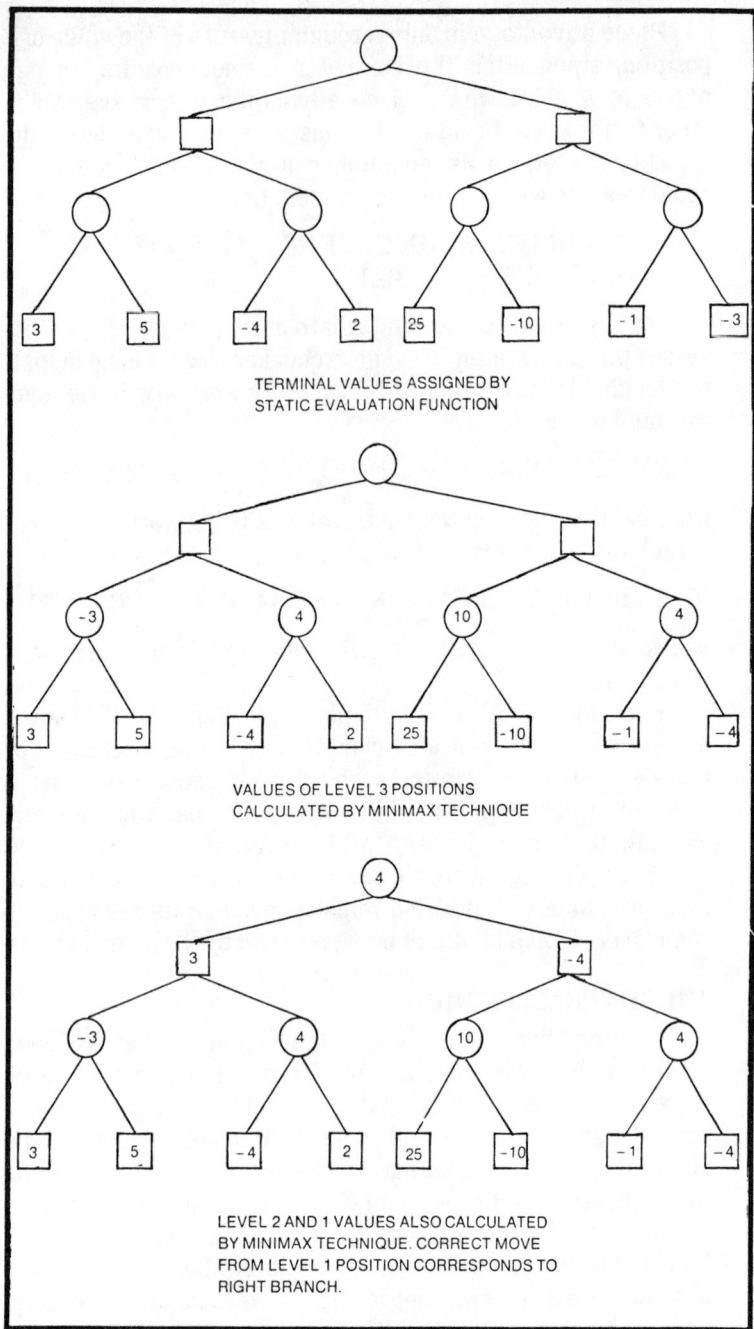

Fig. 22-2. Assigning values to positions in a game tree.

On the other hand, the opponent will always choose the move that leads to the position with *minimal* value for the computer, and hence maximal value for the opponent. We define the value of a position in which the opponent has the move, then, as the *minimum* of the values of all its children.

Having assigned values to the leaves of the tree, then, we can work upward, assigning a value to each node by the above rules as soon as values have been assigned to all its children. Because of the alternate minimization and maximization required, this is known as the *minimax* technique.

Actually, it is clumsy to have our program minimizing at some nodes and maximizing at others. A better technique is to let the value of a position be its value to *the player that is to move*.

Thus the static evaluation function will yield a positive value when the player that is to move has the advantage, and a negative value when the other player has the advantage. In terms of our checkers example, when the computer is to move MEN would be calculated by

MEN = COMPUTERS_MEN − OPPONENTS_MEN;

whereas when the opponent was to move it would be calculated by

MEN = OPPONENTS_MEN − COMPUTERS_MEN;

and likewise for KINGS and MOBILITY.

The rule for calculating the value of a position which is not a leaf is as follows: Change the algebraic signs of all the values of the position's children, so that these values apply to the player who is to move now, and not the one that will move next. The largest of these values is the value of the current position. Now the computer has only to maximize rather than maximizing sometimes and minimizing others. Figure 22-2 illustrates this method.

A procedure for calculating the value of a position is a recursive procedure, since the value of a nonterminal position is defined in terms of the values of its children. Program 22-1 shows the function VALUE (P, LEVEL). P is a pointer to a position and LEVEL is the level at which that position occurs in the game tree. VALUE returns the value of the position.

```
VALUE: PROCEDURE (P, LEVEL) RECURSIVE;
   DECLARE (P, Q, LEVEL, V, W) WORD;
   /* IF P IS A TERMINAL POSITION, RETURN ITS TERMINAL
      VALUE.  OTHERWISE RETURN THE VALUE OF THE MOST
      FAVORABLE POSITION THAT CAN BE OBTAINED FROM P
      IN ONE MOVE */
   IF TERMINAL (P, LEVEL) THEN
        RETURN TERMINAL _ VALUE (P);
   ELSE;
      DO;
         P = NEXT _ POSITIONS _ FROM (P);
         V = -32768;
         DO WHILE P < > NIL;
            W = - VALUE  (P, LEVEL + 1);
            IF V < W THEN V = W;
            Q = P;
            P = P - > POSITION.LINK;
            CALL DISPOSE _ OF (Q);
         END;
         RETURN V;
      END;
END VALUE;
```

Program 22-1. VALUE computes the backed up value of the position pointed to by P.

A position is defined as follows:

DECLARE  POSITION,
          2 BOARD(8, 8) BYTE,
          2 MOVE BYTE,
          2 LINK WORD;

BOARD is an appropriate representation for the game board of whatever game is at hand; the details of its declaration would vary from one game to another. MOVE is TRUE for positions in which the computer is to move, and FALSE for others. LINK is used to link the children of a position into a chain.

VALUE calls three functions which are dependent on the particular game at hand, and hence are not given here.

TERMINAL (P, LEVEL) returns TRUE if the position pointed to by P is terminal, that is, is a leaf, and FALSE otherwise. The argument LEVEL is necessary since the termination criterion often depends on the level at which a position occurs in the tree.

TERMINAL_VALUE (P) is the static evaluation function; it returns the static value of the position pointed to by P.

NEXT_POSITIONS_FROM (P) returns a pointer to a chain of the children of the position pointed to by P. The children are linked together using the LINK component of position.

VALUE uses the now familiar DISPOSE_OF (P) function to return a position to the free space list.

Because of space limitations, we can cover here only the elements of searching game trees. Many techniques for improving the efficiency of the search exists, including the important "alpha-beta" technique. For further details see the book by Nilsson listed in the bibliography.

# Part VI
# Sorting

# Chapter 23
# Internal Sorting

Computers, like people, frequently need to "put things in order." It has been estimated that 25% of all computer time is spent on sorting, and at some installations this figure is as high as 50%. Business data processing accounts for much of the time spent on sorting. But sorting problems arise in other kinds of programs too. We have already seen the need for sorting in the garbage collector of a string manipulation system. And—to give another perhaps unexpected example—artificial intelligence programs often must sort a list of possible courses of action according to their estimated likelihoods of success.

We distinguish two kinds of sorting: *internal sorting,* for lists stored in main memory; and *external sorting,* for lists stored on tape or disk. As we have seen, main memory is a truly random access storage medium, while tape and disks are not. These different kinds of access demand different sorting techniques:

The most widely used techniques of internal sorting are:

1) *Selection.* We *select* the smallest element on the list-to-be-sorted, and move it to the first position of the sorted-list. We then select the smallest element remaining on the list-to-be-sorted, and move it to the second position on the sorted-listed. The process continues until the list-to-be-sorted is exhausted.
2) *Insertion.* We remove the elements from the list-to-be-sorted one by one, and *insert* each in its proper position in the sorted-list.

3) *Exchange*. We compare two elements on the list-to-be-sorted, and *exchange* them if they are out of order. We repeat this, following some particular scheme for choosing pairs of elements to be compared, until the list is in order.

A complete discussion of internal sorting techniques would easily fill a book as large as this one. In a single chapter we can barely scratch the surface. Therefore, we shall concentrate on one sorting method—exchange—and consider several progressively more sophisticated applications of it. In the process we shall construct a set of procedures that will meet most of the internal sorting needs of the computer hobbyist.

**DEFINITIONS**

The procedures we construct in this chapter will be designed to sort a list of records defined as follows:

DECLARE 1 LIST(/* DESIRED SIZE */),
          2 KEY WORD,
          2 DATA,
               /* SUBDIVISIONS OF DATA */;

The records are to be sorted in ascending order according to the value of the KEY component. Thus two records of LIST, LIST(I) and LIST(J), where I is less than J, are in order if

$$\text{LIST(I) .KEY} <= \text{LIST(J) .KEY}$$

and out of order if

$$\text{LIST(I) .KEY} > \text{LIST(J) .KEY}$$

As was done in previous chapters, we assume our keys to be single words. This allows us to write out comparisons simply, using the $<$, $=$, $>$ and $>$ operators. In business data processing applications, however, the keys will often be character strings, and subroutines will have to be called to do the comparisons.

**SORTING LISTS OF TWO OR THREE RECORDS**

If a list consists of only two or three elements, we should not call a general purpose sorting routine, but simply write out the statements to do the sorting "in line" at the point in the program where they are needed.

For two items we simply compare their keys, and exchange the items if they are out of order:

```
IF LIST(0) .KEY > LIST(1) .KEY THEN
    DO;
        TEMP = LIST(0);
        LIST(0) = LIST(1);
        LIST(1) = TEMP;
    END;
```

Since such comparisons and exchanges will be the basis of all the routines discussed in this chapter, it is well to spend a few moments on the details. We compare two records, here LIST(0) and LIST(1). If the key of the first is greater than the key of the second, then they are out of order and must be exchanged.

To do the exchange we first save the contents of LIST(0) in TEMP. Then we move the current contents of LIST(1) to LIST(0). Finally, LIST(1) gets the contents of LIST(0), which was saved in TEMP.

The temporary location TEMP is essential; to exchange the contents of two locations we always need a third for temporary storage. TEMP holds a list record and so must have the same structure as the records being sorted:

DECLARE 1 TEMP LIKE LIST;

Now we turn to sorting three records: LIST(0), LIST(1), and LIST(2). For the sake of an example, let us assume that the keys of these records are 1, 2, and 3. Then these may be in any of six possible orders:

```
        1 2 3           2 1 3
        2 3 1           3 2 1
        1 3 2           3 1 2
```

We start by comparing LIST(0) and LIST(1) and exchanging them if they are out of order:

```
IF LIST(0) .KEY > LIST(1) .KEY THEN
    /* EXCHANGE LIST(0) AND LIST(1) */;
```

where the exchange is done as just described. This will change 2 1 3 to 1 2 3, 3 2 1 to 2 3 1, and 3 1 2 to 1 3 2. We are now left with three possibilities:

```
                1 2 3
                2 3 1
                1 3 2
```

Now we compare LIST(1) and LIST(2), and exchange them if they are out of order. This reduces the possibilities to

1 2 3
2 1 3

Finally, we compare LIST(0) and LIST(1) again, and exchange them if they are out of order, which reduces us to the single possibility 1 2 3.

But notice that the last comparison is unnecessary if, after the second comparison, LIST(1) and LIST(2) were in order. For before that comparison the possibilities were 1 2 3, 2 3 1, and 1 3 2; of these, the only one in which LIST(1) and LIST(2) are in order is 1 2 3. Therefore, the last comparison need be made only if LIST(1) and LIST(2) were out of order when tested.

These considerations give us the complete routine for sorting three items:

IF LIST(0) .KEY > LIST(1) .KEY THEN
　　/* EXCHANGE LIST(0) AND LIST(1) */;
IF LIST(1) .KEY > LIST(2) .KEY THEN
　　DO;
　　　　/* EXCHANGE LIST(1) AND LIST(2) */
　　　　IF LIST(0) .KEY > LIST(1) .KEY THEN
　　　　　　/* EXCHANGE LIST(0) AND LIST(1) */;
　　END;

## THE BUBBLE SORT

The bubble sort is the simplest of the exchange sorting routines to program, but it is also the least efficient. The time required to do a bubble sort is proportional to $N^2$, where N is the number of records to be sorted. Thus if we double the number of records, the sorting time will be multiplied by 4; if we triple the number of records, the sorting time will be multiplied by 9, and so on.

The bubble sort is at its best for lists of 4 through 10 elements. It should be used for larger lists only if the sorting time is much less important than the simplicity of the sorting routine. This is often the case when the sorting routine is coded in assembly language, so that a simple routine is desired, and where—because of the speed of the computer—even a grossly inefficient routine will take up only a few seconds of computer time.

|  | | | |
|---|---|---|---|
| FIRST PASS | 5-1 3 2 6 4<br>1 5-3 2 6 4<br>1 3 5-2 6 4<br>1 3 2 5-6 4<br>1 3 2 5 6-4<br>1 3 2 5 4 6 | SECOND PASS | 1-3 2 5 4 6<br>1 3-2 5 4 6<br>1 2 3-5 4 6<br>1 2 3 5-4 6<br>1 2 3 4 5-6<br>1 2 3 4 5 6 |
| THIRD PASS<br>(No exchanges<br>made so sort<br>terminates) | 1-2 3 4 5 6<br>1 2-3 4 5 6<br>1 2 3-4 5 6<br>1 2 3 4-5 6<br>1 2 3 4 5-6<br>1 2 3 4 5 6 | Fig. 23-1. A bubble sort. | |

The basic operation of the bubble sort is a *pass*, which consists of working through the list from beginning to end, comparing adjacent records. If any adjacent records are out of order, they are exchanged.

Suppose we are sorting a list of 6 records, and the keys of those records are initially 5 1 3 2 6 4. If we place a hyphen between the two records that are being compared at any step, a pass would go like this:

```
5-1 3 2 6 4
1 5-3 2 6 4
1 3 5-2 6 4
1 3 2 5-6 4
1 3 2 5 6-4
1 3 2 5 4 6
```

Notice that the 5 is carried to the right until it runs up against the 6. The 5 is then abandoned and the 6 is carried on until the end of the list. This is where we get the name "bubble sort". If we think of the beginning of a list at its "bottom," and its end as its "top," then an element "bubbles up" until it is stopped by the presence of a larger element.

A complete bubble sort consists of making passes until the list is in order. Figure 23-1 illustrates a bubble sort.

In any bubble sort routine, we must have some way to determine when the list is in order, so the sorting routine can be terminated. Different termination conditions give different versions of bubble sort.

Program 23-1, BUBBLE_SORT_1 uses the simplest termination condition: when a pass is completed without having made any exchanges, then the list is in order and the sort can be terminated. The flag NO_EXCHANGES is set to

TRUE before commencing a pass. Whenever an exchange is made, NO_EXCHANGES is set to FALSE. If a pass can be completed, then, with NO_EXCHANGES still TRUE, no exchanges were made on that pass and the sort can terminate. We have:

```
DO UNTIL NO_EXCHANGES;
   NO_EXCHANGES = TRUE;
   /* MAKE A PASS */
END;
```

A pass consists of the following,

```
DO I = 0 TO LAST (LIST) - 1;
   /* IF LIST(I) .KEY > LIST(I + 1) .KEY THEN
      EXCHANGE LIST(I) AND LIST(I + 1), AND
      SET NO_EXCHANGES TO FALSE */
END;
```

We only let I go to LAST (LIST) $-$ 1, since it is LIST(I) and LIST(I + 1) that we compare and exchange.

Program 23-2, BUBBLE_SORT_2, applies the above idea to a part of a list, as well as the entire list: if a part of a list can be passed over without making any exchanges, then that part of the list is in order and can be omitted in future passes. The

```
BUBBLE_SORT_1: PROCEDURE;
   DECLARE I WORD,
           NO_EXCHANGES BYTE;
   DO UNTIL NO_EXCHANGES = FALSE;
      NO_EXCHANGES = TRUE;
      DO I = 0 TO LAST (LIST) - 1;
         IF LIST (I).KEY > LIST(I + 1).KEY THEN
            DO;
               TEMP = LIST(I);
               LIST(I) = LIST(I + 1);
               LIST(I + 1) = TEMP;
               NO_EXCHANGES = FALSE;
            END;
      END;
   END;
END BUBBLE_SORT_1;
```

Program 23-1. BUBBLE_SORT_1.

```
BUBBLE_SORT_2: PROCEDURE;
    DECLARE (I, J, BOUND) WORD;
    BOUND = LAST(LIST);
    DO UNTIL BOUND = 0;
        J = 0;
        DO I = 0 TO BOUND - 1;
            IF LIST(I).KEY > LIST(I + 1).KEY THEN
                DO;
                    TEMP = LIST(I);
                    LIST(I = LIST(I + 1);
                    LIST(I + 1) = TEMP;
                    J = I;
                END;
        END;
        BOUND = J;
    END;
END BUBBLE_SORT_2;
```

Program 23-2. BUBBLE_SORT_2.

part we can conveniently omit is a segment at the end of the list.

On each pass we set a variable BOUND to the position I at which the last exchange was made, or to 0 if no exchanges were made on that pass. Then the succeeding pass need go no further than BOUND. Also BOUND can replace NO_EXCHANGES, since BOUND = 0 implies the list is sorted:

```
BOUND = LAST (LIST);
DO UNTIL BOUND = 0;
    J = 0;
    DO I = 0 TO BOUND - 1;
        /* IF LIST(I) .KEY > LIST(I + 1) .KEY THEN
           EXCHANGE LIST(I) AND LIST (I + 1) AND
           SET J = I */
    END;
    BOUND = J;
END;
```

Finally, Program 23-3, BUBBLE_SORT_3, uses this idea: after the first pass the largest element will be in the last position, so this position may be omitted on the second pass.

After the second pass, the next-to-largest element will be in the next-to-last position, so on the third pass the last two positions may be omitted. Eventually, the part of the list we are sorting gets down to two elements, and after sorting them the routine terminates.

BUBBLE_SORT_3 has no way of detecting when a list has been sorted, so it will take just as long on a list with only a few elements out of order as on one in reverse order—the worst case. On the other hand, it uses only iterative DOs for control, and so is easy to program in languages which feature only that repetitive construct.

The control scheme is:

```
DO BOUND = LAST (LIST) − 1 DOWNTO 0;
   DO I = 0 TO BOUND;
      /* COMPARE LIST(I) AND LIST(I + 1) AND
         EXCHANGE IF OUT OF ORDER */
   END;
END;
```

Other variations of the bubble sort are possible. But one should bear in mind that the bubble sort is a quick and dirty sort. If greater performance is required, another algorithm should be used.

```
BUBBLE_SORT_3: PROCEDURE;
   DECLARE (I, BOUND) WORD;
   DO BOUND = LAST (LIST) − 1 DOWNTO 0;
      DO I = 0 TO BOUND;
         IF LIST(I).KEY > LIST(I + 1).KEY THEN
            DO;
               TEMP = LIST(1);
               LIST(I + 1) = LIST(I);
               LIST(I + 1) = TEMP;
            END;
      END;
   END;
END BUBBLE_SORT_3;
```

Program 23-3. BUBBLE_SORT_3.

```
SHELL__SORT: PROCEDURE;
    DECLARE (I, GAP) WORD,
            NO__EXCHANGES BYTE;
    GAP = LENGTH(LIST)/2;
    DO UNTIL GAP = 0;
        DO UNTIL NO__EXCHANGES;
            NO__EXCHANGES = TRUE;
            DO I = 0 TO LAST(LIST) - GAP;
                IF LIST(I).KEY > LIST(I + 1).KEY THEN
                    DO;
                        TEMP = LIST(I);
                        LIST(I) = LIST(I + 1);
                        LIST(I + 1) = TEMP;
                        NO__EXCHANGES = FALSE;
                    END;
            END;
        END;
        GAP = GAP/2;
    END;
END SHELL__SORT;
```

Program 23-4. SHELL__SORT.

## THE SHELL SORT

The Shell sort—named after its inventor, D. L. Shell—is an excellent sort for routine use. It is almost as easy to program as the bubble sort, and is far more efficient.

The time required to sort N elements with a Shell sort is (approximately) proportional to $N^{1.2}$. This is considerably better than the $N^2$ for the bubble sort. If we double the number of elements to be sorted, the sorting time will be multiplied by 2.3, instead of 4 as for the bubble sort. If we triple the number of elements to be sorted, the sorting time is multiplied by 3.7, instead of 9 as for the bubble sort. Only for very large lists—say more than 500 records—and where speed is more of a consideration than program complexity is one likely to be tempted by the more efficient Quicksort discussed in the next section.

The reason the bubble sort is so slow is that only adjacent elements are compared and exchanged. Thus if an element is far out of place it will move to its proper position very slowly. This is particularly true if it must move from back to front—contrary to the direction of the "bubbling." An element is moved backward by only one position per pass!

A Shell sort does a whole sequence of bubble sorts, but instead of comparing adjacent elements, it compares LIST(I) and LIST(I + GAP), where GAP is halved on each successive bubble sort. The final sort is a true bubble sort, with GAP equal to 1.

Program 23-4 shows the procedure SHELL_SORT. Figure 23-2 illustrates a Shell sort.

At first thought the Shell sort may seem somewhat paradoxical. After all, we complained that the bubble sort was slow, and now we are doing a whole series of bubble sorts—9, in fact, for a list of 512 records. How can this be faster?

The early sorts with large gaps are faster because fewer elements must be put in order. When we sort with a gap other than 1, we are sorting a series of sublists whose elements are separated by a gap. These sublists have fewer elements and hence can be sorted faster than the full list.

The sorts with small gaps, including the final bubble sort with GAP = 1, run faster because of the "presorting" which use has moved items far out of place much closer to their correct places. Somewhat surprisingly, the whole series of sorts goes much faster than a single bubble sort.

### QUICKSORT

Quicksort lives up to its name. It is one of the fastest of internal sorts. On the other hand, it is definitely more complicated than the Shell sort.

```
                 8* 7  6  5  4* 3  2  1
                 4  7* 6  5  8  3* 2  1
FIRST PASS       4  3  6* 5  8  7  2* 1     SECOND PASS
GAP = 4          4  3  2  5* 8  7  6  1*    GAP = 2           (Omitted)
                 4  3  2  1  8  7  6  5

                                                        2* 1* 4  3  6  5  8  7
SECOND PASS                                             1  2* 4* 3  6  5  8  7
GAP = 4                    (Omitted)                    1  2  4* 3* 6  5  8  7
                                             FIRST PASS 1  2  3  4* 6* 5  8  7
                                             GAP = 1    1  2  3  4  6* 5* 8  7
                 4* 3  2* 1  8  7  6  5                 1  2  3  4  5  6* 8* 7
                 2  3* 4  1* 8  7  6  5                 1  2  3  4  5  6  8* 7*
FIRST PASS       2  1  4* 3  8* 7  6  5                 1  2  3  4  5  6  7  8
GAP = 2          2  1  4  3* 8  7* 6  5
                 2  1  4  3  8* 7  6* 5
                 2  1  4  3  6  7* 8  5*    SECOND PASS
                 2  1  4  3  6  5  8  7     GAP = 1            (Omitted)
```

Fig. 23-2. A Shell sort. Values being compared are marked with asterisks. Passes which do not produce any exchanges are omitted.

The time required for sorting N elements with Quicksort is proportional to $N*\log_2 N$. Since $N^{1.2} = N*N^{.2}$, and $N^{.2}$ increases more rapidly with N than does $\log_2 N$, Quicksort will beat Shell sort for a large enough list. Quicksort is recommended for large lists where sorting speed is a more important considerations than programming complexity.

Quicksort approaches sorting much like the binary search approaches searching. The list to be sorted is arranged into two parts, such that every element in the first part precedes every element in the second part. (See Fig. 23-3. There may possibly be a single element which is not in either part, but lies between them.) If these two parts can be sorted, then the entire list can be sorted.

Now the process is repeated with each of the two parts. Each part is itself divided into two parts, with every element in the first preceding every element in the second. If those four parts—obtained from dividing the list in two and then dividing each part in two again—are sorted, then the entire list will be sorted.

The subdivision process continues until partitions of two elements are obtained. When a two element partition is arranged so that the smaller element precedes the larger, then it is sorted. If this is done for all two element partitions then all

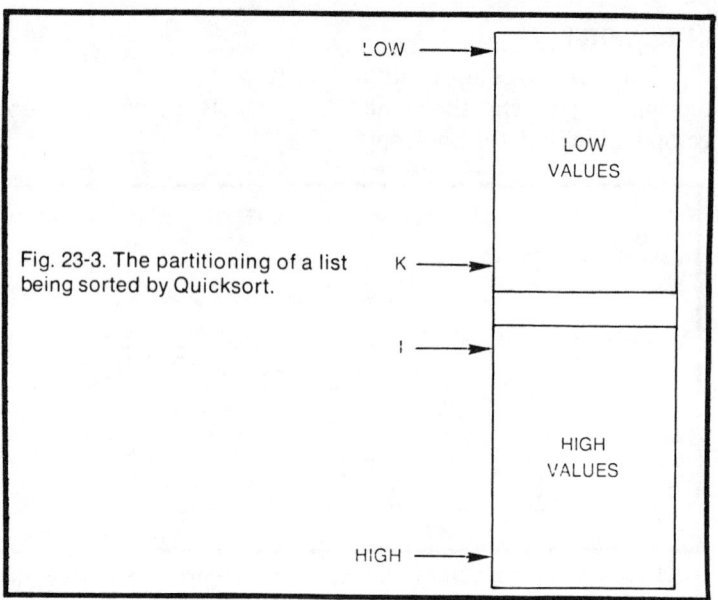

Fig. 23-3. The partitioning of a list being sorted by Quicksort.

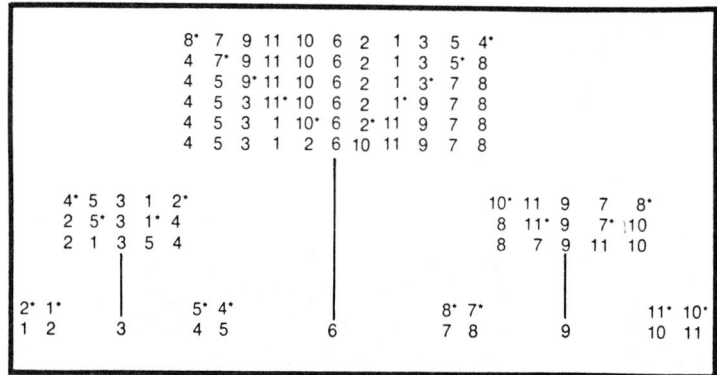

Fig. 23-4. A Quicksort. In each partition the middle element was taken as the trial median. For the sake of the example, the data was chosen to give the "ideal" Quicksort. Things would not work out so neatly with other data.

the larger partitions, and hence the entire list, will be sorted. Figure 23-4 illustrates a Quicksort.

Quicksort lends itself well to a recursive formulation, since the same operation—sorting—must be done on the partitions of the list as Quicksort was called to do on the entire list. If LOW and HIGH are the limits between which we are to sort, then we have:

QUICKSORT: PROCEDURE (LOW, HIGH) RECURSIVE;
   DECLARE (LOW, HIGH, I, K) WORD;
   /* PARTITION THE LIST FROM LOW THROUGH HIGH INTO TWO PARTS. SET K TO THE SUBSCRIPT OF THE LAST ELEMENT IN THE FIRST PART, AND I TO THE SUBSCRIPT OF THE FIRST ELEMENT IN THE SECOND PART */

   IF LOW < K THEN CALL QUICKSORT (LOW, K);
   IF I < HIGH THEN CALL QUICKSORT (I, HIGH);
END QUICKSORT;

As has been mentioned before, when a recursive call occurs at the end of a procedure, the recursion can be changed to a repetition, since there is nothing that has to be saved on a stack for later use. This idea gives:

```
QUICKSORT: PROCEDURE (LOW, HIGH) RE-
CURSIVE;
    DECLARE (LOW, HIGH, I, K) WORD;
    DO WHILE LOW < HIGH;
        /* PARTITION THE LIST FROM LOW
           THROUGH HIGH INTO TWO PARTS.
           SET K TO THE SUBSCRIPT OF THE
           LAST ELEMENT IN THE FIRST PART, AND
           I TO THE SUBSCRIPT OF THE FIRST
           ELEMENT IN THE SECOND PART */
        IF LOW < K THEN CALL QUICKSORT (LOW,
        K);
        LOW = I;
    END;
END QUICKSORT;
```

Now we turn to the partitioning process, which we do by means of exchanges. We start by setting the variables I and K at the ends of the partition to be sorted, and J to its midpoint:

```
I = LOW;
J = (LOW + HIGH)/2;
K = HIGH;
```

We would like very much to choose M to be the median key, the one such that there are just as many elements with keys less than or equal to M as there are with keys greater than or equal to M. Unfortunately, there is no simple way of finding the true median without doing an elaborate sorting procedure. There are several ways to estimate the median. The one we shall use is to choose the median of the first, middle, and last elements. We do this by sorting LIST(I), LIST(J), and LIST(K), using the in-line, three element sort discussed previously, and then setting:

$$M = LIST(J) .KEY;$$

We shall partition the list so that all elements with keys less than M will be in the first part, and all those with keys greater than M will be in the second part. Elements with keys equal to M may be in either part. Also, one such element may be in between the two parts, not belonging to either.

We do this by moving I forward in the list until an element with key greater than or equal to M is encountered, and moving K backwards until an element with key less than or

```
QUICKSORT: PROCEDURE (LOW, HIGH) RECURSIVE;
    DECLARE (LOW, HIGH, I, J, K, M) WORD;
    I = LOW;
    DO WHILE LOW < HIGH;
        J = (LOW + HIGH)/2;
        K = HIGH
        /* ESTIMATE MEDIAN, M, OF PARTITION (I, K) BY SORTING
            LIST(I), LIST(J), AND LIST(K) AND SETTING M
            TO LIST (J).KEY */
        IF LIST(I).KEY > LIST(J).KEY THEN
            DO;
                TEMP = LIST(I);
                LIST(I) = LIST(J);
                LIST(J) = TEMP;
            END;
        IF LIST(J).KEY > LIST(K).KEY THEN
            DO;
                TEMP = LIST(J);
                LIST(J) = LIST(K);
                LIST(K) = TEMP;
                IF LIST(I).KEY > LIST(J).KEY THEN
                    DO;
                        TEMP = LIST(I);
                        LIST(I) = LIST(J);
                        LIST(J) = TEMP;
                    END;
            END;

        M = LIST(J).KEY;
        /* PARTITION (LOW, HIGH) INTO (LOW, K) AND (I, HIGH) */
        DO UNTIL I > K;
            DO UNTIL LIST(I).KEY > = M;
                I = I + 1;
            END;
            DO UNTIL LIST(K).KEY < = M:
                K = K - 1;
            END;
            IF I < K THEN
                DO;
                    TEMP = LIST(I);
                    LIST(I) = LIST(K);
                    LIST(K) = TEMP;
                END;
        END;
        /* SORT PARTITION (LOW, K) */
            IF LOW < K THEN CALL QUICKSORT (LOW, K);
        /* ON NEXT REPETITION WE WILL SORT PARTITION (I, HIGH) */
            LOW = I;
    END;
END QUICKSORT;
```

Program 23-5. QUICKSORT

equal to M is encountered. The two elements are exchanged. The process is repeated until I and K pass each other. We have:

```
DO UNTIL I > K;
    DO UNTIL LIST(I) .KEY > = M;
        I = I + 1;
    END;
    DO UNTIL LIST(K) .KEY < = M;
        K = K - 1;
    END;
    IF I < K THEN CALL EXCHANGE (I, K);
END;
```

EXCHANGE (I, J) exchanges the contents of LIST(I) and LIST(J), using the method discussed earlier.

Program 23-5 shows the complete procedure, QUICKSORT.

Actually, we can improve our execution time by not letting QUICKSORT work its way all the way down to two element partitions. For lists in which no element is more than 10 positions out of place, the bubble sort is faster than QUICKSORT, due to its smaller bookkeeping requirements. We modify the termination condition of QUICKSORT so that it will terminate when it has obtained partitions of 11 elements or less. In Program 23-5, we replace

DO WHILE LOW < HIGH;

by

DO WHILE HIGH - LOW > 10;

When this version of QUICKSORT terminates the list elements will be at most 10 places out of position. Thus 10 bubble sort passes will complete the sorting. It is not worthwhile to attempt to test for an earlier termination:

```
DO N = 1 TO 10;
    DO I = 0 TO LAST (LIST) - 1;
        /* IF LIST(I) AND LIST(I + 1) ARE OUT OF
           ORDER, EXCHANGE THEM */
    END;
END;
```

# Chapter 24
# External Sorting

The internal sorting routines of the previous chapter are totally unsuited for *external sorting*, the sorting of records stored on auxiliary storage devices, such as tapes or disks.

The internal sorts demand random access, in which the time required to access the records does not depend on the order in which they are processed. Auxiliary storage devices, on the other hand, favor sequential access, where records are processed in the order in which they are stored. For some devices—such as most magnetic tape units—sequential access is the only kind possible. For other devices, such as disks, it is by far the more efficient.

Although it is *possible* to use internal sorting routines with a disk, the sort will be very slow for moderately large files. Sorting a file of several thousand records would take many hours.

Fortunately there is a sorting technique that requires only sequential access to files, and that technique is *merging*. Although other techniques have been proposed from time to time, the most widely used external sorting techniques are all based on merging.

In this chapter we shall examine several external sorting techniques. We shall concentrate on principles, and not attempt to develop explicit programs. This is for two reasons: First, our programming language has no provisions for describing the manipulation of data on auxiliary storage

```
                            17 25 41 58
                            15 27 58 60 75

        15                  17 25 41 58
                            27 58 60 75

        15 17               25 41 58
                            27 58 60 75

        15 17 25            41 58
                            27 58 60 75

        15 17 25 27         58
                            58 60 75

        15 17 25 27 58      58 60 75

        15 17 25 27 58 58 60 75
```

Fig. 24-1. Merging two sequences.

devices. And second, external sorting programs devote so much space to bookkeeping—calculations that do not directly contribute to the sorting, but are necessary for the program to keep track of what is going on—that the principles are often obscured. Completely worked out programs can be found in the book by Wirth (see bibliography).

## MERGING

The principle behind all external sorting routines is this: Given two (or more) ordered sequences of records, we can merge them into a single sequence which is also ordered.

Figure 24-1 illustrates this. The sequences to be merged are shown on the right, the result of the merging on the left. At each step the next records in each of the two sequences on the right are compared, and the smaller of the two is placed in the sequence on the right. If the two records have the same key, then an arbitrary choice is made. If one of the input sequences is exhausted before the other, then the remainder of the other sequence is merely copied into the output.

We may merge any number of sequences, as shown in Fig. 24-2. Here again the next record in each input sequence is examined, and the one with the smallest key is placed into the output. This process is repeated until all input sequences have been exhausted. Any input sequences that become exhausted early are simply ignored thereafter

Thus if we start with a three-way merge, then after one sequence becomes exhausted we continue with a two-way merge, and when another sequence becomes exhausted, then whatever remains of the third sequence is merely copied into the output.

**RUNS**

Consider the sequence:

    5   8   12   4   8   21   25   40   59   1   2

Although the sequence itself is unsorted, it contains

|  |  |
|---|---|
|  | 17 58 |
|  | 15 41 60 |
|  | 25 27 58 75 |
|  |  |
|  | 17 58 |
| 15 | 41 60 |
|  | 25 27 58 75 |
|  |  |
|  | 58 |
| 15 17 | 41 60 |
|  | 25 27 58 75 |
|  |  |
|  | 58 |
| 15 17 25 | 41 60 |
|  | 27 58 |
|  |  |
|  | 58 |
| 15 17 25 27 | 41 60 |
|  | 58 75 |
|  |  |
|  | 58 |
| 15 17 25 27 41 | 60 |
|  | 58 75 |
|  |  |
| 15 17 25 27 41 58 | 60 |
|  | 58 75 |
|  |  |
| 15 17 25 27 41 58 58 | 60 |
|  | 75 |
|  |  |
| 15 17 25 27 41 58 58 60 |  |
|  | 75 |
| 15 17 25 27 41 58 58 60 75 |  |

Fig. 24-2. Merging three sequences.

subsequences that are. These already sorted subsequences are called *runs*. If we break the sequence down into runs we have

                5  8  12  .  4  8  21  25  40  59  .  1  2

The original sequence contains three runs: 5-8-12, 4-8-21-25-40-59, and 1-2.

In the examples in this book I will use a period between runs to make them stand out to the eye. But no one is nice enough to do this for the computer! It has to be able to detect the end of one run and the beginning of the next.

The end of a run is signaled by a *stepdown*, a smaller element following a larger one. In the example, just given, the stepdown 12 4 signals the end of the first run, and 59 1 signals the end of the second. The end of the third, of course, is the end of the sequence.

## SORTING BY MERGING

We are now in a position to state the fundamental principle of external sorting: A file is sorted by successively merging runs into larger and larger runs until eventually only one run, the entire file, is left.

Let us consider the simplest possible sort using merging. Suppose we have three files as shown in Fig. 24-3: File 1, File 2, and File 3. Initially, the data to be sorted is in File 1. File 2 and File 3 are empty.

We wish to merge the successive runs in File 1 into larger and larger runs. Since runs can only be merged if they are in separate files, we must *distribute* the runs from File 1 onto File 2 and File 3. The first run from File 1 goes in File 2, the second in File 3, the third in File 2 again, and so on. Every other run will be placed in File 2, and those in between will go in File 3.

Now we *merge* the runs in File 2 and File 3, and place the result back in File 1. Thus the first run in File 2 is merged with the first run in File 3, and the result becomes the first run in File 1. The next run in File 2 is merged with the next run in File 3, and the result becomes the next run in File 1. And so on.

Now we are back where we started, with all the data in File 1, but with this difference: There are only (approximately) half as many runs and the runs are (approximately) twice as long.

We now repeat the entire process—distributing runs into Files 2 and 3, and merging them back into File 1. Each

```
Initial Situation
    File 1: 8.7.6.5.4.3.2.1
    File 2:
    File 3:
Distribute Runs:
    File 1:
    File 2: 8.6.4.2
    File 3: 7.5.3.1
Merge:
    File 1: 78.56.34.12
    File 2:
    File 3:
Distribute Runs:
    File 1:
    File 2: 78.34
    File 3: 56.12
Merge:
    File 1: 5678.1234
    File 2:
    File 3:
Distribute Runs:
    File 1:
    File 2: 5678
    File 3: 1234
Merge:
    File 1: 12345678
    File 2:
    File 3:
```

Fig. 24-3. Sorting by merging.

repetition at least halves the number of runs. Soon we are down to one run and the records are sorted. For instance, if the original data had consisted of 64 runs, approximately 6 repetitions, or *passes*, would be required.

Two technicalities: If the number of runs on File 1 is odd, then after distribution File 2 will contain one more run than File 3. To make them come out even, we add a *dummy run* to the end of File 3. This is just a matter of bookkeeping; we record somewhere that File 3 has a dummy run at the end. When merging a dummy run with a real one, the real run is merely copied into the output file, in this case, File 1.

When two runs are placed one after another on a file, they may coalesce into a single run. If, for instance, the runs 2 3 4 5 and 6 7 8 9 were placed one behind the other we would have

2 3 4 5 6 7 8 9

365

```
Initial Situation:
    File 1: 8.7.6.5.4.3.2.1
    File 2:
    File 3:
    File 4:
Initial Distribution:
    File 1:
    File 2:
    File 3: 8.6.4.2
    File 4: 7.5.3.1
Merge and Distribute:
    File 1: 78.34
    File 2: 56.12
    File 3:
    File 4:
Merge and Distribute:
    File 1:
    File 2:
    File 3: 5 6 7 8
    File 4: 1 2 3 4
Final Merge:
    File 1: 1 2 3 4 5 6 7 8
    File 2:
    File 3:
    File 4:
```

Fig. 24-4. Balanced merging.

which is one run, not two. This means that when we distribute runs from one file into others, it is possible for some of the runs to combine into larger ones.

Desirable as this effect is from the point of view of reducing sorting time, it can complicate the bookeeping, particularly for some of the more sophisticated sorts which must always have a certain number of runs in each file.

## BALANCED MERGING

The process of distributing runs from File 1 into Files 2 and 3 contributes nothing to the actual job at hand—the reordering of the records. We can eliminate it—or at least do it only once—by using an extra file.

Figure 24-4 illustrates the process. The data to be sorted is initially in File 1. As before we start by distributing, in this case, the runs from File 1 into Files 3 and 4.

Now, however, when we merge the runs in File 3 and File 4, instead of putting them all back in File 1, we distribute them alternately between File 1 and File 2. The first run on File 3 is merged with the first run in File 4, and the result is placed in File 1. The next run in File 3 is merged with the next run in File 4, and the result goes in File 2. The result of merging the next runs would go back into File 1, and so on.

Now suppose that all the runs from File 3 and File 4 have been merged and distributed into File 1 and File 2. We now repeat the process and merge the runs from File 1 and File 2 and distribute them into File 3 and File 4. The data moves back and forth between File 1 and File 2, on the one hand, and File 3 and File 4 on the other. Eventually only one run is left and the sort is complete.

We can reduce the number of passes, and hence the sorting time, by using more files. If we used 6 files, for instance, we would do a three-way merge on each pass, and hence divide the number of runs by 3 instead of 2. Even more files—in the range 8-16—are not uncommon. As a rule, the more the better.

## THE POLYPHASE SORT

Balanced merging does not make the best use of the available files. With four files, for instance, we will at any time be doing a two-way merge from two of the files, and distributing the result into the other two. But with four files, we could reduce the sorting time by doing a three-way merge from three of the files into the fourth. In general, for N files, we will get the best performance by spending as much time as possible doing $N - 1$ way merges from $N - 1$ of the files into the remaining one. The sorting method based on this idea is called the *polyphase sort*.

We pay for the increased efficiency of the polyphase sort with a considerable increase in bookkeeping. The bookkeeping does not slow the sort down: auxiliary storage devices are so slow compared to the computer that the bookkeeping can easily be done while records are being transferred back and forth between the files and the computer. But the bookkeeping does make the program a lot more complicated.

Figure 24-5 illustrates a polyphase sort. For simplicity, we will hereafter concentrate on just the runs, and not write out the keys of the records making up the runs. We use (Run 1), (Run 2), (Run 3), (Run 4), and (Run 5) to denote the 5 initial runs. After some merging has taken place, we will use (Runs 1 & 4) to denote the result of merging (Run 1) and (Run 4), (Runs 1, 3, & 4) to denote the result of merging (Run 1), (Run 3), and (Run 4) (not all in the same step), and so on.

> Initial Situation:
>     File 1: (Run 1) (Run 2) (Run 3) (Run 4) (Run 5)
>     File 2:
>     File 3:
>
> Distribute Runs:
>     File 1:
>     File 2: (Run 1) (Run 2) (Run 3)
>     File 3: (Run 4) (Run 5)
>
> Merge into File 1 until File 3 is empty:
>     File 1: (Runs 1 & 4) (Runs 2 & 5)
>     File 2: (Run 3)
>     File 3:
>
> Merge into File 3 until File 2 is empty:
>     File 1: (Runs 2 & 5)
>     File 2:
>     File 3: (Runs 1, 3 & 4)
>
> Final Merge into File 2:
>     File 1:
>     File 2: (Runs 1, 2, 3, 4 & 5)
>     File 3:

Fig. 24-5. A polyphase sort.

Now let us work through Fig. 24-5. Initially we have 5 runs on File 1. We distribute these in File 2 and File 3, putting (Run 1), (Run 2), and (Run 3) in File 2 and (Run 4) and (Run 5) in File 3.

File 1 is now empty. So we start by merging File 2 and File 3 and putting the result in File 1. We merge (Run 1) and (Run 4) and put (Runs 1 & 4) in File 1. We merge (Run 2) and (Run 5) and put (Runs 2 & 5) in File 1.

Now File 3 is empty, although File 2 is not. We therefore start merging runs from File 1 and File 2, and putting the results in File 3. Since File 2 contains only one run, only one merge takes place; (Runs 1 & 4) are merged with (Run 3), and (Runs 1, 3, & 4) goes into File 3.

Now File 2 is empty, and there is one run each in File 1 and File 3. We merge those two files and put the single run that results—the sorted file—into File 2.

We see, then, the principle of the polyphase sort: Whenever one file becomes exhausted, we immediately switch to using it as a destination, and merging into it from the other files.

The problem now is to determine how the runs should initially be distributed among the files so that the sorting process will "come out right" in the end with a single run on one file, and with all the others empty.

We work the problem backward. In the above example, for instance, the final result we want is 1 run on File 2 and 0 runs on File 1 and File 3. We can symbolize this state of affairs by:

File 1: 0    File 2: 1    File 3: 0

Just before the final merge File 2 had to be empty and File 1 and File 3 had to contain one run each, so that they could merge into the single run that will go into File 2. Just before the final merge, then we must have:

File 1: 1    File 2: 0    File 3: 1

Now the reasoning becomes slightly trickier. At the end of the preceding phase one file must be empty. This could be either File 1 or File 3. We will let the files be empty in 1-2-3 order, and so choose File 3. We now have:

File 1: ?    File 2: ?    FILE 3: 0

What should be in File 1 and File 2? File 1 must contain at least 1 run, and File 2 at least 0 runs (it always will, of course) since these are what are left over after the merge into File 3 takes place.

In addition, File 1 and File 2 must contain as many runs as will be in File 3 after merging, since each run in File 3 comes from merging a run from File 1 and a run from File 2.

File 1 and File 2, then, must each contain the number of runs that will be left over in each *plus* the number that will be in File 3. To get the number of runs in File 1 and File 2 we take the number that will be in File 3 in the following step and add it to the number that will be left in File 1 and File 2. This gives:

File 1: 2    File 2: 1    File 3: 0

At the end of the next previous phase it is File 1's turn to be empty. The number of runs in File 2 and File 3 will be the number currently in each *plus* the number currently in File 1:

File 1: 0    File 2: 3    File 3: 2

This is the initial distribution of runs that we need. If we do the polyphase sort, we will reproduce all the distributions just given, in reverse order, until we end up with a single run in File 2.

| DISTRIBUTION OF RUNS | | | TOTAL NUMBER OF RUNS |
|---|---|---|---|
| FILE 1 | FILE 2 | FILE 3 | |
| 0 | 1 | 0 | 1 |
| 1 | 0 | 1 | 2 |
| 2 | 1 | 0 | 3 |
| 0 | 3 | 2 | 5 |
| 3 | 0 | 5 | 8 |
| 8 | 5 | 0 | 13 |
| 0 | 13 | 8 | 21 |
| 13 | 0 | 21 | 34 |
| 34 | 21 | 0 | 55 |
| | (and so on) | | |

Fig. 24-6. Computing the initial distribution of runs for three files. Each line is a possible initial distribution.

Let us carry the "working backward" process a step further. It is now File 2's turn to be empty. Therefore we must add 3, the number of runs in File 2, to the number of runs in File 1 and File 3. We get:

File 1: 3    File 2: 0    File 3: 5

This tells us that if we had 8 runs, we would distribute them 3 in File 1 and 5 in File 3, in order to eventually come out with a single run on File 2.

We can, in fact, carry the calculation as far as we wish. See Fig. 24-6. Also, we may carry it out for any number of files. Figure 24-7 shows the calculation carried out for 5 files.

We are not through with the problems of the polyphase sort, however. When we examine Fig. 24-6 and Fig. 24-7, we see that there are only certain numbers of initial runs that will allow the polyphase sort to "come out right". These are the numbers that appear in the Total column in the two figures. From Fig. 24-6, for instance, we see that a polyphase sort using 3 files must start with 1, 2, 3, 5, 8, 13, . . . and so on runs. (Each number in this sequence is the sum of the preceding two. For 5 files you can readily verify that each number in the total column is the sum of the preceding 4, except near the beginning of the sequence.)

So what if we don't have 5 or 8 or 13 runs, or some other number in this sequence, to start off with? We must make up the difference in dummy runs. If we had 6 initial runs, then, we would add 2 dummy runs to make up 8 runs in all. Or if we had 10 initial runs, we would add 3 dummy runs to make 13 runs in all.

But now we come to still another question: How should the dummy runs be distributed in the files for best performance? When a dummy run participates in a merge, the effect is to reduce the order of the merge. If we are merging 4 files, for instance, and 2 of them contain dummy runs, then only 2 real runs will be merged. Our 4-way merge has been temporarily reduced to a 2-way merge, with a corresponding loss in efficiency. On the other hand, if 4 dummy runs were merged, then this would only be a bookkeeping operation, and no data would be moved (so efficiency would not be affected).

Therefore, we place the dummy runs at the beginnings of the files, so that dummy runs will be merged with each other as much as possible. Also the runs at the beginnings of the files are subject to more manipulation than those at the ends. If these are dummy runs, which do not actually have to be manipulated, so much the better.

The usual technique for assigning dummy runs is the so-called *horizontal method*. It is not optimal, but it is close to being so, and doing any better means a tremendous increase in the complexity of the bookkeeping.

We assume three files, which means we will be distributing runs from the file which initially contains the records to be sorted into the other two files.

Suppose we have 6 runs to distribute. The next highest number of runs that will give a valid distribution is 8, so 2 dummy runs are needed.

Imagine the two files into which runs are to be distributed to be two containers. One container is 5 runs deep; the other is 3 runs deep. We assume that their tops are aligned. We fill the

| DISTRIBUTION OF RUNS | | | | | TOTAL NUMBER OF RUNS |
|---|---|---|---|---|---|
| FILE 1 | FILE 2 | FILE 3 | FILE4 | FILE 5 | |
| 0 | 1 | 0 | 0 | 0 | 1 |
| 1 | 0 | 1 | 1 | 1 | 4 |
| 2 | 1 | 0 | 2 | 2 | 7 |
| 4 | 3 | 2 | 0 | 4 | 13 |
| 8 | 7 | 6 | 4 | 0 | 25 |
| 0 | 15 | 14 | 12 | 8 | 49 |
| 15 | 0 | 29 | 27 | 23 | 94 |
| 44 | 29 | 0 | 56 | 52 | 181 |
| 100 | 85 | 56 | 0 | 108 | 349 |
| (and so on) | | | | | |

Fig. 24-7. Computing the initial distribution of runs for five files.

containers with runs, letting each run go into the lowest available position. After all the real runs have been distributed, then the containers are filled up to the top with dummy runs. If the tops of the containers correspond to the beginnings of the files, then this distribution accomplishes our goal of keeping the dummy runs at the beginning.

Only one more problem remains. When we start distributing we may not know how many runs we will end up with. As we shall see in the next section, the initial runs are themselves produced by a computational process. We would like to distribute them as they are generated, without having counted them in advance.

The solution (for the case of 3 files) is shown in Fig. 24-8. We start out by assuming that there will be only 1 run, and setting up a container 1 run deep. If it becomes filled, then we assume 2 runs, and set up the containers appropriately. When they are filled we assume 3 runs, and if they are filled then 5 runs, and so on. Thus the containers grow deeper as we go along. When we give out of runs, then we fill the containers as they are presently constituted to the top with dummy runs.

Of course our containers exist only in the "mind" of the computer. It merely distributes runs into files, keeping track of the number of runs in each file. It uses the container model to calculate where the next run should go, and after all the runs have been distributed, to calculate how many dummy runs should be assumed to be at the beginning of each file.

As we have seen, it is possible for two runs to accidentally coalesce into a single run. The computer must detect this, since it has to place an exact number of different runs in each file.

## GENERATING THE INITIAL RUNS

When we examine the original file to be sorted, we find that it already contains many runs. But we can greatly increase the length of these, and correspondingly reduce their number, by the use of internal sorting in main memory.

One obvious solution is to read as many records from the file to be sorted as will fit into main memory, sort these using some internal sort—Quicksort, perhaps—and output the result as a single run. The process repeats until the file to be sorted is exhausted. The length of each initial run, then, equals the space available for sorting in main memory.

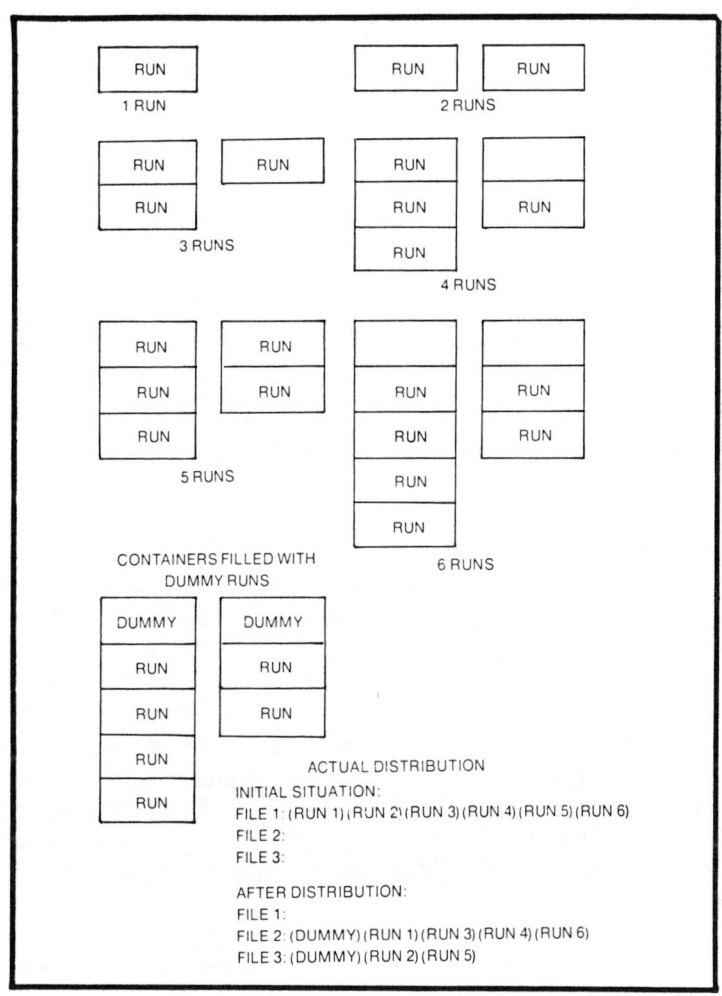

Fig. 24-8. The initial distribution problem for 6 runs and 3 files.

This technique has much to recommend it for disk files. A disk file is already divided up into large blocks: the tracks. Assuming the disk drive will read or write an entire track in one revolution, it is both convenient and efficient to read each track into memory, sort it, and write it back on disk.

Nevertheless, if we wish to process records individually, we can generate runs *longer* than the space available in main memory, twice as long on the average.

(Of course we do not ever read and write records one by one on tape or disk. Instead we read and write whole sectors,

| OUTPUT | MEMORY | INPUT |
|---|---|---|
|  |  | 9 8 7 6 5 4 3 2 1 |
|  | 9 8 7 | 6 5 4 3 2 1 |
| 7 | 9 8 6* | 5 4 3 2 1 |
| 7 8 | 9 5*6* | 4 3 2 1 |
| 7 8 9 | 4 5 6 | 3 2 1 |
| 7 8 9 . 4 | 3*5 6 | 2 1 |
| 7 8 9 . 4 5 | 3*2*6 | 1 |
| 7 8 9 . 4 5 6 | 3 2 1 |  |
| 7 8 9 . 4 5 6 . 1 | 3 2 |  |
| 7 8 9 . 4 5 6 . 1 2 | 3 |  |
| 7 8 9 . 4 5 6 . 1 2 3 |  |  |

Fig. 24-9. Replacement selection.

tracks, or other blocks. We need buffers in memory to hold these blocks, from which records will be passed one by one to and from the sorting routines. The space taken up by these buffers will be unavailable for other purposes, such as internal sorting.)

Figure 24-9 illustrates the technique that allows us to generate runs averaging twice as long as the available space in main memory. It is called *replacement selection*.

We begin by filling the available memory space with records from the input file, the file to be sorted. Now the record in memory with the smallest key is *selected*, and written on the output file. This record is replaced with the next record from the input file. The selection and replacement process is then repeated, at each step selecting the smallest record in main memory for output and replacing it with the next input record.

It may happen that the record read from the input file is smaller than the one it is replacing. In this case it cannot belong to the current run. We put this record in memory anyway, but distinguish it in some way from those in the current run. (In Fig. 24-10, such records are enclosed in boxes.)

In selecting a record for output, we *ignore* those belonging to the next run, and select only from among those belonging to the current run. Eventually, memory is filled with records belonging to the next run; at that time a new run is started.

## A PRIORITY QUEUE

We have still said nothing about how to select the smallest record for output from those in memory. Since we anticipate a *large* list of records in memory—as large as possible, in fact—we need something more efficient than merely scanning a list from one end to the other.

What we are implementing is called a *priority queue*. An ordinary queue has a first-in first-out behavior. What we need is a smallest-in first-out discipline. Or, put another way, the record with the highest priority is the next removed from the queue. We of course assign the highest priority to the record with the smallest key.

A priority queue can be implemented using a *heap*. A heap—illustrated in Fig. 24-10—is a binary tree such that the key of any record is less than or equal to the keys of its two children.

We recall that a complete binary tree can be conveniently stored as an array, and hence so can a heap. The number outside each node is the subscript of that node in the array. Node 1, the root, is the record with the smallest key, the one to be output next.

When we output the root, we replace it with the next record from the input file. We then move this record to its proper place in the tree through a process known as *sifting*. The key of the record is compared with the key of the smallest of its two

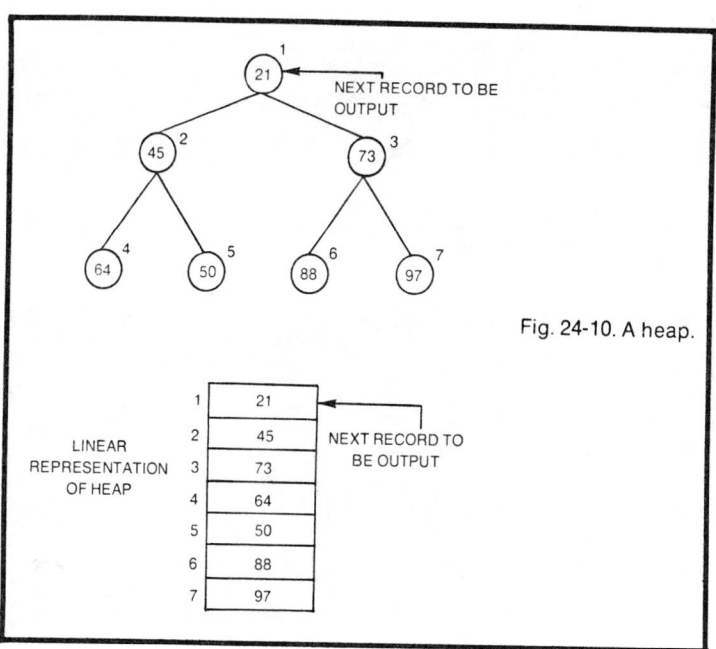

Fig. 24-10. A heap.

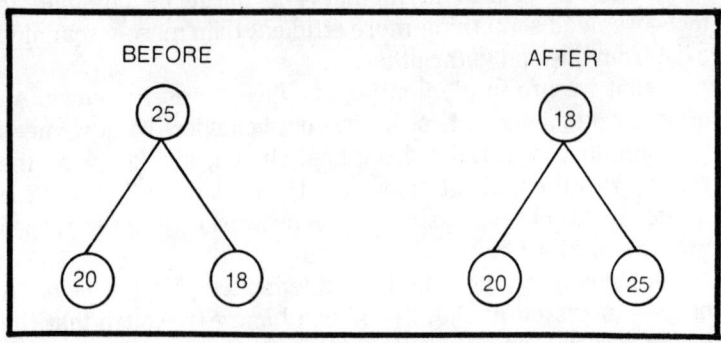

Fig. 24-11. The sifting process, whereby a parent is exchanged with the smaller of its two children.

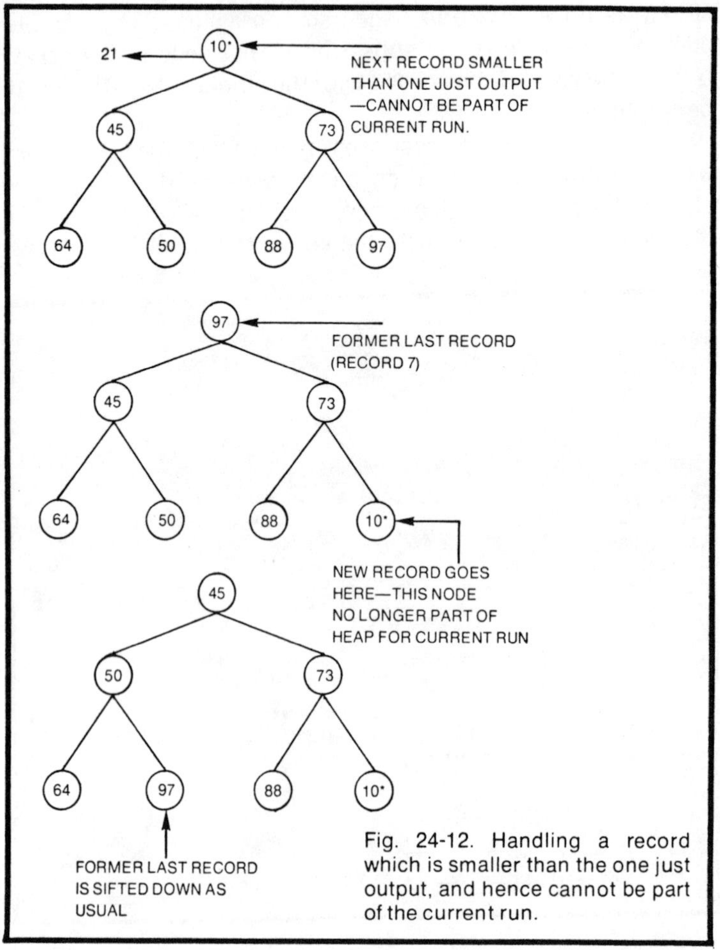

Fig. 24-12. Handling a record which is smaller than the one just output, and hence cannot be part of the current run.

children. If the record in question is larger than the smallest of its two children, it is exchanged with that child. The sifting process continues until the record either reaches the bottom of the tree, or reaches a position where it is less than or equal to both its children. Figure 24-11 illustrates sifting.

Sifting a record into place requires on the order of $2*\log_2 N$ comparisons. This is a tiny fraction of the N comparisons that would be required if we scanned all the records.

To create a heap initially, we fill it with records from the input file without regard to their order. Then we apply the sifting algorithm, first to the records on the level just above the leaves, then to the records just above those, and so on, until the algorithm is finally applied to the root.

Figure 24-12 illustrates what happens when we input a record which is smaller than the last one output. We exchange it with the last record in the heap (considered as a linear array), Record 7 in this case. The heap of records in the current run has been reduced to 6 records; Record 7 is no longer in the heap. The record that formerly occupied position 7 is placed in the root, and sifted down as usual.

When the next record not in the current run is read, it is exchanged with Record 6, and position 6 in the heap is removed from the current run heap and added to the next run heap.

As we proceed, the current run heap diminishes and the next run heap grows. When we start putting next run records in positions that are not leaves, we sift them down as they are added. Eventually, the current run heap disappears, signaling the end of the current run. But the next run heap is already built and awaiting use.

# Bibliography

1. O. J. Dahl, E. W. Dijkstra, and C. A. R. Hoare, *Structured Programming* (Academic Press, London, 1971).
2. D. E. Knuth, *The Art of Computer Programming*
   Volume 1. *Fundamental Algorithms* (1968)
   Volume 2. *Seminumerical Algorithms* (1969)
   Volume 3. *Sorting and Searching* (1973)
   (Addison-Wesley, Reading, Mass.).
3. James Martin, *Computer Data-Base Organization* (Prentice-Hall, Englewood Cliffs, New Jersey, 1975).
4. Nils J. Nilsson, *Problem Solving Methods in Artificial Intelligence* (McGraw-Hill, New York, 1971).
5. Niklaus Wirth, *Algorithms + Data Structures = Programs* (Prentice-Hall, Englewood Cliffs, New Jersey, 1976).
6. Edward Yourdon, *Techniques of Program Structure and Design* (Prentice-Hall, Englewood Cliffs, New Jersey, 1975).

# Index

## A

| | |
|---|---|
| Absolute machine addresses | 313 |
| Acyclic | 260 |
| Addition | 62, 110 |
|    binary | 18 |
| Address | 43, 61, 168 |
|    calculations | 168 |
| Algorithms, recursive | 253 |
| Arcs | 258 |
| Arcs, labeled | 260 |
| Arguments | 68, 92, 312 |
| Arithmetic | |
|    binary | 18 |
|    multiple precision | 108 |
|    operations | 61 |
| Arrays | 50 |
|    circular | 191 |
|    designated by pointers | 176 |
|    linear | 171 |
|    multidimensional | 53, 180 |
|    of structures | 173 |
|    two-dimensional | 180 |
| Assignment operator | 59 |
| Attributes | 274 |

## B

| | |
|---|---|
| Balanced merging | 366 |
| Base | 13 |
|    powers of | 14 |
| Base conversion | 28 |
|    basic techniques | 28 |
| BASED attribute | 54 |
| Basic designation | 14 |
| Basic techniques of base conversion | 28 |
| Binary | |
|    addition | 18 |
|    arithmetic | 18 |
|    correspondence | 16 |
|    division | 20 |
|    multiplication | 20 |
|    search | 282 |
|    subtraction | 19 |
|    systems | 13 |
| Binary trees | 299 |
|    complete | 240 |
|    definition | 240 |
|    deletions | 302 |
|    insertions | 302 |
|    performance | 308 |
|    searching | 301 |
| Bit table | 246, 264, 332 |
| Blank space | 43 |
| Blocks | 314 |
|    search | 281 |
| Bottom | 184 |
| Bottomless stack | 199 |
| Branches | 238 |
| Bubble sort | 349 |
| Bucket address | 313 |
| Byte | 18 |

## C

| | |
|---|---|
| Calculations, address | 168 |
| Carry bit | 19 |
| Case study | 100 |
| Cells | 18 |
| Cellular multilist | 314, 334 |
| Chained files | 333 |
| Chains | 220, 221 |
|    doubly linked | 224, 233 |
|    singly linked | 221, 230 |
| Child | 238 |
|    and twin pointers | 249 |
| Circular | |
|    lists | 191 |
|    arrays | 191 |
| Collision handling | 288 |
| Comments | 97 |
| Complete binary tree | 240 |
| Completely inverted files | 325 |
| Components | 47 |
| Computing large powers | 32 |
| Concatenation | 208 |
| Condition | 75 |
| Connected | 260 |
| Connected strongly | 260 |
| Constants | 61 |
| Control structures | 73 |
| Conversion | |
|    base | 28 |
|    from decimal | 31 |
|    to decimal | 30 |
| Correspondence | 16 |
| Cycle | 258 |
| Cylinders | 314 |

379

## D

Data
- definition — 41
- manipulation — 59
- movement — 59
- structure — 166
- types — 41

Decimal
- to binary conversion — 34
- to hexadecimal conversion — 35
- to octal conversion — 35
- value to digits — 29

Declarations — 44, 202
Deletion — 227
- binary tree — 302

Deques — 199
Descendant — 238
Descriptors — 201
Digits — 13
- to decimal value — 29

Directed graph — 258
Displacement — 168
- field — 171

Distributed free space — 318
Division — 63
- binary — 20
- binary fractions — 119

Documentation — 97
Doubly linked chains — 224, 233
Dummy run — 365

## E

Eight-bit bytes — 18
Entities — 273
Equal sign, uses of — 61
Evaluating conditions — 80
Exchange — 347
Exponent — 14, 27
Exponential notation — 14
Expressions — 71
Extended place value system — 25
External sorting — 361

## F

Fields — 274
File — 311
Floating point numbers — 26
Forest — 240
Fractions — 24
Free space list — 227
Front — 193
Functional notation — 67
Functions — 94, 312, 313

## G

Game trees — 338
Garbage
- collection — 215
- collector for lists — 271

Global names — 93
Graphs — 258
- directed — 258
- nodes — 258
- representations — 262

## H

Hashing — 285
Header node — 222
Height-balanced — 309
Hexadecimal
- correspondence — 16
- to decimal conversion — 33

High order byte — 42
Horizontal method — 371

## I

Immediate
- predecessor — 258
- successor — 258

Incrementation — 111
Index — 51, 311
Initialization — 58
Initial node — 258
Inputs — 261
- buffering — 196

Insertion — 227, 346
- binary tree — 302

Integers — 13
- divide — 116
- multiplication — 114

Internal
- sorting — 346
- states — 261

Interrupt procedures — 95
Inverted
- files — 325
- lists — 325

Iterative DO statement — 88

## K

Key — 275
- to address transformations — 276

## L

Large power computation — 32
Left
- child — 240
- subtree — 240

Least
- significant bit — 42
- significant byte — 42

Leaves — 238
Level — 239
- numbers — 48

Lineal charts — 238
Linear
- arrays — 171, 276
- representations of trees — 240
- sweep phase — 271

Linked lists — 221
Lists — 267
- of immediate successors — 262
- of ordered pairs — 262
- of ordered triples — 262

Local names — 93
Log — 37
Logarithms — 36
Logical operations — 63
Low order byte — 42

## M

| | |
|---|---|
| Macros | 58 |
| Mantissa | 27 |
| Marking phase | 271 |
| Mask | 64 |
| Maximum level, game trees | 339 |
| Merge | 329 |
| Merging | 361, 362 |
| Minimax method | 341 |
| Minimum level, game trees | 340 |
| Most significant | |
|     bit | 42 |
|     byte | 42 |
| Multidimensional | |
|     arrays | 53, 180 |
|     binary trees | 334 |
| Multilevel indexes | 322 |
| Multilist | 314 |
|     chain | 314 |
| Multiple | |
|     assignment | 61 |
|     child pointers | 247 |
| Multiple precision | |
|     arithmetic | 108 |
|     numbers | 108 |
| Multiplication | 63 |
|     binary | 20 |
|     binary fractions | 119 |
| Multiway slection | 78 |

## N

| | |
|---|---|
| Name value | 46 |
| Negation | 63, 111 |
| Negative powers | 25 |
| Nodes | 220, 238 |
|     for graphs | 258 |
|     initial | 258 |
|     terminal | 258 |
| Nonrestoring division | 122 |
| Nonsequential file | 317 |
| Notation, exponential | 14 |
| Numbers, signed | 21 |

## O

| | |
|---|---|
| Octal | |
|     correspondence | 16 |
|     to decimal conversion | 33 |
| Offset | 168 |
| Ones complement representation | 24 |
| Open addressing | 293 |
| Operations | |
|     arithmetic | 61 |
|     on strings | 207 |
| Operator notation | 67 |
| Overflow areas | 318 |

## P

| | |
|---|---|
| Parallel | |
|     arrays | 179 |
|     linear arrays | 178 |
| Parent | 238 |
| Partially inverted files | 325 |
| Path | 258 |
| Pattern matching | 211 |
| Pedigrees | 238 |
| Performance, binary tree | 308 |
| Phase | |
|     marking | 271 |
|     linear sweep | 271 |
|     sweep | 271 |
| Place | |
|     value system | 15 |
|     value system, extended | 25 |
| Plexes | 220 |
| Plex representations | 247, 265 |
| Pointers | 53 |
|     additional | 251 |
|     child and twin | 249 |
|     multiple child | 247 |
| Polish notation | 246 |
| Polyphase sort | 367 |
| Pop | 227 |
| Postorder | |
|     representations | 242 |
|     traversal | 242 |
| Powers | |
|     negative | 25 |
|     of the base | 14 |
| Preorder | |
|     representations | 242 |
|     traversal | 242 |
| Primary | |
|     index | 312 |
|     key | 275, 312 |
| Primitive data types | 41 |
| Priority | 71 |
| Priority queue | 374 |
| Probes | 279 |
| Procedures | 91 |
|     calls and returns | 188 |
|     recursive | 253 |
| Program | |
|     design | 96 |
|     with comments | 99 |
| Programming, recursive | 253 |
| Push | 227 |

## Q

| | |
|---|---|
| Qualifying | 48 |
| Quanta | 312 |
| Queues | 193 |
| Quicksort | 355 |

## R

| | |
|---|---|
| Radix | 13 |
| Random access | 177 |
| Ranges | 24 |
| Rear | 193 |
| Record | 274 |
|     type | 274 |
| Recursive | |
|     algorithms | 253 |
|     procedures | 95, 253 |
|     programming | 253 |
| Recursively | 251 |
| Relational | |
|     data bases | 275 |
|     operations | 69 |
| Relations | 275 |

| | |
|---|---|
| Relative addresses | 313 |
| Repetition | 85, 96 |
| Replacement selection | 374 |
| Representating lists | 269 |
| Representation | |
|    ones complement | 24 |
|    sign-magnitude | 21 |
|    twos complement | 21 |
| Reversed Polish notation | 246 |
| Right | |
|    child | 240 |
|    justified | 43 |
|    subtree | 240 |
| Rings | 224 |
|    with pointers to header record | 224 |
| Root | 238 |
| Rotate and shift operations | 65 |
| Rounding | 38 |
|    binary | 38 |
|    hexadecimal | 39 |
|    octal | 38 |
| Runs | 363 |
|    time | 169 |

**S**

| | |
|---|---|
| Savelist | 271 |
| Scaling | 36 |
| Searching | |
|    binary trees | 301 |
|    game trees | 338 |
|    lists | 273 |
| Secondary | |
|    index | 312 |
|    key | 276, 312 |
|    key dictionary | 325 |
| Sectors | 314 |
| Selection | 96, 346 |
|    statements | 74 |
| Sentinel | 222 |
| Sequencing | 73, 96 |
| Sequential | |
|    file | 316 |
|    search | 276 |
|    search, chains | 279 |
|    traversal | 308 |
| Shell sort | 354 |
| Shift operations | 65 |
| Shifting | 112 |
| Short | |
|    chain | 334 |
|    occurrence | 334 |
| Sibling | 239 |
| Sifting | 375 |
| Sign-magnitude representation | 21 |
| Signed | |
|    numbers | 21 |
|    relationals | 70 |
| Simple path | 258 |
| Singly linked chains | 221, 230 |
| Sorting | |
|    by merging | 364 |
|    lists, two or three records | 347 |

| | |
|---|---|
| Specifying values | 60 |
| Stack | 227, 184 |
|    implementations | 185 |
| State transition graph | 261 |
| Static | |
|    evaluation | 340 |
|    evaluation function | 340 |
| Strings | 201 |
|    input | 205 |
|    output | 205 |
| Strongly connected | 260 |
| Structured programming | 96 |
| Structures | 47, 166 |
|    data | 166 |
|    designated by pointers | 170 |
|    in fixed locations | 170 |
| Subgraph | 260 |
| Subroutine invocation | 96 |
| Subscript | 51 |
| Subscripts vs pointers | 177 |
| Substrings | 210 |
| Subtraction | 62, 111 |
| Subtraction, binary | 19 |
| Subtree | 239 |
| Sweep phase | 271 |
| Symbolic address | 313 |
| Systems | |
|    binary | 13 |
|    place value | 15 |

**T**

| | |
|---|---|
| Tracks | 314 |
| Translation time | 169 |
| Transition table | 264 |
| Traverse | 242 |
| Trees | 238 |
| Terminal node | 258 |
| Termination criterial, game trees | 339 |
| Token | 285 |
| Top | 184 |
| Top-down design | 96 |
| Twin | 238 |
| Two-dimensional array | 180 |
| Twos complement | |
|    overflow | 23 |
|    representation | 21 |
| Type conversion | 61 |

**U**

| | |
|---|---|
| Unsigned | |
|    numbers | 69 |
|    relationals | 69 |

**V**

| | |
|---|---|
| Value | 167, 275 |
| Variable | 46 |

**W**

| | |
|---|---|
| Word | 18, 43 |

## DATE DUE

| | | | |
|---|---|---|---|
| | | | |
| | | | |
| | | | |
| | | | |
| | | | |
| | | | |
| | | | |
| | | | |
| | | | |
| | | | |
| | | | |
| | | | |
| | | | |
| | | | |
| | | | |
| | | | |
| | | | |
| | | | |
| GAYLORD | | | PRINTED IN U.S.A. |